CULTURE COUNTS

A Concise Introduction to Cultural Anthropology

Second Edition

Serena Nanda
John Jay College of Criminal Justice
City University of New York

Richard L. Warms
Texas State University—San Marcos

WADSWORTH
CENGAGE Learning™

Australia • Brazil • Japan • Korea • Mexico • Singapore • Spain • United Kingdom • United States

Culture Counts: **A Concise Introduction to Cultural Anthropology, Second Edition**
Serena Nanda and Richard L. Warms

Acquiring Editor: Erin Mitchell

Developmental Editor: Lin Gaylord

Assistant Editor: Linda Stewart

Editorial Assistant: Mallory Ortberg

Media Editor: Melanie Cregger

Marketing Manager: Andrew Keay

Marketing Assistant: Dimitri Hagnere

Marketing Communications Manager: Tami Strang

Content Project Manager: Cheri Palmer

Design Director: Rob Hugel

Art Director: Caryl Gorska

Print Buyer: Mary Beth Hennebury

Rights Acquisitions Specialist: Roberta Broyer

Production Service: MPS Content Services

Text Designer: Norman Baugher

Photo Researcher: Billie Porter

Text Researcher: Sarah D'Stair

Copy Editor: Heather McElwain

Illustrator: MPS Limited, a Macmillan Company

Maps: Graphic World

Cover Designer: Riezebos Holzbaur/ Angelyn Navasca

Cover Image: Peter Mattison/"Household Interview"

Compositor: MPS Limited, a Macmillan Company

For product information and technology assistance, contact us at
Cengage Learning Customer & Sales Support, 1-800-354-9706.
For permission to use material from this text or product,
submit all requests online at **www.cengage.com/permissions.**
Further permissions questions can be e-mailed to
permissionrequest@cengage.com.

Library of Congress Control Number: 2010933733

ISBN-13: 978-1-111-30153-8

ISBN-10: 1-111-30153-0

Wadsworth
20 Davis Drive
Belmont, CA 94002-3098
USA

Cengage Learning is a leading provider of customized learning solutions with office locations around the globe, including Singapore, the United Kingdom, Australia, Mexico, Brazil, and Japan. Locate your local office at **www.cengage.com/global.**

Cengage Learning products are represented in Canada by Nelson Education, Ltd.

To learn more about Wadsworth, visit **www.cengage.com/wadsworth**

Purchase any of our products at your local college store or at our preferred online store **www.CengageBrain.com.**

Printed in the United States of America
1 2 3 4 5 6 7 14 13 12 11

Dedication

To the grandchildren:
Alexander, Adriana,
Charlotte, Kai, and
Waverly. —SN—

To my professors at
Bates College and
Syracuse University,
particularly George
Fetter, Deborah Pellow,
and Michael Freedman.
—RW—

BRIEF CONTENTS

FEATURES CONTENTS

DETAILED CONTENTS

CHAPTER 3

DOING CULTURAL ANTHROPOLOGY   47

CHAPTER 4

COMMUNICATION   73

CHAPTER 7

MARRIAGE, FAMILY, AND KINSHIP   151

CHAPTER 10

STRATIFICATION: CLASS, RACE, ETHNICITY, AND CASTE   229

CHAPTER 11

RELIGION   255

CHAPTER 12

POWER, CONQUEST, AND A WORLD SYSTEM   281

CHAPTER 13

GLOBALIZATION AND CHANGE   305

PREFACE

ANTHROPOLOGY is the study of all people, in all places, and at all times. Students and scholars alike are drawn to anthropology as part of the realization that our lives and experiences are limited, but human possibilities are virtually endless. We are drawn to anthropology by the almost incredible variability of human society and our desire to experience and understand it. We are drawn by the beauty of other lives and sometimes by the horror as well. We write *Culture Counts,* Second Edition, to transmit some of our sense of wonder at the endless variety of the world and to show how anthropologists have come to understand and analyze human culture and society.

Culture Counts, Second Edition, is a brief introduction to anthropology written particularly for students in their first two years of college, but is accessible to and appropriate for other audiences as well. Our goal has been to write in a clean, crisp, jargon-free style that speaks to readers without speaking down to them. Each chapter is relatively brief but is packed with ethnographic examples and discussions that keep readers involved and focused. Although it is written in an extremely accessible style, *Culture Counts* sacrifices none of the intellectual rigor or sophistication of our longer work, *Cultural Anthropology*, now in its Tenth Edition. Each chapter of *Culture Counts* opens with an ethnographic situation, circumstance, history, or survey designed to engage the readers' interest and focus their attention on the central issues of the chapter. These chapter opening essays raise questions about the anthropological experience, the nature of culture, and the ways in which anthropologists understand society. Passages later in each chapter refer readers back to the opening examples to show the ways in which they are illuminated by anthropological thinking.

Each chapter concludes with a feature entitled "Bringing It Back Home," which contains a relatively brief example of a current controversy, issue, or debate. Each example is followed by a series of three critical thinking questions entitled "You Decide." The questions encourage students to apply anthropological understandings as well as their own life experiences and studies to the issue under discussion. Through these exercises, students learn to use anthropological ideas to grapple with important issues facing our own and other cultures. They learn to apply anthropology to the realities of the world.

Design is an important feature of *Culture Counts*. One of our goals is to present students with a clear, easy-to-follow text that is uncluttered and that highlights the main source of anthropology—ethnographic data.

To address the visual orientation of contemporary students, we have taken considerable care to choose visually compelling photographs and to include high-quality maps and charts that provide visual cues for content and help students remember what they have read. Each image is linked to a specific passage in the text. Each photo has an explanatory caption identifying its source and importance. Extended ethnographic examples are accompanied by maps that provide the specific geographical location of the group under discussion.

▊ PERSPECTIVE AND THEMES

As with *Cultural Anthropology*, our main perspective in this book is ethnographic, and our theoretical approach is eclectic. Ethnography is the fundamental source of the data of anthropology, and the desire to hear about and read ethnography is one of the principal reasons students take anthropology courses. Ethnographic examples have the power to engage students and encourage them to analyze and question their own culture. Ethnographic examples chosen to illuminate cultures, situations, and histories, both past and present, are used extensively in every chapter of *Culture Counts*. *Culture Counts* describes the major issues and theoretical approaches in anthropology in a balanced manner, drawing analysis, information, and insight from many different perspectives. It takes a broad, optimistic, enthusiastic approach and promotes the idea that debates within the field are signs of anthropology's continued relevance rather than problems it must overcome.

Additionally, we believe that issues of power, stratification, gender, and ethnicity are central to understanding contemporary cultures. These topics are given chapters of their own as well as integrated in appropriate places throughout the text.

Culture Counts continues the collaboration between Serena Nanda and Richard Warms. Warms's specialties in West Africa, anthropological theory, and social anthropology complement Nanda's in India, gender, law, and cultural anthropology. The results have been synergistic. Our experiences, readings, discussions, and debates, as well as feedback from reviewers and professors who have adopted our other books, have led to the production of a book that reflects the energy and passion of anthropology.

Both Nanda and Warms have extensive experience in writing textbooks for university audiences. In addition to *Cultural Anthropology*, now in its tenth edition, Nanda writes *American Cultural Pluralism and Law*, now in its third edition, with Jill Norgren. Warms, with R. Jon McGee, is author of *Anthropological Theory: An Introductory History*, now in its fourth edition, and of *Sacred Realms: Readings in the Anthropology of Religion*, second edition, with James Garber and R. Jon McGee. Collaborative writing continues to be an exciting intellectual adventure for us, and we believe that the ethnographic storytelling approach of this book will promote students' growth as well.

▊ NEW IN THIS EDITION

We have made a number of significant changes and additions to the second edition, based partly on recent developments in the field of anthropology and partly on the valuable feedback we have received from our adopters and reviewers. Two are of particular importance. We have combined the two chapters on inequalities, "Class and Caste" and "Race and Ethnicity," into a single chapter called "Stratification: Class, Race, Ethnicity, and Caste." This reorganization of the material will make these topics more easily accessible to students and will draw attention to the degree to which the critical concepts of class, race, ethnicity, and caste overlap and relate to one another. In combining these chapters, we have been careful to retain the rich ethnography of ethnicity, race, and caste in the United States and in India. The second major change is the addition of a new chapter called "Anthropology Makes a Difference," highlighting some of the many activities that anthropologists are engaged in today. Far more than a chapter on job possibilities in anthropology, "Anthropology Makes a Difference" is designed to bring anthropology into the lives of students, and to encourage them to see the ways in which anthropological knowledge and the work of anthropologists is an active force in the social, political, and economic lives of people around the world. In addition to these changes, we have provided a running glossary at the bottom of the pages to make important terms more easily accessible to students, and we have carefully edited each chapter again to include new references and new examples.

Following, are some of the most important changes to each chapter:

In Chapter 1, we have reorganized the chapter so that the section on archaeology now falls directly after the section on cultural anthropology to make the close connections between these two fields more apparent. We've increased the focus on globalization and added information and references on immigration. We've added information about recent Neanderthal gene discoveries and new photographs as well.

In Chapter 2, we've increased coverage of Temple Grandin's experiences and added more information on Inuit child rearing and enculturation. We've increased the information on the role of football in American culture and added commentary on the idea of the "magical Negro" in American media. We have written a new "Bringing It Back Home" section on the role of science in anthropology and the degree to which cultural anthropology can be considered a science.

Chapter 3 begins with a new opening story about the feelings of anger and frustration that sometimes accompany arriving in a new field situation. We have trimmed a little of the information about the history of anthropology so that we could offer a more complete section on ethical considerations in fieldwork. We've added a new named section on anthropology and the military.

In Chapter 4, we have streamlined some of the technical information about phonology. We have added a brief note describing new research on the FOXP2 gene as well as information on minimal pairs. We have increased our coverage of sociolinguistics, adding information on the relation of speech to identity and the use of certain kinds of speech as resistance to the dominant culture. We have modified our presentation of the Sapir-Whorf hypothesis to take account of new information.

Chapter 5 has been substantially rewritten. The opening story has been condensed, and each of the five principal sections of the chapter has been rewritten so they are of approximately equal length. A new example of foragers, the Pintupi, has been added. We have dropped the use of the terms *intensive* and *extensive* agriculture in favor of *horticulture* and *agriculture*. There is a new "Bringing It Back Home" section on food choice and globalization.

In Chapter 6, we have brought all statistical information up to date. We have placed additional emphasis on the division of labor, and reorganized information on the household and the firm, and on gender and work. We have rewritten the section on the Kula trade to increase students' appreciation of this practice from the point of view of culture members.

Chapter 7 begins with an updated and revised introductory story about the Na. Information about the changing American family has been updated, and new information about surrogate parenthood has been added. There are two new photos and two new annotations for instructors.

Chapter 8 has several substantial changes. The section on factory workers in China found in the first edition has been moved to Chapter 14 in this edition. There are new sections on masculinity and bullfighting in Spain and on "Gender, Culture, and Art." Additionally, there is a new discussion of Muslim women and the wearing of the hijab in the section on gender ideology and women's sexuality.

Chapter 9 begins with a new opening scenario on nationalism and ethnic conflict using the example of Turkey and the Armenians. The chapter has been substantially reorganized to give it better flow and a more logical sequence of ideas. There are new sections on the "Emergence of the Nation-State," "The Nation-State and Ethnicity," and "The Nation-State and Indigenous People."

Chapter 10 integrates Chapters 10 and 11 in the first edition to simplify the presentation of the material on inequality and to make the connections between caste, class, race, and ethnicity more transparent. Some of the material that was part of Chapters 10 and 11 in the first edition (including sections on ethnicity and ethnic conflict, and indigenous people and the nation-state) has been moved to Chapter 9.

Although the structure of our chapter on religion (Chapter 12 in the first edition, Chapter 11 in the current edition) remains unchanged, much of the material has been rewritten. There is new information on the biology of religious experience and on Wiccans and neo-pagans. There are new sections on rites of passage and on fundamentalism. Although the title of the "Bringing It Back Home" feature remains "Religion, Art, and Censorship," almost all of the information in the section is new.

Our chapter on "Power, Conquest, and a World System" (Chapter 13 in the first edition, but Chapter 12 in the current edition) has been streamlined, and small organizational changes have made it more readable. Information on the role of disease in the Western expansion has been consolidated. There is a new "Bringing It Back Home" feature that considers neocolonialism and the idea of charter cities. Additionally, map colors have been modified for clarity, and a new photograph illustrates the "Bringing It Back Home" section.

Much of our chapter on "Globalization and Change" (Chapter 14 in the first edition, but Chapter 13 in this edition) has been streamlined and slightly shortened so that we might add two new sections: one on tourism and the global art market and a second on the effect of the revolution in electronic communication on global culture.

As we noted previously, we are very pleased to present an entirely new Chapter 14 called "Anthropology Makes a Difference." In this chapter, we focus on some of the exciting activities in which today's anthropologists are engaged. Far more than a chapter on job possibilities in anthropology, this chapter is designed to bring anthropology into the lives of students. There are sections on race, on the roles anthropologists play in identifying and preserving human remains, on museum representations of indigenous people, pollution, domestic violence, exploited children, anthropology and medicine, and advocating for workers. The "Bringing It Back Home" section explores domestic violence and the cultural defense.

CHAPTER OVERVIEWS

Each chapter is organized so that the main ideas, secondary ideas, important terms and definitions, and ethnographic material stand out clearly. Although we have a deep appreciation for classic ethnography and cite it frequently, each chapter also presents current work in anthropology and includes many references to books and essays published in the past five years.

Chapter 1, "What Is Anthropology and Why Should I Care?" introduces the major perspectives of anthropology and the subfields of the discipline. It highlights race as a social construction and the many ways anthropology contributes to a sensitive understanding of human differences. The chapter explains the importance of anthropology as a university discipline and the reasons that understanding anthropology is critical in the world today. The chapter opens with the classic essay on the Nacirema, and the "Bringing It Back Home" feature is about homelessness.

Chapter 2, "Culture Counts," exposes students to a range of theoretical positions in anthropology by examining the ways different anthropologists have understood the idea of culture. It demonstrates that different theoretical positions lead anthropologists to ask different sorts of questions and do different sorts of research. The chapter concludes with a discussion of the cultural change mechanisms of innovation and diffusion. A full discussion of culture change and the expansion of capitalism is found in Chapters 12 and 13. The chapter opening essay explores the relationship between culture and autism, and the "Bringing It Back Home" feature raises questions about the degree to which anthropology can be considered a science.

Chapter 3, "Doing Cultural Anthropology," considers the history and practice of fieldwork in anthropology. The chapter opens with historical background, describing the contributions of Boas, Malinowski, and others. It provides a brief analysis of the different techniques anthropologists use in the field, including participant observation, survey techniques, mapping, photography, and cross-cultural analysis. Issues in anthropological methodology and theory, including feminist anthropology, postmodernism, collaborative anthropology, and the problems of studying one's own culture, are discussed. The chapter concludes with an extended discussion of anthropological ethics. The chapter opening essay recounts the story of an anthropologist arriving at his fieldwork site, and the "Bringing It Back Home" feature raises critical issues about human rights.

Chapter 4, "Communication," provides a solid background for anthropological linguistics. Phonology, morphology, and other elements of linguistics are briefly discussed. Much of the chapter focuses on sociolinguistics, particularly the performance of language and the complex interrelationships among culture, language, and social hierarchies. The chapter also explores nonverbal communication and the relationship of language change to political and technological changes. The chapter opens with a dialogue from African American English Vernacular, or Ebonics, and the "Bringing It Back Home" feature concerns the English-only movement.

Chapter 5, "Making a Living," brings cultural adaptation into focus. It examines subsistence strategies, including foraging, pastoralism, horticulture, agriculture, and the industrial food industry, using extended ethnographic examples from the Maasai of East Africa, the Lua' of Thailand, Egyptian villagers, and the American meatpacking industry. The chapter opening essay focuses on the effects of global warming in the Arctic, and the "Bringing It Back Home" essay is about food choice and globalization.

Chapter 6, "Economics," explores the nature of economic behavior and economic systems in cross-cultural perspective. Special attention is paid to issues of access to resources, the organization of labor, systems of distribution and exchange (including classic examples such as the potlatch and the kula ring), and reactions to the spread of capitalism. The chapter opening essay explores the results of experiments in which people from very different cultures play economic simulation games. The "Bringing It Back Home" feature is about the use of anthropology by large corporations.

Chapter 7, "Marriage, Family, and Kinship," focuses on types of family systems, emphasizing the diversity of forms and functions of families. It includes sections on marriage rules, the exchange of goods at marriage, and family composition and residence rules, using extended examples from the Na of China, the contemporary American family, and the Hopi of the southwestern United States, among others. A section on kinship introduces the major kinship ideologies and the kinds of social groups formed by kinship. The chapter opening essay discusses the Na of China, a culture that seems to have no marriage practices, and the "Bringing It Back Home" feature discusses polygamy in the United States.

Chapter 8, "Sex and Gender," begins with an explanation of the cultural construction of gender, using ethnographic data from cultures with more than two genders. It explores initiation rites for men and women and the relationship among gender, power and prestige, and the complex and variable nature of gender roles in foraging, pastoralist, horticulturalist, agricultural, and industrial societies. Key ethnographic examples come from India, New Guinea, Spain, Polynesia, and Mexico. The chapter opening essay examines Nanda's work with the hijras, a third gender group in India, and the "Bringing It Back Home" feature discusses the issues raised by female genital operations.

Chapter 9, "Political Organization," begins with a discussion of authority and the nature of social control. It then turns to a systematic discussion of leadership, social control, and conflict resolution in bands, tribes, chiefdoms, and states. It concludes with a discussion of the emergence of the nation-state and the ways in which states have dealt with ethnicity and with indigenous people. The chapter opening essay discusses the ethnic conflict between Turkey and the Armenians, and the "Bringing It Back Home" exercise discusses illegal immigration and the construction of a barrier along the Mexico–United States border.

Chapter 10, "Stratification," begins by introducing functionalist and conflict perspectives on social stratification and continues with an exploration of the relationship among power, wealth, and prestige. It then explores class and the cultural construction of race. This is followed by a discussion of ethnicity in America focusing on the importance of assimilationist and multicultural models. The chapter then turns to a discussion of the Indian caste system, emphasizing ritual purity as well as recent changes in the caste system. The chapter opening essay explores how ethnicity, class, and race intersected in a court case in Hawaii in the 1930s. The "Bringing It Back Home" essay examines the debate between those who favor and those who oppose strong government intervention to help the poor.

Chapter 11, "Religion," moves from a brief consideration of the functions of religion to a definition of religion that includes stories and myths, symbolism, supernatural beings and powers, rituals, practitioners, and change. It then looks at each of these aspects of religion using examples from different cultures. This is followed by an exploration of the ways in which religion changes and the relationship between social change and religious change. The chapter opening essay about cargo cults raises questions about religion and materialism, and the "Bringing It Back Home" exercise raises questions about religion and the censorship of art in the United States.

Chapter 12, "Power, Conquest, and a World System," takes a historical perspective, exploring the ways in which the expansion of the power of today's wealthy nations fundamentally changed cultures throughout the world. It begins with an exploration of the motives and means for European expansion and discusses the effects of this expansion on people in the 15th through 18th centuries. This is followed by an analysis of the colonialism of the 19th and early 20th centuries and its effect on patterns of wealth and poverty in the world today. The chapter concludes with the decolonization movement of the mid-20th century. The chapter opening essay describes Warms's work with veterans of an African colonial army. The "Bringing It Back Home" essay describes the controversy over Ghana's 50th anniversary celebrations.

Chapter 13, "Globalization and Change," examines the challenges and prospects faced by peoples and cultures in the globalized contemporary world. It begins with a historical overview of development efforts and continues with an exploration of some of the key issues facing people in poor nations today. They include the presence of powerful multinational corporations, urbanization, population pressure, environmental degradation, migration, the effects of tourism, and of the revolution in electronic communication. The chapter opening essay describes wealth and poverty in several locations around the world. The "Bringing It Back Home" essay explores whether or not advances in technology are creating a world of increasing opportunity and equity.

Chapter 14, "Anthropology Makes a Difference," explores some of the many ways that anthropological knowledge and the work of anthropologists are having an effect on the world. The topics explored include race and racism, museum representations of indigenous people, the relationships among pollution, race, and class, domestic violence, the lives of working children living in desperately poor conditions and those of child sex workers, and the living conditions of female factory workers in China. The chapter begins with an essay about the Chagossians, a group of people forcibly removed from their home on islands in the Indian Ocean, and the "Bringing It Back Home" essay focuses on domestic violence and the cultural defense.

▊▊TEACHING FEATURES AND STUDY AIDS

Each chapter includes outstanding pedagogical features to help students identify, learn, and remember key concepts and data. The following learning aids are designed to help students better understand and retain the chapter's information:

- Full-color opening photos with captions are placed at the beginning of each chapter.
- An outline at the beginning of each chapter clearly shows the organization of the chapter and the major topics covered.

- Each chapter opens with an essay that focuses on an ethnographic situation, circumstance, or history designed to capture students' interest and launch them into the chapter.
- Each chapter concludes with a brief essay and questions that encourage the application of anthropological thinking to a current controversy, issue, or debate. The questions can be used as assignments or to promote classroom discussion.
- Summaries, arranged as numbered points at the end of each chapter, recap critical ideas and aid study and review.
- Key terms are listed alphabetically at the end of each chapter, for quick review.
- A running glossary of key terms is found at the bottom of the pages.
- References for every source cited within the text are listed alphabetically at the end of the book.

SUPPLEMENTS

Instructor Resources

- **Online Instructor's Manual and Test Bank for *Culture Counts*, Second Edition**. This instructor resource, written by Marjorie Snipes of the University of West Georgia, provides detailed chapter outlines, learning objectives, lecture suggestions, key terms, student activities, and test questions that include multiple choice, true/false, fill in the blank, short answer, and essay. In addition, there are over 100 instructor's annotations to help speed class preparation. Using their years of teaching experience, the authors have provided from 5 to 10 ideas for assignment and active student engagement for each chapter to help simplify your class preparation.
- **Online PowerPoint® slides.** These slides will help you prepare for class in record time. Each chapter features a detailed outline of chapter content, photos and figures from the textbook, discussion questions to encourage student participation, and "quick quizzes" to review chapter concepts.
- **ExamView® Computerized Test Bank**. Create, deliver, and customize tests in minutes with this easy-to-use assessment and tutorial system. ExamView offers both a Quick Test Wizard and an Online Test Wizard that guide you step by step through the process of creating tests, while its unique "WYSIWYG" capability allows you to see the test you are creating on screen exactly as it will print or display online. You can build tests of up to 250 questions using up to 12 question types. Using ExamView's complete word-processing capabilities, you can enter an unlimited number of new questions or edit existing questions.
- **The Wadsworth Anthropology Video Library, Volume 1**. The Wadsworth Anthropology Video Library drives home the relevance of course topics through short, provocative clips of current and historical events. Perfect for enriching lectures and engaging students in discussion, many of the segments on this volume have been

gathered from BBC Motion Gallery. Ask your Cengage Learning representative for a list of contents.

- **AIDS in Africa DVD.** Expand your students' global perspective of human immuno-deficiency virus (HIV)/acquired immunodeficiency syndrome (AIDS) with this award-winning documentary series that focuses on controlling HIV/AIDS in southern Africa. Films focus on caregivers in the faith community; how young people share messages of hope through song and dance; the relationship of HIV/AIDS to gender, poverty, stigma, education, and justice; and the story of two HIV-positive women helping others.

Student Resources

- **Student Companion Website for *Culture Counts, Second Edition*.** This site provides students with basic learning resources including tutorial quizzes, a final practice exam, learning objectives, web links, flash cards, and more! Go to **www.cengagebrain.com** and search for this title.
- **Anthropology Resource Center**. This hands-on online center offers a wealth of information and useful tools for both instructors and students in all four fields of anthropology: cultural anthropology, physical anthropology, archaeology, and linguistics. It includes interactive maps, learning modules, video exercises, a Case Study Forum with abstracts and critical thinking exercises, and breaking news in anthropology.
- **Additional Student Resources**. For a complete listing of our case studies and modules, go to www.cengagebrain.com.
- ***Case Studies in Cultural Anthropology,*** edited by George Spindler and Janice E. Stockard, offers a diverse array of case studies that emphasize culture change and the factors influencing change in the peoples depicted. New topics include *Life in a Muslim Uzbek Village: Cotton Farming after Communism* by Russell Zanca (ISBN 0-495-09281-9) and *New Cures, Old Medicines: Women and the Commercialization of Traditional Medicine in Bolivia* by Lynn Sikkink (ISBN 0-495-83711-3).
- ***Case Studies on Contemporary Social Issues,*** edited by John A. Young, offers a variety of case studies that explore how anthropology is used today in understanding and addressing problems faced by human societies around the world. Melissa Cheyney looks at homebirth midwifery in the United States in *Born at Home: The Biological, Cultural and Political Dimensions of Maternity Care in the United States* (ISBN: 0-495-79366-3), while Sunil K. Khanna explores family planning in *Fetal/Fatal Knowledge: New Reproductive Technologies and Family-Building Strategies in India* (ISBN: 0-495-09525-7).
- ***Classic Readings in Cultural Anthropology,*** Third Edition (ISBN 1-111-29792-4). Practical and insightful, this concise and accessible reader by Gary Ferraro presents a core selection of historical and contemporary works that have been instrumental in shaping anthropological thought and research over the past decades. Readings are organized around eight topics that closely mirror most introductory textbooks and are selected from scholarly works on the basis of their enduring themes and contributions to the discipline.

- *Current Perspectives: Readings from InfoTrac® College Edition: Cultural Anthropology and Globalization* (ISBN 0-495-00810-9). Ideal for supplementing your cultural anthropology textbook, this reader will evoke lively classroom discussions about real-world challenges and opportunities of globalization. Selected articles about globalization are drawn from InfoTrac College Edition's vast database of full-length, peer-reviewed articles from more than 5,000 top academic journals, newsletters, and periodicals.
- **Wadsworth's Modules for Anthropology Series.** This series includes modules entitled *Medical Anthropology in Applied Perspective* by Lynn Sikkink (ISBN 0-495-10017-X) and *Human Environment Interactions: New Directions in Human Ecology* by Kathy Galvin (ISBN 0-534-62071-X). Each freestanding module is actually a complete text chapter, featuring the same quality of pedagogy and illustration that is contained in Wadsworth/Cengage Learning anthropology texts.

ACKNOWLEDGMENTS

It gives us great pleasure to thank the many people who have been associated with this book. We are most appreciative of the helpful comments made by our reviewers: Stephen Fadden, Santa Fe Community College; Douglas Hume, Northern Kentucky University; Velesta Jenkins, Wiley College; John McDermott, Fullerton College and California State, Fullerton; Shawn Parkhurst, University of Louisville; Amanda Paskey, Cosumnes River College; Rita Sakitt, Suffolk County Community College; Lois Stanford, New Mexico State University; and Denice Szafran, SUNY College at Buffalo.

For their support and assistance, we thank Raksha Chopra, Douglas Feldman, Stanley Freed, and Joan Gregg. For the use of photographs, we thank Soo Choi, Ronald Coley, Douglas Feldman, Chander Dembla, Joan Gregg, James Hamilton, Jane Hoffer, Ray Kennedy, Judith Pearson, and Jean Zorn.

We gratefully acknowledge the support of our universities and the help of the staffs of our departments at John Jay College of Criminal Justice and Texas State University–San Marcos. In addition, many of our students have contributed ideas, reflections, and labor to this project.

Our families continue to form an important cheering section for our work, and we thank them for their patience and endurance and for just plain putting up with us.

We are deeply grateful to the people at Wadsworth, particularly our Development Project Manager, Lin Marshall Gaylord, and our Acquisitions Editor, Erin Mitchell, for their support, their encouragement, and their insight. In addition, we thank Andrew Keay, Marketing Manager; Mallory Ortberg, Editorial Assistant; Linda Stewart, Assistant Editor; Melanie Cregger, Media Editor; and Cheri Palmer, Content Production Manager.

Finally, we thank Jill Traut of MPS Content Services who shepherded us through the production process, and Billie Porter, photo researcher *extraordinaire*.

The knowledge, editing skills, and superb suggestions made by the many people involved in the production of this book have greatly contributed to it.

ABOUT THE AUTHORS

Serena Nanda is professor emeritus of anthropology at John Jay College of Criminal Justice, City University of New York. In addition to *Cultural Anthropology*, tenth edition, her published works include *Neither Man nor Woman: The Hijras of India*, winner of the 1990 Ruth Benedict Prize; *American Cultural Pluralism and Law;* and *Gender Diversity: Cross-Cultural Variations*. She is also the author of *New York More Than Ever: 40 Perfect Days in and around the City* and *The Gift of a Bride: A Tale of Anthropology, Matrimony and Murder,* an ethnographic novel set in an Indian immigrant community in New York City. She has always been captivated by the stories people tell and by the tapestry of human diversity. Anthropology was the perfect way for her to immerse herself in these passions and, through teaching and writing, to spread the word about the importance of understanding both human differences and human similarities.

Richard L. Warms is professor of anthropology at Texas State University–San Marcos. In addition to *Cultural Anthropology*, tenth edition, his published works include *Anthropological Theory: An Introductory History* and *Sacred Realms: Essays in Religion, Belief, and Society* as well as journal articles on commerce, religion, and ethnic identity in West Africa; African exploration and romanticism; and African veterans of French colonial armed forces. Warms's interests in anthropology were kindled by college courses and by his experiences as a Peace Corps volunteer in West Africa. He has traveled extensively in Africa, Europe, and Japan. He continues to teach Introduction to Cultural Anthropology every year but also teaches classes in anthropological theory, the anthropology of religion, economic anthropology, and film at both the undergraduate and graduate levels. Students and faculty are invited to contact him with their comments, suggestions, and questions at r.warms@txstate.edu.

© Jialiang Gao

Anthropologists study cultural practices including dances and religious festivals. Here, women in New Guinea decorate themselves in preparation for a dance. Notice the use of materials such as feathers and cowry shells along with manufactured products such as whiteout.

CHAPTER **1**

WHAT IS ANTHROPOLOGY AND WHY SHOULD I CARE?

THE NACIREMA

ANTHROPOLOGISTS have become so familiar with the diversity of ways different peoples behave in similar situations that they are not apt to be surprised by even the most exotic customs. However, the magical beliefs and practices of the Nacirema present such unusual aspects that it seems desirable to describe them as an example of the extremes to which human behavior can go. The Nacirema are a North American group living in the territory between the Canadian Cree, the Yaqui and Tarahumare of Mexico, and the Carib and Arawak of the Antilles. Little is known of their origin, although tradition states that they came from the east.

Nacirema culture is characterized by a highly developed market economy, but Naciremans spend a considerable portion of the day in ritual activity. The focus of this activity is the human body, the appearance and health of which loom as a dominant concern in the ethos of the people.

The fundamental belief underlying the whole system appears to be that the human body is ugly and has a natural tendency to debility and disease. People's only hope is to avert these through the use of ritual and ceremony, and every household has one or more shrines devoted to this purpose. The rituals associated with the shrine are secret and are discussed with children only when they are being initiated into these mysteries. I was able, however, to establish sufficient rapport with the natives to examine these shrines and to have the rituals described to me.

The focal point of the shrine is a box or chest built into the wall in which are kept the many charms and magical potions no native believes he could live without. Beneath the charm box is a small font. Each day, every member of the family, in succession, enters the shrine room, bows his head before the charm box, mingles different sorts of holy water in the font, and proceeds with a brief rite of purification. The holy waters are secured from the Water Temple of the community, where the priests conduct elaborate ceremonies to make the liquid ritually pure.

The Nacirema have an almost pathological horror of and fascination with the mouth, the condition of which is believed to have a supernatural influence on all social relationships. Each day, Naciremans perform a complex set of rituals devoted to the mouth. Were it not for these rituals, they believe that their teeth would fall out, their gums bleed, their jaws shrink, their friends desert them, and their lovers reject them.

In addition to daily mouth rites, the people seek out a holy-mouth-man once or twice a year. These practitioners have an impressive set of paraphernalia, consisting of a variety of augers, awls, probes, and prods. The use of these objects in the exorcism of the evils of the mouth involves almost unbelievable ritual torture of the client. The holy-mouth-man uses these tools to scrape, prod, and cut particularly sensitive areas of the mouth. Magical materials believed to arrest decay and draw friends are inserted in the mouth. The extremely sacred and traditional character of the rite is evident in the fact that the natives return to the holy-mouth-men year after year, despite the fact that their teeth continue to decay. One has but to watch the gleam in the eye of a holy-mouth-man, as he jabs an awl into an exposed nerve, to suspect that a certain amount of sadism is involved in these practices. And indeed much of the population shows definite masochistic tendencies. For example, a portion of the daily body ritual performed only by men involves scraping and lacerating the surface of the face with a sharp instrument.

Nacirema medicine men have an imposing temple, or latipsoh, in every community of any size. The more elaborate ceremonies required to treat very sick patients can be performed only at this temple. These ceremonies involve not only the priests who perform miracles but also a permanent group of vestal maidens who move sedately about the temple chambers in distinctive costume.

Hospital

The latipsoh ceremonies are so harsh that it is surprising that sick adults are not only willing but eager to undergo the protracted ritual purification, if they can afford to do so. No matter how ill the supplicant or how grave the emergency, the guardians of the temple will not admit a client if he cannot give a rich gift to the custodian. Even after one has gained admission and survived the ceremonies, the guardians continue to demand gifts, sometimes pursuing clients to their homes and businesses.

Supplicants entering the temple are first stripped of all their clothes. Psychological shock results from the fact that body secrecy is suddenly lost. A man whose own wife has never seen him in an excretory act suddenly finds himself naked and assisted by a vestal maiden while he performs his natural functions into a sacred vessel. Female clients find their naked bodies are subjected to the scrutiny, manipulation, and prodding of the medicine men. The fact that these temple ceremonies may not cure, and may even kill, in no way decreases the people's faith in the medicine men.

In conclusion, mention must be made of certain practices that have their base in native esthetics but depend upon the pervasive aversion to the natural body and its functions. There are ritual fasts to make fat people thin and ceremonial feasts to make thin people fat. Still other rites are used to make women's breasts larger if they are small, and smaller if they are large. General dissatisfaction with breast shape is symbolized by the fact that the ideal form is virtually outside the range of human variation. A few women afflicted with almost inhuman hypermammary development are so idolized that they make a handsome living by simply going from village to village and permitting the natives to stare at them for a fee.

Our review of the ritual life of the Nacirema has shown them to be a magic-ridden people. It is hard to understand how they have managed to exist so long under the burdens they have imposed upon themselves. But even exotic customs such as these take on real meaning when they are viewed with the insight Malinowski provided when he wrote: "Looking from far and above, from our high places of safety in civilization, it is easy to see all the crudity and irrelevance of magic. But without its power and guidance early man could not have mastered his practical difficulties as he has done, nor could man have advanced to the higher stages of civilization."

The essay you've just read is adapted from a classic piece of American anthropology by Horace Miner. Despite being a half century old, it has lost none of its bite. The essay is good because it plays upon two critical themes that continue to draw people to anthropology: our quest to gain knowledge and to understand people who are vastly different from ourselves, and our desire to know ourselves and our own culture better.

Miner's essay draws you in as you read about the strange and bizarre customs of people who at first appear utterly different from yourself. You're titillated by the details of the exotic practices of the other but also comforted by the scientific writing style that seems to assure you that somehow this all makes sense. At some point in your reading, you may have realized that Miner is, in fact, describing American customs as they might be seen from the point of view of an unknowing but perhaps quite perceptive observer. Your first reaction might be to chuckle at the narrator's misunderstandings and treat the essay as an example of just how deeply an outside observer might be in error about a culture. But if you're a reflective person, you might have also wondered if the narrator hadn't turned up some fairly penetrating insights about the nature of our society. Clearly, the narrator has misunderstood some of the ways Americans think about bathrooms, dentists, and hospitals. But is the narrator so far off in describing the American attitude toward disease, decay, and death? Finally, if you caught the joke early enough, you might have pondered the meaning of the quote that ends the essay: Have we really "advanced to the higher stages of civilization?" What does that mean anyway?

Miner's essay deals with some of the critical questions and desires at the heart of anthropology: How do we understand other people and actions that seem different, odd, or strange? Why do people do what they do? And, perhaps more profoundly, how do we go about describing other people's cultural worlds, and how do we know if these descriptions are accurate? We will return to these issues in many places in this book. But first, a brief definition and description of anthropology: **Anthropology** is the scientific and humanistic study of human beings. It encompasses the

anthropology The scientific and humanistic study of human beings.

evolutionary history of humanity, physical variation among humans, the study of past societies, and the comparative study of current-day human societies and cultures.

A **society** is a group of people who depend on one another for survival or well-being. **Culture** is the way members of a society adapt to their environment and give meaning to their lives.

Some critical goals of anthropology are to describe, analyze, and explain different cultures, to show how groups live in different physical, economic, and social environments, and to show how their members give meaning to their lives. Anthropology attempts to comprehend the entire human experience. Through human paleontology, it describes the evolutionary development of our species. Through archaeology, it reaches from current-day societies to those of the distant past. Through primatology, it extends beyond humans to encompass the animals most closely related to us.

Human beings almost everywhere are **ethnocentric**. That is, they consider their own behavior not only right but also natural. We often want other people to behave just like we do, and we feel troubled, insulted, or outraged when they do not. Indeed, part of our reaction to the Nacirema essay stems from the fact that the Nacerimans seem to do things that, to us, seem neither right nor natural. However, as the essay suggests, the range of human behavior is truly enormous. For example, should you give your infant bottled formula, or should you breast-feed not only your own child but, like the Efe of Zaire, those of your friends and neighbors as well (Peacock 1991:352)? Is it right that emotional love should precede sexual relations? Or should sexual relations precede love, as is normal for the Mangaian of the Pacific (Marshall 1971)? If a child dies, should we bury it, or, as Wari' elders say was proper, should it be eaten (Conklin 1995)? And what about sex? Are boys naturally made into men through receipt of semen from older men, as the Sambia claim (Herdt 1987)? For anthropologists, these examples suggest that what is right or natural for human beings is not easily determined and that attempts to understand human nature and theories of human behavior cannot be based simply on our own cultural assumptions. To accurately reflect humanity, they also must be based on studies of human groups whose goals, values, views of reality, and environmental adaptations are very different from our own. We can achieve an accurate understanding of humanity only by realizing that other groups of people who behave differently from us and have different understandings also consider the things they do and the ways they understand the world to be normal and natural.

One job of anthropology is to understand what actions and ideas mean within their contexts and to place these within the broader framework of human society, environment, and history. Anthropologists refer to the practice of attempting to understand cultures within their contexts

society A group of people who depend on one another for survival or well-being as well as the relationships among such people, including their status and roles.

culture The learned behaviors and symbols that allow people to live in groups; the primary means by which humans adapt to their environment; the ways of life characteristic of a particular human society.

ethnocentrism Judging other cultures from the perspective of one's own culture. The notion that one's own culture is more beautiful, rational, and nearer to perfection than any other.

Ethnocentrism is the belief that one's own culture is superior to any other.

cultural relativism The notion that cultures should be analyzed with reference to their own histories and values rather than according to the values of another culture.

holism In anthropology, an approach that considers culture, history, language, and biology essential to a complete understanding of human society.

as **cultural relativism**. It is important to understand that practicing cultural relativism does not mean that anthropologists believe all cultural traditions to be good or to be of equal worth. People around the world, and indeed in our own society, do terrible things. Slavery, human sacrifice, and torture are all cultural practices. Anthropologists do not defend such customs on the basis of cultural relativism. However, anthropologists do try to understand how all cultural practices, even those that horrify us, developed, how they work in society, and how they are experienced by the people who live them. Both ethnocentrism and cultural relativism are examined in greater detail in Chapter 3.

Anthropologists bring a holistic approach to understanding and explaining. To say anthropology is **holistic** means that it combines the study of human biology, history, and the learned and shared patterns of human behavior and thought we call culture in order to analyze human groups. Holism separates anthropology from other academic disciplines, which generally focus on one factor—biology, psychology, physiology, or society—as the explanation for human behavior.

Because anthropologists use this holistic approach, they are interested in the total range of human activity. Most anthropologists specialize in a single field and a single problem, but together, they study the small dramas of daily living as well as spectacular social events. They study the ways in which mothers hold their babies or sons address their fathers. They want to know not only how a group gets its food but also the rules for eating it. Anthropologists are interested in how people in human societies think about time and space and how they see and name colors. They are interested in health and illness and the significance of physical variation as well as many other things. Anthropologists maintain that culture, social organization, history, and human biology are tightly interrelated. Although we can never know absolutely everything about any group of people, the more we know about the many different facets of a society, the clearer picture we are able to draw and the greater the depth of our understanding.

SPECIALIZATION IN ANTHROPOLOGY

In the United States, anthropology has traditionally included four separate subdisciplines: cultural anthropology, anthropological linguistics, archaeology, and biological or physical anthropology. In this section, we briefly describe each of them.

Cultural Anthropology

Cultural anthropology is the study of human society and culture. As we have said, a society is a group of people who depend upon one another for survival or well-being. Anthropologists also understand society as a set of social relationships among people—their statuses and roles. Societies are often thought of as occupying specific geographic locations. For example, we might think of the Ashanti Kingdom as located around the city of Kumasi in the modern nation of Ghana, West Africa; however, due to rapid transportation and electronic communication, societies are increasingly global. Yes, there are still Ashanti living around Kumasi, but there are also Ashanti living in New York, Los Angeles, London, and perhaps most other major world cities. Today, a society is perhaps best described as what Ajun Appadurai (1990) has called an **ethnoscape**: a global distribution of people associated with each other by history, kinship, friendship, and webs of mutual understandings.

Culture is the way members of a society adapt to their environment and give meaning to their lives. It includes behavior and ideas that are learned rather than genetically transmitted as well as the material objects a group of people produces. Cultural anthropologists attempt to understand culture through the study of its origins, development, and diversity. Just as societies have become global, cultures too are increasingly globalized. Cultures have always borrowed traits and practices from one another. However, today, travel and electronic communication mean that styles, customs, and practices of one part of the world can rapidly appear in other places. Consider the case of Tuva, located north of Mongolia in the former USSR. For

cultural anthropology The study of human thought, behavior, and lifeways that are learned rather than genetically transmitted and that are typical of groups of people.

ethnoscape Global distribution of people associated with each other by history, kinship, friendship, and webs of mutual understandings.

Westerners, Tuva used to be one of the world's most isolated places. Nobel Prize-winning physicist Richard Feynman tried famously, and unsuccessfully, to get there in the 1980s (Leighton 2000). Today, anyone with sufficient money and taste for adventure can go to Tuva. Additionally, Tuva is known for a particular kind of music called throat singing. The Tuvan throat singing group *Alash* regularly tours in both Europe and the United States, sometimes appearing with jazz, rock, and classical artists. Tuvan culture is based around herding, and *Alash*'s American-born manager, Sean Quirk, reports that the band is particularly well received in places in the United States where ranching plays an important role in people's lives (pers. comm.). The members of *Alash* say they've been heavily influenced by Sun Ra (an American Jazz ensemble) and Jimi Hendrix. You can hear some of *Alash*'s music on their website: www.alashensemble.com.

As the Tuvan example illustrates, change is a basic attribute of culture and is evident in any examination of recent society. Understanding the dynamics of change is critical for individuals, governments, and corporations. Many anthropologists study such dynamics. For example, Scott Atran (2003, 2007) studies the origins and development of suicide terrorism in the Middle East; Caitlin Zaloom (2006) studies the ways in which technology affects the dynamics of stock and commodity trading in

Anthropologists study cultural practices all over the world in their attempt to understand the similarities and differences among human beings. Today, like these Maasai tribesmen, members of cultures throughout the world are deeply affected by the global market and by technological change. Anthropologists are particularly interested in the ways in which cultures respond to such changes.

Chicago and London; and Michael Wesch (2007) studies the development of social networks on Facebook. Thus, cultural anthropology contributes to public understanding and debate about our promotion of and reaction to change.

Ethnography and ethnology are two important aspects of cultural anthropology. Ethnography is the description of society or culture. An ethnographer attempts to depict an entire society or a particular set of cultural institutions or practices. Ethnographies may be either emic or etic, or they may combine the two. An **emic** ethnography attempts to capture what ideas and practices mean to members of a culture. It attempts to give readers a sense of what it feels like to be a member of the culture it describes. An **etic** ethnography describes and analyzes culture according to principles and theories drawn from Western scientific tradition, such as ecology, economy, or psychology. For example, the Nacirema essay is an etic analysis drawn from a psychological perspective. **Ethnology** is the attempt to find general principles or laws that govern cultural phenomena. Ethnologists compare and contrast practices in different cultures to find regularities.

Although most cultural anthropologists focus on current-day cultures, studying the ways in which societies change demands a knowledge of their past. As a result, many cultural anthropologists are drawn to historical ethnography: description of the cultural past based on written records, interviews, and archaeology.

Archaeology

A friend of ours once had a T-shirt with the logo "All that remains is archaeology," a pun that gets close to explaining what **archaeology** is about. Human beings in every culture make physical changes to their environment and leave traces of their activities behind them. In some cases, these changes are large and easily visible . . . like New York City. In other cases, the changes are very small: only a fire circle, small objects of stone, remains of meals, and, perhaps, places where wooden poles were stuck in the ground.

One of the fundamental insights of anthropology is that, although surprising things may happen, our lives are not random. The things we do form some sort of pattern. Consider two simple examples. Every day, most professors leave their homes and go to their offices. The vast majority of their possessions are in one of these places with little scattered between the two. If you were to make a guess at professorial behavior based on the distribution of professors' belongings, you'd guess correctly that professors spent most of their time at their home or at their office. Similarly, if you were to look at professors' homes, you would find that in most cases pots

ethnography The major research tool of cultural anthropology; includes both fieldwork among people in a society and the written results of such fieldwork.

emic Examining societies using concepts, categories, and distinctions that are meaningful to members of that culture.

etic Examining societies using concepts, categories, and rules derived from science; an outsider's perspective.

ethnology The attempt to find general principles or laws that govern cultural phenomena.

archaeology The subdiscipline of anthropology that focuses on the reconstruction of past cultures based on their material remains.

and pans are located in the kitchen and the books are located in the den. You might occasionally find a book in the kitchen or a pot in the den, but that would be rare. From this distribution, you probably would conclude that, in general, professors cooked in the kitchen and read in the den. These simple examples get at a central insight: The patterns of our lives impress themselves on our material belongings.

The key focus of archaeology is looking at the material remains people leave behind and trying to infer their cultural patterns from them. Understanding this is important for at least two reasons. First, most people probably have an "Indiana Jones" conception of archaeology. In the movies, archaeology is about collecting exciting or beautiful objects for museums and personal collections. Although it is perhaps true that every researcher likes finding a really beautiful artifact, archaeology is not really about finding objects; it is about interpreting their patterns to provide insights into the lives and cultural ways of other people in other times. Second, a focus on pattern provides a small moral reminder. Archaeological sites are a highly limited resource. Once they are destroyed, they are gone for good. Looters and amateur collectors disturb sites to take artifacts. The loss of the artifacts is bad, but these objects rarely have scientific importance in themselves. The loss of the patterns is far worse. A site that has been looted or otherwise disturbed cannot tell us much about the lives and culture that went on there.

Anthropological Linguistics

anthropological linguistics The study of language and its relation to culture.

Anthropological linguistics is the study of language and its relation to culture. The human ability to use language is one of our most fascinating attributes. Other animals make noise too: Birds chirp and elephants trumpet, but human noise differs from animal noise in important ways. First, humans have a huge number of words and we put them together in complex patterns. As far as we know, no other animal has as large a repertoire of sound. Second, we form communities of speech. Different groups of humans speak different languages, and each has culturally based customs for determining what kinds of speech are appropriate for different social situations. Finally, although researchers have been able to teach other animals to use very limited humanlike vocabularies and language structures, the use of complex language is central to being a human being. There are no groups of humans who don't use complex language. And, as far as we know, there are no other animals that, in their natural setting, do.

Anthropological linguists try to understand how words work in human communities. Sometimes they are interested in the histories of language. Sometimes they focus on the structure of language. More often, they are concerned with discerning the patterns of speech and rules of verbal interaction that guide communication in different groups and in different social settings within a group. They focus on the social learning that enables people to know when it is appropriate to speak and what is appropriate to say.

Physical or Biological Anthropology

The fourth subdiscipline of anthropology is **physical** or **biological anthropology**. Anthropologists in this subdiscipline study humans as physical and biological entities. Understanding human biology is critical to anthropology because all human culture rests on a biological base. For example, we have highly accurate depth perception, hands with opposable thumbs, and the ability to manipulate objects with great precision. These features are fundamental to making tools, and without them, human culture would be vastly different, if it existed at all. Anthropologists are engaged in an often fierce debate about the biological origins of specific behaviors, but no one doubts that the form of the human body and the capacities of the human mind both shape and are shaped by culture.

There are numerous foci within physical and biological anthropology, some of which are very well known. When we think about humans as biological organisms, one of the first things we'd like to understand is where we came from, our evolutionary history. **Human paleontology** is a focus within biological anthropology that tries to answer this question. Human paleontologists search for fossils to discover and reconstruct the evolutionary history of our species. They extract biological and chemical data from ancient bones or from living humans to help discover the biological histories of humanity and the relationships among different human groups. The findings of human paleontologists often make spectacular news and lead us to rethink what it means to be human. For example, the recent sequencing of the Neanderthal genome and subsequent discovery that Neanderthals are more closely related to modern people than previously thought (Green et al. 2010, Callaway 2010) made news across the world. This finding will give us additional information on the things that make human beings unique as well as the characteristics we share with others.

Primatology is a second well-known focus in biological anthropology. Humans are primates, and other primates, such as apes, Old World and New World monkeys, and prosimians, are biologically very close to us. We share about 98 percent of our genes with our closest ape relations. Studying these relatives may give us important insights into the behavior of our evolutionary ancestors. It is useful to keep in mind that although the 2 percent genetic difference between us and our nearest ape relations sounds like a small amount, it is clearly extraordinarily important. In some critical way, that 2 percent makes us who we are. We learn more about what it means to be not an ape, but to be human, by studying our nonhuman relations.

physical (or biological) anthropology The subdiscipline of anthropology that studies people from a biological perspective, focusing primarily on aspects of humankind that are genetically inherited.

human paleontology The focus within biological anthropology that traces human evolutionary history.

primatology The focus within biological anthropology that is concerned with the biology and behavior of nonhuman primates.

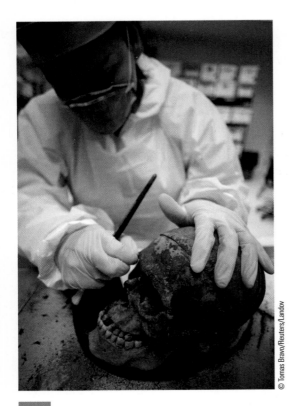

© Tomas Bravo/Reuters/Landov

Forensic anthropologists advise law enforcement agencies and other organizations about the identity of victims of crime, political violence, and natural disaster. Here a forensic anthropologist cleans a skull exhumed from a mass grave near Juarez, Mexico.

forensic anthropology The application of biological anthropology to the identification of skeletalized or badly decomposed human remains.

applied anthropology The application of anthropology to the solution of human problems.

Forensic anthropology, a third focus, is concerned with using the tools of physical anthropology to aid in the identification of skeletal or badly decomposed human remains. Forensic anthropologists identify the victims of crimes, warfare, and genocide. Their work often is critical in bringing those guilty of crimes against individuals or crimes against humanity to justice. Books, including Mary Manhein's *The Bone Lady* (1999) and William Maples and Michael Browning's *Dead Men Do Tell Tales* (1995), and television shows, such as *Bones and Forensic Files,* have brought forensic anthropology to the public's attention.

There are numerous other fields within physical and biological anthropology. These include the study of human variation, population genetics, and anthropometry: the measurement of human bodies.

Applied Anthropology

From the start, anthropologists have been interested in the application of their studies. Anthropologists such as Franz Boas contributed to debates on race and foreign policy at the turn of the 20th century. Margaret Mead, Ruth Benedict, and others did studies aimed at helping America's efforts during World War II. However, in the first half of the 20th century, almost all anthropologists worked in universities. In the past fifty years, anthropology has increasingly become a full-time profession for people outside of academe. **Applied anthropology** is the use of cultural anthropology, linguistics, archaeology, and biological anthropology to solve practical problems in business, politics, delivery of services, and land management. There are anthropologists who analyze factory floors and decision-making structures for large corporations. There are those who try to determine the best ways to sell products or deliver services. There are anthropologists who work for hospitals and health care organizations, improving the ability of these agencies to serve their patients. Some anthropologists work in politics, performing foreign and domestic policy analysis for governmental agencies. Some are employed in trying to find effective ways to deliver aid to people in poor nations. There are anthropologists who work in museums and those who work on public lands, uncovering our archaeological heritage and both preserving it and making it available to the public.

In all of these cases and many others besides, anthropologists take the knowledge and the methodological skills they have learned in the classroom and through fieldwork and apply them to the real-world tasks of making money, providing better services to people, and, we would like to think, making the world a bit better.

ANTHROPOLOGY AND "RACE"

One thing that anthropology can help us understand is "race." In the United States, most people see humanity as composed of biological "races." Census forms, applications, and other documents ask us to indicate our "race." Although "race" is clearly an important social and historical fact in America, most anthropologists believe that "race" is not a scientifically valid system of classification. Despite more than a century of attempts, no agreed-on, consistent system of "racial" classification has ever been developed. We have put the word "race" in quotation marks in this paragraph to begin to focus your attention on these problems. To make reading easier, we dispense with the quotation marks for the remainder of the book.

There are many problems in developing a scientifically valid racial classification scheme. First, most Americans understand race as a bundle of traits: light skin, light hair, light eyes, and so on. But, if this is so, the races you create are the result of the traits you choose. For example, races based on blood type would be very different than races based on skin color. However, there is no biological reason to think that skin color is more important than blood type. Almost all traits we use to assign people to a race are facial traits. It is hard to imagine a biological reason why the shape of one's eye or nose should be more important than the characteristics of one's gallbladder or liver. It is easy to find a social reason: traits easily visible on the face enable us to rapidly assign individuals to a racial group. This is a good clue that race is about society, not biology.

There are many other problems with racial classifications. For example, if race is biological, members of one race should be genetically closer to one another than to members of different races. But, measurement reveals that people are as different from others classified in their same race as they are from those in different races. Or consider people from Central Africa, Melanesia (islands in the Western Pacific), and France. Most Central Africans and most Melanesians have dark-colored skin. Most French are light. However, Africans are more closely related to the French than either is to Melanesians. This isn't surprising considering the geographical distances involved, but it suggests that traits like skin color have arisen at many times and many places in the past. Furthermore, although the characteristics of our species, Homo sapiens, were fully present 35,000 to 40,000 years ago, a 2004 study by Rohde, Olson, and Chang argues that all current-day humans have common ancestors who lived only 2,000 to 5,000 years ago. At a time depth of more than 5,000 years, all people alive today have exactly the same ancestors. Thus, differences among people are very recent and unlikely to be of great biological importance.

Anthropology teaches us that the big differences among human groups result from culture, not biology. Adaptation through culture, the potential for cultural richness, and creativity are universal. They override physical variation among human groups. We explore issues surrounding race and ethnicity many places in this book, particularly in Chapter 11.

WHY STUDY ANTHROPOLOGY

Let's be honest. If you're reading this book for a course at a college or university, what happened when you told your friends you were taking anthropology? Some certainly thought it was cool, but others no doubt said something like, "Why would you do that? What's that good for?" If you're a traditional student (age 18 to 23) and you told your parents that you're planning on majoring in anthropology, they might have told you it was a great idea, but they more likely threw up their hands and conjured up visions of you moving back into their house in your mid-20s. So what did you tell them? Why should you major in anthropology or even take a course in it? Well, you might have told them that you want to work in some aspect of applied anthropology or you want to become a college professor, but we think there are other good answers as well.

In most colleges, anthropology is part of a liberal arts curriculum. The liberal arts generally also include English, geography, history, modern languages, philosophy, political science, psychology, and sociology. They may include many other departments and programs as well. Some liberal arts programs teach skills that are directly applicable to job requirements. For example, if you want to teach middle school English, you will probably need a degree in English in most places. Geography departments may offer training in remote sensing and analysis of aerial photography, complex skills with very specific job applications. However, the vast majority of liberal arts programs produce generalists. An undergraduate degree in psychology does not generally get you a job as a psychologist. Most people who study political science do not go on to become politicians, and few who study sociology go on to work as sociologists. In fact, survey data show that there often is little connection between people's undergraduate major and their eventual career. For example, in a survey of 3,000 alumni from the University of Virginia School of Arts and Sciences, 70 percent reported that there was little such connection. This survey included many who had majored in subjects that required specific technical skills (University of Virginia 2006; Tang 2007).

Both job prospects and the careers that people eventually pursue are about the same for students who study anthropology and for those who major in other liberal arts disciplines. Like the others, anthropology graduates go on to government, business, and the professions. Some are executives at large corporations, some are restaurateurs, some are lawyers, some are doctors, some are social service workers, some sell insurance, some are government officials, some are diplomats, and yes, no doubt, some still live with their parents. And you could say the same of every other liberal arts program.

To refocus the question, we might ask: What are the particular ways of thought that anthropology courses develop and that are applicable to the very broad range of occupations that students who study anthropology follow? How is anthropology different from other social science disciplines? Although there certainly are many ways to answer these questions, it seems to us that three are of particular importance.

First, anthropology is the university discipline that focuses on understanding other groups of people. This focus on culture is one of the most valuable contributions anthropology can make to our ability to understand our world and to analyze and solve problems.

Although America has always been an ethnically and culturally diverse place, for most of the 20th century the reins of wealth and power were held by a dominant group: white Protestant men of northern European ancestry. Members of other groups sometimes did become rich, and many white Protestants certainly were poor. However, wealthy white Protestants held the majority of positions of influence and power in American society, including executive positions at most large corporations, high political offices at both state and national levels, and seats on the judiciary. As a result, if you happened to be born white, Protestant, and male, you had an advantage. Of course, you might inherit great wealth. But, even if (as was more likely) you were the son of a factory hand or a shopkeeper, you were a representative of the dominant culture. The ways of the powerful were, more or less, your ways. If members of other cultural groups wanted to speak with you, do business with you, or participate in public and civic affairs with you, they had to learn to do so on your terms . . . not you on theirs. They had to learn your style of English, the customs of your religion, the forms of address, body language, clothing, manners, and so on, appropriate to their role in your culture. Because others had to do the work of changing their behavior, you probably were almost completely unaware of this; you simply accepted it as the way things were. *Miami Herald* columnist Leonard Pitts (2007) has pointed out that "if affirmative action is defined as giving preferential treatment on the basis of gender or race, then no one in this country has received more than white men." Although such preferences were obvious to those who did not receive them, they were generally invisible to those who did.

The white, Protestant, northern European male is hardly an endangered species in America (such people today still control most of the nation's wealth); however, by the late 20th century, their virtual monopoly on power began to break up. In America, members of minority groups have moved to stronger economic and political positions. Moreover, America increasingly exists in a world filled with other powerful nations with very different histories and traditions. It is less and less a world where everyone wants to do business with America and is willing to do so on American terms. Instead, corporations, workforces, and institutions are increasingly spread across the globe. Capital and information crosses spacial, national, and cultural boundaries in milliseconds. Americans who wish to understand and operate effectively in such a world must learn other cultures and other ways; failure to do so puts them at a distinct disadvantage.

At home, America once again is a nation of immigrants. Immigration flourished in America in the late 19th and early 20th centuries. However, in the early 1920s, Congress passed a series of laws that greatly limited it. These laws persisted until 1965, but since then, immigration has steadily increased. In 2009, 1.1 million people became permanent legal residents of the United States. Individuals born in Mexico accounted for less than 15 percent of this total. Other countries that contributed large numbers of immigrants include China, the Philippines, India, Cuba, and Vietnam (Monger 2010:4). Until the late 20th century, most immigrants were cut off from their homelands by politics and by the expense and difficulty of communication. In this condition, assimilation to the dominant American culture was essential. Although politics will always be an issue, today's immigrants can, in most cases, communicate freely and inexpensively with family and friends in their homelands and may be able to travel back and forth on a regular basis. Thus, complete assimilation is far less necessary or desirable.

Some people may applaud multiculturalism; others may bemoan what they feel is the passing of the "American" way of life. What no one can really dispute is that the world of today is vastly different from the world of 1950. Given the increasing integration of economic systems, the declining costs of communication and transportation, and the rising economic power of China and other nations, we can be sure that people of different ethnic, racial, and cultural backgrounds will meet more and more frequently in arenas where none has clear economic and cultural dominance. Thus, an understanding of the nature of culture and a knowledge of the basic tools scholars have devised to analyze it are essential, and anthropology is the place to get them.

In addition to this first, very practical application, there is a second, more philosophical concern of anthropologists. Like scholars in many other disciplines, anthropologists grapple with the question of what it means to be a human being. However, anthropologists bring some unique tools to bear upon this issue. Within anthropology, we can look for the answer to this question in two seemingly mutually exclusive ways. We can look at culture as simply the sum total of everything that humans have done, thought, created, and believed. In a sense, as individual humans, we are heirs to the vast array of cultural practices and experiences humans have ever had. Anthropology is the discipline that attempts to observe, collect, record, and understand the full range of human cultural experience. Through anthropology, we know the great variety of forms that cultures can take. We know the huge variation in social organization, belief systems, production, and family structures that is found in human society. This gives us insight into the plasticity of human society as well as the limits to that plasticity.

Alternatively, we can answer the question by ignoring the variability of human culture and trying to find and focus on the characteristics that all cultures share, traits that are universal in human societies. In the 1940s, George Murdock listed 77 characteristics that he believed were common to all cultures. These included such things as dream interpretation, incest taboos, inheritance rules, and religious ritual. More recent authors (Brown 1991; Cleaveland, Craven, and Danfelser 1979) have developed other lists and analyses. Brown (1991:143) notes that human universals are very diverse, and there likely is no single explanation for them. However, thinking about commonalities among cultures may guide us in our attempt to understand human nature.

Finally, anthropology presents many useful ways of thinking about culture. One effective way of understanding culture is to think of it as a set of answers to a particular problem: How does a group of human beings survive together in the world? In other words, a culture is a set of behaviors, beliefs, understandings, objects, and ways of interacting that enable a group to survive with greater or lesser success and greater or lesser longevity. At some level, all human societies must answer the critical question of survival together, and to some degree, each culture is a different answer to it.

In the world today and in our own society, we face extraordinary problems: problems of hunger, poverty, inequality, violence between groups, violence within families, drug addiction, pollution, crime; the list is long. However, we are not the only people in the world ever to have faced problems. At some level, all of these problems are the result of our attempt to live together as a group on this planet. Learning how other peoples in other places, and perhaps other times as well, solved their problems may give us the insight to solve our own; we might learn lessons, both positive and negative, from their cultural experiences.

In some ways, the cultures of today are unique. Societies have never been as large and interconnected as many are today. They have never had the wealth that many societies have today. They have never had the levels of technology, abilities to communicate, and abilities to destroy that our current society has. These characteristics make it naive for us to imagine that we could simply observe a different culture, adopt their ways as our own, and live happily ever after. We can no more re-create tribal culture or ancient culture or even the culture of industrialized nations of fifty years ago than we can walk through walls. But it does not follow that the answers of others are useless to us.

In Greek drama, the notion of hubris is critical. Hubris probably is best understood as excessive pride or confidence that leads to both arrogance and insolence toward others. In Greek tragedy, the hubris of characters is often their fatal flaw and leads to their downfall. Heroes such as Oedipus and Creon were doomed by their hubris.

We surely won't find that the members of other cultures have provided ready-made answers to all the problems that confront us. But to imagine ourselves as totally unique, to imagine that the experiences of other peoples and other cultures have nothing to teach us, is a form of hubris and, as in tragedy, could well lead to our downfall.

The ancient Greeks contrasted hubris with arete. Arete implies a humble striving for perfection along with the realization that such perfection cannot be reached. With this notion in mind, we approach the study of anthropology cheerfully and with a degree of optimism. From anthropology, we hope to learn new ways of analyzing, understanding, celebrating, and coming to terms with the enormous variations in human cultural behavior. We hope to be able to think creatively about what it means to be human beings and to use what we learn to provide insight into the issues, problems, and possibilities of our own culture. We hope that, with the help of such understanding, we will leave the world a better place than we found it.

BRINGING IT BACK HOME:
ANTHROPOLOGY AND HOMELESSNESS

Most anthropologists would like their work to further a deep understanding of the human condition. But they also want to provide practical help that enables people to live their lives and do their jobs more effectively. They want to help find meaningful solutions for problems in our own society. The work of Vincent Lyon-Callo, an anthropologist who studies social services for homeless people, is a good example. Lyon-Callo hopes to understand homelessness but also to move attention on its causes to the center of American culture and politics.

Lyon-Callo believes that most homelessness in the United States results from a cultural and political philosophy that embraces the free markets and private initiative as the solution to social problems. He argues that most Americans believe the problem of homelessness can be solved through charity or services aimed at reforming homeless people, who are seen as deviant or disabled. This understanding undercuts attempts to see homelessness as a result of systemic inequalities, such as increasing unemployment, declining relative wages, and exploitation of workers. Lyon-Callo argues that, by distracting action from these issues, the social services orientation helps to maintain homelessness.

Working in collaboration with community members and homeless people in Northampton, Massachusetts, Lyon-Callo promoted new understandings of homelessness. His emphasis on structural causes of homelessness, such as lack of jobs and lack of housing, led to the creation of a winter cot program in community churches, a living-wage campaign, and new job opportunities for the homeless.

Lyon-Callo suggests that anthropological analysis can challenge routine understandings, raise new questions, and get people to think in new ways. He argues that in the absence of political efforts to transform the economy, caring and helping cannot themselves end homelessness. Anthropologists must work in public political forums to expose the connections between social problems, political ideologies, and inequality. However, promoting profound change is slow and discouraging work. Even those who basically agree with Lyon-Callo note that the current social service approach at least offers a degree of immediate hope for homeless people.

YOU DECIDE

1. Lyon-Callo promotes a politically engaged anthropology in which the researchers become advocates for their subjects. What are the advantages and disadvantages of such an approach?

2. Lyon-Callo's research focuses on a critique of American society, and the critical problems he identifies are very difficult to correct. Have you ever had a problem that seemed impossible to solve? Did you wish the problem would go away, or did you enjoy "digging in" and finding a solution? Is it fair to be critical of your society? Are you?

3. What are some specific American cultural values that underlie both the causes and the treatment of homelessness in the United States? How might an understanding of those cultural values help provide solutions to the problem of homelessness? Have you ever spent the night outside? Was it because you wanted to, or was it beyond your control? Was it fun? Were you scared? What did others think? Would you do it again? Could you live like that?

CHAPTER SUMMARY

1. The essay "Body Ritual among the Nacirema" by Horace Miner illustrates two critical themes that continue to draw people to anthropology: our quest to gain knowledge and understanding of people who are vastly different from ourselves, and our desire to know ourselves and our own culture better.

2. Anthropology is a comparative study of humankind. Anthropologists study human beings of the past and of the present and in every corner of the world.

3. Anthropology is holistic. Anthropologists study the entire range of human social, political, economic, and religious behavior as well as the relationships among the different aspects of human behavior.

4. Anthropology is divided into subfields: cultural anthropology, anthropological linguistics, archaeology, physical or biological anthropology, and applied anthropology.

5. Anthropology stresses the importance of culture in human adaptation. It asserts that critical differences among individuals are cultural rather than biological.

6. Anthropology demonstrates that race is not a valid scientific category but rather is a social and cultural construct.

7. Anthropology is part of the liberal arts curriculum. Both the job prospects and the careers of those who study anthropology are similar to the job prospects and careers of those who study other liberal arts disciplines.

8. Anthropology courses develop three important ways of thought that are applicable to the broad range of occupations followed by anthropologists: (1) Anthropology focuses on understanding other groups of people. (2) Anthropologists grapple with the question of what it means to be a human being. Anthropology is the discipline that attempts to observe, collect, record, and understand the full range of human cultural experience. (3) Lastly, anthropology presents many useful ways of thinking about culture.

9. Learning how other peoples in other places solved their problems may give us insight into solving our own problems. In addition, we can learn lessons, both positive and negative, from their cultural experience.

KEY TERMS

Anthropological linguistics	Archaeology
Anthropology	Cultural anthropology
Applied anthropology	Cultural relativism

Culture
Emic
Ethnocentrism
Ethnography
Ethnology
Ethnoscape
Etic

Forensic anthropology
Holism
Human paleontology
Physical (or biological)
   anthropology
Primatology
Society

© adrian arbib/Alamy

Many dimensions of culture are expressed in the ritual dress of these Masaai men participating in an initiation ritual. They are dressed in styles and patterns that the Masaai have used for many years, but each wears a wristwatch as well.

CHAPTER 2

CULTURE COUNTS

CHAPTER OUTLINE

AUTISM AND CULTURE

AUTISM is a developmental disorder characterized by difficulties in both verbal and nonverbal communication, impairment of social interaction, and a host of other symptoms. It is generally diagnosed in children between the ages of 18 and 36 months. The incidence of autism is increasing rapidly in the United States, and a government report issued in early 2007 states that autism may affect as many as one in 150 children. Given that statistic, you likely either know or know of someone with autism.

Autism can occur at many different levels of severity. Some individuals with profound autism are silent and deeply withdrawn. However, many others have a mild-to-moderate form of autism called *Asperger's syndrome*. People with Asperger's syndrome can master language and learn to participate in society.

Some individuals with autism or Asperger's have exceptional intellectual skills. Dr. Temple Grandin is among the best known of such people. Dr. Grandin is a professor of animal science at Colorado State University. As a researcher, Grandin is best known for her work on the humane slaughter of cattle. However, Grandin has also written extensively on her experience with autism and the ways in which she has learned to interact with other people and navigate her social world. In 2010, she was the subject of an HBO movie and was on *Time Magazine*'s list of the world's 100 most influential people (*Time* 2010).

As Grandin and psychologist Oliver Sacks explain it, people with autism think in extremely concrete terms and have profound difficulty understanding social conventions and cultural presuppositions of every sort. Some researchers say that autistics lack a "theory of mind." That is, they find it very hard to attribute mental states, such as intention, desire, deceit, and belief, to others or perhaps even to themselves. Although Grandin does not agree with this analysis, her work shows that she has learned to relate to others in ways that are fundamentally different from the ways of most people. Writing about Grandin, Sacks (1995:270) says, "The implicit knowledge, which every normal person accumulates and generates throughout life on the basis of experience and encounters with others, Temple seems to be largely devoid of. Lacking it, she has instead to 'compute' others' intentions and states of mind, to try to make algorithmic and explicit, what for the rest of us is second nature." Members of another, highly functioning autistic family interviewed by Sacks (1995:276) said, "We know the rules and conventions of the 'normal' but there is no actual transit. You act normal, you learn the rules and obey them. . . . You learn to ape human behavior . . . [but] don't understand what is behind the social conventions."

Grandin has often described herself as an "anthropologist on Mars." To her, being in human society is like being on a different planet. She is an outsider confronted with a wholly different way of life. She can observe what people do, but their actions make no sense. She has no intuitive feel for the things going on around her. In other words, for Grandin, other people have this thing we call "culture." Either she lacks culture, or her culture is enormously different from what other people have. Grandin has been very successful because she has learned to imitate normality. That is, through observation and analysis (and with the help of mentors), she has learned many of the rules of cultural behavior. She has learned when she needs to say certain things and to perform certain actions. But Sacks reports that, despite her success, Grandin does not think she understands others. She feels that there is something mechanical about her mind and that "the emotion circuit is not hooked up" (Sacks 1995:286). For example, when Sacks and Grandin visit the Rocky Mountains, Grandin tells Sacks, "you look at the brook, at the flowers. I see what great pleasure you get out of it. I'm denied that. . . . You get such joy out of the sunset. . . . I wish I did too. I know it's beautiful, but I don't 'get' it" (Sacks 1995:293–294). The classical music critic Tim Page (2007:36), who has Asperger's syndrome, recently wrote: "I am left with the melancholy sensation that my life has been spent in a perpetual state of parallel play, alongside, but distinctly apart from, the rest of humanity."

Accounts of autistic individuals such as Grandin and Page show that it is extremely difficult for them to become functioning members of society. Grandin's experiences as well as her notion of herself as an anthropologist on Mars strongly suggest that she does not participate in culture in the way that most people do. Such cases make it clear that, without the constraints, assumptions, and patterns imposed by culture, it is extraordinarily difficult to express our human qualities and abilities. But what is culture?

Although it is difficult to come up with a useful brief definition of culture, an anthropologist from Mars observing the many different human cultures might come up with six characteristics shared by all cultures:

1. Cultures are made up of learned behaviors. People are not born knowing their culture. They learn it through a process called **enculturation.**
2. Cultures all involve classification systems and symbols. A **symbol** is simply something that stands for something else. People use cultural symbols to create meaning.
3. Cultures are patterned and integrated. Thus, changes in one aspect of culture affect other aspects. However, elements of culture do not necessarily work smoothly with one another.

enculturation The process of learning to be a member of a particular cultural group.

symbol Something that stands for something else. Central to language and culture.

4. Cultures are shared. Although there may be disagreement about many aspects of a culture, there must be considerable consensus as well.
5. Cultures are adaptive and include information about how to survive in the world. Cultures also contain much that is maladaptive.
6. Cultures are subject to change. Whether propelled by their internal dynamics or acted upon by outside forces, cultures are always in flux.

Based on this list, we might define culture as the learned, symbolic, at least partially adaptive, and ever-changing patterns of behavior and meaning shared by members of a group. Although anthropologists agree on the basic characteristics of culture, they disagree on their relative importance, how to study them, and indeed the goal of anthropology itself. For example, some anthropologists are deeply concerned with observable behavior. For these scholars, what people actually do is far more important than what they say or how they understand the world. Other anthropologists take precisely the opposite view. Their primary goal is to comprehend the ways in which other people understand their world. Some anthropologists hope to find general laws of human cultural behavior. Others are more concerned with describing cultures or describing specific aspects of culture. These disagreements reflect different theoretical positions within anthropology. For our purposes, an **anthropological theory** is a set of propositions about which aspects of culture are critical, how they should be studied, and what the goal of studying them should be. Although those who hold different theoretical perspectives may insist that there is a right way and a wrong way to do anthropology, we suggest that theoretical perspectives are more like different windows through which one may view culture. Just as the view changes as one moves from one window of a building to another, so does the anthropologist's understanding of society change as he or she changes focus from one aspect of culture to another. Just as two windows may have views that overlap or views that show totally different scenes, perspectives on culture may overlap or reveal totally different aspects. In this chapter, we examine each element of our definition of culture. Each is a common characteristic of all human groups. However, each also raises questions, problems, and contradictions. Through examining these elements, we come to a keener appreciation of the nature of culture and, ultimately, what it means to be human.

anthropological theory A set of propositions about which aspects of culture are critical, how they should be studied, and what the goal of studying them should be.

CULTURE IS MADE UP OF LEARNED BEHAVIORS

Just about everything that is animate learns. Your dog, your cat, even your fish show some learned behavior. But, as far as we know, no other creature has as much learned behavior as human beings. Almost every aspect of our lives is layered with learning. Our heart beats, our eyes blink, and our knees respond reflexively to a doctor's rubber mallet, but to get much beyond that, we need learning. Food is a good example. Humans must eat; that much is determined biologically. However, we don't just eat; our culture teaches us what is edible and what is not. Many things that are nutritious, we decline as not being food. Many insects, for example, are perfectly edible. The philosopher Aristotle was particularly fond of eating cicadas, and northern Europeans ate some species of beetles well into the 19th century. Yet most Americans have learned that insects are not food, and they will go hungry, to the point of starvation, before eating them. Further, we eat particular things at particular times, in particular places, and with particular people. For example, although it is acceptable to eat popcorn at the movies, you would be unlikely to have lamb chops and asparagus, or a nice stir-fry at most movie theaters.

We sometimes think of learning as an aspect of childhood, but in every society, human beings learn their culture continuously. We are socialized from the moment of our births to the time of our deaths. Although large demands for labor and responsible behavior may be placed on children in many societies, all humans remain physically, emotionally, and intellectually immature well into their teen years and perhaps into their early 20s. This lengthy period of immaturity has profound implications. First, it allows time for an enormous amount of childhood learning. This means that very few specific behaviors need be under direct genetic or biological control. Second, it demands that human cultures be designed to provide relatively stable environments that protect the young for long periods of time.

Human infants become adults in a particular human society. Thus, the infant grows into a child and later into an adult not simply as a human but as a particular kind of human: a Kwakiutl, Trobriand Islander, Briton, or Tahitian. Child-rearing practices in all cultures are designed to produce adults who know the skills, norms, and behavior patterns of their society—the cultural content. But the transmission of culture involves more than just knowing these things. It also involves patterning children's attitudes, motivations, values, perceptions, and beliefs so that they can function in their society (which itself adapts to external requirements of the physical and social environment). The process of learning to be a member of a particular cultural group is called enculturation.

As an example, we can consider child rearing among the Inuit, a hunting people of the Arctic. The Inuit teach their children to deal with a world that is a dangerously problematic place, in which making wrong decisions might well mean death (Briggs 1991). To survive in this harsh environment, Inuit must learn to maintain a "constant state of alertness" and an "experimental way of living." Therefore, developing skills for solving

The Inuit.

The Inuit ear pull game is a harsh test of physical endurance. Contestants pull against one another until one can no longer endure the pain.

problems quickly and spontaneously is central to Inuit child rearing. Children are brought up to constantly test their physical skills to extend them and to learn their own capacity for pain and endurance (Stern 1999).

Inuit children learn largely through observing their elders. Children are discouraged from asking questions. Rather, when confronted with a problem situation, they are expected to observe closely, to reason, and to find solutions independently. They watch, practice, and then are tested, frequently by adults asking them questions based on the idea of *"isummak-saiyuq,"* a northern Baffin Island Inuit term meaning to "cause (or cause to increase) thought." Some questions are very practical. For example, when traveling on the featureless, snow-covered tundra, an adult may ask a child, "Where are we?" or "Have you ever been here before?" Others are existentially challenging. Adults may ask children, "Why don't you kill your baby brother?" or "Your mother's going to die—look, she's cut her finger—do you want to come live with me?" Such questions are not considered cruel. Rather, they force children to grapple with issues of grave consequence (Briggs 1999:5).

Play is a critical part of Inuit child rearing. Inuit games prepare children for the rigors of the arctic environment by stressing hand–eye coordination, problem solving, and physical strength and endurance. Some games involve learning by taking objects apart and trying to put them back together. This process develops careful attention to details and relationships, to patient trial and error, and to a mental recording of results for future reference. Many games stress the body and test the limits of the individual's psychological and physical endurance (Nelson 1983). For example, in the ear pull game, a thin loop of leather is positioned behind the ears of each of two competitors, who then pull away from each other until one gives up in pain (Canadian Broadcasting Company 1982).

In addition to being physically adept and independent, Inuit children must learn to be cooperative and emotionally restrained. Under the conditions of their closely knit and often isolated camp life, expressions of anger or aggression are avoided. The Inuit prize reason, judgment, and emotional control, and these characteristics are thought to grow naturally as children grow.

The Inuit believe that children have both the ability and the wish to learn. Thus, educating a child consists of providing the necessary information, which the child will remember sooner or later. Scolding is seen as futile. Children will learn when they are ready; there is no point in forcing children to learn something before they are ready to remember it. Inuit elders believe that frequent scolding makes children hostile, rebellious, and impervious to the opinions of others.

The study of enculturation has a central place in the history of anthropology and gave rise to some of its classic works. Margaret Mead's 1928 book, *Coming of Age in Samoa,* was a popular best seller and a landmark work that changed how Americans looked at childhood and culture (Mead 1971/1928). Mead and others who studied childhood learning are known as **culture and personality** theorists. They held that cultures could best be understood by examining the patterns of child rearing and considering their effect on adult lives and social institutions. Culture and personality theory was extremely influential from the 1920s to the 1950s. Although few anthropologists today would call themselves culture and personality theorists, enculturation remains an important topic of anthropological research.

culture and personality A theoretical position in anthropology that held that cultures could best be understood by examining the patterns of child rearing and considering their effect on adult lives and social institutions.

CULTURE IS THE WAY HUMANS USE SYMBOLS TO ORGANIZE AND GIVE MEANING TO THE WORLD

Consider this: Can you really see your environment? For example, when you walk into a classroom, you notice some things but not others. You see your friends and other students, the professor, the video equipment, and so on. You might spend an entire semester without ever seeing the cracks in the ceiling, the pattern of the carpeting, or the color of the walls. Yet these things are as physically present as the chairs and your friends.

You see certain things in the classroom and overlook others because you mentally organize the contents of the classroom with respect to your role as a student. It is virtually impossible to see things without organizing and evaluating them in some manner. If you paid as much attention to the cracks in the wall, the patterns on the floor, and the humming of the ventilation system as you did to the professor's lecture, not only would you likely fail the class, but you would also live in a world that was overwhelming and impossibly confusing. Only through fitting our perceptions and experiences into systems of organization and classification can we comprehend our lives and act in the world. A human without this ability would be paralyzed, frozen by an overwhelming bombardment of sensations. Indeed, this is one of the problems that people with autism such as Temple Grandin often experience.

Methods of organizing and classifying are typical of groups. You are not the only one who thinks that the students and professors in a classroom are more important than the ceiling tiles; all students and professors probably share that perception.

Anthropologists have long proposed that culture is a shared mental model that people use to organize, to classify, and ultimately to understand their world. A key way in which this model is expressed is through language, a symbolic system.

Different cultures have different models for understanding and speaking about the world. For instance, in English, the verb *smoke* describes the action of ingesting a cigarette and the verb *drink* describes the action of consuming a liquid. However, in the Bamana language, spoken by the Bambara of Mali, the verb *min* is used both for smoking and for drinking. Americans classify rainbows as objects of beauty and frequently point them out to one another. However, Lacandon Maya in southern Mexico classify rainbows as dangerous and frightening, and pointing them out to other people is highly inappropriate.

Anthropologists who are particularly interested in describing the systems of organization and classification used by different cultures often use a theoretical perspective called **ethnoscience.** Generally, these anthropologists are interested in capturing the understanding of members of a culture. Ethnoscience is one position or technique within a broader perspective called **cognitive anthropology,** which focuses on the relationship between the mind and society. Understanding classification systems is also extremely important for scholars interested in ethnobotany and ethnomedicine. **Ethnobotany** focuses on the relationship between humans and plants in different cultures. **Ethnomedicine** examines the ways in which people in different cultures understand health and sicknesses as well as the ways they attempt to cure disease. In each case, discovering how people classify and organize their world is a critical element in this process.

Human beings not only classify the world, but they also fill it with meaning. A key way that they do this is through the use of symbols. The simplest definition of a symbol is something that stands for something else.

ethnoscience A theoretical position in anthropology that focuses on recording and examining the ways in which members of a culture use language to classify and organize their cognitive world.

cognitive anthropology A theoretical position in anthropology that focuses on the relationship between the mind and society.

ethnobotany A focus within anthropology that examines the relationship between humans and plants in different cultures.

ethnomedicine A focus within anthropology that examines the ways in which people in different cultures understand health and sicknesses as well as the ways they attempt to cure disease.

Words, both spoken and written, objects, and ideas can all be symbols. Symbols enable us to store information. For example, the book you are currently holding contains a huge amount of information all stored symbolically. Because humans can store information symbolically, as stories and teachings passed from generation to generation or as written words, human cultures can be endlessly large. Nonhuman animals must learn through experience or imitation and, therefore, the amount they can learn is relatively small.

Symbols also have the ability to condense meaning. People may take a single symbol and make it stand for an entire constellation of ideas and emotions. Religious symbols and national symbols often have this characteristic. The meaning of a national flag or a symbol such as the cross cannot be summed up in a word or two. These symbols stand for vast complexes of history, ideas, and emotions. People are often literally willing to fight and die for them.

Symbolic anthropologists try to understand a culture by discovering and analyzing the symbols that are most important to its members. These often reflect the deep concerns of the culture's members in ways that may be difficult for them to articulate. For example, according to Victor Turner (1967), among the Ndembu of East Africa, the mudyi tree is a central symbol and plays an important role in girls' puberty rites. The tree has a white, milky sap that symbolizes breast-feeding, the relationship between mother and child, the inheritance through the mother's family line, and, at the most abstract level, the unity and continuity of Ndembu society itself. It is unlikely that all Ndembu think deeply about all of these meanings during the puberty rites of their girls. However, Turner argues that this complex symbolism helps hold Ndembu society together by reaffirming its central tenets. For anthropologists, understanding the meaning of the mudyi tree and the role it plays in Ndembu society is to have penetrated deeply into the Ndembu view of the world.

Culture can also be analyzed using the tools of literature, and this is the job of **interpretive anthropology**. Clifford Geertz, one of the best-known interpretive anthropologists, said that, in a sense, culture is like a novel. It is an "ensemble of texts . . . which the anthropologist strains to read over the shoulders of those to whom they properly belong" (Geertz 2008/1973a:531). He meant that culture is a story people tell themselves about themselves. Like all good stories, culture engrosses us and helps us understand the nature and meaning of life. It comments on who we are and how we should act in the world. Interpretive anthropologists often find these cultural texts in public events, celebrations, and rituals. Analyzing them gives us clues and insights into the meaning of culture for its participants.

Consider the American fascination with football. American football has little appeal outside the United States, but here it draws more fans than

symbolic anthropology A theoretical position in anthropology that focuses on understanding cultures by discovering and analyzing the symbols that are most important to their members.

interpretive anthropology A theoretical position in anthropology that focuses on using humanistic methods, such as those found in the analysis of literature, to analyze culture and discover the meaning of culture to its participants.

any other sport. Football has lots of excitement and action, but so do many less popular sports. Some anthropologists argue that football's popularity is related to its symbolic meanings, that is, the unique ways in which it presents and manipulates important American cultural themes. Football attracts us because, more than other sports, it displays and manipulates ideas about topics such as the violence and sexuality underlying competition between men, racial character and the relationship of the individual to the group (Oriard 1993:18). Football is just a game, but so is checkers. Millions watch football because it is meaningful in ways that checkers is not. For interpretive anthropologists, its meaning derives from the ways in which it explores and comments on critical themes in American culture. Those who wish to understand American culture would do well to consider the meanings of football.

Interpretive and symbolic anthropologists use methods drawn from the humanities rather than from the sciences to uncover and interpret the deep emotional and psychological structure of societies. Their goal is to understand the experience of being a member of a culture and to make that experience available to their readers (Marcus and Fischer 1986).

◼ CULTURE IS AN INTEGRATED SYSTEM—OR IS IT?

Consider a biological organism. The heart pumps blood, the lungs supply the blood with oxygen, the liver purifies the blood, and so on. The various organs work together to create a properly functioning whole. An early insight in anthropology was the usefulness of comparing societies to organisms. The subsistence system provides food, the economic and political systems determine how the food is distributed, religion provides the justification for the distribution system, and so on. Societies, like bodies, are integrated systems.

organic analogy The comparison of societies to living organisms.

This **organic analogy** has strengths and weaknesses. It allows us to think about society as composed of different elements (such as kinship, religion, and subsistence), and it implies that anthropologists should describe the shape and role of such elements as well as the ways in which changes in one affect the others. For example, subsistence and social structure are two identifiable social elements and are related to each other. Foraging is an activity that is most often done in small groups and requires little direction or coordination. People who forage for their food will probably have relatively loosely defined social groups with changing membership. Farming requires more coordination than foraging; therefore, people who farm will likely have a society with a more rigid structure and a more stable membership. If a group was to move from foraging to farming, we would expect it to develop an increasingly well-defined social structure.

However, the organic analogy also implies that properly functioning societies should be stable and conflict-free. The parts of a biological organism work together to keep the entire being alive and well. The lungs do not declare war on the liver. The result of conflict between the parts of a living thing is sickness or death. If such conflict occurs (an autoimmune disease, for example), we understand that the organism is not functioning properly, and steps should be taken to restore the system. Thinking of cultures as systems may similarly suggest that their parts should work in harmony and that conflict and struggle are deviations from normality. But are cultures really like that? Do their elements really fit well together?

Consider, for example, whether the American family system fits well with the demands made by most American jobs. Most Americans want to maintain long-term marriage commitments, raise families, and live middle-class lifestyles. Most jobs in the United States provide inadequate income for this purpose. Many jobs require mobility, long hours, and flexibility, which come at the expense of the family. Americans must negotiate the contradictions between the lifestyle they desire, the demands of their families, and the requirements of their jobs.

Consider that, in socially stratified societies, different groups have different interests, and this creates conflict. For example, in capitalist societies, both workers and owners want their companies to do well, but within this context, the owners hope to maximize their profit and the workers want to maximize their pay. However, increases in workers' pay come at some expense to owners' profits. Therefore, there is a structural conflict between the owners and the workers. This conflict does not occur because society is not working properly. Rather, it is a fundamental condition of a capitalist society.

There is nothing uniquely American or modern about contradiction and conflict within culture. People in nonindustrialized societies must also handle conflicting commitments to their families and other social groups, such as secret societies or religious associations. Even in societies that lack social groups beyond the family, the interests of men and women, or those of the old and the young, may differ. Thus, in all societies, social life may be characterized by conflict as well as concord. Although culture certainly is patterned and surely is a system, often the parts may rub, chafe, and grind against each other.

Anthropologists who are drawn to the study of the relationships among different aspects of culture have often sought to find laws of cultural behavior. In the first half of the 20th century, **functionalists** such as A. R. Radcliffe-Brown and Bronislaw Malinowski searched for such laws in the mutually supportive relationships among kinship, religion,

functionalism A theoretical position in anthropology, common in the first half of the 20th century, that focuses on finding general laws that identify different elements of society, show how they relate to each other, and demonstrate their role in maintaining social order.

ecological functionalism A theoretical position in anthropology that focuses on the relationship between environment and society.

and politics. For example, Radcliffe-Brown (1965/1952:176) argued that religion supports social structure by giving individuals a sense of dependence on their society.

More recently, **ecological functionalists** have focused on the relationship between environment and society. These anthropologists view social institutions and practices as elements in broader ecological systems. They are particularly concerned with ways in which cultural practices both alter and are altered by the ecosystem in which they occur. For example, Marvin Harris's (1966) classic explanation of the Hindu taboo on eating beef focused on the effect of cattle in the Indian environment rather than on the Hindu belief system. Harris noted that despite widespread poverty and periodic famine in India, Hindus refuse to eat their cattle. Although this seems unreasonable superficially, it makes good ecological sense. Cows are important in India because they provide dung for fertilizer and cooking fuel, and they give birth to bullocks, the draft animals that pull the plows and carts essential to agriculture. If a family ate its cows during a famine, it would deprive itself of the source of bullocks and could not continue farming. Thus, the Hindu religious taboo on eating beef is part of a larger ecological pattern that includes the subsistence system.

Many anthropologists today, although they accept that culture is a patterned system, choose to focus on conflicts within the system. This often reflects the deep influence of the work of Karl Marx and the early 20th-century sociologist Max Weber. Both Marx and Weber saw conflict in society as a key factor driving social change. For example, Marx understood society to be made up of different social groups, such as factory owners and workers, who had opposing interests. Marx believed that, over time, these opposing interests inevitably would lead to both conflict and social change.

CULTURE IS A SHARED SYSTEM OF NORMS AND VALUES—OR IS IT?

What would a person with their own private culture be like? Perhaps he or she would be like Temple Grandin, Tim Page, or other high-functioning autistics: able to exist in the social world but unable to "get it." Alternatively, such a person might live in a world in which everything has one set of meanings to them but different meanings to everyone else. People with certain forms of schizophrenia seem to have just this problem; they live in worlds filled with symbols that are of meaning only to them. In either case, it would be very difficult for such people to interact with others; they would probably be isolated and, in some cases, insane. Clearly, then, at some level, members of a culture must share ways of thinking and behaving. Often, we refer to these as *norms* and *values*.

Norms are shared ideas about the way things ought to be done—rules of behavior that reflect and enforce culture. **Values** are shared ideas about what is true, right, and beautiful. For example, the notion that advances in technology are good is an American value; most Americans agree that humans can and should transform nature to meet human ends. Shaking hands rather than bowing when introduced to a stranger is an American norm.

Human behavior is not always consistent with cultural norms or values. People do not necessarily do what they say they should do. Norms may be contradictory and manipulated for personal and group ends. For example, people in India believe that women should stay in their homes rather than go out with their friends. They also believe that women should spend a lot of time in religious activities. Modern Indian women use the second of these ideals to get around the first. By forming clubs whose activities are religious, they have an excuse to get out of the house, to which their elders cannot object too strongly.

Cultures do share ideas about the correct way to behave, but members of a single culture often show great variability in knowledge, beliefs, and styles.

This example raises important questions. How do we determine the norms and values of a society? Do all people in society agree on these things? How many people must agree on something before it is considered a norm or a value? Research shows that, even in small societies, norms are not always followed and values are not universal. Individuals differ in their knowledge, understanding, and beliefs. For example, one might expect that all members in a small fishing society would agree on the proper names for different kinds of fish, but on Pukapuka, the small Pacific atoll Robert Borofsky (1994) studied, even experienced fishermen disagreed much of the time.

The degree to which people do not simply share a single culture is even more obvious in large societies. Sometimes the term **subculture** is used to designate groups within a single society that share norms and values significantly different from those of the **dominant culture**. The terms *dominant culture* and *subculture* do not refer to superior and inferior but rather to the idea that the dominant culture, because it controls greater wealth and power, is more able to impose its understanding of the world on subcultures than the reverse.

norms Shared ideas about the way things ought to be done; rules of behavior that reflect and enforce culture.

values Shared ideas about what is true, right, and beautiful.

subculture A group within a society that shares norms and values significantly different from those of the dominant culture.

dominant culture The culture with the greatest wealth and power in a society that consists of many subcultures.

Dominant cultures retain their power partly through control of institutions, like the legal system, criminalizing practices that conflict with their own (Norgren and Nanda 1996). In contemporary society, public schools help maintain the values of the dominant culture, and the media plays an important role in encouraging people to perceive subcultures in stereotypical (and usually negative) ways. For example, in a study that focused on television news and reality shows, Oliver (2003) found that images of race and crime systematically overrepresented African Americans as criminal. Furthermore, such shows tended to portray black men as particularly dangerous and presented information about black suspects that assumed their guilt. By contrast, many memorable recent portrayals of African Americans focus on the "magical Negro," "a lower class, uneducated black person who possesses supernatural or magical powers" (Hughey 2009:544). The "magical Negro" appears in films such as *The Green Mile* (1999) and *Pirates of the Caribbean* (2007). Hughey argues that, although such characters are an improvement over earlier stereotypes, they capitalize on traditional stereotypes of African Americans such as poverty, cultural deficiency, and folk wisdom. They treat whiteness as normal, and glorify black characters, only they are placed in racially subservient positions.

Although domination of one group by another is extreme in some situations, rarely is it complete. People contest their subjugation and protect their subcultures through political, economic, and military means. Sometimes, when domination is intense, minorities can protect themselves only through religious faith or by building cultural tales in which they hold positions of power and their oppressors are weak (Scott 1992).

The result of struggles between groups in society is that norms and values, ideas we sometimes think of as timeless and consensual, are constantly changing and being renegotiated. This involves conflict and subjugation as well as consensus. Which norms and values are promoted and which are rejected is particularly important because such cultural ideas influence and are influenced by wealth, power, and status.

For example, what are American norms and values about using drugs to alter one's state of consciousness? Should the use of such drugs be legal? Clearly, these are difficult questions. In the past, Americans considered alcohol a dangerous mind-altering substance. Its manufacture, sale, and transport were prohibited in the United States between 1920 and 1933. Even today, substantial numbers of Americans oppose alcohol. In 2006, the Southern Baptist Convention, which represents about 16 million church members, passed a resolution expressing "total opposition to the manufacturing, advertising, distributing, and consuming of alcoholic beverages" (Southern Baptist Convention 2006). Marijuana, on the other hand, has been illegal in the United States since 1937, but currently, about one-third of Americans say they favor its legalization (Carroll 2005), and medical marijuana is currently legal in 14 states.

Believing that people should consume or not consume either alcohol or marijuana clearly does not make one more or less "American." However, which of these notions is held by those in power is critical. It influences the laws and social policies that shape our lives and history.

The focus on culture as a shared set of norms and values is often associated with the American anthropologists of the first half of the 20th century, a school of thought referred to as **historical particularism**. These anthropologists were interested in presenting objective descriptions of cultures within their historical and environmental context. Their emphasis on norms and values was designed to show that, although other cultures were very different from our own, they were coherent, rational, and indeed often beautiful. In contrast to the logical coherence seen by the historical particularists, some contemporary anthropologists, particularly **postmodernists**, hold that culture is a context in which norms and values are contested and negotiated. Rather than assuming a cultural core of shared beliefs and values, these anthropologists see culture and society as battlegrounds where individuals and groups fight for power and the right to determine what is accepted as true.

historical particularism A theoretical position in anthropology associated with American anthropologists of the early 20th century that focuses on providing objective descriptions of cultures within their historical and environmental context.

postmodernism A theoretical position in anthropology that focuses on issues of power and voice. Postmodernists suggest that anthropological accounts are partial truths reflecting the backgrounds, training, and social positions of their authors.

██ CULTURE IS THE WAY HUMAN BEINGS ADAPT TO THE WORLD

All animals, including human beings, have biologically based needs. All need habitat and food, and each species must reproduce. All creatures are adapted to meet these needs. **Adaptation** is a change in the biological structure or lifeways of an individual or population by which it becomes

adaptation A change in the biological structure or lifeways of an individual or population by which it becomes better fitted to survive and reproduce in its environment.

One way people use culture to adapt to their environment is through house construction. In the fishing village of Nzulezu in Western Ghana, houses are built on stilts in Lake Tadane. People in Nzulezu have adapted to life on lake and most village activities including food preparation, schooling, worship and burial are done on the water.

© John Miles/Getty Images

better fitted to survive and reproduce in its environment. Nonhuman animals fill their needs primarily through biological adaptation. Lions, for example, have a series of biologically based adaptations that are superbly designed to enable them to feed themselves (and their mates). They have large muscles for speed as well as sharp teeth and claws to capture and eat their prey.

Humans are different. We lack offensive biological weaponry, and, if left to get our food like the lion, we would surely starve. There is little evidence that we have an instinct to hunt or consume any particular kind of food, to build any particular sort of structure, or to have a single fixed social arrangement. Instead, human beings, in groups, develop forms of knowledge and technologies that enable them to feed themselves and to survive in their environments. They pass this knowledge from generation to generation and from group to group. In other words, human beings develop and use culture to adapt to the world.

Most of a lion's adaptation to the world is set biologically. The growth of its teeth and claws, its instinct to hunt, and the social arrangement of a pride are largely expressions of the lion's genetic code. Humans also have a biological adaptation to the world: learning culture. All humans automatically learn the culture of their social group. The only exceptions are people with profound biologically based difficulties (such as autism) and, sometimes, victims of extreme abuse. The fact that humans universally learn and use culture strongly suggests that such learning is a manifestation of our genetic code. Although our biology compels us to learn culture, it does not compel us to learn a particular culture. The range of human beliefs and practices is enormous (although perhaps not limitless). However, people everywhere learn to fill their basic needs, such as food and shelter, through cultural practices. Culture everywhere must, to some extent, be adaptive.

Cultural adaptation has some distinct advantages over biological adaptation. Because humans adapt through learned behavior, they can change their approach to solving problems quickly and more easily than creatures whose adaptations are primarily biological. Lions hunt and eat today in much the same way as they have for tens of thousands of years. The vast majority of human beings today do not live like humans of even three or four generations ago, let alone like our distant ancestors. Our means of feeding ourselves, our culture, have changed. **Plasticity**—the ability to change behavior—has allowed human beings to thrive under a wide variety of social and ecological conditions.

plasticity The ability of human individuals or cultural groups to change their behavior with relative ease.

Cultural adaptation has some disadvantages too. Misinformation, leading to cultural practices that hinder rather than aid survival, may creep into human behavior. Cultural practices such as unrestrained logging, mining, or fishing that encourage destruction of the environment, may lead to short-term success but long-term disaster. Furthermore, many human practices are clearly not adaptive, even in the short run. Political policies of ethnic cleansing and genocide that urge people to murder their neighbors may benefit the leaders of the society, but it is hard to see any meaningful way in which these practices are adaptive. A normal lion will always inherit the muscle, tooth, and claw that, given a relatively stable environment, let it survive. Normal humans, on the other hand, may inherit a great deal of cultural misinformation that hinders their survival.

Historically, a focus on the adaptive aspect of culture is associated with a theoretical position called **cultural ecology**, first proposed in the 1930s. Although many of our ideas have changed since then, investigating the adaptive (and maladaptive) aspects of culture continues to be an important aspect of anthropology. Anthropologists who view culture as an adaptation tend to be concerned with people's behavior, particularly as it relates to their physical well-being or the relationship of cultural practices to ecosystems. They investigate the ways in which cultures adapt to specific environments and the ways in which cultures have changed in response to new physical and social conditions.

cultural ecology A theoretical position in anthropology that focuses on the adaptive dimension of culture.

▌CULTURE IS CONSTANTLY CHANGING

Did you ever want to visit a culture where people were untouched by the outside world, living just the same way they have been living for thousands of years? Well, you are out of luck. One of the most romantic notions of anthropology presented in the media is that there are "Stone Age" cultures waiting to be discovered. But this is false. No culture has ever been stuck in time or isolated from others for very long. Cultures are constantly changing. They change because of conflict among different elements within them. They change because of contact with outsiders. Population growth, disease, climate change, and natural disaster all drive culture change. However, cultures do not always change at the same speed. Cultural change may happen in small increments, or it may happen in revolutionary bursts. Historically, in most places and at most times, culture change has been a relatively slow process. However, the pace of change has been increasing for the past several hundred years and has become extremely rapid in the past century.

Since the 16th century, the most important source of culture change has been the development of a world economic system based primarily in the wealthy nations of Europe and Asia. This has involved invasions, revolutions, and epidemic diseases. These historic processes and the resultant global economic system are the primary foci of Chapters 12 and 13. Here, we focus on some of the more traditional ways in which anthropologists have examined culture change.

Anthropologists usually have discussed cultural change in terms of innovation and diffusion. An **innovation** is an object, a way of thinking, or a way of behaving that is new because it is qualitatively different from existing forms (Barnett 1953:7). Although we often think of innovations as technological, they are not limited to the material aspects of culture. New art forms and new ideas are also innovations.

New practices, tools, or principles may emerge from within a society and gain wide acceptance. Anthropologists sometimes call these *primary innovations*, and they are frequently chance discoveries and accidents. In our own society, some examples of accidental discovery include penicillin, found when British researcher Alexander Fleming noticed that bacteria samples he had left by a window were contaminated by mold spores, and Teflon, discovered by Roy Plunkett, who was trying to find new substances to use in refrigeration. All such innovations are based on building blocks provided by culture. For example, although Fleming is justly famous for the discovery of penicillin, this innovation also illustrates the importance of context and incremental discovery. Fleming was not a random person who woke up one morning thinking about mold and bacteria. He was a trained bacteriologist who had been looking for a substance to fight infection for more than a decade. He was very aware of the work of other scientists studying the problem of infection. It does not diminish his achievement to point out that he, like every other inventor or discoverer, did not create something totally new. He realized the critical importance of new combinations of things that already existed. His culture provided him with the training, tools, and context in which his discovery could be made.

Innovations tend to move from one culture to another, a process known as **diffusion**. Diffusion can happen in many ways; trade, travel, and warfare all promote it. Direct contact among cultures generally results in the most far-reaching changes, and cultures located on major trade routes tend to change more rapidly than do those in more isolated places. However, because no human society has ever been isolated for a long time, diffusion has always been an important factor in culture. This implies that "pure" cultures, free from outside influences, have never existed.

Innovation and diffusion are not simple processes. People do not "naturally" realize that one way of doing things is better than another or that one style of dress, religion, or behavior is superior. For innovation and diffusion

© Barry Kaas/Anthro-Photo, Inc.

Innovation often involves crafting familiar things from new materials. In Niger, a craftsman fashions sandals from old tires.

to occur, new ideas must be accepted, and even when the desirability of an innovation seems clear, gaining acceptance is a very complex process. Again, the discovery of penicillin provides a good example. Although Fleming understood some of the importance of his discovery in 1928, human trials did not take place until World War II, and the drug was not widely prescribed until the mid- to late 1950s (Sheehan 1982; Williams 1984).

People may not accept an idea because they do not fully understand it, but other factors are usually involved as well. For psychological reasons, individuals may vary in their willingness to adopt change. Far more importantly, changes rarely provide equal benefits to everyone. For example, new agricultural techniques were introduced in Latin America and Asia from the 1940s to the 1960s (an era known as the "Green Revolution"). The new techniques did radically improve crop yields, but large landowners received the greater part of the benefit. Laborers, many of whom were landless, were often impoverished by the change and, as a result, were very resistant to it (Das 1998).

Change is often promoted or resisted by powerful interests. Innovations that have strong political, economic, or moral forces behind them may be rapidly accepted. But, when those forces are arrayed against an innovation, acceptance can be delayed. New technologies may face resistance from those who have invested heavily in older ones. For example, FM radio broadcasting is clearly superior to AM broadcasting; it has greater fidelity and is much less susceptible to static and interference. Although it was invented in 1933, the opposition of CBS, NBC, and RCA, powerful corporations heavily invested in AM technology, prevented FM from gaining popularity until the late 1960s (Lewis 1991).

Like innovation, diffusion is often accompanied by conflict. People who are colonized or captured by others are often forced to assume new cultural practices. New rulers may require that older traditions be abandoned. Economic demands by governments or creditors often compel the adoption of new technologies and practices. Although these processes happen in most places where cultures confront one another, they have been particularly important in the past 500 years. During this time, cultures have been increasingly tied together in an economic system controlled largely in northern Europe, North America, and Japan, a process we explore further in Chapters 12 and 13.

The rapid pace of cultural change and diffusion, particularly in the past 100 years, raises the question of cultural homogenization. Are cultural differences being erased? Are we all being submerged in a single global culture? There are no simple answers to these questions. On the one hand, modern technological culture now penetrates virtually every place on earth. On the other hand, this penetration is uneven. The wealthy have far greater access to and ability to control technology than the poor.

The world dominance of industrialized nations has affected cultures everywhere, but rather than annihilating local culture, the result may be the creation of new cultures. Cultural traits are transformed as they are adopted, and new cultural forms result. Radio, television, and video recording are good examples. Developed by industrialized societies, these technologies have spread around the world. However, they do not necessarily promote the values and practices of the societies that created them. Recently, Osama bin Laden as well as insurgents and jihadists in Iraq and elsewhere have made extensive use of television, cell phones, and the Internet in their campaign against Western secular society.

Anthropologists have traditionally worked in tribal and peasant societies. Because such cultures have been profoundly affected by their contact with industrial societies, most anthropologists today, whatever their theoretical orientations, are interested in change. The study of cultural change has special interest for applied anthropologists, particularly those who investigate issues related to the economic development of poor nations.

▌▌CULTURE COUNTS

Culture is many different things. It is learning, symbolism and meaning, patterns of thought and behavior, the things we share with those around us, the ways in which we survive in our world, and dynamism and change. It is both consensus and conflict. Culture makes us human and ties us to others everywhere. Ultimately, because all societies are based around fundamental patterns of culture, no society can be utterly incomprehensible to members of another. On the other hand, enormous variability is built into these patterns. The fact that human lifeways are shared, learned, and symbolic, the fact that we don't simply adapt to our environment but fill it with meaning, results in extraordinary differences in human cultures.

Naked mole rats are a highly social species found in the Horn of Africa. Their behavior is extremely complex, but they lack culture in a human sense. Each colony is more or less identical to every other. Imaginary mole rat explorers visiting each colony would understand everything they saw or heard. But the history of human exploration is one of miscomprehension. Because cultures are so different and count for so much in human life, we need tools to help us understand them. One job of anthropology is to provide these tools. In Chapter 3, we examine the methods anthropologists have used to investigate culture.

BRINGING IT BACK HOME:
YES, BUT IS IT SCIENCE?

Early in this chapter, we defined an anthropological theory as a set of propositions about which aspects of culture are critical, how they should be studied, and what the goal of studying them should be. This is a definition that seems to work well for anthropology but is different than the way that people in physics or chemistry understand theory. Much of the current-day understanding of theory is based on the work of the philosopher Karl Popper. For Popper, falsifiability was the most important characteristic of theory. In 1963, he wrote that "Every 'good' scientific theory is a prohibition: it forbids certain things to happen. The more a theory forbids, the better it is. A theory which is not refutable by any conceivable event is nonscientific. Irrefutability is not a virtue of a theory (as people often think) but a vice" (Popper 2002/1963:48). It is clear that many of the ideas we have discussed in this chapter are not really scientific theories by this definition. How, for example, could you possibly falsify underlying tenets of symbolic anthropology: the idea that studying the way people use symbols and their meanings enables anthropologists to understand and analyze their culture? Much the same is true of other anthropological theories.

Franz Boas, often considered the founder of American anthropology, frequently referred to anthropology as a science (for example, see 1906:641). Through the first two-thirds of the 20th century, other anthropologists also promoted a scientific anthropology. Ethnoscientists, for example, devised interview techniques that they believed would create both replicable and falsifiable data. The tradition of scientific anthropology continues today in the work of anthropologists such as Lee Cronk whose work promotes a "science of behavior that includes a clearly defined concept of culture and that uses it . . . to help us understand people's behavior not only in other societies but also in our own" (1999:2). Cronk has recently written on interviews as scientific experiments (Cronk, Gerkey, and Irons 2009).

However, anthropologists began to debate the scientific nature of their field fairly early in its history. Boas's student Ruth Benedict wrote: "once anthropologists include the mind of man in their subject matter, the methods of science and the methods of the humanities complement each other. Any commitment to methods which exclude either approach is self-defeating" (1948:593).

By the last third of the 20th century, many—perhaps most—anthropologists rejected the notion that anthropology should (or could) be a science. For example, Clifford Geertz wrote that the analysis of culture was "not an experimental science in search of law but an interpretive one in search of meaning" (1973b:5), but what is an interpretive science? Can there be an interpretive physics? Some anthropologists even cast doubt on the notion of science itself. Stephen A. Tyler wrote: "scientific thought is now an archaic mode of consciousness surviving for a while yet in degraded form" (1986:123).

▋▋ YOU DECIDE

1. Given that it is impossible to construct laboratory experiments in anthropology the way one might in the natural sciences such as chemistry or social sciences such as psychology, is it possible to construct a science of anthropology?
2. Most people accept that objectivity is a critical hallmark of science. To what degree can anthropology be objective? Do you believe there are limits to anthropological objectivity?
3. Clifford Geertz wrote that the anthropologist's job is to "unsettle" others; to "hawk the anomalous, peddle the strange", to be "Merchants of astonishment" (1984:275). This is an attractive and deeply romantic notion. However, to what degree does the ability of anthropologists to perform these functions depend on our claims of objectivity and scientific knowledge?

▋▋ CHAPTER SUMMARY

1. Culture is the learned, symbolic, at least partially adaptive, and ever-changing patterns of behavior and meaning shared by members of a group. Humans are vitally dependent on culture for their existence.
2. Almost all human behavior is learned. Humans learn throughout their entire life span. The example of the Inuit shows how children are taught to survive in a harsh environment.
3. Humans understand the world by classifying it and using symbols to give it meaning. Different cultures use different systems of classification. People use symbols to give meaning to their lives. Anthropologists analyze and interpret symbols and rituals to understand cultural meanings.
4. Culture is a system of related elements working together. However, cultural systems include contradictions that lead to conflict.

5. Members of a culture must share many things in common, including norms and values. However, there are substantial group and individual differences in understanding.

6. Culture is the way that humans adapt to their world. Unlike other species, adaptation by humans is primarily learned, which enables people to rapidly adapt to change.

7. All cultures change. Innovation and diffusion are two sources of change. Many factors determine the acceptance or rejection of a culture change.

8. Culture makes humans unique. The vast differences between human cultures make cultural understanding a challenge. Anthropology supplies tools to meet that challenge.

KEY TERMS

Adaptation
Anthropological theory
Cognitive anthropology
Cultural ecology
Culture and personality
Diffusion
Dominant culture
Ecological functionalism
Enculturation
Ethnobotany
Ethnomedicine
Ethnoscience

Functionalism
Historical particularism
Innovation
Interpretive anthropology
Norms
Organic analogy
Plasticity
Postmodernism
Subculture
Symbol
Symbolic anthropology
Values

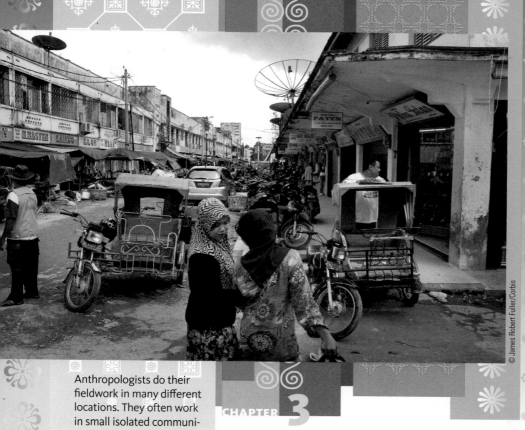

Anthropologists do their fieldwork in many different locations. They often work in small isolated communities but sometimes they work in cities as well. This picture shows a neighborhood in Indonesia, perhaps similar to the ones described in the paragraphs opening this chapter.

CHAPTER 3

DOING CULTURAL ANTHROPOLOGY

CHAPTER OUTLINE

ANGER MANAGEMENT IN INDONESIA

DOING fieldwork is a fundamental part of anthropology, but is often a deeply challenging experience as well. In this passage, Greg Simon describes some of his fieldwork experiences in Bukittinggi, Indonesia:

> When I picture myself moving through the streets of Bukittinggi during my first months of fieldwork, I picture myself angry.
>
> After living several months in this small mountain city, I have found myself thinking: I am being abused. I am like an animal at the local zoo; people stare at me, point, make jokes about me. They comment to each other—as if I were not present—on my skin, my nose, my height, my movements. I tense whenever I go to use the local dialect, knowing that every time I do, they will be sure to laugh and parrot me. Sometimes they greet me, in barely audible tones, only after we have passed each other moving in opposite directions. Or they zoom by in pairs on motorcycles, screaming at me then laughing as they speed away.
>
> When I remember myself during those first months here, I remember myself bracing for attack.
>
> Day after day, I saw red when faced with an enthusiastically smiling visage; I was prone to feel my blood pressure rise when greeted with a hearty, "Hello, Mister!" and I was vulnerable to feeling a prick of irritation at the curious probe of a stranger's questions. Seeing a stranger looking towards me, perhaps about to speak to me, I might find myself turning away as if frightened, or directing a steely stare in their direction as if hardening myself for their approach. It was all done in an effort to protect myself. But it also made what I needed to do—meet people, interact, have conversations—all that much more difficult. So I would despair at my prospects for carrying out successful research, and I would lay blame: Minang people are hostile, unwelcoming, mean-spirited, and indifferent to making any genuine connection with me.
>
> I felt horribly guilty for these thoughts. Wasn't this, after all, exactly the kind of bigotry that anthropology is supposed to confront and defuse? I also knew, rationally, that this characterization of Minang people was not true. Not only did it brush broadly over the behavior of the thousands of people around me, each with a different personality and attitude, but so often it seemed to be exactly the opposite of what I have experienced here from the beginning. In between these failed encounters, I was also spending hours enjoying people's hospitality and conversation and developing genuine friendships. I receive frequent invitations to visit people in their homes, or to attend weddings and parties, and at gatherings I am always an extra-special guest, given the most careful attention and deference.

Greg Simon is challenged by his emotional reaction to fieldwork. On the one hand, he finds that he is often treated extremely well. People tell him that he is "like their very own child." However, he also has many uncomfortable experiences. People laugh at him, treat him as a child, and accuse him of being a spy. Simon finds it difficult to escape the feelings of anger and hostility that these encounters cause. He knows that such feelings will get in the way of being an anthropologist, but anthropologists are humans too, and fieldwork cannot be divorced from individual emotions the way an experiment in chemistry or biology might be. Instead, anthropologists must reconcile their own emotional responses with skills of data collection they need to perform their jobs. Eventually, Simon finds that his experiences of being treated as "less than completely human" gave him some insight into the lives of many Indonesians who themselves "often feel that they live in a world that is liable to dismiss them as less than fully human." A year into his fieldwork, Simon has a deeply disturbing encounter with an Indonesian, the sort of encounter that would have caused him great anger before. Now, although on the one hand he feels no anger and agrees to speak with the man who provoked him again, he still feels lost and confused (Simon, 105–106, 108, 114, 118).

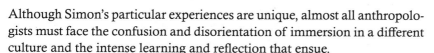

Although Simon's particular experiences are unique, almost all anthropologists must face the confusion and disorientation of immersion in a different culture and the intense learning and reflection that ensue.

If you have any picture of anthropologists at all, you probably think of men and women who share the lives of people who are different than themselves. Indeed, one of the fundamental ways in which anthropologists work is by spending time in other cultures. Psychologists or sociologists may be able to do research without leaving the college campus. They conduct surveys using the telephone, the Internet, or the postal service, or they may bring students into a laboratory and ask them questions or observe their reactions. Philosophers or scholars of literature may work by reading, observing, and pondering. Anthropologists do these things too, but, in addition, must go into the field.

For more than 100 years, anthropologists have gone into other cultures. They have lived among small isolated groups that forage for their food, have joined with societies that travel with their herds, and have spent time in agricultural villages and in bustling modern cities. They have lived among farmers, craftsmen, thieves, and crack cocaine dealers. If you enjoy anthropology, fieldwork is probably one of the key reasons you are attracted to it. There is something profoundly romantic about the idea of living with members of another culture, learning their way of life, and attempting to understand the world in a new and different manner. However, as Simon's description of his experiences shows, there is also confusion, strangeness, alienation, and a host of challenges and dilemmas. Fieldwork is a wonderful experience. It is essential to the ways in which anthropology is done. However, it can also be intensely lonely and disturbing. In this chapter, we explore some of the history and practice of fieldwork. We examine fieldwork techniques and different trends in anthropological data collection and discuss some of the ethical issues raised by the practice of anthropology.

A LITTLE HISTORY

Anthropology was not always based around fieldwork. The first scholars who called themselves anthropologists worked in the second half of the 19th century. Among the most famous of them were Sir Edward Burnett Tylor and Lewis Henry Morgan. Both saw themselves as compilers and analysts of ethnographic accounts rather than as field researchers. They relied largely upon the writings of amateurs—travelers, explorers, missionaries, and colonial officers—who had recorded their experiences in remote areas of the world. Because of this, critics of Tylor and Morgan sometimes referred to them as "armchair anthropologists."

Morgan and Tylor were deeply influenced by the evolutionary theories of Charles Darwin and Herbert Spencer. They assumed that such theories could be applied to human society. Thus, as they analyzed societies, they used type of technology and social institutions, such as family and religion, to place each society on an evolutionary scale of increasing complexity. Their scale began with simple, small-scale societies (classified as "savages"), passed through various chiefdoms (usually classified as "barbarians"), and ended with societies such as their own (classified as "civilization"). Although Morgan and Tylor were deeply critical of many aspects of their own societies, they were also convinced that they lived in the most highly evolved society that had ever existed.

There were numerous problems with Morgan and Tylor's evolutionary anthropology. Explorers, colonial officials, and missionaries had particular interests in playing up the most exotic aspects of the societies they described. Doing so increased the fame of explorers (and the number of books they were able to sell). It made the natives more in need of the "good government" or salvation that colonial officials and missionaries could provide. Perhaps more importantly, the evolutionists were so sure that they had properly formulated the general evolutionary history of society that they twisted and contorted their data to fit their theories.

Franz Boas and American Anthropology

The problems implicit in Morgan and Tylor's evolutionary approach led to a radical reappraisal of evolutionary anthropology at the end of the 19th century. The most important critic of evolutionism was Franz Boas. Born in Minden, Germany, Boas came to the United States after completing his doctorate in geography and living among the Inuit on Baffin Island. In the late 1890s, he became the first professor of anthropology at Columbia University in New York City. From there, he trained many students who became the leading anthropologists of the first half of the 20th century. As a result, Boas's ideas had a profound impact on the development of anthropology in the United States.

Boas's studies and his experiences among the Inuit convinced him that evolutionary anthropology was both intellectually flawed and, because it treated other people and other societies as inferior to Europeans, morally defective. Boas argued that anthropologists should not be collectors of tales and spinners of theories but should devote themselves to objective data collection through fieldwork. Anthropologists must live among the people they study, both observing their activities and, where possible, participating in them. They should record as much information about the group's culture as possible. Boas's style of fieldwork became known as **participant observation** and has been the hallmark of American anthropology. Although few anthropologists today would investigate society in the same way as Boas, almost all do fieldwork in which they both observe members of a culture and participate with them to the greatest extent possible.

One of Boas's core beliefs was that cultures are the products of their own histories. He argued that a culture's standards of beauty and morality as well as many other aspects of behavior could be understood only in light of that culture's historical development. Because our own ideas were also the products of history, they should not be used as standards to judge other cultures. Evolutionists failed partly because they assumed, incorrectly, that the most evolved cultures were those that had values most similar to their own. In other words, the evolutionists failed because of their own ethnocentrism. In one sense, **ethnocentrism** is simply the belief that one's own culture is better than any other. In a deeper sense, it is precisely the application of the historical standards of beauty, worth, and morality developed in one culture to all other cultures.

Franz Boas had a huge impact on American anthropology in the first half of the 20th century. Boas's early fieldwork was done among the Inuit of Baffin Island. Here, in 1883, shortly after his return to Germany, he poses for a photograph wearing Inuit clothing.

participant observation The fieldwork technique that involves gathering cultural data by observing people's behavior and participating in their lives.

ethnocentrism Judging other cultures from the perspective of one's own culture. The notion that one's own culture is more beautiful, rational, and nearer to perfection than any other.

The American tourist who, presented with a handful of Mexican pesos, asks, "How much is this in real money?," is being ethnocentric—but there is nothing uniquely American or Western about ethnocentrism. People all over the world tend to see things from their own culturally patterned point of view. For example, when the people living in Highland New Guinea first saw European outsiders in the 1930s, they believed them to be the ghosts of their ancestors. It was the only way they could initially make sense of what they were seeing (Connolly and Anderson 1987).

Although most people are ethnocentric, the ethnocentrism of Western societies has had greater consequences than that of smaller, less technologically advanced, and more geographically isolated peoples. Wealth and military technology have given Westerners the ability to impose their beliefs and practices on others. It may matter little, for example, to the average Frenchman if the Dogon (an ethnic group in Mali) believe their way of life to be superior. The Dogon have little ability to affect events in France. However, French ethnocentrism mattered a great deal to the Dogon. The French colonized Mali and imposed their beliefs and institutions on its people.

Some ethnocentrism seems necessary. A group's belief in the superiority of its own way of life binds its members together and helps them to perpetuate their values. However, to the extent that ethnocentrism prevents building bridges between cultures and leads members of one culture to force their ways of life on another, it is maladaptive. It is but a short step from this kind of ethnocentrism to **racism**—beliefs, actions, and patterns of social organization that exclude individuals and groups from the equal exercise of human rights and fundamental freedoms.

racism The belief that some human populations are superior to others because of inherited, genetically transmitted characteristics.

Boas insisted that anthropologists free themselves, as much as possible, from ethnocentrism and approach each culture on its own terms. This position came to be known as **cultural relativism** and is one of the hallmarks of anthropology. Boas and his followers maintained that anthropologists must suspend judgment to understand the logic and dynamics of other cultures. Researchers who view the actions of other people simply in terms of the degree to which they correspond to their own notions of the ways people should behave systematically distort the cultures they study.

cultural relativism The notion that cultures should be analyzed with reference to their own histories and values rather than according to the values of another culture.

Boas was a tireless campaigner for human rights and justice. He argued that all human beings have equal capacities for culture and that although human actions might be considered morally right or wrong, no culture was more evolved or of greater value than another. He was an unwavering supporter of racial equality. His work and that of his students, notably Ruth Benedict and Margaret Mead, were widely used by Americans who argued for the equality of men and women and for the rights of African Americans, immigrants, and Native Americans. Today, virtually all anthropologists rely on Boas's basic insights.

From Haddon to Malinowski in England and the Commonwealth

While Boas was forming his ideas in America, a separate fieldwork tradition was developing in Britain. In the late 19th century, Alfred Cort Haddon mounted two expeditions to the Torres Straits (between New Guinea and Australia). Haddon originally was a biologist, but his travels turned his interest to **ethnography**, the gathering and interpretation of information based on intensive firsthand study. Haddon and his colleagues became professors at Cambridge and the London School of Economics, where they trained the next generation of British Commonwealth anthropologists. Like Boas, their understandings were based in fieldwork, and they made it a basic part of their students' training.

Bronislaw Malinowski was one of the most prominent students of the Torres Straits scholars. Malinowski grew up in Krakow, then part of the Austro-Hungarian Empire (now in Poland). He came to England to study ethnography, and his mentor, Charles Seligman, sent him to do fieldwork on the Trobriand Islands (in the Torres Straits). Malinowski arrived in the Trobriands in 1914, as World War I broke out. Because Australia governed the Trobriands and Malinowski was a subject of the Austro-Hungarian Empire, he was considered an enemy national. As a result, he was unable to leave the islands until the end of the war. Thus, what he had intended as a relatively short fieldwork expedition became an extremely long one.

Malinowski's time on the Trobriands was a signal moment in British Commonwealth anthropology. A diary he kept during those years shows that, like Greg Simon many years later, he was frequently lonely, frustrated, and angry. Despite his problems, he revolutionized fieldwork. The Torres Straits scholars had studied culture at a distance, observing and describing it for a short time. Malinowski spent years with native Trobrianders, learning their language, their patterns of thought, and their cultural ways. He developed a form of ethnography centered on empathic understandings of native lifeways and on analyzing culture by describing social institutions and showing the cultural and psychological functions they performed.

In an era when non-Europeans were often considered incomprehensible and illogical, Malinowski forcefully promoted the idea that native cultural ways were logical. For example, in a famous essay on science and magic, he argued that natives used magic only for goals they were unable to attain by more rational means (such as controlling the weather) (Malinowski 1948).

London School of Economics Archives, Malinowski/3/18/2

Bronislaw Malinowski, one of the pioneers of participant observation, worked in the Trobriand Islands between 1915 and 1918.

ethnography The major research tool of cultural anthropology; includes both fieldwork among people in a society and the written results of such fieldwork.

The Trobriand Islands

The anthropologies of Malinowski and Boas were quite different. Boas and his students focused on understanding cultures with respect to their context and histories. Malinowski and his students emphasized the notion of function: the contribution made by social practices and institutions to the maintenance and stability of society. However, both developed traditions of fieldwork and participant observation. Both traditions have strong histories of opposition to racism. Both see other cultures as fully rational and as neither superior nor inferior to their own. Despite the great many new approaches in anthropology since the days of Boas and Malinowski, their fundamental insights remain basic to the discipline.

ANTHROPOLOGICAL TECHNIQUES

Today, anthropologists work in a wide variety of settings. They work for universities, for businesses, for government, and for nongovernmental organizations. You still find anthropologists investigating the relations among kin and the meanings of religious rituals. However, you also find them researching shopping behavior and the ways in which people relate to their computers. Because of the multiplicity of anthropologies, it would be impossible to describe all of the different ways that anthropologists go about their work. Anthropologists began by studying small communities, and the techniques they develop in so doing form the framework for other techniques. Therefore, we will focus on the ways in which fieldwork is done in such communities.

Most anthropologists begin to do fieldwork as part of their graduate training and continue fieldwork as a basic element of their careers. Fieldwork is often funded by grants given by universities, government agencies, and nonprofit organizations that promote social science research.

Decisions about which communities anthropologists investigate are based on factors including personal history, geographical preferences, political stability, cost, physical danger, and connections their professors and other mentors may have. However, the most critical aspect of choosing a location has to do with the particular research questions that the anthropologist wishes to answer.

In the early 20th century, anthropologists studying relatively small groups often attempted to write complete descriptions of societies. Their books, with titles such as *The Tiwi of North Australia* (Hart and Pilling 1960), *The Sebei* (Goldschmidt 1986), and *The Cheyennes* (Hoebel 1960), had chapters on subjects such as family, religion, farming, and legal affairs. In a sense, it did not matter much where anthropologists chose to work; any small-scale community or society could be described.

Today, few anthropologists attempt to write such descriptions. This is partly because most feel that societies are so complex that they cannot be adequately described in a single work. But, more importantly, although societies never were really isolated, they are so interconnected today and so changed by these connections that they must be seen in regional and global contexts. Current ethnographies focus on specific situations, individuals, events, and, frequently, on culture change. For example, recent ethnographies describe Native Americans and casino gambling (Darian-Smith 2004), the ways in which people in Jamaica use cell phones (Horst and Miller 2006), and the survival techniques of drug addicts on the streets of San Francisco (Bourgois and Schonberg 2009). As research has narrowed, both the questions anthropologists ask and the conditions and locations where they can be answered have become more specific.

After they have identified an area of interest, anthropologists spend time reading the existing research on their subject. It is no exaggeration to say that most researchers spend several hours reading for each hour they spend doing active field research. From their studies, they gain an understanding of the geography, history, and culture of their chosen area. They find out what is known and what remains to be learned about the subjects of their interest. They then try to design projects that help to close the gaps in existing knowledge. It is a bit like filling in pieces of a jigsaw puzzle, with one important exception: You can finish a puzzle, but good research leads to the posing of interesting questions and, thus, more research.

Arriving at a field location can be a disorienting experience. For most people, living in another culture and trying to learn its ways are difficult. Most anthropologists probably have at least some experiences like those Greg Simon describes in the passage that opens this chapter. Anthropologists are objects of curiosity and sometimes hostility. Perhaps more importantly, culture is learned behavior, and we have been learning our culture since the moment of our births. When we move to a radically different culture, much of that learning is no longer relevant.

Anthropologists arriving in new cultures are in many ways like children. Their language skills are often weak, and their speech is sometimes babyish. Their social skills are undeveloped. They are ignorant of many aspects of their environment and their new culture. One almost universal result of this situation is the syndrome called **culture shock**—the feelings of alienation, loneliness, and isolation common to one who has been placed in a new culture. For graduate students, sometimes the journey stops there. You can be an outstanding scholar—well versed in literature and able to think and write creatively—yet be unable to do fieldwork.

culture shock Feelings of alienation and helplessness that result from rapid immersion in a new and different culture.

Getting past culture shock is a process of learning the language, customs, and social organization, of gaining the fundamental grounding knowledge that it takes to be an adult in a different culture. Most anthropologists never truly become members of the cultures they study. We are separated from our subjects by our backgrounds, by our education, and sometimes by the color of our skin. We are also separated by the knowledge that our time in the field is temporary and that we will leave to rejoin our other lives. However, in our best moments, anthropologists do come close to acting and feeling like members of the cultures we study.

In most cases, as anthropologists begin to adapt to new cultures, they develop networks of friends and contacts who both guide them in their new surroundings and offer insights into the culture. Traditionally in anthropology, these people are called **informants**. They may also be called **respondents**, interlocutors, **consultants**, and sometimes partners. These terms emphasize the collaborative nature of fieldwork and suggest that the people who work with anthropologists are active and empowered. Much of what anthropologists know they learn from such people, who frequently become enduring friends. In some cases, anthropologists work with a few individuals whom they believe to be well informed and eager to talk with them (called "key informants"). Alternatively, they may construct statistical models and use techniques such as random sampling to choose their consultants. Sometimes, they are able to interview all members of a community.

Working with consultants is often informal, but anthropologists also use an arsenal of more formal tools, depending on their theoretical interests.

informant A person from whom anthropologists gather data. Also known as a consultant or sometimes an interlocutor.

respondent A person from whom anthropologists collect data. Also known as informant, consultant, or sometimes interlocutor.

consultant A person from whom anthropologists gather data. Also known as an informant or sometimes an interlocutor.

In fieldwork, anthropologists both observe culture and participate in it, as with this anthropologist living with the Mentawai in Sumatra, Indonesia. The tattoos usually are incised with needles and vegetable dye, but these are being done with washable pigments.

Much of anthropology is done by interviewing, and there are many different interview techniques. Some anthropologists prepare exhaustive inventories and questionnaires; however, more frequently, they design a series of open-ended questions that allow their subjects to talk freely and extensively on a topic. Sometimes, they use interview techniques drawn from ethnoscience and designed to help identify the objects and ideas their consultants think are important. Because kinship structures are important in many societies, anthropologists become adept at gathering genealogical information.

In addition to interviewing, anthropological data gathering includes participating in activities with culture members, mapping, photography, careful observation of activities, measurements of various kinds of production, and, occasionally, serving apprenticeships. It all depends on the nature of the problem the anthropologists are investigating.

As with the techniques used, analysis of data also depends on the questions being asked and the theoretical perspective of the researcher. Anthropological data generally come in the form of extensive field notes, tape recordings, and photographs. In most cases, organizing data presents substantial challenges. Notes have to be indexed, recordings transcribed, and data entered in spreadsheets. Successful anthropologists often spend more time working with their data than they did collecting it in the first place. Recording an interview may take only an hour or two. Transcribing and indexing that recording may take several days.

Ethnographic Data and Cross-Cultural Comparisons

Boas and his students were interested in describing cultures in their contexts. Because they understood each culture as the product of its unique history, they did not attempt systematic comparison of one culture to another, and they were not very interested in discovering laws or principles of cultural behavior. However, some comparison has always been implicit in anthropology. For example, one goal of the Boasians was to use their research to cause Europeans and Americans to think about their own societies in a new light.

British and European anthropologists were more explicitly interested in **ethnology**, the attempt to find general principles or laws that govern cultural phenomena. They compared societies in the hope of finding such laws and principles. Starting in the 1860s, Herbert Spencer began to develop a systematic way of organizing, tabulating, and correlating information on a large number of societies, a project he called *Descriptive Sociology*. The American scholar William Graham Sumner, his student Albert Keller, and Keller's student George Murdock brought this idea to the United States. In the late 1930s, Murdock and Keller created a large, indexed ethnographic

ethnology The attempt to find general principles or laws that govern cultural phenomena.

Human Relations Area Files
An ethnographic database that
includes cultural descriptions of
more than 300 cultures.

database at Yale University. First called the *Cross-Cultural Survey*, in the late 1940s, the project was expanded and its name was changed to the **Human Relations Area Files** (HRAF).

The HRAF is an attempt to facilitate cross-cultural analysis. It provides a single index to ethnographic reports and other sources on 710 numbered subject categories. Some examples of categories are 294 (techniques of clothing manufacture) and 628 (traditional friendships and rivalries within communities). Using the HRAF, researchers can find information on these and many other topics for a wide range of current and historic societies.

The HRAF frequently comes under fire as critics charge that the project takes cultural data out of context and therefore corrupts it. They say that the works indexed in the HRAF were written from different perspectives, for different purposes, and in different eras. In consequence, the indexing is often inconsistent and analyses based on it are suspect. Despite these problems, work based on the HRAF is often both interesting and insightful. For example, back in the 1950s, the rising divorce rate in the United States was causing alarm. Was divorce truly something new and different, a product of modernity? Murdock used the HRAF to show that almost all societies had some form of divorce and that the divorce rate in America (in the 1950s) was lower than average. Thus, his use of the HRAF allowed people to think about divorce in a comparative context. In recent years, the HRAF, now available online, has been used to consider a wide variety of issues including family violence (Levinson 1989), corporal punishment of children (Ember and Ember 2005), patterns of cultural evolution (Peregrine, Ember, and Ember 2004), and adolescent gender and sexuality (Schlegel and Barry 1991).

CHANGING DIRECTIONS AND CRITICAL ISSUES IN ETHNOGRAPHY

Feminist Anthropology

By the 1960s, the role of fieldwork in anthropology was extremely well established. Additionally, the position of women within academic anthropology was relatively good, particularly in comparison to other areas of the university. Franz Boas had trained several female anthropologists who had gone on to become well known within the discipline. One, Margaret Mead, had become a household name outside of anthropology as well. Despite this (or perhaps because of it), the political movements of the 1960s, particularly the civil rights movement and the feminist movement, caused anthropologists to begin thinking about gender and their discipline in new ways.

Feminists soon discovered that the presence of some very high-profile women within anthropology did little to counteract the fact that the over-whelming majority of anthropologists were men and that their areas of interest tended to focus on the social roles, activities, and beliefs of men in the societies they studied. There were several reasons why anthropologists had focused on men. First, in many societies, men and women live quite segregated lives. Because they were men, most anthropologists had little access to the lives of women. Second, anthropologists tended to assume that men's activities were political and therefore important, whereas women's activities were domestic and therefore of less importance. Third, in most societies, men's activities were far more public than women's activities. Anthropologists tended to assume that what was public and visible was more important than what was more behind the scenes and less visible. However, this clearly is not always (or even often) the case.

The result of taking men more seriously than women was a systematic bias in anthropological data and understandings. Anthropologists had often reported with great detail and accuracy about men's social and cultural worlds, but they had barely scratched the surface of women's worlds. Furthermore, the assumption that men spoke for all of society that is frequently implicit in ethnographies often made cultures appear more harmonious and homogeneous than they actually were.

Starting in the 1970s, increasing numbers of women joined university anthropology faculties. By the late 1990s, more than 50 percent of new anthropology PhDs and more than 40 percent of all anthropology professors were women (Levine and Wright 1999). They began paying greater attention to women's lives in the societies they studied and to the nature of sexuality and gender. We will address these issues more fully in Chapter 8.

Postmodernism

Ultimately, the issue of women in anthropology focused on ways of knowing. Feminists argued persuasively that male anthropologists had missed vital dimensions of society because their gender and their academic interests predisposed them to see certain things and not others. These ideas dovetailed well with **postmodernism**, a critique of both natural and social sciences that gained prominence in the 1980s. Postmodernists hold that all knowledge is influenced by the observer's culture and social position. They claim fieldworkers cannot discover and describe an objective reality because such a thing does not exist (or exists but cannot be discovered or comprehended by human beings). Instead, postmodernists propose that there are many partial truths or cultural constructions, which depend on frame of reference, power, and history.

postmodernism A theoretical position in anthropology that focuses on issues of power and voice. Postmodernists suggest that anthropological accounts are partial truths reflecting the backgrounds, training, and social positions of their authors.

Postmodernists urged anthropologists to examine the ways they understood both fieldwork and writing. They demanded that anthropology become sensitive to issues of history and power. Some postmodernists challenged the ethnographer's role in interpreting culture, claiming that anthropological ethnographies were just one story about experienced reality and the ethnographer's voice was only one of many possible representations.

The publication of Edward Said's *Orientalism* in 1978 was a critical moment in opening anthropology to postmodern ideas. The "Orient" of Said's title refers to the colonial British name for what is now called the Middle East. Said argued that European art and drama as well as anthropology and other social sciences gave a simplified, distorted, and romanticized view of Middle Eastern cultures, portraying them as timeless societies full of savagery and exotic wonder. Said believed that this portrayal was politically and culturally motivated, demonstrating western European superiority and justifying military conquest and colonization. However, it also drew attention from the area's actual history, economics, and politics. It particularly ignored the roles the British and other colonizers had played in shaping Middle Eastern politics and culture. One area of Western fascination was gender and sexuality. Because they focused on multiple wives, the harem, and the role of Islam, Western observers almost entirely misunderstood the actual lives of Middle Eastern women.

During the 1990s, reflection on the nature of fieldwork and the anthropological enterprise became a central focus of writing in anthropology. Work such as Said's encouraged anthropologists to think about the ways in which their own status, personality, and culture shape their view of others and how ethnographers interact with members of other cultures to produce data. In many cases, anthropologists turned from writing about culture to writing about anthropology itself, and critical analyses of earlier anthropological literature became common. In other cases, rather than trying to describe culture or to find principles underlying cultural practices, anthropologists wrote about their own experience of living in other cultures.

The claims of postmodernists have been a subject of intense debate in anthropology. Few anthropologists accept the postmodern critique in its entirety. To do so would be to understand anthropology as a rather peculiar sort of travel writing or a school of literary criticism. However, some of the ideas of postmodernism have become part of the mainstream. For example, almost all anthropologists today agree that ethnographers need to reflect critically on their positions as observers and be aware of the moral and political consequences of their work. Most ethnographies now include information about the conditions under which the fieldwork was carried out and the nature of the relationships between the anthropologists and their consultants. Most are sensitive to issues of voice and power and the ways anthropology is written.

Engaged and Collaborative Ethnography

Engaged and **collaborative ethnography** reflect some of the concerns just noted. Collaboration is the process of working closely with other people and in a sense describes all anthropological research. Collaborative anthropologists highlight this aspect of their work. They consult with their subjects about shaping their studies and writing their reports. They attempt to displace the anthropologist as the sole author representing a group, turning research into a joint process between researcher and subject. The work of James Spradley (1934–1982) is an important contribution to collaborative, engaged anthropology. His classic ethnography, *You Owe Yourself a Drunk* (Spradley 1970), was aimed at getting the public to understand and help the homeless alcoholics who were the subject of the book.

Luke E. Lassiter, an anthropologist inspired by Spradley, has done collaborative work with the Kiowa Indians in Oklahoma. The Kiowa were particularly interested in an ethnography of Kiowa song. They stipulated that it be written so that it could be read and understood by the Kiowa people themselves and that they would be acknowledged for their contributions. Lassiter emphasizes that a critical aspect of his collaboration with the Kiowa was to give the highest priority to representing the Kiowa cultural consultants as they wished to be represented, even if this meant adding or changing information or changing his interpretations. For Lassiter (2004), collaborative ethnography is not just eliciting the comments of the cultural consultants but, even more importantly, integrating these comments back into the text.

Although many anthropologists practice some elements of collaborative anthropology, there are deep problems with the notion that anthropologists' primary job is to write and say what their consultants want. First, most probably would agree that anthropologists have an obligation to accurately report what people say and do to the best of their ability. They may have an additional obligation to not knowingly falsify information. Furthermore, communities are rarely so homogeneous that they speak with a single voice. Collaborative anthropology may give voice and legitimacy to one element of a community over another. Often, writing what consultants want really means choosing their side in a political contest.

collaborative ethnography
Ethnography that gives priority to cultural consultants on the topic, methodology, and written results of fieldwork.

Studying One's Own Society

When most people think of anthropologists, they imagine researchers who study others in exotic locations, but, since the early 20th century, anthropologists have also studied their own societies. W. Lloyd Warner, Solon T. Kimball, Margaret Mead, Zora Neale Hurston, and Hortense Powdermaker were all American anthropologists who wrote about

Contemporary anthropologists work in a wide range of communities and use many different methods.

American culture. Kenyan anthropologist (as well as freedom fighter and first president of Kenya) Jomo Kenyatta wrote about the Gikuyu of Kenya in 1936, and Chinese anthropologist Francis Hsu wrote extensively on Chinese society. In recent years, writing about one's own culture has become even more common. This trend is driven by many factors, including the training of more anthropologists from more different cultures, the increasing total number of anthropologists, the rise of interest in ethnicity in America and Europe, as well as the dangers of violence in some areas where anthropologists have studied in the past.

The emphasis on more reflective fieldwork and ethnography affects all anthropologists but particularly those who study their own societies. Traditionally, anthropologists doing fieldwork try hard to learn the culture of the people with whom they are working. In a sense, anthropologists working in their own culture have the opposite problem: They must attempt to see their culture as an outsider might. This is challenging because it is easy to take cultural knowledge for granted. In addition, it may be as difficult to maintain a neutral stand in one's own culture as it is in a different one. As Margaret Mead once noted, it may be easier to remain culturally relativistic when we confront patterns, such as cannibalism or infanticide, in other cultures than when we confront problematic situations such as child neglect, corporate greed, or armed conflict in our own.

Some of the problems and the rewards of studying one's own culture can be seen in Barbara Myerhoff's books and films. Myerhoff contrasted her work with the Huichol of northern Mexico (1974) with her work among elderly Jewish people in California (1978). She notes that, in the first case, doing anthropology was "an act of imagination, a means for discovering what one is not and will never be." In the second case, fieldwork was a glimpse into her possible future, as she knew that someday she would be a "little old Jewish lady." Her work was a personal way to understand that condition and to contemplate her own future. Tragically, it was a future that never arrived. Myerhoff died of cancer when she was only 49.

Another dilemma experienced by many anthropologists, but particularly poignant for native anthropologists, is whether one should be a disinterested researcher or an advocate for the people one studies. Can the two be combined? Delmos Jones, an African American anthropologist who worked in the United States, was deeply concerned with improving the position of African Americans. He studied voluntary organizations whose goal was to create political and social change in African American urban communities (Jones 1995). He was able to get access to such organizations both because he was an African American and because he shared their goals. One of his important findings was that, for a variety of reasons, there was considerable dissent between the leadership and the rank and file in the groups he studied. Furthermore, he found that leaders used many different means to stifle this dissent. Jones's findings left him with a variety of unpleasant choices. If he publicized problems within the organizations, he risked both alienating the leaders who had befriended him and potentially damaging causes in which he believed deeply. On the other hand, if he failed to publicize such problems, he would be omitting an important aspect of his findings and supporting leadership practices he considered troubling.

Reflecting on his research experience, Jones concluded that although being a cultural insider offers certain advantages, such as access to the community, it also poses special dilemmas, particularly when the group being studied has been oppressed by the larger society. Indeed, he noted that the very concept of a native anthropologist is itself problematic. An individual has many identities, including race, culture, gender, and social class. Being a native in one identity does not make one a native in all one's identities (Cerroni-Long 1995; Narayan 1993).

ETHICAL CONSIDERATIONS IN FIELDWORK

Jones's position as a native anthropologist involved him in a delicate ethical situation. This is not unusual. Ethical issues frequently arise in anthropological research. Anthropologists have obligations to the standards of their discipline, to their sponsors, to their own and their host governments, and to the public. However, their first ethical obligations are usually to the people they study and to the people with whom they work. Under some circumstances, these obligations can supersede the goal of seeking new knowledge. According to the American Anthropological Association *Code of Ethics* (1998), "Anthropological researchers must do everything in their power to ensure that their research does not harm the safety, dignity, or privacy of the people with whom they work. . . ." This includes safeguarding the rights, interests, and sensitivities of those studied, explaining the aims of the investigation as clearly as possible to the people involved; respecting anonymity of informants, not exploiting individual informants for personal gain; and giving "fair return" for all services. It also includes the responsibility to communicate the results of the research to the individuals and groups likely to be affected, as well as the general public.

Informed consent is a critical aspect of anthropological ethics. Generally, obtaining the informed consent of study participants requires anthropologists to take part in ongoing and dynamic discussion with their consultants about the nature of study as well as the risks and benefits of participation in it (Clark and Kingsolver n.d.). In particular, informed consent means that study participants should understand the ways in which release of the research data are likely to affect them. Further, individuals must be free to decide whether or not they will participate in the study (and, if they begin to participate, they must always be free to stop).

Anthropologists also have obligations to the discipline of anthropology. Two of these seem both particularly important and particularly problematic. First, anthropologists should conduct themselves in ways that do not endanger the research prospects or lives of other anthropologists. Anthropologists who violate the mores and ethics of the communities where they work make it unlikely that those communities will accept other anthropologists in the future. Anthropologists who become involved with and identified with governments, military forces, or political platforms may endanger not only their own safety but also the work and lives of others. People may come to believe that because some anthropologists are identified with specific political actors, all are.

Most anthropologists also believe that the primary purpose of research is to add to the general store of anthropological knowledge. Thus they have an obligation to publish their findings in forms that are available to other anthropologists and to the general public. Publishing usually involves review of the work by other anthropologists to help assure the validity and quality of research. Anthropologists acknowledge that certain forms of secrecy are acceptable, and, on occasion, even required. For example, to protect both the communities where they work and the individuals with whom they work, anthropologists may decide to not reveal the precise location of their research or the actual names of the individuals they discuss. However, research in which the methods and findings are secret is a far greater problem. Not only does it fail to contribute to anthropological knowledge, but the scientific community has no way of assessing its validity.

The obligations to protect other anthropologists and to publish research findings both pose dilemmas. The engaged anthropologists described in this chapter believe that anthropologists must work for the communities they study. However, this may make it impossible for future anthropologists to work at all. For example, governments may not grant anthropologists research visas and organizations may not allow research if they believe anthropologists will promote political action against them. Applied anthropologists wish to work for businesses and governments. Often anthropological findings have greatest value for these entities when they are not shared with other businesses or the general public. There may be very few jobs available for applied anthropologists who insist on the right to publish all of the results of their research.

Numerous projects have tested the boundaries of ethics in anthropology, both in regard to the people anthropologists study and to the discipline itself. One of the best known of these was "Project Camelot," a mid-1960s attempt by the army and Department of Defense to enlist anthropologists and other social scientists in achieving American foreign policy goals. Project Camelot's purpose was to create a model for predicting civil wars but it was also implicated in using military and cultural means to fight insurgency movements and prop up friendly governments (Horowitz 1967). When Project Camelot was made public in 1965, the United States had recently invaded the Dominican Republic and was escalating the war in Vietnam.

Project Camelot created controversy both inside and outside of anthropology. In countries where anthropologists worked, people began to see them as spies whose presence presaged an American invasion. At the American Anthropological Association, Project Camelot led to vitriolic debate, where members raised concerns for the integrity of research, the safety of anthropologists in the field, and the purposes to which anthropological knowledge might be put. These concerns eventually led to the issuing of the first official statement on anthropological ethics in 1971.

Anthropology and the Military

Recently, concerns similar to those raised by Project Camelot have recurred over the engagement of some anthropologists with the American military. Anthropologists and other social scientists are involved with the military in two different ways. Some anthropologists have worked at military colleges and bases, providing anthropological training for officers or analyses of the culture of the military itself. Other anthropologists and social scientists have worked on the ground collecting data in zones of active conflict. Most of these individuals work for a program called Human Terrain Systems (HTS). As of this writing (summer of 2010), three social scientists working in this program have been killed.

The use of anthropologists in the training of military officers is the less controversial of the two forms of engagement. Anthropologists who favor this form of working with the military argue that such anthropologists generally present information that is publically available. Military personnel are free to enroll in anthropology courses at public and private universities. Presenting anthropology courses as part of military training is no different. Additionally, supporters of such engagement argue that soldiers of all ranks who understand the dynamics of culture, the importance of critical meanings and symbols, and the structure and distribution of power within a society are liable to be more successful and less destructive than those who do not. Where are they to get this knowledge if not from anthropology? However, such engagement also raises important questions. No professor can ever control the uses to which students put the information and skills received in classes. However, the military's interest in anthropological knowledge is related to conquest, domination, and control of other populations. Some anthropologists argue that engagement with the military is wrong because it actively promotes such ends. David Price (2008) notes that although anthropologists working in universities and in the military face similar issues, anthropologists in universities seek knowledge for its own sake whereas those working for the military seek it for victory, security, and defense, at least in theory.

The use of anthropologists and other social scientists as part of HTS teams on the ground raises much deeper problems than their presence in military training. Starting in early 2007, the Pentagon has employed HTS teams to help its combat brigades. According to some, this program has been very successful. For example, the obituary of Michael Bhatia, one of the HTS members who died while performing their duties, reports that Bhatia's work helped save the lives of both U.S. soldiers and Afghan civilians. Colonel Martin Schweitzer testified before Congress that the HTS team helped the 4-82 airborne brigade reduce its lethal operations by 60 to 70 percent, increase the number of districts supporting the Afghan government from 15 to 83, and reduce Afghan civilian deaths from over 70 during the previous brigade's tour to 11 (Fondacaro and McFate 2008). However, the use of anthropologists in such circumstances continues to be extremely problematic. A recent American Anthropological Association report notes that engagement with the military raises concerns about obligations to those who anthropologists study; perils for the discipline, one's colleagues, the broader academic community; as well as issues of secrecy and transparency (Peacock et al. 2007).

It is indeed difficult to see how many of anthropology's ethical requirements can be met under conditions of warfare. How, for example, are participants to give coercion-free consent while subject to military occupation? How can anthropologists honestly inform participants about the ways the research data will be used and are likely to affect them? Are individuals in a conflict ever really free to decide whether or not they will participate in a study? Can anthropologists working under such circumstances assure, within reason, that the information they supply will not harm the safety, dignity, or privacy of the people with whom they work? Isn't the point of their work sometimes just the opposite of that? What about anthropologists' obligation to publish their research? Aren't the results of this sort of research necessarily secret? Historically, anthropologists have been concerned with protecting the rights and safety of the people they study. The primary concern of anthropologists working in HTS must be the safety, security, and goals of their employers instead.

Given all of the problems with HTS, it is probably safe to say that a strong majority of anthropologists oppose this use of anthropology. Anthropologists voiced opposition to HTS and other forms of involvement with the military at the annual meetings of the American Anthropological Association (AAA) in 2007 and 2008. It seems very likely that, in the next few years, the AAA will revise its code of ethics to take a stronger position against this kind of anthropology. However, ultimately, ethical behavior is the responsibility of each individual anthropologist. The members of the American Anthropological Association are supposed to subscribe to its code of ethics. Universities and some other research organizations have institutional review boards that examine all research involving human subjects for ethical violations. However, not all anthropologists are subject to the AAA or to institutional review boards. Lawyers who behave unethically can be disbarred. Doctors can have their medical licenses revoked. In both cases, they violate laws and can be punished if they continue to practice. There is no comparable sanction for anthropologists (and, indeed, for members of most disciplines). Therefore, there will always be a great diversity of anthropological practice.

NEW ROLES FOR THE ETHNOGRAPHER

Although there have been native anthropologists for a long time, until the 1970s, the prevailing model of fieldwork was a European or North American ethnographer visiting a relatively isolated and bounded society who reported on that society to other Europeans and North Americans. In the past several decades, this model has become unrealistic. Immigration, inexpensive communication, and relatively cheap airfare have altered the world and the nature of the anthropologist's job.

Whether working in cities, villages, or with tribal groups, almost all ethnographers must take into account the interaction of these local units with larger social structures, economies, and cultures. Such connections may extend from the region to the entire world. Thus, research may mean following consultants from villages to their workplaces in cities or collecting genealogies that spread over countries or even continents. In addition to expanding the research site, contemporary ethnographers must often use techniques such as questionnaires, social surveys, archival material, government documents, and court records in addition to participant observation. The deep connections among cultures and the global movement of individuals means that we must constantly reevaluate the nature of the cultures we are studying, their geographical spread, their economic and political position, and their relation to each other.

Today, not only are native anthropologists much more common, but the people anthropologists study generally have far greater knowledge of the world than they did in earlier times. Often they understand what anthropology is and what anthropologists do, something not true in the past. In some cases, this has led to difficulties as people struggle over the question of who has the right to speak for a group. In other cases, people from the groups that anthropologists have described have publicly taken issue with their analysis. For example, in the early 2000s, a fierce controversy broke out over anthropological descriptions of the Yanomamo, an often studied Amazonian group. Had their primary ethnographer, Napoleon Chagnon, portrayed them accurately? Was the research team that he was part of responsible for spreading disease and decimating Yanomamo villages? Anthropologists, journalists, and Yanomamo tribe members debated these questions at meetings and in the popular press (for a review of the debate, see Borofsky 2005).

Despite controversies, for the most part, natives' increased knowledge of the outside has resulted in closer relations among anthropologists and the people they study as well as more accurate ethnography. Ethnographic data are often useful to a society. Sometimes they serve as the basis for the revitalization of cultural identities that have been nearly effaced by Western impact (Feinberg 1994). Sometimes they play important roles in establishing group claims to "authenticity" and are useful in local political and economic contexts. For example, when Kathleen Adams (1995) carried out her fieldwork among the Toraja of Sulawesi, Indonesia, she became a featured event on tourist itineraries in the region. Toraja tour guides led their groups to the home of her host, both validating his importance in the village and bolstering the tourists' experience of the Toraja as a group sufficiently "authentic" and important to be studied by anthropologists.

In the past, anthropologists sometimes worried about their subject disappearing. They argued that the main thing anthropology was designed to study was small-scale, relatively isolated "primitive" societies. They worried that, as economic development spread around the world, such societies would go out of existence and anthropology would essentially be done. In a small sense they were right, but in the larger sense they were wrong. Any anthropologist today looking to study a society untouched by the outside world would be out of luck. No such societies have existed for a long time. On the other hand, the forces of globalization have been as productive of diversity as they have been of homogeneity. Economic, political, and social forces bring groups of people together in new ways, in conflict and in cooperation. New cultural forms are created and old ones modified. Human cultural diversity, imagination, and adaptability show no signs of dying out, so anthropologists will always have material to study. Wherever human cultures exist and however they change, anthropologists will be there, devising means to study, understand, and think about them.

BRINGING IT BACK HOME:
ANTHROPOLOGISTS AND
HUMAN RIGHTS

What could be more obvious than that anthropologists should support human rights and be actively engaged in their promotion? For most Americans, doubting the value of human rights is like arguing against freedom of speech or claiming that children are not important. Yet, human rights pose ethical dilemmas for anthropologists. Almost all anthropologists believe firmly in their duty to promote human rights in our own society. Many also believe that they have an obligation to promote the interests of those they study. For example, Laura R. Graham (2006:5) writes that "[o]ur privileged position, specialized training, and unique skills . . . carry with them specific ethical obligations to promote the well-being of the people who are collaborators in our anthropological research and in the production of anthropological knowledge." Ida Nicolaisen points out that standing for human rights is often a matter of life and death. For example, she notes that in the Philippines between 2005 and late summer 2006, at least 73 indigenous people were "subjected to extra-judicial killings" and concludes that "[w]e owe it to indigenous peoples and other marginalized groups to stand up for their basic human rights when needed" (Nicolaisen 2006:6).

But there often are difficulties determining what the rights are and whether or not we should stand up for them. Laura Nader (2006:6) writes that ideas about human rights were developed in a largely western European context and are often conceived of as "something Euro-Americans take to others." Promoting Western notions of human rights may mean denying people in other societies what they consider to be their rights to pursue individual and cultural choices. Female genital operations are a good example and are covered in more detail in Chapter 8, but there are many others. Consider Islamic hadd ("to the limit") punishments, such as stoning for adultery, amputation of limbs for theft, and flogging for moral offenses. Hadd punishments deeply offend many people (including many Muslims), yet they form a core component of ethical belief and practice for many people in some Islamic nations. The organization Human Rights Watch reports that courts in Saudi Arabia continue to impose punishments such as amputations of hands and feet for robbery and floggings for lesser crimes such as "sexual deviance" and drunkenness (Human Rights Watch 2001:14). In northern Nigeria, between 2000 and 2004, courts passed more than 60 amputation sentences (Human Rights Watch 2004:38). Anthropologist Carolyn Fluehr-Lobban (2005) interviewed attorneys, judges, social scientists, and journalists in Sudan, a country that has practiced hadd punishments. She notes that most Sudanese Muslims oppose the use of hadd, and see it as an abuse of religion by the state. However, they also think that Western interest in eliminating such punishment is unwarranted interference in their right to determine their own culture. They point to a double standard: Westerners, particularly Americans, see hadd punishments as "barbaric" while they ignore their own abuses of human rights, such as the death penalty, waterboarding, Abu Ghraib, and Guantanamo.

YOU DECIDE

1. Given the diversity of culture and the anthropological importance of cultural relativism, can there be such a thing as universal human rights?
2. If anthropologists have moral obligations to the people with whom they work, should they ever work with people whose beliefs and practices they disapprove of? If yes, then what obligations do they have to such people? If no, how are we to accurately represent such people?
3. What sorts of things do you consider to be universal human rights? How good is our society at assuring the rights you have identified? Do you think there is a core set of universal rights upon which most people could or should agree?

CHAPTER SUMMARY

1. Anthropology began in the 19th century. In that era, anthropologists were compilers of data rather than fieldworkers. Their goal was to describe and document the evolutionary history of human society. There were numerous problems with their data and methods.
2. In the United States, Franz Boas established a style of anthropology that rejected evolutionism. Boas insisted that anthropologists collect data through participant observation. He argued that cultures were the result of their own history and could not be compared to one another, a position now called *cultural relativism.*
3. In Britain, Bronislaw Malinowski and others also developed a tradition of fieldwork. Although their focus was different than Boas's, they also saw members of other cultures as fully rational and worthy of respect.
4. Almost all anthropologists today do fieldwork, and many continue to work in small communities. Most focus on answering specific questions rather than describing entire societies. Anthropological techniques include participant observation, interviews, questionnaires, and mapping.

5. Cross-cultural comparison has always been an aspect of anthropology. The Human Relations Area File (HRAF) is a large database that facilitates cross-cultural research.
6. Despite the presence of important women in early 20th-century anthropology, women were historically underrepresented in anthropological writing. This situation began to be redressed in the late 1960s.
7. In the 1980s, postmodernists urged anthropologists to become more sensitive to issues of voice, history, and power. Postmodernists' insistence that the objective world was unknowable and that the anthropologist's voice was uncertain created intense debate but ultimately enriched ethnography.
8. One response to postmodernism was collaborative anthropology. Some anthropologists placed special emphasis on the political dimensions of their work. They often took great pains to involve members of the group being studied in the production of ethnographic knowledge.
9. Anthropologists who study their own society have become more numerous. Although native anthropologists may have advantages of access and rapport in some cases, they also experience special burdens more intensely, such as whether to expose aspects of the culture that may be received unfavorably by outsiders.
10. Doing anthropology often raises ethical questions. Anthropological ethics require protecting the dignity, privacy, and anonymity of the people one studies. However, anthropological ethics are rarely simple. The use of anthropologists in pursuit of foreign relations goals is sometimes extremely problematic.
11. Anthropologists are increasingly enmeshed in a global society. Those they study are rarely isolated and are often quite knowledgeable about anthropology. Anthropological knowledge is often important in the ways people understand their identity and, as such, is increasingly political.

KEY TERMS

Collaborative ethnography
Consultant
Cultural relativism
Culture shock
Ethnocentrism
Ethnography
Ethnology

Human Relations Area Files
Informant
Participant observation
Postmodernism
Racism
Respondent

Human language consists of words and gestures as illustrated by this interaction between two Tajik men in a square on the outskirts of Dushanbe, the capital of Tajikistan.

© Associated Press

CHAPTER **4**

COMMUNICATION

INNER-CITY EBONICS

ARRY H., a 15-year-old core member of the Jets (a teenage gang in Philadelphia) is one of their loudest and roughest members. He gives the least recognition to conventional rules of politeness. Most of you meeting Larry for the first time probably wouldn't like him any more than his teachers do, and the dislike would be mutual. Larry causes trouble in and out of school. He was put back from the eleventh grade to the ninth and has been threatened with further action by the school authorities. In the dialogues that follow, John Lewis (JL) interviews Larry:

JL: What happens to you after you die? Do you know?

Larry: Yeah, I know. (What?) After they put you in the ground, your body turns into—ah—bones an' shit.

JL: What happens to your spirit?

Larry: Your spirit—soon as you die, your spirit leaves you. (And where does the spirit go?) Well, it all depends. . . . (On what?) You know, like some people say if you're good an' shit, your spirit goin' t'heaven. . . . 'n' if you bad, your spirit goin' to hell. Well, bullshit. Your spirit goin' to hell anyway, good or bad.

JL: Why?

Larry: Why? I'll tell you why. 'Cause, you see, doesn' nobody really know that it's a God, y'know, 'cause I mean I have seen black gods, pink gods, white gods, all color gods, and don't nobody know it's really a God. An' when they be sayin' if you good, you goin' t'heaven, tha's bullshit, 'cause you ain't goin' to no heaven, 'cause it ain't no heaven for you to go to.

Larry is a paradigmatic speaker of African American English Vernacular (AAEV) as opposed to Standard English. His grammar shows a high concentration of such characteristic AAEV forms as negative inversion ("don't nobody know"), negative concord ("you ain't goin' to no heaven"), invariant *be* ("when they be sayin'"), dummy *it* for standard *there* ("it ain't no heaven"), optional copula deletion ("if you're good . . . if you bad"), and full forms of auxiliaries ("I have seen"). . . .

Our particular interest here is on the logical form of this passage. Larry presents a complex set of interdependent propositions that can be explained by setting out the Standard English equivalents in linear order: Everyone has a different idea of God, therefore no one knows if God exists. A God that doesn't exist couldn't have made a heaven; therefore you can't go there. Thus, you are going to hell.

This hypothetical argument is not carried on at a high level of seriousness. It is a game played with ideas as counters in which opponents use a wide variety of verbal devices to win. Lewis challenges Larry's logic:

JL: Well, if there's no heaven, how could there be a hell?

Larry: I mean—ye-eah. Well, let me tell you, it ain't no hell, 'cause this is hell right here, y'know. (This is hell?) Yeah, this is hell right here.

Despite the fact that Larry does not believe in God and has just denied all knowledge of him, Lewis advances the following hypothetical question:

JL: . . . but, just say that there is a God, what color is he? White or black?

Larry: Well, if it is a God . . . I wouldn' know what color, I couldn' say,—couldn' nobody say what color he is or really would be.

JL: But now, jus' suppose there was a God—

Larry: Unless'n they say . . .

JL: No, I was jus' saying jus' suppose there is a God, would he be white or black?

Larry: . . . He'd be white, man.

JL: Why?

Larry: Why? I'll tell you why. 'Cause the average whitey out here got every-thing, you dig? And the nigger ain't got shit, y'know? Y'unnerstan'? So—um—for—in order for that to happen, you know it ain't no black God that's doin' that bullshit.

No one can hear Larry's answer to this question without being convinced that they are in the presence of a skilled speaker with great "verbal presence of mind," who can use the English language expertly for many purposes. Larry's answer to John Lewis is a complex argument. The formulation is not in Standard English, but it is clear and effective, even for those not familiar with the vernacular.

In these passages from *Language in the Inner City*, linguist William Labov (1972) analyzes African American English Vernacular (AAEV), sometimes called *Ebonics*. AAEV has deep roots in the African American community, particularly among rural and urban working-class blacks. Although not all Americans of African origin speak it, AAEV is emblematic of black speech in the minds of many. There are lots of different ways of speaking English in the United States, but few have been as widely criticized as AAEV.

From the 1950s to the 1970s, a group of linguists, psychologists, and educators called *cultural deficit theorists* argued that African American children did poorly in school because of the way they spoke English. They argued that the poor speech of these children, which they characterized as coarse, simple, and irrational, was due to a culturally deprived home environment (Ammon and Ammon 1971). They proposed that if people could be taught to speak Standard English, they would be able to think more logically, and this would help lift them from poverty (Bereiter and Engelmann 1966; Engelmann and Engelmann 1966).

The work of William Labov and others was central to countering the arguments of the deficit theorists. Through analysis of dialogues such as those with Larry, Labov showed that inner-city black speech was no more or less complex, rational, or orderly than that of other English speakers. It simply followed different rules, many of which were also found in other languages. Labov demonstrated that AAEV was just a different way of speaking and, from a linguistic point of view, neither better nor worse than any other.

So, what is good English? Consider the double negative. Almost everyone reading this book has heard someone (perhaps a teacher) claim that a double negative is really a positive. Thus, saying "I don't want no" is really saying "I want some." This is simply incorrect. When Mick Jagger sings, "I can't get no satisfaction," no native English speaker believes he is saying how satisfied he is. And no one imagines that the kids singing in Pink Floyd's "The Wall" are telling us how much they want to go to school.

But sometimes, two negatives do make a positive, as when a child who refuses to do her homework says: "I won't not do my homework if you buy me some ice cream." And two or more positives can sometimes make a negative, as in:

Speaker A: "Yes, I will do it."

Speaker B: "Yeah, yeah, yeah, sure you will."

The point is that, from a linguistic perspective, one way of speaking is as good as the next. There is no reason to prefer "I don't have any money" to "I ain't got no money," and there is no reason that saying "I'm about to go get lunch" is better than saying "I'm fixin' to get me some lunch." All the statements are fully logical and comprehensible, and communicate the information the speaker desires.

So why does society act as if one statement is good and the other bad? Because speech often identifies the speaker's ethnic background, social class, geographical location, and other aspects of their life. Our judgments are really about people, based on their speech, not on the comprehensibility of the speech itself.

Although all humans who are physically able to do so communicate through language, speech is not just biology. The language we speak, the style of our speaking, to whom we speak, and how we speak to them are all aspects of culture.

THE ORIGINS AND CHARACTERISTICS OF HUMAN LANGUAGE

Although passing information is critical to the survival of most living things, members of other species communicate very differently than humans. No·member of any other species can make up a story and tell it to another, understand a piece of poetry, or discuss what it would like to eat tomorrow, yet these are things that people in all human cultures do regularly.

Animal vocalizations are referred to as *calls*, and animal **call systems** may have up to 60 sounds. However, even large call systems are restricted to a fixed number of signals generally uttered in response to specific events. Human language, on the other hand, is capable of re-creating complex thought patterns and experiences in words.

call system A form of animal communication composed of a limited number of sounds that are tied to specific stimuli in the environment.

So, when did humans first begin to speak? Anthropologists offer several answers to this question. Certainly our most distant ancestors communicated, but they probably used call systems similar to modern-day primates. Some believe that language might have begun as early as two million years ago, when the genus *Homo* emerged (Schepartz 1993:119), but most anthropologists think that language like our own has been limited to members of our own species. The earliest *Homo sapiens* date from about 200,000 years ago, so language may well have emerged at that time. A third position (Bickerton 1998) holds that modern human language emerged about 50,000 years ago, in connection with a big jump in the sophistication of human toolmaking and symbolic expression. Work in biology suggests a relationship between language and a gene called FOXP2. Although the ability to acquire and use language is controlled by many genes, FOXP2 is the only one that has been clearly identified (Dominguez and Rakic 2009). Interestingly, the human form of FOXP2 has also been found in Neanderthals (Krause et al. 2007).

Regardless of the date at which humans acquired language, anthropologists generally agree that language is part of our biological adaptation. Although in any culture, some people talk with greater or lesser artistry than others, all physiologically normal individuals in all cultures develop adequate language skills.

Language is more than simply a human capacity or ability. For example, people have the capacity to learn algebra or ice-skating. They may or may not do it as their culture and their individual choices dictate. Language is different. Unless prevented by total social isolation

Colorado University

Some nonhuman animals show surprising linguistic abilities. Here a chimpanzee signs "double apple" to his trainer. However, human language is uniquely complex, sophisticated, and abstract.

or physical incapacity, all humans learn a first language as part of the developmental process of childhood. All go through the same stages of language learning in the same sequence and at roughly the same speed regardless of the language being learned. Language is an innate property of the mind.

Humans have what Steven Pinker (1994) calls a "language instinct." Pinker points out that the language "instinct" in humans is very different from instinctive communication in other animals. Among animals, the instinct for communication means that dogs do not *learn* to wag their tails when they are content and growl when they are angry: They do these things as an expression of their underlying genetic code. Dog behavior is species-wide. A growl means the same thing to a dog in Vladivostok as it does to a dog in Manhattan. But language is not instinctual in this way. The human "instinct" is to learn the language of the group into which the individual is socialized. There is no biological basis for learning one language over another. For example, an infant born to French-speaking parents but raised in an English-speaking family has no predisposition to speak French.

universal grammar A basic set of principles, conditions, and rules that form the foundation of all languages.

The universality of the process of learning a first language as well as the underlying similarities that unite all human languages led Noam Chomsky (1975) and many others to propose that there is a **universal grammar**—a basic set of principles, conditions, and rules that form the foundation of all languages. Children learn language by applying this unconscious universal grammar to the sounds they hear.

The social element of language learning is critical. To learn language, we must be able to interact verbally with others. There is a particularly important period from our birth until about 6 years of age. Children deprived of contact during these years never learn to speak like other members of their community. This is illustrated by the case of Genie, a child discovered in the 1970s by social workers in California. Genie had been locked in an attic for the first 12 years of her life. With training and good living conditions, she acquired a large vocabulary, but she was never able to master English syntax; she created sentences like "Genie have momma have baby grow up" (Pinker 1994:292). Children like Genie demonstrate that although language is a biological capacity, it can only be activated within a social group. Thus, language provides an outstanding example of the interrelation of biology and culture.

symbol Something that stands for something else. Central to language and culture.

conventionality The notion that, in human language, words are only arbitrarily or conventionally connected to the things for which they stand.

Human language is first and foremost a system of symbols. A **symbol** is just something that stands for something else. Words are symbols, and they stand for things, actions, and ideas because speakers of a language agree that they do, a feature of human language called **conventionality**. An animal is no more a dog than it is a *chien* (French), a *perro* (Spanish), or a *kutta* (Hindi).

This seemingly trivial fact is critical for two reasons. First, because the relationship between a series of sounds (a word) and their meaning is symbolic, relatively few sounds can be used to refer to an infinitely large number of meanings. For nonhuman animals, there is a direct connection between a sound and its meaning; 60 sounds equals 60 meanings. Most human languages have only 30 to 40 sounds. However, used in combination, these sounds can produce an endless variety of words and meanings. There is no maximum number of words or sentences in any human language. People constantly create new ones, a characteristic known as **productivity**.

Second, symbols enable humans to transmit and store information, a capacity that makes our cultures possible. If humans had to learn everything they know by trial and error or by watching others, our lives would be vastly different and much simpler than they are. Human beings do learn by these methods, but they also learn by talking. We tell each other our experiences and the stories passed down to us. We discuss the past and plan for the future using words. This human ability to speak about different times and places is called **displacement**.

The ability of humans to use symbols allows us to store information. In cultures with writing, such stored information is vast. Consider, for example, that no one individual could possibly know everything written in the books in even a relatively small university library. However, because we can store our knowledge symbolically as words, we can have access to everything that is there. And with the Internet . . . well, you get the point!

THE STRUCTURE OF LANGUAGE $\rightarrow$ stop

Although there are enormous differences among languages, there are also some compelling similarities. Every language has a structure: an internal logic and a particular relationship among its parts. Descriptive, or structural, linguistics is the study of the internal workings of language. A basic insight of structural linguistics is that all languages are composed of four subsystems: **phonology** (a system of sounds), **morphology** (a system for creating words from sounds), **semantics** (a system that relates words to meanings), and **syntax** (a system of rules for combining words into meaningful sentences).

At a very basic level, all language is made up of sounds. Humans use a vast array of sounds in their languages. For example, the International Phonetic Alphabet (IPA), a system designed to represent the sounds of all human languages in writing, has more than 100 base symbols, which can be altered by about 55 modifiers. The total set of sounds found in human language is called the **phones** of language. No individual language uses

productivity (linguistics) The idea that humans can combine words and sounds into new, meaningful utterances they have never before heard.

displacement The capacity of all human languages to describe things not happening in the present.

phonology The sound system of a language.

morphology A system for creating words from sounds.

semantics The system of a language that relates words to meaning.

syntax A system of rules for combining words into meaningful sentences.

phone Smallest identifiable unit of sound made by humans and used in any language.

phoneme The smallest unit of sound that serves to distinguish between meanings of words within a language.

minimal pair Two words that differ in only one sound but have different meanings.

allophones Two or more different phones that can be used to make the same phoneme in a specific language.

morpheme The smallest unit of language that has a meaning.

isolating language A language with relatively few morphemes per word and fairly simple rules for combining them.

agglutinating language A language that allows a great number of morphemes per word and has highly regular rules for combining morphemes.

more than a small subset of this huge number of possible sounds. The sounds that are used in any individual language are called the **phonemes** of that language.

Phonemes distinguish meaning within a given language. For example, the English words *den* and *then* are a **minimal pair**: two words that differ in only one sound but have different meanings. In this case, the difference is indicated by the sounds that are made when we produce the consonants /d/ or /th/ at the beginning of the word. The fact that changing this sound changes the meaning of the word indicates that /d/ and /th/ are two different phonemes in English. In other languages, Spanish for example, both of these sounds exist, but they are not separate phonemes. Interchanging them may make you sound strange, but will not change the meaning of the word. Thus, they are **allophones**; that is, both phones indicate only one phoneme. In Spanish, their proper usage depends on whether they are found at the beginning or in the middle of a word.

At some level, almost everyone is aware of the phonemic differences among languages. For example, the "rolled r" common in Spanish is not found in most varieties of English, and many English speakers find the sound difficult to make. On the other hand, the /th/ sound (as in the word *the*) is common in most varieties of English but does not exist in French or Japanese (as well as many other languages). Attempting to speak one language using the phonemes of another results in an accent.

At a more profound level, phonemes are probably the first aspect of language that an infant learns. Every child has the biological capacity to acceptably make all the sounds of all human language. However, they learn the breathing and the tongue and lip positions associated only with the sounds of their own language. Learning as an adult to hear and make new sounds can be very difficult.

All languages are made up of units that have meaning called **morphemes**. Morphemes can be composed of any number of phonemes. Some are as simple as a single phoneme (the English morphemes "A" and "–s" for example), and most are relatively brief. Words are composed of any number of morphemes. Some are extremely simple: "A" is a phoneme, a morpheme, and a word. The word *teacher* has two morphemes: "teach" and "–er" (here, "–er" refers to someone who does what came before it). Long words, such as antidisestablishmentarianism, for example, are simply strings of morphemes.

Languages differ in the way morphemes and words are related. An **isolating language** such as English or Chinese tends to have few morphemes per word and fairly simple rules for combining them. An **agglutinating language** has a great number of morphemes per word. In languages such as Inuktitut (an Arctic Canadian language), translating a single word may require an entire English sentence. For example, the Inuktitut word *qasuirrsarvigssarsingitluinarnarpuq* contains ten morphemes and is best translated as "someone did not find a completely suitable resting place" (Bonvillain 1997:19).

The total stock of words in a language is known as its **lexicon**. A lexicon often provides clues to culture because it tends to reflect the objects and ideas that members of that culture consider important. For example, the average American can name 50 to 100 types of plants, but members of foraging societies can often name 500 to 1,000 types (Harris 1989:72). Germans in Munich have a vocabulary of more than 70 words to describe the strength, color, fizziness, clarity, and age of beer because it is so central to their culture (Hage 1972, cited in Salzmann 1993:256). Americans have large numbers of words to describe cars or money but have far fewer to describe bicycles.

Anthropologists sometimes use vocabulary as a clue to understanding different cultures. For example, the words people use for their kin tell us something of the nature of their families. In English, a woman uses the term brother-in-law to speak about her sister's husband, her husband's brother, and the husbands of all her husband's sisters. The use of a single term for all of these relations reflects the similarity of a woman's behavior toward the men in these kinship statuses. In Hindi, a language of North India, a woman uses separate terms for her sister's husband (*behnoi*), her husband's elder brother (*jait*), her husband's younger brother (*deva*), and her husband's sisters' husbands (*nandoya*). The variety of words in Hindi reflects the fact that a woman treats the members of each of these categories differently.

Sounds and words alone do not make up a language. To convey meaning, every language has syntax, rules that structure the combination of words into meaningful utterances. Languages differ in their syntactic structures. In English, word order is a basic element of syntax, so statements such as "The dog bit the man" and "The man bit the dog" have very different meanings. Word order is not equally important in all languages. In Japanese, the subject and object of a sentence are indicated by word endings, and order is less important. For example, "John gave Mary the book" is translated *John-san ga Mary-san ni hon o ageta*. The same word order, with the word endings ga and ni reversed *(John-san ni Mary-san ga hon o ageta)* would be "Mary gave John the book."

Parts of speech (nouns, verbs, and so on) are a critical aspect of syntax. All languages have a word class of nouns, but different languages have

© Reuters/Corbis

Languages build vocabularies around ideas and things important to their speakers. Germans in Munich have more than 70 words to describe beer.

lexicon The total stock of words in a language.

different subclasses of nouns, frequently referred to as *genders*. (In linguistics, the word *gender* does not refer to masculine and feminine traits but rather to the category or "class" of a word.) For example, Papago, a Native American language, divides all the features of the world into two genders: "living things" and "growing things." Living things include all animated objects; growing things refer to inanimate objects. Spanish, French, Italian, and many other languages divide nouns into masculine and feminine subclasses. German and Latin have masculine, feminine, and neuter subclasses. Some languages have many more subclasses. Kivunjo, a language spoken in East Africa, has 16 of them (Pinker 1994:27, Corbett 2008).

Applying the rules of grammar turns meaningless sequences of words into meaningful utterances, but we can recognize a sentence as grammatical even if it makes no sense. To use a now-classic example (Chomsky 1965), consider the following sentences: "Colorless green ideas sleep furiously," and "Furiously sleep ideas green colorless." Both sentences are meaningless in English, but English speakers easily recognize the first as grammatical, whereas the second is both meaningless and ungrammatical.

LANGUAGE AND CULTURE

Phonemes, morphemes, syntax . . . these are essentially elements of the biology of language, but language is much more than just its structure. Consider the following exchange:

Scene: It's a clear, hot evening in July. J and K have finished their meal. The children are sitting nearby. There is a knock at the door. J rises, answers the knock, and finds L standing outside.

J: Hello, my friend! How're you doing? How are you feeling, L? You feeling good? *(J now turns in the direction of K and addresses her.)*

J: Look who here, everybody! Look who just come in. Sure, it's my Indian friend, L. Pretty good, all right. *(J slaps L on the shoulder and, looking him directly in the eyes, seizes his hand and pumps it wildly up and down.)*

J: Come right in, my friend! Don't stay outside in the rain. Better you come in right now. *(J now drapes his arm around L's shoulder and moves him in the direction of a chair.)*

J: Sit down! Sit right down! Take your loads off you ass. You hungry? You want crackers? Maybe you want some beer? You want some wine? Bread? You want some sandwich? How about it? You hungry? I don't know. Maybe you sick. Maybe you don't eat again long time. *(K has now stopped what she is doing and is looking on with amusement. L has seated himself and has a look of bemused resignation on his face.)*

J: You sure looking good to me, L. You looking pretty fat! Pretty good all right! You got new boots? Where you buy them? Sure pretty good boots! I glad. . . . *(At this point, J breaks into laughter. K joins in. L shakes his head and smiles. The joke is over).*

The Western Apache.

The joke is over. . . . So what was the joke? This joke, from the Western Apache, recorded by Keith Basso (1979), is about how the Apache see white people as communicating with them and with each other. In the joke, *J* pretends he is a white man. The joke is that white speech, as *J* presents it, is highly inappropriate and offensive. For starters, you do not publicly call someone a friend or ask how he or she is feeling. For the Western Apache, these are very personal statements and questions. To use them in a highly public way as *J* does here conveys insincerity. The Apache believe that one should enter and leave a room as unobtrusively as possible, so *J* making a big to-do about *L* coming into the room is inappropriate as well. Actions such as putting an arm around another man's shoulder or asking repeatedly if he wants something to eat are understood as both violations of individual dignity and overwhelming bossiness. To the Apache, such actions suggest that the speaker thinks the person he or she is talking to is of no account and that his wishes can be safely ignored. Perhaps worst of all is suggesting that another might be sick. Not only is this a violation of privacy; the Apache fear that talking about misfortune may well bring it on.

Knowing only the technical grammatical aspects of language would not help much in understanding *J* and *L's* speech. Their speech embeds critical cultural concepts and values. Without understanding their culture, an observer cannot possibly get the joke.

Language is so heavily freighted with culture that understanding one is almost always a key to understanding the other. One way anthropologists analyze this relationship is to think in terms of speech performance. Such performance includes what people are saying as well as what they are communicating beyond the actual words. **Sociolinguistics** is the study of the relationship between language and culture. Sociolinguists study speech performances and attempt to identify, describe, and understand the ways in which language is used in different social contexts.

sociolinguistics The study of the relationship between language and culture and the ways language is used in varying social contexts.

The ways in which people actually speak are highly dependent on the context of their speech as well as issues such as class, ethnicity, and geography. For example, a public political speech has different purposes and is limited by different norms than a political discussion among friends. And different cultures have different norms regarding political speeches: who can participate as speaker and audience, the appropriate topics and cultural themes for such a speech, where such speeches can take place, the relationship between the speaker and hearer, the language used in a multilingual community, and so forth.

Speech is critical in the construction of identity. Penelope Eckert (2000) has studied the way children and adolescents in American schools use language to create and enforce social roles and identities. This process starts with teasing in elementary and junior high schools. It continues for girls in the form of both true and false compliments that "establish and enforce social hierarchies and boundaries" (Eckert 2004), and for boys with increased use of language styles specifically opposed by teachers and other powerful adults, including sexual references and obscenities. In high schools, verbal labels indicate social terrain and frequently physical location within the school. In the Detroit high school Eckert studied, the critical labels were jocks and burnouts. Jocks identified with the institution, with adolescence, and with the white suburban middle class. Burnouts saw themselves as opposed to the institution, wanting to be adults, and identified with the urban working class. Jock and burnout groups used language differently: Jock girls were the most standard speakers, and burnout girls used the most vernacular language. Boys' language was between these two groups. Burnout girls made frequent use of multiple negatives and other stigmatized speech forms. These differences involved not only the use of different vocabularies but changes in the sounds of the languages they used as well (Eckert 1989).

In some cultures, different speech forms are used depending on whether the speaker and hearer are intimate friends, acquaintances on equal footing, or people of distinctly different social statuses. French, German, and Yoruba, among many other languages, have formal and informal pronouns that are not found in English. The rules for their use vary among cultures. In France, parents use the informal term to address their children, but children use the formal term to address their parents. In the Spanish spoken in Costa Rica, many people use three forms: the informal *tú* is used by an adult speaking to a child (or lover), the formal *usted* is used among strangers, and the intermediate term *vos* can be used among friends. In India, the status of a husband is higher than that of a wife, and among most Hindi speakers, a wife never addresses her husband by his name (certainly not in public) but uses a roundabout expression that would translate into English as something like "I am speaking to you, sir."

Language and Social Stratification

From a linguistic perspective, all languages are equally sophisticated and serve the needs of their speakers equally well, and every human being speaks with equal grammatical sophistication. Despite this, in complex stratified societies such as the United States, some speech is considered "correct" and other speech is judged inferior (see the example that opens this chapter).

In hierarchical societies, the most powerful group generally determines what is "proper" in language. Indeed, the grammatical constructions used by the social elites are considered *language,* whereas deviations from them are often called *dialects.* Because the power of the speaker rather than any inherent qualities of a speech form determines its acceptability, linguist Max Weinreich has defined a language as "a dialect with an army and a navy" (quoted in Pinker 1994:28).

The relation of language usage to social class and power is reflected in the speech of different social classes in the United States. In a classic study, sociolinguist William Labov (1972) noted that elites and working-class people have different vocabularies and pronounce words differently. The forms associated with higher socioeconomic status are considered "proper," whereas forms spoken by those in lower socioeconomic statuses are considered incorrect and stigmatized.

Labov found that speakers often vary their vocabulary and pronunciation in different contexts and that the degree of such variation is related to their social class. At the bottom and top of the social hierarchy, there is little variation. Elites use privileged forms of speech and the poor use stigmatized forms. However, members of the lower–middle class often use stigmatized forms in casual speech but privileged forms in careful speech. One interpretation is that people at the bottom and top of the social hierarchy do not vary their speech because their social position is stable. The very poor do not believe they have much chance to rise, and the wealthy are secure in their positions. Members of the lower–middle class, however, are concerned with raising their social position and in consequence copy the speech patterns of the wealthy in some social situations. However, they are also concerned with maintaining connections to family and friends and therefore use stigmatized speech with them. Labov's study makes clear what many of us know but do not like to admit: We do judge a person's social status by the way he or she speaks. What we say and how we say it are ways of telling people who we are socially or, perhaps, who we would like to be.

Although there are many stigmatized variants of American English, including Appalachian English, Dutchified Pennsylvania English, Hawaiian Creole, Gullah, and emergent Hispanic Englishes, the most stigmatized is African American Vernacular English (AAVE), also called *Ebonics.* As we noted earlier, AAVE is simply a variant of Standard English, neither better nor worse than any other. Further, from Mark Twain and William Faulkner to Toni Morrison and Maya Angelou, from George Gershwin to Public Enemy and Run DMC, Ebonics has had deep influences on American art, speech, fiction, and music.

Since the 1970s, controversy over Ebonics has frequently been politicized. For example, in the mid-1990s, the Oakland School Board in California encouraged its teachers to *make use of* Ebonics in teaching Standard English (Monaghan 1997). Many Americans misunderstood the Oakland School Board as encouraging the teaching of Ebonics, and this misunderstanding ignited a national furor. A North Carolina legislator denounced Ebonics as "absurd," an *Atlanta Constitution* editorial referred to "the Ebonic plague," and laws banning the teaching of Ebonics were introduced in several state legislatures (Matthews 1997; Sanchez 1997).

Individuals who speak only Ebonics are at a disadvantage in the larger society, and most realize that AAVE is stigmatized as symbolizing ignorance while standard spoken American English (SSAE) is considered "normal" and symbolizes intelligence. Fordham (1999) found that successful students at a predominantly black high school in Washington DC learned to switch rapidly between using SSAE in the classroom and AAVE with friends and in social settings. Often they attempted to hide their proficiency in SSAE from their friends. In fact, most AAVE speakers do become effective speakers of several varieties of English. AAVE and SSAE have similar capacities to deliver both "formal and informal knowledge as well as local knowledge and wisdom" (Morgan 2004), but speakers of AAVE, like others who are bilingual, must learn **code switching**, to move seamlessly between two languages, and this ability is often central to their identities and their interactions inside and outside of their communities.

code switching Moving seamlessly and appropriately between two different languages.

The Sapir-Whorf Hypothesis

The close relationship between culture and language raises interesting questions about the connections between language and thought. At

The connection between language, thought, and perception seems weak. However, Gordon (2004) reports that members of the Piraha tribe he studied had difficulty understanding and recalling numbers for which they had no words.

© Daniel L. Everett

the opening of the chapter, we pointed out that some social scientists in the 1950s and 1960s believed, incorrectly, that AAVE was less logical than SSAE and that, as a result, AAVE speakers thought illogically. In so doing, they assumed a strong relationship between speaking and thinking. The existence of such a relationship is an old and controversial idea in anthropology. It is often associated with the work of Edward Sapir and his student Benjamin Lee Whorf.

In the early 20th century, Sapir and Whorf argued that, because language played a critical role in determining the way people understand the world, then people who spoke different languages must understand the world in different ways. They proposed that the ability to think about things such as time, space, and matter are conditioned by the structure of the languages people speak. They argued that we perceive the world in certain ways because we talk about the world in certain ways. This idea has come to be known as the **Sapir-Whorf hypothesis**.

We clearly choose our words to guide and direct the thoughts of others. Politicians, for example, routinely search for derogatory words and phrases to characterize their opponents. Or consider the term *side effect*. A side effect is an unwanted consequence of something such as a drug. However, the phrase *side effect* encourages us to think of it as off to the side and therefore less important than the *"central" effect* of the drug. But is it less important? In the late 1950s and early 1960s, thalidomide was prescribed to calm the stomachs of pregnant mothers. The drug was effective but had the horrible side effect of causing severe malformations in babies born to those mothers. Calling the deformities *side effects* did not prevent people from thinking that they were more important than the drug's effect. In fact, the thalidomide case led to special testing of drugs prescribed during pregnancy. This makes an important point: Word choice can encourage people to think certain ways. However, words cannot force people to think in one way or another. Even a government that controlled all the words people used could not control their thoughts. People would merely invent new words or give the old ones new and ironic meanings.

Sapir and Whorf also argued that the grammatical structure of languages compelled their speakers to think and behave in certain ways. For example, Whorf (1941) claimed that because tenses in the Hopi language were very different from tenses in English, Hopi speakers necessarily understood time in ways very different from English speakers. This position is sometimes called "strong determinism," and it has some deep problems. For example, consider the differences in the way we speak about missing a person in English and in French. In English, we say "I miss you." "I," the person doing the missing, is the subject; "you," the person being missed, is the object. In French, however, the order is reversed: You say "Tu me manques." The person being missed is the subject, and the person doing

Sapir-Whorf hypothesis The hypothesis that perceptions and understandings of time, space, and matter are conditioned by the structure of a language.

the missing is the object. Literally translated, the French sentence appears to mean "you miss me." A strong determinist would expect this structural difference to indicate that speakers of French and English have different understandings of missing a person. However, no evidence suggests that this is so.

This is not to say that language structure and thought are completely unrelated. Bowerman (1996) argues that space is understood differently in English and Korean, and Gordon (2004) reports that members of the Brazilian tribe he studied have difficulty understanding and recalling numbers for which they have no words. Other interesting work argues that some kinds of perception are partially universal and partially mediated by specific languages. Experiments done by Gilbert et al. (2006) suggest that language affects color perception in the right visual field, but not the left. This corresponds to the fact that language processing is located primarily on the left side of the brain. Casasanto (2008) conducted studies on the way that Greek and English speakers estimate time. He argues that the association of time with distance or with quantity is given by people's experience of the physical world (all humans experience that it takes a certain amount of time to move a certain distance and that material such as rain or snow accumulates over time). All languages use space and material as metaphors for time (for example, in English we talk about a long time, or visualize time as sand in an hourglass). However, languages use these metaphors unequally. English uses mostly distance metaphors whereas Greek uses mostly material metaphors. Casasanto showed that, in an experimental situation, Greek and English speakers estimated time differently because of this. However, a brief training session caused these differences to disappear. Casasanto's work, like that of Gilbert et al., shows the complexity of the relationship between language and perception. It shows both universal and language-specific elements. But, it also shows that the relationship of language to perception is fairly weak.

NONVERBAL COMMUNICATION

Before returning to our discussion of spoken language, it is important to note that anthropologists also study the nonverbal ways in which humans communicate. Our use of our bodies, interpersonal space, physical objects, and even time can communicate worlds of information: "Time talks" and "space speaks" (Hall 1959). Nonverbal communication includes artifacts, haptics, chronemics, proxemics, and kinesics.

In the context of nonverbal communication, **artifacts** such as clothing, jewelry, tattoos, piercings, and other visible body modifications send messages. For example, among the Tuareg, a people of the Sahara, men

artifacts (in communications studies) Communication by clothing, jewelry, tattoos, piercings, and other visible body modifications.

often wear veils and use their position as an important part of nonverbal communication (Murphy 1964). A Tuareg man lowers his veil only among intimates and people of lower social status. He raises it high when he wishes to appear noncommittal. The use of artifacts to send messages is familiar to every American. Tattoos, piercings, and jewelry all provide information about those who wear them.

Haptics refers to the study and analysis of touch. Handshakes, pats on the back or head, kisses, and hugs are all ways we communicate by touch. Many American males, for example, believe that the quality of a handshake communicates important information. Firm handshakes are taken to indicate self-confidence, and strength of character, whereas limp handshakes often suggest indecisiveness, or effeminacy.

Some anthropologists suggest that societies can be divided into "contact" cultures, where people tend to interact at close distances and touch one another frequently, and "noncontact" cultures, where people interact at greater distance and avoid touching (Hall 1966; Montagu 1978). Contact cultures are common in the Middle East, India, and Latin America. Noncontact cultures include those of northern Europe, North America, and Japan. But this dichotomy is simplistic. In India, for example, social equals may touch, but nonequals almost never do. In the United States, equality and inequality also play an important role in touch. Your boss may pat you on the back, but you will rarely pat your boss (Leathers 1997:126).

Chronemics refers to the study of cultural understandings of time. For example, in North American culture, what does it say when a person shows up for an appointment 40 minutes late? Does it mean something different if he or she shows up 10 minutes early? Is a Latin American who shows up late for an appointment saying the same thing?

Edward Hall (1983) divided cultures into those with monochronic time (M-time), such as the United States and northern European countries, and those with polychronic time (P-time). Hall argued that in M-time cultures, time is perceived as inflexible and people organize their lives according to schedules. In P-time cultures, time is understood as fluid. The emphasis is on social interaction, and activities are not expected to proceed like clockwork. Thus, being late for an appointment in P-time cultures does not convey the unspoken messages that it conveys in an M-time culture (Victor 1992).

© Jeff Greenberg/PhotoEdit

In addition to speaking, people use hands and facial expressions as well as interpersonal space to communicate.

haptics The analysis and study of touch.

Chronemics The study of the different ways that cultures understand time and use it to communicate.

Like the contact/noncontact dichotomy, M-time and P-time seem to capture a basic truth about cultural variation but fail to account for the enormous variability within cultures. How long an individual is kept waiting for an appointment may have more to do with power than with cultural perceptions of time. People are likely to be on time for their superiors but may keep their subordinates waiting.

proxemics The study of the cultural use of interpersonal space.

Proxemics is the social use of space. Hall (1968) identified three different ranges of personal communicative space. *Intimate distance,* from 1 to 18 inches, is typical among intimates. Personal distance, from 18 inches to 4 feet, characterizes relationships among friends. *Social distance,* from 4 to 12 feet, is common among relative strangers. These distances are affected by circumstances, culture, gender, and individual personality. We speak to strangers at a much closer distance in a movie or a classroom than in an unconfined space. In the United States, women and mixed-gender pairs talk at closer distances than do men. In Turkey, on the other hand, men and women talk at close distances with members of their own sex but at very large distances with members of the opposite sex (Leathers 1997).

kinesics The study of body position, movement, facial expressions, and gaze.

Finally, **kinesics** refers to body position, movement, facial expressions, and gaze. We use our posture, visual expression, eye contact, and other body movements to communicate interest, boredom, and much else. Smiling and some other facial expressions likely are biologically based human universals. There are no societies in which people do not smile. In all societies, social interactions are more likely to have a positive outcome if people are smiling than if they are frowning or scowling. Smiling is also found in chimpanzees and gorillas, our nearest nonhuman relations.

Smiling also shows the powerful effects of culture on biology, however. A smile does not mean the same thing in all cultures. Americans generally equate smiling with happiness, but people in many cultures smile when they experience surprise, wonder, or embarrassment (Ferraro 1994). A guidebook on international business advises American managers that the Japanese often smile to make their guests feel comfortable rather than because they are happy (Lewis 1996:267). Despite this, Japanese and Americans agree that smiling faces are more sociable than neutral faces (Matsumoto and Kudoh 1993), and most often interpret smiles in the same way (Nagashima and Schellenberg 1997).

LANGUAGE CHANGE

Fæder ure þu þe eart on heofonum
Si þin nama gehalgod
to becume þin rice
gewurþe ðin willa

on eorðan swa swa on heofonum.

urne gedæghwamlican hlaf syle us todæg

and forgyf us ure gyltas

swa swa we forgyfað urum gyltendum

and ne gelæd þu us on costnunge

ac alys us of yfele soþlice[1]

This 11th-century version of the Lord's Prayer shows how much English has changed in the past thousand years. The sounds, structures, and vocabulary of all languages are constantly changing, and some of this change happens in patterned ways.

Consider sound. When we imagine people speaking English hundreds of years ago, we often think of them using different words than we do but otherwise sounding pretty much like us. But English spoken in the 14th century sounded very different from the English of today. Between 1400 and 1600, there was a change in sound of English called the **great vowel shift**. A correct reading aloud of the Lord's Prayer at the beginning of this section would involve speaking the words using the sounds of 11th-century English. For example, the fifth word of the last line, *yfele*, gives us the modern English word *evil*. The medieval pronunciation is close to "oo-vah-la." Shifting sounds are not just something out of the past. Language sounds are constantly changing. For example, since about 1950, some vowel sounds in U.S. cities around the Great Lakes have been changing, a process linguists call the *northern city shift* (Labov, Ash, and Boburg 2005).

The grammatical structures of a language (its syntax) also change. For example, as we have seen, meaning in modern English is tightly tied to word order. But in Old English, as in Latin, the endings of nouns indicated whether they were subjects or objects, making word order within sentences less important. Thus, in Old English, "The dog bit the child" and "The dog the child bit" would have the same meaning and be equally grammatical.

Vocabulary, particularly slang, is the most noticeable aspect of language change. Consider slang terms from the 1950s and 1960s, such as "boss" to mean great (as in "The new Little Richard album is really boss") or "bag" to mean something that an individual likes (as in "What's your bag?"). We may still understand slang from the 1960s, but terms from the

great vowel shift A change in the pronunciation of English language that took place between 1400 and 1600.

---

[1]In Modern English, the Lord's Prayer is: "Our father who art in heaven, hallowed be thy name. Thy kingdom come, thy will be done on earth as is in heaven. Give us this day our daily bread and forgive us our trespasses as we forgive those who trespass against us; and lead us not into temptation but deliver us from evil, amen." The nonstandard symbols are from the International Phonetic Alphabet mentioned on page 79. You can find additional information on the IPA at www.omniglot.com.

19th century and early 20th century are almost entirely lost: Would you know what "ramstuginous" or "kafooster" means?

New words are constantly added to language. In the past 10 to 20 years, an entire vocabulary has grown up around computers and the Internet. Words such as *software, dot-com, disk drive, gigabyte,* and *email* would have been unintelligible to most people in 1980. *WiFi, spyware, domain name, texting,* and many others would have been meaningless to people in the mid-1990s.

Language and Culture Contact

The meeting of cultures through travel, trade, war, and conquest is a fundamental force in linguistic change. Languages thus reflect the histories of their speakers. Current-day English has French words such as *reason, joy, mutton,* and *liberty*, which came into the language after the Norman Conquest of England in the 11th century. Other words speak of more recent political events. For example, *cot, pajamas,* and *jungle* come from Hindi and reflect the British colonization of India. *Gumbo, funky,* and *zebra* come from Kongo and reflect the slave trade. Nahuatl, a language spoken in Mexico and Central America, gives us *tomato, coyote, shack,* and *avocado*. Most Americans in 1970 probably did not know the meanings of words such as *sunni, mujahidin,* or *fatwa*. Today, we do.

© Frederick Atwood

Pidgins develop when people who speak different languages come together. This church banner in Papua New Guinea, where people speak more than 750 different languages, means "Jesus is Lord."

When societies where different languages are spoken meet, they often develop a new language that combines features of each of the original ones. Such languages are called *pidgins*. No one speaks a pidgin as a first language, and the vocabulary of pidgins is often limited to the words appropriate to the sorts of interactions engaged in by the people speaking it.

As culture contact deepens and time passes, pidgins are sometimes lost, and people speak only the language of the dominant power. Or pidgin languages may become creoles. A *creole* is a language composed of elements of two or more different languages. But, unlike a pidgin, people do speak creoles as their first languages, and the vocabulary of these languages is as complex and rich as any others.

Many creoles were formed as Europeans expanded into Asia and the Americas. Often, in countries that were colonized, upper classes speak the language of the colonizing power, while the lower classes speak creoles. For example, in Haiti, 70 to 90 percent of the population speaks only Creole, but almost all governmental and administrative functions are performed in French, the language of the elite.

Tracing Relationships among Languages

Comparative linguistics is a field of study that traces the relationships of different languages by searching for similarities among them. When such similarities are numerous, regular, and basic, it is likely that the languages are derived from the same ancestral language.

Linguists have identified a **core vocabulary** of 100 or 200 words, such as *I, you, man, woman, blood, skin, red,* and *green,* which designate things, actions, and activities likely to be named in all the world's languages. Many believe that core vocabularies change at a predictable rate (about 14 percent per 1,000 years). **Glottochronology** is a statistical technique that uses this idea to estimate the date of separation of related languages. Linguists use glottochronology to discover historic relationships among languages and to group languages into families. However, the accuracy of the technique has long been controversial, and many modifications have been used to improve it (Renfrew, McMahon, and Trask 2000).

Considering the history of language raises two interesting questions. First, at any point, was there a single original human language? Second, in the future, will there be a world with one language? Neither of these questions is fully answerable, but we can speculate about each of them.

We do not know if there was a single original human language. However, the development of language almost certainly involved specific genetic changes. Such changes probably happened in a single small group. If this is the case, an original language probably did exist. What might it have been like? Well, again, we cannot say with any confidence. There are no established techniques for discovering the patterns and content of language that can reach back tens of thousands of years.

The question of whether a single world language is emerging is provocative. We are certainly moving toward a world of linguistic homogenization. The number of languages in the world has clearly declined. About 10,000 years ago, there may have been as many as 15,000 different languages. Today there are only about 6,500, and half of these are under threat of extinction in the next 50 to 100 years (Krauss 1992). Today, 95 percent of the world's languages are spoken by only 5 percent of the world's population. Almost one-third of the world's languages are spoken by fewer than

comparative linguistics The science of documenting the relationships between languages and grouping them into language families.

core vocabulary A list of 100 or 200 terms that designate things, actions, and activities likely to be named in all the world's languages.

glottochronology A statistical technique that linguists have developed to estimate the date of separation of related languages.

1,000 people. At the same time, more than half of the world's population speaks one of the 20 most common languages (Gibbs 2002).

Languages may disappear for various reasons: All their speakers may be killed by disease or genocide. Government policies may deliberately seek to eliminate certain languages. For example, in 1885, the American government explicitly forbade the use of Indian languages in Bureau of Indian Affairs schools. Children were beaten and otherwise punished for speaking their tribal languages (Coleman 1999).

Nation states often try to suppress linguistic diversity within their borders, insisting that government, the court system, and other aspects of public life be conducted in the language of the most numerous and politically powerful groups. Global trade favors people who speak the languages of the wealthiest and most populous nations. Similarly, the vast majority of television and radio broadcasts, as well as the Internet, are in a very few languages. In the face of such forces, people who are members of linguistic minorities often abandon their languages because they find it more convenient, prestigious, or profitable to speak the languages of wealth and power.

In some ways, linguistic homogenization is a positive development. Today, more people are able to speak to each other than ever before. In the future, this may be true to an even greater extent. However, the global movement toward fewer languages is troubling. There is generally a strong connection between language and ethnic identity. Language often is rooted in culture and is entwined with it. As language is lost, so are important elements of cultural identity. Additionally, the disappearance of languages reduces our ability to understand the underlying structures of language and the range of variability they enable.

Not all global forces lead toward language homogenization. First, there is no language spoken by the majority of the world's people. Mandarin Chinese, with more than one billion speakers, is by far the most commonly spoken language, while hundreds of millions of people speak English, Spanish, Russian, French, Hindi/Urdu, Arabic, Portuguese, and several other languages. None of these languages seems likely to disappear in the foreseeable future. Second, although the number of languages spoken in the world has diminished, the diversity within each language has increased. People in New York City; Kingston, Jamaica; Glasgow, Scotland; and Mumbai, India may all speak English, but that does not necessarily mean they can understand what each other says. Perhaps more importantly, the nature of language, the human ability to create new meanings, new words, and new grammatical structures, means that language adapts to the needs, interests, and environments of its speakers. Thus, even as globalizing forces move humans toward cultural and linguistic homogeneity, spaces are created in which diversity can flourish.

BRINGING IT BACK HOME:
ENGLISH ONLY

Language has become an important political issue in America. As of summer 2010, 30 states have enacted legislation to make English their state's official language. No federal bill making English the national language has yet passed both chambers of Congress, but the House and the Senate have, at different times, both voted to make English the national language or require the federal government to conduct all of its official business in English. A recent survey suggests that 87 percent of Americans believe English should be the official national language (Rasmussen Reports 2010).

U.S. ENGLISH, Inc., a lobbying group that promotes English-only legislation, claims to have 1.8 million members. According to U.S. ENGLISH, Inc. (n.d.): "Official English benefits every resident of this wonderful melting pot called America. The melting pot works—because we have a common language. English is the key to opportunity in this country. It empowers immigrants and makes us truly united as a people. Common sense says that the government should teach people English rather than provide services in multiple languages. What would happen if our government had to provide services in all 322 languages spoken in the U.S.? Without a common language, how long would we remain the 'United' States?"

Many, and perhaps most, anthropologists believe the legislative program of groups such as U.S. ENGLISH, Inc., is misguided and their claims inaccurate. Graham et al. (2007) say that when people talk about language, they really are talking about race: "People in positions of social advantage feel free to say things about the language of stigmatized groups that they would never say about race or ethnicity." Furthermore, Graham et al. claim that promoters of English-only legislation assume that difficulties in communication are caused by people speaking many languages, ignoring the simple fact that sharing the same language does not create effective communication. Finally, critics of English-only legislation say the idea that requiring official English will unify the nation and help provide answers to problems of racism gets things backwards. The underlying problem is not language; it is inequality. Official English, in the name of promoting unity and opportunity, actually disadvantages the poor and the powerless, making it harder for them to gain access to education and public services.

YOU DECIDE

1. Do you speak a language other than English as a first language? If so, do you want your children and grandchildren to speak that language?

If English is your first language, did your parents or grandparents speak a different first language? How do you feel about your abilities (or lack of ability) in that language?

2. In the United States, how closely is language linked both to American identity and to ethnic identity? To what degree can a person be a full citizen of America without speaking English as a primary language?

3. The United States has never had an official national language. Are there good reasons why this should change? Multiple languages are great assets in the global economy. Instead of mandating English only, would it be better to mandate increased second language training for Americans?

CHAPTER SUMMARY

1. The use of language is basic to what it means to be a human being. Language is at the same time deeply biological and profoundly cultural. From a scientific point of view, no way of speaking is better or worse than any other.

2. Human language is different from the communication systems of other animals. It is complex and symbolic, and it is able to describe abstract times, places, and ideas in ways that animal communications are not.

3. Despite great variability, all human languages are based around similar patterns and show deep similarities. All are composed of a phonology (a system of sounds), morphology (a system for creating words from sounds), semantics (a system that relates words to meanings), and syntax (a system of rules for combining words into meaningful sentences).

4. Culture exerts a profound influence upon language. Environment, cultural ideas, values, and beliefs are encoded in the way people speak. The meaning of conversation usually is much more than simply the words that are spoken.

5. Cultural aspects of language are heavily influenced by wealth and identity. Privileged and stigmatized ways of speaking reflect the power dynamics of different groups. Individuals who move between social groups must often learn multiple forms of speech and the correct times and places to use them.

6. Speakers choose words to encourage others to think in certain ways. Early 20th-century theorists believed that the structure of language had a critical influence on culture, but this does not seem to be the case. Because language can be changed rapidly, it can neither force people to think in one way nor prevent them from thinking in others.

7. In addition to speaking, people communicate in many different ways. Some of these ways are through touch, the use of time, the use of space, and the use of body position. There is substantial variability in nonverbal aspects of communication both within and between cultures.

8. The sounds, words, and structures of language all are subject to change. Comparative linguists study the ways language changes and are able to describe the historical relationships among different languages. However, no agreed-upon technique has been found to determine or describe very early human language.

▮▮▮ KEY TERMS

Agglutinating language
Allophones
Artifacts
Call system
Code switching
Chronemics
Comparative linguistics
Conventionality
Core vocabulary
Displacement
Glottochronology
Great vowel shift
Haptics
Isolating language
Kinesics
Lexicon

Minimal pair
Morpheme
Morphology
Phone
Phoneme
Phonology
Productivity
Proxemics
Sapir-Whorf hypothesis
Semantics
Sociolinguistics
Symbol
Syntax
Universal grammar

The key to human survival is extracting food from the environment. Here a farmer in the Nile Valley in Egypt harvests his alfalfa crop.

© Robert Caputo/Aurora Photos

CHAPTER 5

MAKING A LIVING

CHAPTER OUTLINE

WHERE HAVE ALL THE ICEBERGS GONE?

"GWICH'IN elders long ago predicted that a day would come when the world would warm and things would not be the same with the animals. That time is now. . ." says Matthew Gilbert of the Gwich'in, an Athabascan people of northeastern Alaska and northwest Canada. "The lakes, the rivers, the waterfowl and, most of all, the caribou that we depend on are under threat" (Gilbert 2007).

The 8,000 Gwich'in live in small villages spread across the huge arctic and subarctic tundra and forest, which contains thousands of lakes and scores of rivers. The main source of Gwich'in subsistence is the caribou herds that also occupy this area. The Gwich'in also hunt small animals for their pelts, which they sell for cash. Global warming has negatively affected the sources of Gwich'in subsistence, decreasing the number of caribou, which are less healthy than they were formerly. Because of early river thaws, many caribou calves are drowned crossing the rushing river waters, the glaciers and snow pockets that provide essential resting places for mothers and their calves are disappearing, and the caribou must move further north, out of their usual territory. This makes it harder for the hunters to find them, and hunting has to begin later in the season than normal.

The subsistence strategies of these Arctic populations are well adapted to their harsh environment. Their knowledge and ingenious technology enabled them to be successful hunters. For thousands of years, the Gwich'in, the Inuit, and other peoples of the Arctic hunted large land

Polar bear crossing from one ice floe to another in summer pack ice. The warmer water due to climate change has led to the starvation of many polar bears.

© Bryan and Cherry Alexander Photography

and sea animals including caribou, polar bear, seal, walrus, and whales. They devised technologies that effectively utilized the materials of their environment for survival, building shelters of snow, which hold the heat and keep out the wind, and expertly fashioning layered clothing that keeps out the cold yet prevents overheating.

Their culture and social organization are also adapted to their environment and foraging strategy. Their values emphasize cooperation and mutual aid; their religious rituals provide effective outlets for the isolation and tension of the long dark winters; and their flexible kinship organization allows local populations to expand and contract in response to the seasonal variation in resources. For the Inuit of Baffin Island, this involves a set of economic practices called *ningiqtuq*, best translated as sharing. *Ningiqtuq* orders the flow of goods and food across individuals, families, and entire communities. Among the Inuit, no one need go without food or shelter. Inuit subsistence isn't just about food. It is also about practices that provide individuals with security (Wenzel 2009:92–93).

As with many other foragers, however, the 20th century and the global economy have brought significant changes to Arctic subsistence strategies (Chance 1990; Condon et al. 1996). Most now base their livelihoods on a combination of cash income and foraging. Commercial trapping and fur sales became dependable sources of income, providing cash, which they used to buy guns and ammunition, food, tobacco, tea, canvas tents, and clothing. Other sources of income today are handicrafts, tourism, work for oil corporations, various kinds of government subsidies, and, for the Alaska natives, payments from the Alaska Native Claims Settlement Act.

Subsistence hunting and use of wild foods still provide at least half of the diet for Arctic peoples, and current-day foraging techniques make use of modern technology, such as snowmobiles, gasoline, fishing nets, and sleeping bags. Many Arctic households also enjoy modern conveniences, and this requires that household members work full-time or seasonally in the cash economy (Kofinas 2007). However, Arctic lifestyles are threatened by global warming. Hunting is dependent on the transformation of water areas into ice during the long, cold winters. Sea ice is used as a highway, formerly for dog sleds and now for snowmobiles, as building materials, and as hunting platforms. As the climate warms, this ice is less and less available, making hunting more difficult and the cultural patterns it sustains more fragile. Warmer weather also affects the animals on which the people prey. The shrinking ice makes it harder for polar bears to fatten up on seals, and the bears are becoming emaciated. Alaskan whale hunters in the open seas have seen walruses try to climb onto their white boats, mistaking them for ice floes. The pelts of fox, marten, and other game are thinning, and even seasoned hunters are falling into water that used to be ice.

In addition to climatic changes, Arctic peoples also face challenges to their subsistence from drilling for oil in the Arctic. Some (but not all) of them have become locally active in resisting the exploitation of oil reserves in the Arctic National Wildlife Refuge and other areas where oil companies now have access to offshore energy resources revealed by global warming (Matthiessen 2007).

It is not clear how Arctic peoples will cope with the challenges that confront them. On the one hand, people regret the changes in hunting patterns that will inevitably happen as the earth warms. One Canadian Inuit said: "The next generation . . . is not going to experience what we did. . . . We can't pass the traditions on as our ancestors passed on to us" (Myers et al. 2005). On the other, Arctic peoples have faced climate changes before and it is worth remembering that they collectively have thousands of years of experience adapting to an extremely difficult environment. Arctic peoples have shown great flexibility in the past. Although global warming will lead to the disappearance of some species, it is also likely to lead to abundance in others, and Arctic hunters will likely adapt (Ford, Smit, and Wandel 2005). In fact, the most important challenges may come less from environmental change and more from the increased presence of governments and the effects of international economics. Arctic peoples may struggle to maintain cultural values such as *ningiqtuq* in the face of the increasing presence of global corporations and of government regulations which, though often well meant, have destructive cultural impact (Wenzel 2009:97).

Anthropologists seek to understand the interactions between humans and their physical environments, both the effects of the environment on culture and the effects of culture on the environment. All societies must utilize the physical environment to provide their people with the basic material requirements of life: food, clothing, and shelter. Different societies have different **subsistence strategies**, or ways of transforming the material resources of the environment into food. These subsistence strategies may be stable for hundreds, even thousands, of years, but they must change in response to new challenges in the environment.

subsistence strategies The pattern of behavior used by a society to obtain food in a particular environment.

HUMAN ADAPTATION AND THE ENVIRONMENT

Unlike most other animals, humans live in an extremely broad range of environments. Some, such as the Arctic or the Great Australian Desert, present extreme challenges to human existence and are relatively limited in the numbers of people and types of subsistence strategies they can support.

The productivity of any particular environment, however, is related to the type of technology used to exploit it. For example, the Arctic can sustain only a relatively small population with the traditional Inuit technology. With modern technology and transportation, however, the circumpolar Arctic supports more than four million people, engaged in indigenous hunting and herding strategies as well as modern industrial pursuits (UNEP/GRID-Arendal 2008).

Technology enables humans to transform a wide range of materials into sources of usable energy. As a result, humans have built many environments, such as farms and cities, and developed many different economic systems and forms of social organization. These human cultural adaptations have resulted in great increases in population that, in turn, have further altered the environment, frequently in unintentional ways.

For most of the history of our species, humans and our ancestors lived by **foraging**—fishing, hunting, and collecting vegetable food. As populations increased, foragers spread out into many environments, created new tools, and developed diverse cultures. By 16,000 to 12,500 years ago, humans had spread to every continent except Antarctica (see Stanyon, Sazzini, and Luiselli 2009). About 11,000 to 10,000 years ago, human groups in the Old World began to domesticate plants and animals, a change that occurred about 1,000 years later in the New World (Bryant 2003, Temple University 2009). Called the agricultural "revolution," the transition to food production was really more like a gradual evolution, although it was revolutionary in the possibilities it opened up for the development of complex social organization.

foraging (hunting and gathering) Fishing, hunting, and collecting vegetable food.

Foraging sets significant limits on population growth and density and, consequently, on the complexity of social organization. The domestication of plants and animals supported much increased populations, and **sedentary** village life became widespread. Over time, more intensive means of cultivation and animal management developed, and human labor was more closely coordinated and controlled, leading eventually to complex social forms such as the state. Within this general outline of growing control over the environment and human population increase, however, only specific environmental, cultural, and historical conditions can explain the exact sequence of events in any particular place (Diamond 1998).

sedentary Settled, living in one place.

Why cultivation did not arise everywhere—and why some populations, such as the aboriginal peoples of Australia or the Inuit, never made the transition from foraging to food production—has several answers. It is important to understand that, under many conditions, foraging is far less work than agriculture and the benefits of agriculture are not always apparent. In the Arctic, climate and soil composition precluded agriculture, whereas in the fertile valleys of California, aboriginal foraging was so productive that there was little pressure to make the transition to food production. Sometimes foraging strategies actually were more dependable than cultivation or animal husbandry, which are more adversely affected by drought. For example, with the introduction of the horse by the Spaniards in the 16th century, some Native American Plains cultures, such as the Cheyenne, did so well with bison hunting that they gave up their traditional cultivation strategy. Even today, many foraging and pastoral populations resist abandoning these occupations for cultivation because they prefer the economic, social, and psychological satisfactions of a foraging or pastoral way of life. In these societies, hunting and pastoralism are highly valued occupations, intimately connected to a people's cultural identity, and are more productive than agriculture in some circumstances.

Another dramatic change in human subsistence strategies was the Industrial Revolution, which involved the replacement of human and animal energy by machines. Industrialism greatly increased human productivity: In a typical nonindustrial society, more than 80 percent of the population is directly involved in food production; in industrial societies, this number declines dramatically.

However, the price of industrialization has been high. A primary source of environmental degradation today is the consumer desires and energy needs of industrialized nations. The demands for tropical hardwoods are leading to devastating logging in tropical forests (Brosius 1999); dam building in the American Pacific Northwest impedes the ability of salmon to spawn, decreasing the food supply of Native Americans in this area (Duncan 2000); and the carbon emissions of modern transport and industrial production have already resulted in global warming affecting not just the Arctic but also areas much closer to home, such as America's shorelines and weather systems (Gore 2006).

The environmental problems resulting from industrial and postindustrial society have led to a reawakened interest in and respect for the ways in which nonindustrial people have adapted. Through vast knowledge of the web of life in which they live and with ingenious, if simple, technology, many nonindustrial societies live in ways that are sustainable and create many fewer environmental problems than industrialization.

■ MAJOR TYPES OF SUBSISTENCE STRATEGIES

Anthropologists identify five basic types of subsistence strategies: foraging, pastoralism, horticulture, agriculture, and industrialism (Cohen 1971). Foraging depends on the use of plant and animal resources naturally available in the environment. **Pastoralism** primarily involves the care

pastoralism A food-getting strategy that depends on the care of domesticated herd animals.

of domesticated herd animals, whose dairy and meat products are a major part of the pastoralist diet. **Horticulture** (extensive cultivation) is the production of plants using a simple, nonmechanized technology. **Agriculture** (intensive cultivation) involves the production of food using the plow, draft animals, and more complex techniques of water and soil control so that land is permanently cultivated and usually needs no fallow period. Finally, **industrialism** involves the use of machine technology and chemical processes for the production of food and other goods. Within these basic types of subsistence strategies, however, there is much diversity. Furthermore, whereas any society normally uses one dominant strategy, many societies combine strategies to meet their material needs. Today, no society, however seemingly remote, remains unaffected by industrialism and the global economy.

Each subsistence strategy generally supports a characteristic level of **population density** (number of people per unit of land) and has a different level of **productivity** (yield per person per unit of land) and **efficiency** (yield per person per hour of labor invested). These criteria, in turn, tend to be associated with characteristic forms of social organization and certain cultural patterns. For example, where local technology allows only limited exploitation of the environment and where safe and reliable methods of artificial contraception are unknown, cultural practices such as sexual abstinence, abortion, infanticide, late weaning, and prohibitions on sexual intercourse after the birth of a child may be used to limit population growth.

In addition to limiting population, a society can extend its resource base by exchange. Trade occurs in all types of societies and forms the basis of historical and contemporary globalization, which incorporates people all over the world as they engage in many kinds of food production, manufacturing, and financial exchanges.

Foraging

Foraging is a diverse strategy that includes hunting large and small game, fishing, and collecting various plant foods. Foragers do not produce food, either directly by planting or indirectly by keeping domestic animals. In most cases, foragers use simple tools including digging sticks, spatulas, spears, and bows and arrows. However, in some places, such as the Arctic, foraging technology can be quite complex. Because foragers do not consciously alter their surroundings to produce food, they have little impact on the environment in most cases.

Foragers use a variety of strategies. In some extreme environments, like the Arctic peoples described in the chapter opening, they may depend almost solely on hunting. However, in most cases, they rely primarily on

horticulture Production of plants using a simple, nonmechanized technology and where the fertility of gardens and fields is maintained through long periods of fallow.

agriculture A form of food production in which fields are in permanent cultivation using plows, animals, and techniques of soil and water control.

industrialism The process of the mechanization of production.

population density The number of people inhabiting a unit of land (usually given as people per square mile or kilometer).

productivity (food production) Yield per person per unit of land.

efficiency (in food production) Yield per person per hour of labor invested.

gathered vegetable foods and women are responsible for gathering. Successful foraging requires extensive and highly detailed knowledge of the environment. Studies among Ju/'hoansi foragers show that women can identify over 150 species of edible plants, and men recognize over 40 species of edible animals (Lee 1979).

In most cases, foraging can only support a low population density. Foragers generally live in communities of between 20 and 50 individuals. Even at this low density, few of the marginal areas where current-day foragers are found can support a year-round human population. Therefore, foraging almost always involves seasonal movement to gain access to water or food. Thus, foraging requires independence and mobility. For this reason, foraging bands tend to have highly flexible social arrangements, and values like *ningiqtuq* (see the chapter opening) are common. Seasonal movement is also a strong disincentive for the accumulation of material goods. Because they must transport everything they own frequently, their material possessions tend to be limited to items essential to their survival.

In some environments, foraging is unquestionably a harsh and dangerous way of life. However, in less demanding places, foragers often live in relative abundance. Further, the extreme flexibility of forager social arrangements means that there is very little hierarchy in foraging societies.

At one time, all human beings lived by foraging, and foragers occupied fertile plains and river valleys. However, as other forms of production developed, the number of foragers declined. Today, they constitute only a very small proportion of the world's population and are mostly found in marginal areas such as deserts and arctic tundra into which they have been pushed by expanding, militarily superior agricultural peoples and states.

The Pintupi, A Foraging Society in Australia

The Pintupi people of the Gibson Desert of Australia were more typical of foraging than the Inuit described in the opening of this chapter. In the Gibson Desert, a wide range of vegetal foods provided most of their diet. The key to their adaptation was the use of a wide variety of seasonally available plant and animal foods and their detailed knowledge of their environment. Even with simple technology, this made foraging a reliable strategy, though a very difficult way of life at certain seasons.

These Australian foragers have an intimate knowledge of their environment. They recognize and can name 126 plants serving 138 different social, economic, and medicinal functions. They use more than 75 different plants for edible seeds. Their diet also includes tubers, fruits, nectars, sap, and edible insects as well as birds, bird eggs, and small mammals. The main constraint on them

© David Austen/Stock, Boston Inc.

A wide variety of plant foods and small animals permits people to survive in the harsh environment of the Gibson Desert.

is the scarcity of water during the driest and hottest months. Thus, the Western Desert societies consist of small, isolated family groups, and have a population density as low as one person per 150 to 200 square miles.

Climatic changes are extreme. Summer temperatures reach 120 degrees, and winter temperatures average around 72 degrees. Rainfall is very low, unpredictable, and evaporates quickly. The availability of food, and particularly water, is the most important influence on the distance people travel, the places they camp, and the length of time they stay in one place. In the wet season, December through February, water is available and families spread across the desert. They move great distances to search for food and to attend ceremonies. Although water is easily available, food is scarce at this time of year, limited mainly to foods left over from the previous year. Men and women gather lizards and edible toads, which are relatively easy to collect.

At the end of the wet season, when temperatures moderate, families move near the large surface water holes. June and July bring the greatest material prosperity, as tubers, fruits, and grass seeds are all abundantly available. Edible fruits are collected from 12 different plants and stored for the "hungry time." People live around the water holes until August, when food availability decreases and temperatures rise steadily, reaching over 100 degrees. The landscape begins to dry out and people fall back to large rock holes where there is water. They set fires on the plains to attract game and to stimulate the growth of new grass seeds and tubers for the following year. Both men and women spend most of the day in the food quest, hunting monitor lizards and kangaroos and gathering fruits, bulbs, tubers, and grass seeds, which are both eaten and stored. In November, temperatures continue to rise, sometimes reaching 120 degrees. This is the harshest time of year, called the "hungry time." Families travel to the largest rock holes for water, but even these occasionally run dry. Food becomes less available, and many seeds and tubers run out completely. If the rain has not come by December, foraging ceases almost entirely. People try to take it easy to conserve food and water. Women remain in camp looking after the children and the elderly while the men search for food, sometimes traveling as far as 12 miles a day from camp. Average daily intake may be reduced to 800 calories per person. Heat stress and the shortage of water prevent the whole camp from moving to areas where food might be more available, and people are thus "trapped" in the areas around the larger water holes. Under conditions of starvation, weak individuals may be fed blood from healthier people to get them through the worst weeks.

The Pintupi and other Australian foragers demonstrate the extraordinary ability of human beings to adapt to the most extreme environments. Though constrained by their simple technology, foragers' detailed knowledge of their environment has permitted them to survive for thousands

Gibson Desert, Australia.

of years, as well as to develop highly complex ceremonial, religious, kinship, and artistic cultural patterns. These Australian tribes survived using traditional foraging strategies until the mid-20th century. Beginning in the 1920s, because of prolonged drought, the Pintupi began moving to mission stations, cattle stations, government settlements, and towns around the desert fringe. The last Pintupi left the Western Desert in 1984 (Myers 1986, Adam 2007). From their point of view, food was easier to get elsewhere.

The Pintupi subsistence strategy demonstrates that foraging in extreme environments can be a harsh existence with periods of desperation. However, in less extreme environments where predictable vegetal foods can be supplemented by hunting, foragers may experience abundant leisure time and generally good health. For example, Richard Lee estimated that an adult Dobe Ju/'hoansi of the Kalahari Desert in southern Africa spends an average of only two and a half six-hour days per week in subsistence activities, and a woman can gather enough in one day to feed her family for three days (1984:50–53).

Today, like the Pintupi, most foragers have moved to permanent settlements, either by choice or as the result of government pressure. Old trading relationships between foragers and nonforaging people have, in most places, disappeared or become greatly diminished. Although people throughout the world continue to forage when they can, members of contemporary foraging bands rely on the market for much of their food.

In East African cattle cultures, like the Maasai, the blood and milk of cattle are the major dietary elements. Cattle are killed for meat only on very special ceremonial occasions.

Pastoralism

Pastoralists depend primarily on the products of domesticated herd animals. Theirs is a specialized adaptation to an environment that, because of hilly terrain, dry climate, or unsuitable soil, cannot support a large human population through agriculture but can support enough native vegetation for animals if they are allowed to range over a large area. Because human beings cannot digest grass, raising animals that can live on grasses makes pastoralism an efficient way to exploit semiarid natural grasslands. Unlike ranching (commercial animal husbandry), in which livestock are fed grain that could be used to feed humans, pastoralism does not require direct competition with humans for the same resources (Barfield 1993:13).

Pastoralists may herd cattle, sheep, goats, yaks, or camels, all of which produce both meat and milk. Because the herd animals of the New World, such as bison, could not be domesticated (except for the llama and alpaca in Peru), pastoralism did not develop as a subsistence strategy there. The major areas of pastoralism are found in East Africa (cattle), North Africa (camels), southwestern Asia (sheep and goats), central Asia (yaks), and the subarctic (caribou and reindeer).

Pastoralism is either transhumant or nomadic. In **transhumant pastoralism**, found mostly in East Africa, men and boys move the animals regularly throughout the year to different areas as pastures become available at different altitudes or in different climatic zones, while women and children and some men remain at a permanent village site.

In **nomadic pastoralism**, the whole population—men, women, and children—moves with the herds throughout the year, and there are no permanent villages.

Pastoralism involves a complex interaction among animals, land, and people. With domestication, animals became dependent on their human keepers for pasture, water, breeding, shelter, salt, and protection from predators. Pastoralists must be highly knowledgeable about the needs of their animals, the carrying capacity of the land, and the subsistence demands of the human population (Barfield 1993:6).

The key to the pastoralist economy is herd growth. The number of animals needed to support a family is a constant concern of pastoralists. Eating or selling too many animals in a single year may lead to insolvency, so pastoralists must always balance their present needs against future herd production. Pastoralism is a risky business; weather disasters such as drought or storms, disease, or theft can easily decimate a herd.

Many pastoral nomads engage in mixed subsistence strategies, rarely existing solely on the products of their herds. The survival of pastoralists depends on their relationships with their sedentary neighbors, with whom they trade meat, animals, wool, milk products, and hides for manufactured goods and grain.

transhumant pastoralism A form of pastoralism in which herd animals are moved regularly throughout the year to different areas as pasture becomes available.

nomadic pastoralism A form of pastoralism in which the whole social group (men, women, children) and their animals move in search of pasture.

The Yarahmadzai: A Nomadic Pastoralist Society in Iran

The Yarahmadzai, who live in the southeastern corner of Iran known as Baluchistan, are an example of a mixed pastoralist adaptation that has undergone changes due to both a global economy and the restraints of adapting to the control of the national state (Salzman 2000). Yarahmadzai territory occupies a plateau at 5,000 feet high, where their chief problem is finding adequate water and pasture year-round. They solve this by moving to seek pasture according to the seasons. The Yarahmadzai live in small camps of between five and twenty families. When information about good pasture becomes available, the whole

Baluchistan, Iran.

Yarahmadzai camp migrates. Because even good pasturage quickly gets exhausted, the camp migrates constantly, anywhere from 5 to 25 miles in each move.

Most of the maximum 6-inch annual rainfall occurs in winter and some years there is no rain at all. This means that there is good pasturage on the Yarahmadzai's high plateau in the spring. However, by June and July, the animals have eaten all of the spring's growth and the season has turned very dry and hot. In response, the Yarahmadzai migrate to areas served by government irrigation projects to earn money by harvesting grain. They remain there until the harvest ends in early autumn. Then they migrate to the lowland desert where there are groves of date palms, leaving their tents, as well as their goats and sheep, on the plateau in the care of young boys. They harvest dates and prepare date preserves for the return journey to their winter camps. At this time, the Yarahmadzai plateau is almost completely barren with very little for the animals to eat. They live on their accumulated fat and the small quantities of roots, grains, dates, and processed date pits their keepers provide. The people depend on food stores from the previous year, but because winter is the rainy season, water is normally available.

Milk is the staple food of the Yarahmadzai and is consumed in many different forms and preserved as dried milk solids and butter. Milk and milk products are also sold and exchanged for grain. Milk is the main source of protein, fat, calcium, and other nutrients; the Yarahmadzai, like most other pastoral peoples, do not eat much meat. Their flocks are their capital, and the Yarahmadzai hope to increase their size. Because killing animals for food works against this objective, the Yarahmadzai rarely do it (Salzman 1999:24).

Like most contemporary pastoralists, the Yarahmadzai combine herding with other subsistence strategies to earn a living. Many pastoralists now depend less than before on consuming the direct products of their herds. Instead, they are often successful in adapting their products to local and even global markets. Nomads in Afghanistan and Iran, for example, are highly integrated into national and international trade networks. They specialize in selling meat animals to local markets, lambskin to international buyers, and sheep intestines to meet the huge German demand for natural sausage casings (Barfield 1993:211). Thus, they are becoming ranchers: pastoral specialists in a cash economy.

Pastoralism cannot support an indefinitely increasing population, and many pastoralists have already become sedentary. With their knowledge of their environment, their creative use of multiple resources, and the global demand for their products, however, pastoralism as a subsistence strategy has a strong future in exploiting the planet's large arid and semi-arid zones.

Horticulture

Horticultural societies depend primarily on the production of plants using a simple, nonmechanized technology, such as hoes or digging sticks, but not draft animals, irrigation techniques, or plows. Fields are not used year after year but remain fallow for some time after being cultivated. Horticulture produces a lower yield per acre and uses less human labor than nonmechanized agriculture.

Horticulturalists usually grow enough food in their fields or gardens to support the local group, but they do not produce surpluses that involve the group in a wider market system. Population densities among horticultural peoples are generally low, usually not exceeding 150 people per square mile (Netting 1977). Despite this, horticultural villages may be quite large, ranging from 100 to 1,000 people.

Horticulture may be practiced in dry lands, such as among the Hopi Indians of northeastern Arizona, who cultivate maize, beans, and squash, but is typically a tropical forest adaptation. In these environments, people practice **swidden (slash-and-burn) cultivation**, clearing fields by felling the trees and burning the brush. The burned vegetation is allowed to remain on the soil, which prevents it from drying out. The resulting bed of ash also acts as a fertilizer, returning nutrients to the soil. Fields are used for a few (1 to 5) years and then allowed to lie fallow for a longer period (up to 20 years) so that the forest cover can be rebuilt and soil fertility restored. Swidden cultivators require five to six times as much fallow land as they are actually cultivating.

swidden (slash-and-burn) cultivation A form of cultivation in which a field is cleared by felling the trees and burning the brush.

Swidden cultivation *can* have a debilitating effect on the environment if fields are cultivated before they have lain fallow long enough to recover their forest growth. Eventually, the forest will not grow back, and grasslands will replace the tree cover. Because of this, governments often consider swidden cultivation both inefficient and destructive. However, modern industrial strategies such as logging and agribusiness, not swidden cultivation, are mainly responsible for the deterioration and disappearance of tropical forests (Sponsel 1995). New studies report that soil fertility is better preserved using long-fallow swidden agriculture than under annual cropping or tree plantations (Bruun et al. 2009), and that replacing swidden with intensified agriculture can lead to swift environmental deterioration (Ziegler et al. 2009).

Horticulture is also a mixed subsistence strategy. Most swidden cultivators grow several crops. They may also hunt, fish, or raise some domestic animals. In New Guinea, for example, domestic pigs are an important source of protein, and the horticulturalist Kofyar of Nigeria keep goats, chickens, sheep, and cows. The Yanomamo of the Amazon rain forest hunt monkeys and other forest animals.

Because of the very diverse environments of swidden cultivation, horticulturalists have diverse cultures.

The Lua': A Horticultural Society in Southeast Asia

The Lua' of northern Thailand are swidden cultivators. Swidden gardens are cultivated in a regular rotational sequence. After using a block of land for one or two years, villagers allow it to lie fallow for about nine years before planting again.

In January, village elders inspect the gardens they expect to use the following year to confirm that the forest regrowth is adequate for cultivation. Using long steel-bladed knives, the men clear their fields by felling small trees. They leave strips of trees along watercourses and at the tops of ridges to prevent erosion and provide seed sources for forest regrowth during the fallow period. They leave taller trees standing, but trim their branches so they will not shade the crops. Such Lua' practices encourage ecosystem diversity (Rerkasem et al. 2009).

The fields cleared in January and February dry until the end of March when a day is chosen to burn them. First a firebreak is cleared around the field so that fire does not accidentally spread into the forest. Then the swidden is burned.

Swidden, or slash-and-burn, horticulture, as practiced traditionally in northern Thailand, is based on a deep understanding of the forest environment. All the features of the landscape are taken into account as Lua' build their houses and plant their fields with a variety of crops used for subsistence, for cash, and for animal fodder.

The cultivators first plant cotton and corn on the slopes of the fields, and plant yams on the lower, wetter portions. By mid-April, they begin to plant the main subsistence crop, upland rice, jabbing the earth loose with 10-foot iron-tipped planting poles. They hope the rice will take root and sprout before the heavy monsoon rains come. Different types of rice are sown in different areas of the field. Quick-ripening rice is planted near the field shelter, where it can be easily watched. Drought-resistant varieties are planted on the drier, sandier tops of the slopes, along with millet. In addition, there are gardens with mustard greens, peppers, beans, and other vegetables. Vine plants are grown in places particularly susceptible to erosion.

By May, weeding begins, with mainly women and older children using a short-handled tool to scrape and hack at the weeds on the surface; weeds are not dug or pulled out by the roots.

Both men and women harvest the rice, using small, handheld sickles, cutting the stems of each bunch of rice close to the ground. The stalks are spread out to dry for a few days, and then young men beat them against a threshing mat to knock the rice grains loose, separating them as completely as possible. After a second winnowing, the cleaned rice is loaded into baskets and kept in a temporary barn near the field shelter.

After the harvest, swiddens are allowed to lie fallow. However, villagers use the plants that grow on fallow fields for grazing, as traditional medicines, and for other purposes. Such plants are also particularly important during food shortages. The Lua' also keep pigs, water buffalo, cattle, and chickens, which they may sell at local markets. In earlier times, the Lua' hunted and fished, but environmental changes and increased population in the last 50 years has greatly reduced these activities.

By the mid-twentieth century, many newcomers had begun to settle in Lua' territory. They were less careful about their swidden practices than the Lua', and the quality of the land began to deteriorate. Additionally, through environmental regulations and the promotion of development projects, the government pressured the Lua' to limit their use of swiddens (Delcore 2007:96). The result has been an increase in intensive agriculture and cattle herding. Many crops such as sorghum and cotton have been severely reduced or eliminated. Cattle now graze the fallow swiddens, leaving few plants for human use. The increase of cash cropping in soybeans has transformed the previously clear and free-flowing streams to muddy, polluted pools, which the Lua' consider too dirty to wash their clothes in, and year-round irrigation has brought in year-round mosquitoes.

The changes in swidden practices among the Lua' are typical of trends in Southeast Asia, and perhaps, worldwide. Rising population, pressure toward industrial agriculture from governments and corporations, and the desire of farmers to raise and sell cash crops all work against swidden

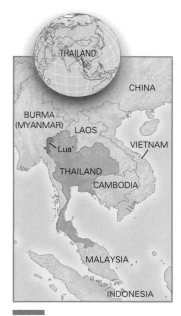

The Lua' of northwestern Thailand.

agriculture. A recent analysis shows that other agricultural systems are replacing swidden farming in Southeast Asia, and that fallow times are growing shorter where it is still being practiced. The authors note, however, that farmers maintain short fallow swidden farming alongside other agricultural practices, so it is unlikely to disappear entirely (Schmidt-Vogt et al. 2009). Despite this, the move away from swidden farming will have profound cultural consequences for the Lua' and other groups.

Agriculture

In agriculture, the same piece of land is permanently cultivated with use of the plow, draft animals, and more complex techniques of water and soil control than horticulturalists use. Plows are more efficient at loosening the soil than are digging sticks or hoes, and turning the soil brings nutrients to the surface. Irrigation is often important in agriculture. Irrigation may require elaborate terracing in hilly areas and sophisticated systems of water control. Preindustrial agriculture also uses techniques of natural fertilization, selective breeding of livestock and crops, and crop rotation, all of which increase productivity.

Intensive cultivation generally supports higher population densities than horticulture. In Indonesia, for example, the island of Java, with 9 percent of the nation's land area, is able to support more than two-thirds of the Indonesian population through intensive wet rice cultivation using elaborate irrigation terraces. The Javanese population density of well over 2,000 people per square mile (Republic of Indonesia 1997) contrasts sharply with the maximum population density of swidden areas in Indonesia, which is about 145 people per square mile.

The greater productivity of agriculture also results from more intensive use of labor. Farmers must work long and hard to make the land productive. For example, growing rice in an irrigated paddy requires about 233 person days of labor per year for each hectare (a hectare is about 2.5 acres) (Barker, Herdt, and Rose 1985:128). In addition to human labor, agriculture requires more capital investment than horticulture. Plows must be bought and draft animals raised and cared for. Although agriculturalists may have more control over food production than horticulturalists, they are more vulnerable to the environment. When people depend on the intensive cultivation of one or two crops, one crop failure or a disease that strikes draft animals may become an economic disaster.

Agriculture is generally associated with sedentary villages, the rise of cities and states, occupational diversity, social stratification, and other complex forms of social organization. In contrast to horticulturalists, who grow food mainly for the subsistence of their households, farmers (agriculturalists) are enmeshed within larger complex societies. Part of their food production is used to support non–food-producing occupational specialists, such as religious or ruling elites. Rural cultivators who produce for the subsistence of their households but are also integrated into larger, complex state societies are called **peasants**.

Musha: A Peasant Agricultural Village in Egypt

Musha is an agricultural village about 250 miles south of Cairo in the Nile Valley. Musha's farmers practice a two-year crop rotation system based on both summer and winter crops. The cycle begins with cotton in the first summer, followed by wheat in the winter. Maize or sorghum follows in the second summer, or the land may be left fallow. The cycle is completed in the second winter with millet, lentils, and chickpeas. In addition, farmers grow grapes and pomegranates and raise a variety of vegetables for home consumption. They also depend on the milk, cheese, and butter from water buffalo, cows, sheep, and goats. Only water buffalo are regularly eaten and sold.

Historically, Musha farmers relied on either animal power or human effort and a few basic wooden tools. Shallow plows and threshing sleds were pulled by cows. Winnowing relied on the wind and a winnowing fork and sieves for the final cleaning. Donkeys and camels were also used to haul crops, people, and equipment.

Many changes occurred in Musha starting in the 1950s. By 1980, almost all farmers used machines at least some of the time. They also came to depend on chemical fertilizers and pesticides as well as animal manure.

In the 1960s, when the completion of the Aswan High Dam brought an end to the flooding of the Nile, the government constructed feed canals and these became the main source of water for the fields. The government is responsible for maintaining these canals and cleans them once a year. However, the farmers must raise water from the canals to the level of the fields. Pumps that perform this task are generally owned by several people, who share the work involved in their maintenance and operation. After arranging for the distribution of water to his fields, the farmer must hire a driver and tractor to plow the fields if he, like many small farmers, does not own one. Fertilizer and seed are hauled from the village bank to his home and from his home to the field. The fertilizer is then spread by hand.

Wheat is one of the most important crops in Musha. It is planted in November and harvested in May and June, and is used for both grain and straw. Hired laborers usually harvest wheat using a small sickle. The reaped wheat is bundled into sheaves, which are transported by camel or wagon to the threshing ground where it is fed into a threshing machine. The threshed grain is winnowed and sifted by specialists who are paid piece rates. Finally, the grain and straw are hauled from the threshing ground back to the farmer's storeroom.

Egypt.

The household is central in Musha cultivation, with extra laborers hired as needed. Women do not work in the fields, but keep house, care for animals, and make cheese. Children, recruited by labor contractors, cut clover for animals and help harvest cotton. The household head plays a key managerial role supervising others, making agricultural purchases, hiring labor, scheduling the use of machinery, and arranging for the water flow into his fields.

In deciding on their strategies for making a living, Musha farmers must also adapt to government policies. At one time, the government controlled prices for key crops such as wheat and cotton. However, direct government intervention was greatly reduced or eliminated in the 1980s and 1990s. Despite this, the government is still heavily involved in agriculture. Indeed, through investments in irrigation systems and other infrastructure, the government has remodeled the very landscape on which the farmer works. Government organizations make loans to farmers, distribute agricultural inputs such as seed and fertilizer, subsidize the production of particular agricultural products, and buy some of the farmers' crops. State policies such as importing wheat from the United States affect the prices farmers receive. The state sets landownership laws, makes rules governing land tenancy, and affects the labor market through policies that encourage migration.

Profits from farming are uncertain, and most families have several sources of income. Sales of animals, fruits and vegetables, and handicrafts supplement household income. In fact, 70 percent of village households derive their major income from activities other than farming: day labor, government jobs, craft trades, specialist agricultural work, as well as remittances from family members who have migrated, or from rents and pensions.

Farmers today must know the skills of farming as well as how to manage a wide range of other activities. They must interact with family members and government officials and negotiate with the owners of tractors, day laborers, and many others. They supervise agricultural work and manage a wide range of activities, making important decisions at every step. Farmers are affected by global prices for the commodities they produce as well as the policies of their own national government and foreign governments. All over the world, farmers are increasingly part of a globalized, industrialized economy.

Industrialism

In industrialism, the focus of production moves away from food to the production of other goods and services. Investments in machinery and technologies of communication and information become increasingly important. In foraging, pastoralism, horticulture, and agriculture, most of the population is involved in producing food. Although the food industry is very large in industrial societies, only a very small percentage of the population is directly involved in food production. In the United States, in the early 1900s, more than one-third of families lived on farms. Today, fewer than 2 percent do, and most of these derive the bulk of their income from nonfarm sources (Lobao and Meyer 2001). In 2005, fewer than one million people, less than one-half of 1 percent of the population, listed farming as their primary occupation (U.S. Census Bureau 2008, Statistical Abstract).

Industrialism has an explosive effect on many aspects of economy, society, and culture. It has led to vastly increased population growth, expanded consumption of resources (especially energy), increased occupational specialization, and a shift from working for subsistence and selling the products of one's labor to selling the labor itself for hourly or yearly wages. In every industrialized society, most people work for wages that they use to purchase food, goods, and services. Although cash transactions are found in other production systems, almost all transactions in industrial economies are mediated by money.

Industrial economies are based on the principles that consumption must constantly expand, and material standards of living must always rise. This contrasts with economies created by the production systems previously discussed, which put various limits on both production and consumption and thus make lighter demands on their environments. Industrialism today has vastly outgrown national boundaries. The result has been great movement of resources, capital, and population, as the whole world has gradually been drawn into the global economy, a process we call **globalization**.

globalization The integration of resources, labor, and capital into a global network.

Contemporary industrial and postindustrial societies are characterized by well-coordinated specialized labor forces that produce goods and services and by much smaller elite and managerial classes that oversee the day-to-day operations of the workplace and control what is produced and how it is distributed. Government bureaucracies become important economic and social strata. Increasingly, mobility, skill, and education are required for success.

Because industrialized societies generate much higher levels of inequality than societies based on foraging, pastoralism, or horticulture and because industrial systems require continued expansion, wealth and poverty become critical social issues. Unequal distributions of opportunity, economic failure, illness, and misfortune limit the life chances of vast numbers of people in industrialized societies. Conversely, economic success creates lifestyles well above poverty for large numbers and conditions of truly extraordinary wealth for a very small number. Inequalities characterize relations among as well as within nations. The creation of complex global systems of exchange between those who supply raw materials and those who use them in manufacturing, as well as between manufacturers and consumers, has resulted in increasing disparities of wealth around the world.

In industrial agriculture, food is processed using techniques similar to other manufacturing processes.

© Ed Lallo

The Beef Industry: Industrialized Agriculture in the United States

The American beef industry is a good if disturbing example of industrialism. Americans have long had a love affair with beef. Because meat was expensive for the average family during much of America's past, beef became both the symbol and the substance of having made it into the middle class. For Americans, steak is symbolic of manliness, and "meat and potatoes" are considered the iconic American meal.

As the standard of living in the United States rose after World War II, so did the demand for inexpensive beef. The postwar era brought the rise of the suburbs and the entry of large numbers of women into the workforce. This increased the complexity of American family life and reduced the amount of time available for cooking and dining together, thus favoring packaged convenience foods and meat that could be rapidly prepared. Additionally, beginning in the 1960s, the expansion of the fast-food industries greatly increased American consumption of hamburgers and the demand for beef. In 2007, McDonald's purchased close to one billion pounds of beef in the United States alone (Roybal 2007).

American dinner tables had been supplied with meat that came through a production chain that started on a family farm and ended in the neighborhood retail butcher shop. However, this system of production could not generate the levels of supply that families now demanded. These favored large corporations that could employ mass production technologies. By the late 1980s, most family farms were no longer economically viable and many small farmers lost their land. Rural America became dominated by large farming operations, tied to multinational corporations. Looking to preserve jobs and stem the flow of people leaving the countryside, local governments recruited agribusinesses with free land and tax breaks, but this put greater revenue burdens on those who remained and did not stop the downward economic spiral.

The cost of labor is a significant factor in the production of meat. Through the 1970s and 1980s, meat processors succeeded in driving down the wages paid to workers. The key to this was their use of nonunion workers, frequently immigrants from Latin America and Southeast Asia. Such workers were not easily (or very willingly) absorbed into tightly knit farm communities and small towns. As the rural economy declined, resentment of immigrants and social problems increased. There were strains on health care, schools, and social services (Artz, Orazem, and Otto 2007).

In many cases, large-scale meatpacking had disastrous environmental impacts. U.S. livestock production creates about 900 million tons of waste annually. In Iowa, hog farming alone produces 50 million tons of manure annually. This waste often seeps into local streams and groundwater supplies, polluting critical resources (Bittman 2008). Although some rural regions experienced short-term job increases from the meatpacking industries, there was a hidden cost and a long-term downside for rural communities (Stull and Broadway 2004).

The efficiency of assembly line beef processing has high human costs as well. The meatpacking industry has a long history of horrific working conditions. In 1906, Upton Sinclair described the deeply impoverished lives, terrible working conditions, and hopelessness of workers in Chicago's slaughterhouses. Although the meatpacking industry today is vastly different from the industry of 100 years ago, working conditions are still deeply disturbing in many cases. The low costs and high availability of American meat is made possible by cheap labor and getting the maximum product out the door. "On the floor," this translates into a large proportion of unskilled, poorly trained, low-paid hourly workers; a speeded-up "disassembly" line; and few break periods for workers.

Work in the meatpacking industry is difficult and dangerous even in the best plants. The processing operations involve thousands of moving animals being stun-gunned by a "knocker," axed in half by "splitters" on a moving platform, and deboned and cut up with sharp knives wielded by an assortment of specialists such as "stickers," "gutters," "tail rippers," and "head droppers." The working conditions of this sector of American agribusiness are so severe that Human Rights Watch has deemed them in violation of international standards and basic human rights. These conditions affect not only the health of the workers, but also the quality of the product. This was dramatically demonstrated in early 2008, when the Westland/Hallmark Meat Packing Company recalled 143 million pounds of contaminated meat, some of which was used in school lunch programs. Despite this, demand for inexpensive beef remains high, and meaningful reform of the industry does not seem likely in the near future.

THE GLOBAL MARKETPLACE

The contemporary world is characterized by connectedness and change of a magnitude greater than anything seen earlier. For some people, the expansion of the global economy has meant new and more satisfying means of making a living. However, these opportunities are not equally available to all peoples or to all individuals within a culture. For many people, the promise of prosperity offered by the global economy has yet to be fulfilled.

Anthropology is particularly sensitive to the complex linkages among local, regional, national, and global contexts that structure the modern world. Anthropologists today can play an important role in shaping government and global economic policies that take into account the environmental impact of different ways of making a living, the values and practices of local cultures, international plant and animal conservation efforts, and corporate- and state-driven efforts to participate in global markets. In the postindustrial globalized society, individuals, governments, and business must call for new responses as they adapt to significant changes in the production and distribution of goods. We explore some of these changes in Chapter 6 on economics.

BRINGING IT BACK HOME:
GLOBALIZATION AND FOOD CHOICE

In the recent past, much of the food on American tables was locally produced and seasonally available. Today, our food is produced on large farms located in rich agricultural regions thousands of miles away from the populations they serve. For example, more than half of all fruit produced in the United States comes from California, which, together with Washington and Florida, accounts for 80 percent of U.S. fruit production (Perez and Pollack 2008). However, our culinary net spreads far wider than the United States. In the fiscal year 2007, the United States imported 70 billion dollars worth of agricultural products.

The presence of so much food from distant places is one of the great triumphs of globalization. Fruits and vegetables are available all year long. We dine on frozen Indian meals actually prepared in India and accompany them with water from Fiji and fruit from Chile. However, this global food network also extracts a high price. Although determining the carbon footprint of individual products is extremely difficult (Economist 2007), moving food around the world may have high environmental costs. For example, the average tomato imported into Canada has traveled almost 3,000 miles and, in so doing, produced more than three times more carbon dioxide than a locally grown tomato (Brandt 2008:26). As our dependence on imported food increases, so does our reliance on the fuel necessary to move it. This means that changes in the price of oil can result in large jumps in the price of food, making our food supply more vulnerable than ever to global economics and politics.

Dependence on food shipped long distances also favors foods that look pretty and are easy to ship. Along with this comes the loss of indigenous and traditional varieties. Although estimates about the percentage of plant species that have disappeared vary, one study found that 97 percent of the vegetable varieties on a United States Department of Agriculture (USDA) list from the early 20th century are extinct today (Brandt 2008:56).

The varieties that are extensively grown along with the fertilizers and pesticides necessary to grow them are produced by large multinational corporations such as Monsanto, ADM, Cargill, DuPont, and Bayer. These companies make huge profits, sometimes at the expense of workers. According to the United Nations Environmental Programme (2004), between one and five million people are poisoned by pesticides yearly, and as many as 20,000 of them die (World Bank 2006). Poor nations account for only 25 percent of the world's pesticide use but 99 percent of the deaths from pesticide poisoning. Buying globally does provide jobs for agricultural workers around the world, but working conditions in such jobs are often very harsh and the key beneficiaries are the corporations that organize food production and transportation.

In recent years, food alternatives have become more mainstream. These include vegetarianism, the slow food movement, and community-supported and local agriculture. All of these are probably healthier for both individuals and the environment than large-scale globalized food production (Wilk 2006). However, thus far, they affect relatively few people in wealthy nations, often cost more than alternatives, and increasing their use involves the difficult task of changing culturally ingrained food habits.

■■■ YOU DECIDE

1. What are the cultural patterns and values that underlie America's food choices and how do they affect what you eat?
2. Locavores are people who eat only food grown within a relatively short distance of their home. Would you become a locavore? Why, or why not?
3. Do you believe movements in favor of local agriculture, organic foods, and slow foods are likely to have success in America? What factors might favor or retard their success?

▌ CHAPTER SUMMARY

1. All societies must adapt to their physical environments, which present different problems, opportunities, and limitations to human populations. The subsistence (food-getting) pattern of a society develops in response to seasonal variations in the environment and environmental variations over the long run, such as drought, flood, animal diseases, climate, demographic changes, and the presence of other groups.

2. The five major patterns of using the environment to support human populations are foraging (fishing, hunting, and gathering), pastoralism, horticulture, agriculture, and industrialism. As a whole, humankind has moved in the direction of using more complex technology, increasing its numbers, and developing more complex sociocultural systems.

3. Foraging, which relies on food naturally available in the environment, has been the major food-getting pattern most of the time humans have been on earth. Although this way of life is rapidly disappearing, foraging is still a useful adjunct to other subsistence strategies for many societies. The Pintupi people of the Gibson Desert of Australia were a foraging culture.

4. Pastoralism involves the care of domesticated herd animals. Most pastoralists must move their herds. Nomadism and transhumance are two patterns of movement. Because it is difficult to live on animal products alone, pastoralism either is found along with cultivation or involves trading relations with food cultivators. The Yarahmadzai are an example of a nomadic mixed pastoralist economy.

5. Horticulture typically is a tropical forest adaptation that uses simple technology and requires the cutting and burning of jungle to clear fields for cultivation. Fields are not used permanently but are allowed to lie fallow after several years of productivity. The Lua' are swidden cultivators in Thailand.

6. Agriculture, or intensive cultivation, usually involves complex technology often including plows and irrigation. Agriculture generally supports high population densities and is associated with sedentary village life. Agricultural societies are stratified and farmers constitute only one element of them. Musha, an Egyptian village, is an example of peasant agriculture.

7. In industrialism, machines and chemical processes are used for the production of goods. Food production constitutes only a small percentage of total production and occupies little of the population. Industrial societies are characterized by complex systems of exchange, by bureaucracies, and by high levels of social stratification. The American beef industry is an example of industrial food production.

KEY TERMS

Agriculture

Efficiency

Foraging (hunting and gathering)

Globalization

Horticulture

Industrialism

Nomadic pastoralism

Pastoralism

Peasants

Population density

Productivity

Sedentary

Subsistence strategies

Swidden (slash-and-burn) cultivation

Transhumant pastoralism

Specialization and the creation of markets are a critical aspect of the development of large-scale economies. In earlier times, cheeses were made and consumed locally. Now they enter a network of international trade. The Amsterdam Cheese Market, pictured here, is an important node in that network.

CHAPTER **6**

ECONOMICS

ULTIMATE DICTATOR

HE notion that human beings are "economic men" underlies much of Western economic theory. The idea is that people are rational, individual economic actors. They are capable of assessing the economic choices facing them, and, when they do so, they make decisions that maximize their wealth and minimize their labor. There is certainly some truth to this idea, and all of us can think of cases where we behave precisely this way. But, economic choices do not occur in a vacuum. Real economic decisions are made in a cultural context and are influenced by ideas about what is right, valuable, and moral, not just about how much we can profit. However, as we have seen in the previous chapters of this book, what is right, valuable, and moral is not the same for everyone.

Economists and anthropologists have developed interesting tools to test the degree to which people in different cultures really behave like the "economic men" of the theory. Two examples are the dictator game and the ultimatum game.

In the dictator game, there are two individuals: a "proposer" and a "responder." The proposer is given a sum of money, say the equivalent of one day of wages, and is told to split it with the responder. The proposer and the responder are unknown to each other and they play the game only once, so there is no chance that generosity will be reciprocated. If people behave like "economic men" and try to maximize their wealth and minimize their work, we would expect that the proposer would keep the entire sum, offering nothing to the responder. In fact, that doesn't always happen. In the United States and other wealthy nations, about 30 to 40 percent of the players take the whole pot. However, most proposers leave between 20 and 30 percent for the responders. Jean Ensminger (2002) found that among the Orma, a group of cattle pastoralists living in Kenya, only 9 percent took the whole pot; the others gave an average of 31 percent to the responders.

The ultimatum game is also played with a proposer and a responder. However, in this case, the proposer offers to split a sum of money, and the responder may either accept or reject the split. If the responder accepts the split, the money is divided and the game is over. If the responder rejects the split, neither player receives any money and the game ends. As in the dictator game, players are anonymous and play only once, so generosity cannot be returned. In the ultimatum game, respondents who behaved like "economic men" would always accept the proposer's offer because accepting the offer involves no financial cost, and even a very low offer is greater than nothing. But, real people do not play like "economic men."

In the past 15 years, anthropologists and economists have played the ultimatum game with members of many different cultures. Results from 15 cultures show large amounts of variation between cultures and show no culture that plays the game as the "economic man" model would predict. For example, among the Machiguenga of the Peruvian Amazon, proposers rarely offered more than 15 percent, and offers were almost never rejected. American college students, on the other hand, offered 42 to 48 percent of the pot to their responders, and responders tended to reject offers of less than 30 percent.

Some of the results may seem counterintuitive. For example, in foraging groups, there is a high degree of equality, but foragers were not generous game players. The Hadza, foragers who live in Tanzania, made some of the lowest proposals of any groups tested. On the other hand, industrialized economies are highly stratified and unequal, but their members are likely to offer almost half the pot to responders. In fact, the results show an interesting trend. The greater the degree to which a group is involved in a market economy, the more likely proposers were to give a larger share of the money to responders. Later in this chapter, we will explore some of the reasons why this is the case.

The results of the dictator and ultimatum games demonstrate the social and cultural dimensions of economic decision making. The fact that cross-culturally a strong majority of proposers give responders something may show that all people have a bias toward at least a little generosity. However, the systematic differences among cultures demonstrate that decisions are set in cultural contexts that determine moral and appropriate behavior and that these are different in different economic systems.

Economics is the study of the ways in which the choices people make as individuals and as members of societies combine to determine how their society uses its resources to produce and distribute goods and services. But, as our example shows, this process is always set within a cultural context. How we make these decisions depends on the values we give to both goods and ideas. And that depends upon culture.

Every society must have an **economic system** in the sense that each group of people must produce, distribute, and consume. However, cultural context determines what is produced and how it is produced. Cultures establish the ways in which goods and services are distributed. And cultural values are critical in determining the meanings of consumption.

economics The study of the ways in which the choices people make combine to determine how their society uses its resources to produce and distribute goods and services.

economic system The norms governing production, distribution, and consumption of goods and services within a society.

▊▊ECONOMIC BEHAVIOR

Economists assume that because human wants are unlimited and the means for achieving them are not, organizations and individuals must make decisions about the best way to apply their limited means to meet their unlimited desires. As we saw in the opening story, one way of understanding economic decisions is to assume that decision makers will always maximize their financial benefit and minimize their work (Dalton 1961). Will a business firm cut down or expand its production? Will it purchase a new machine or hire more laborers? Such decisions are assumed to be motivated by the desire to maximize profit.

However, the opening story also shows us that this understanding misses critical factors. As human beings, we only have so much time and so much energy to expend in meeting our desires. But, we do not always allocate our time and effort to maximize our financial wealth. Consider a choice you may make today. After you finish reading this chapter, you might confront a series of decisions: Should you reread it for better comprehension? Should you study for another course? Call and get a pizza delivered? Play with your kids? Socialize with your friends? You will make your choice based on some calculation of benefit. However, that benefit probably cannot be reduced to financial profit. You may believe that you will make more money if you study and get higher grades. However, your choice is set in a context in which money is unlikely to be the most important element of value; we value our friends, our children, our leisure time, and many other things as well. If you choose to socialize instead of hitting the books, your choice is not irrational, but it does not necessarily lead to greater profit. We cannot assume that you will always act to increase your material well-being. Rather, we need to find out what motivates you.

Just as you might value an evening spent with friends over an "A" in this class, members of other cultures might value family connections, cultural tradition, social prestige, leisure time, or other things over monetary profit. For example, the Hadza, mentioned earlier, live in an area of Tanzania with an abundance of animal and vegetable food. They have considerable leisure time but make no attempt to use it to increase their wealth. Although they know how to farm, they don't do it because it would require too much work (Woodburn 1968).

Leisure time is only one of the ends toward which people expend effort. They may also direct their energies toward increasing social status or respect. In Western society, **prestige** is primarily tied to increased consumption and display of goods and services, but this is not universal. In many societies, prestige is associated with giving goods away. Conspicuous consumers and stingy people become objects of scorn and may be shunned or accused of witchcraft (see Danfulani 1999; Offiong 1983, for examples). The notion that prestige can be gained through giving is well established in our own society. Universities have buildings bearing the names of their most generous donors. Bill Gates is not only the chairman of Microsoft, but he is also the head of the world's largest charitable foundation.

prestige Social honor or respect.

To understand the economies of various cultures, anthropologists face two related problems. First, they must analyze the broad institutional and social contexts within which people make decisions, and second, they must determine and evaluate the factors that motivate individual decision making.

One way we can think about any given economic system is to consider a series of fundamental issues that all societies must face. Because all societies must acquire the food and other materials necessary to their lives, all must engage in production. To do so, all societies must acquire resources, such as land and water, and all must have some system through which the rights to use such resources are allocated.

However, resources in and of themselves do nothing. Rather, people must be organized in specific ways to use resources in the production of goods and services. Thus, each society has a **division of labor**: a pattern by which different tasks are given to different members of a society. For example, foragers rely on the plants and animals in their environment. But, foragers never simply gather and eat the plants and animals randomly. In each group, specific groups of people do specific tasks. Most often, men hunt and women gather. Thus, they are organized to produce.

division of labor The pattern of apportioning different tasks to different members of a society.

Additionally, people in all societies exchange and consume the products of production. Thus, each society has a system of distribution, and in each, there are distinct styles and patterns of consumption. In the remainder of this chapter, we will explore how different societies tackle the problems of allocating resources, organizing labor, and distributing and consuming the results of production.

ALLOCATING RESOURCES

Productive resources are the things that members of a society need to participate in the economy, and access to them is basic to every culture. The most obvious productive resources are land, water, labor, and tools. However, knowledge is also an important productive resource. We can see the effects of access to knowledge in current-day society by looking at the relationship between university degrees and income. According to the U.S. Bureau of Labor Statistics (2010), the median income for high school graduates in 2009 was about $32,500. The median income for those with a college degree was almost $53,300. The median for those with master's and doctoral degrees was substantially higher. Of course, the university is not the only source of knowledge in our society. But still . . .

productive resources Material goods, natural resources, or information used to create other goods or information.

An important point of contrast between economic systems is the extent to which the members of a society have access to productive resources. In general, differential access to resources develops as population and social complexity increase. Small-scale economies have a limited number of productive resources and most everyone has access to them. Large-scale societies have a great many more resources, but access to them is limited. Again, considering differential access to knowledge in the United States, we see that only 3 percent of the students at America's most selective universities come from households in the lowest 25 percent of the income scale, and only 10 percent come from the bottom 50 percent (Lexington 2005). Thus, family wealth plays a critical role in accessing knowledge and is a powerful predictor of future wealth and social position.

Access to the knowledge that allows one to make and use tools plays an important role in all societies. There may be additional important forms of knowledge that can be controlled as well, such as the knowledge of healing or of religious rituals. In preindustrial societies, however, the most basic resources are land and sometimes water. Examining the ways in which people access these particular resources can give us insight into the social organization and other aspects of a culture.

The requirements of a foraging lifestyle generally mean that a group of people must spread out over a large area. Boundaries are generally flexible so that they can be adjusted as the availability of resources changes. Abundance and scarcity shape people's relationship to land. Where resources are scarce and large areas are needed to support the population, boundaries usually are not defended. Where resources are more abundant and people move less, groups may be more inclined to defend their territory (Cashdan 1989:42).

Among pastoralists, the most critical resources are livestock and land. Livestock are owned and managed by individual heads of households. Animals, in turn, produce goods that are directly consumed, such as milk. They are also kept as a form of wealth, to produce other animals and to exchange goods and services. Land and water are generally not owned. In many cases, during the summer or the rainy season, cattle graze in deserts and highland areas unsuitable for farming. In the winter or dry season, they move to areas that are occupied by settled farmers. There, agreements with landowners and village leaders allow animals to graze on crop waste and the stubble from harvested fields. Most such agreements specify rights, payments, and schedules for all parties.

In most societies characterized by horticulture (extensive cultivation), land is communally owned by an extended kin group. Designated elders or officials of the group allocate the rights to use land to individuals or heads of households. But such land may not be sold. Because almost everyone belongs to some land-controlling kin group, few people are deprived of access to this basic resource. Thus, control over land is not a means by which one group can exploit or exert permanent control over another.

Horticulture often involves investing a great deal of labor in clearing, cultivating, and maintaining land. Generally, the rights to cleared land

and its products are vested in those who work it. Since such individuals may die while the land is still productive, some system of inheritance of use rights is usually provided. Among the Lacandon Maya, for example, individuals can farm any unused piece of land. However, clearing virgin land is difficult, so people retain rights to land they have cleared even if it is not currently in production. Maya who migrate may lose their land rights, but their families retain ownership of any fruit trees that they have planted. Should a man die after investing time and labor in clearing and planting land, his wife and children retain rights to use the land (McGee 1990).

In more politically and technologically complex societies, agriculture dominates production. Enormous amounts of labor are invested in the land and very large quantities of food produced. When this happens, control of the land becomes an important source of wealth and power. Landownership moves from the kin group to the individual or family. Within the limits of law or custom, the owner has the right to keep others off the land and to dispose of it as he or she wishes.

In agricultural societies, land and other productive resources are often owned by an elite group. Landowners usually do not work their fields themselves. Most fieldwork is done by laborers who often are referred to as *peasants*. Today, peasants typically pay cash rent to their landlords, but in the past, they also provided goods and services, including a portion of their agricultural production, labor, finished craft goods such as cloth, and raw material such as lumber. As a result, landowners enjoy relatively high standards of living but peasants do not.

Many current-day societies rely on industrialized agriculture. But in these cases, as we saw in Chapter 5, only a minuscule percentage of the

In complex societies, enormous amounts of labor are often invested in land. This results in high levels of production, and landownership becomes an important source of wealth and power. This picture shows rice paddies in Yunnan, China.

© Jailiang Gao www.peace-on-earth.org/Getty

population is directly involved in farming. Therefore, access to productive land is not important for most people in these societies. In industrialized economies, most people earn their livelihood by working for wages for businesses and other organizations that provide goods and services. These usually are organized as capitalist enterprises. We will discuss capitalism at some length later in this chapter.

ORGANIZING LABOR

In small-scale preindustrial and peasant economies, the household or some extended kin group is the basic unit of production and of consumption (White 1980). The **household** is an economic unit—a group of people united by kinship or other links who share a residence and organize production, consumption, and distribution of goods among themselves. A household is different from a family because it may include lodgers, servants, and others. Household members use most of the goods they produce themselves.

household A group of people united by kinship or other links who share a residence and organize production, consumption, and distribution among themselves.

Households and kin groups do seek financial gain, but this is not their primary purpose. Their goals are often social or religious rather than monetary. Labor is not a commodity bought and sold in the market; rather, it is an important aspect of membership in a social group. The labor that people both perform and receive situates them with respect to others in their family and gives them both a sense of identity and a sense of meaning.

In economies where households are the units of production, there can be little economic growth. Households cannot easily expand or contract as the economy fluctuates. They cannot easily fire their members or acquire new ones. Thus, large-scale production and distribution systems tend not to develop under such conditions. However, as we will see in the ethnography of Turkey later in this chapter, household social relations can play an important role in an industrialized economy.

In Western society, work also has very important social implications. Of course people work to put food on their table and a roof over their head. But, as anthropologist Pamela Crespin notes, an individual's self-image and social status are bound up with work in our society. Joblessness or the inability to earn a living wage diminishes an adult's identity and status (Crespin 2005:20). This is a particularly important issue in a nation such as the United States, where in 2008, about 8.9 million adults were classified as "working poor," about 1.4 million more than in 2007 (U.S. Department of Labor 2010).

Gender may also play an important role in organizing labor. In all human societies, some tasks are considered appropriate for women and others appropriate for men. At some level, the sexual division of labor is biological since only women can bear and nurse children. However, beyond this, the specific tasks defined as men's or women's work vary widely from group to group. For example, in Aztec Mexico, weaving was a female task. Newborn girls were presented with tools for weaving, and weaving equipment was placed with women when they died (Brumfiel 1991, 2006:866). However, in most West African societies, weaving is considered men's work.

Specialization in Complex Societies

The division of labor in society becomes more specialized and complex as the population increases and agricultural production intensifies. This is particularly the case where a society is dependent on grain agriculture. Grains are hard, durable, and storable. Those who are able to control them have access to wealth and power in new and important ways. Landowners and rulers are able to support many people. Occupational specialization spreads through society as individuals are able to exchange their services or the products they produce for food and wealth. Specialists are likely to include soldiers, government officials, and members of the priesthood as well as artisans, craftspeople, and merchants.

Traditional areas of contemporary India provide an excellent example of occupational specialization. There, only people belonging to particular hereditary kinship groups can perform certain services or produce certain kinds of goods. Literally thousands of specialized activities—washing clothes, drumming at festivals, presiding over religious ceremonies, making pots, painting pictures—are traditionally performed by specific named hereditary groups.

Much of the world's population today lives in industrial or postindustrial societies, and almost everyone is a specialist of one kind or another. A quick glance at the yellow pages of the phone book of a major American city gives a good indication of the degree of specialization in American society. Each entry represents at least one specialty.

Although specialization undoubtedly has advantages in terms of efficiency and the ability to produce large quantities of goods, it can take a large physical and emotional toll on members of a society. Since the beginnings of the industrial age many factory jobs have involved repetitious and mind-numbing labor often performed under hazardous conditions. In the American automobile plants of the early 20th century, for example, almost all skilled tasks were mechanized. Workers simply inserted pieces into machines, turned a switch and waited until the machine completed its task, removed the finished pieces, and passed them on to the next worker. The machinery determined the pace of work and the tasks performed. In the 1920s, one worker said simply, "The machine is my boss" (Meyer 2004).

In the past 200 years, jobs have become increasingly specialized. Repetitive, monotonous factory labor, such as the work in this sneaker factory in Mexico, altered people's lives and led to new understandings of identity.

© Jeff Greenberg/PhotoEdit, Inc.

Factory labor often led to new notions of identity. For example, in the 19th century, many American workers associated masculinity with skilled labor, independence, and decision-making power at work. On the assembly lines in early 20th-century America, labor was boring and monotonous, and workers had little decision-making ability. Companies such as Ford Motors, through public speeches, company policies, and employment practices, sought to redefine masculinity, associating it with "working hard in the company of other men, on a useful product, and being paid well for it" (Lewchuk 1993:852), rather than with skill and independence.

DISTRIBUTION: SYSTEMS OF EXCHANGE AND CONSUMPTION

In all societies, goods and services are exchanged. In fact, some anthropologists have long theorized that the exchange of goods is one of the fundamental bases of culture. The great French anthropologist Marcel Mauss (1990/1924) theorized that societies were held together by patterns of giving and receiving. He pointed out that because gifts invariably must be repaid, we are obligated to each other through exchange. And in many situations, it is better to give than to receive.

The three main patterns of exchange are reciprocity, redistribution, and the market. Although more than one kind of exchange system exists in most societies, each system is predominantly associated with a certain kind of political and social organization (Polyani 1944). Let us look first at reciprocity.

Reciprocity

Reciprocity is the mutual give-and-take among people of similar status. Three types of reciprocity can be distinguished from one another by the degree of social distance between the exchanging partners (Sahlins 1972).

Generalized reciprocity usually is carried out among close kin and carries a high moral obligation. It involves a distribution of goods in which no overt account is kept of what is given, and no immediate or specific return is expected. In our culture, the relationship between mother and child is usually a good example. Ideally, such transactions are without any thought of self-interest.

Generalized reciprocity involving food is an important social mechanism among foraging peoples. In these societies, hunters distribute meat among members of the kin group or camp. Each person or family gets an equal share or a share dependent on its kinship relationship to the hunter. We might wonder what the hunter gets out of this arrangement. Aren't some people always in the position of providing and others always receiving? Part of the answer is that hunters gain satisfaction from accomplishing a highly skilled and difficult task (Woodburn 1998) and that this is accompanied by a degree of prestige. Additionally, because all people in the society are bound by the same rules, the system provides everyone with the opportunity to give and receive, although this does not necessarily mean that people do so equally.

Balanced reciprocity involves greater social distance than generalized reciprocity and entails a clear obligation to return, within a reasonable time limit, goods of nearly equal value to those given. In the United States, we participate in balanced reciprocity when we give gifts at weddings or birthdays, exchange invitations, or buy a round of drinks for friends. The economic aspect of these exchanges is repressed; we say it is the spirit of the gift that is important. However, we also know that accepting a gift involves the obligation to return a gift of approximately the same value. If we fail to do so, our relationship with the gift giver is unlikely to last very long.

Balanced reciprocity is often characteristic of trading relations among nonindustrialized peoples without market economies. Such trade is frequently carried out over long distances and between different tribes or villages. It is often in the hands of trading partners, men or women who have a long-standing and personalized relationship with one another.

Bronislaw Malinowski's (1984/1922) analysis of the **kula ring**, an extensive system of intertribal trade

reciprocity A mutual give-and-take among people of equal status.

generalized reciprocity Giving and receiving goods with no immediate or specific return expected.

balanced reciprocity The giving and receiving of goods of nearly equal value with a clear obligation of a return gift within a specified time limit.

kula ring A pattern of exchange among trading partners in a ring of islands off Papua New Guinea.

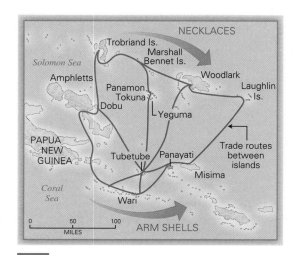

The kula trade binds people in a ring of islands off Papua New Guinea in a network of reciprocal trading relationships.

among the inhabitants of a ring of islands off Papua New Guinea, is one of the most famous anthropological studies of reciprocal trading. The kula trade moves two types of prestige goods from island to island around the kula circle. *Soulava*, long necklaces of red shell, always move in a clockwise direction. *Mwali*, bracelets of white shell, move counterclockwise. Participants receive the necklaces or bracelets from their trading partners. Although kula items can be permanently owned and can be taken out of circulation (Weiner 1976), people generally hold them for a while and then pass them on. Kula valuables are not simple objects. Each item is known by its history and associations, and some are much more valuable and important (and famous) than others. The gift or receipt of an important *soulava* or *mwali* is an action heavily loaded with prestige and politics. Kula exchanges can carry a deep emotional importance, and issues of jealousy, anger, sickness, and witchcraft are sometimes involved (Munn 1990).

Although the central drama of trading involves the gift or receipt of a kula valuable, *mwali* are never simply exchanged for *soulava*. A visiting trader hoping to receive an important kula valuable instead brings goods that may include canoes, axe blades, pottery, and pigs, as well as other items. Traders are likely to bring things not found on the island where the trading is taking place, because these are likely to be particularly valuable to their recipients. The presentation of goods by the visiting trader, as well as declarations of alliance and support, encourages the kula partner to give a *mwali* or *soulava* to the visitor. Such a gift (especially if it is an important or famous valuable) demonstrates and confirms the political importance and allegiances of both giver and recipient. Critically, the receipt of such a gift also implies the obligation to present gifts of equal or greater importance to the kula partner when he or she comes as a visiting trader.

Kula exchanges thus have economic, social, and political functions. They bring kula partners into systems of balanced reciprocity and, in so doing, create alliances that are critical in settling disputes and maintaining peace. This is particularly important because there is no formal government incorporating the different groups that take active roles in the kula. In addition, by moving products from island to island, kula exchanges increase the islanders' consumption of a wide range of goods, particularly those they do not produce, thus raising their standard of living.

negative reciprocity Exchange conducted for the purpose of material advantage and the desire to get something for nothing.

Negative reciprocity is the unsociable extreme in exchange. It happens when trade is conducted for the purpose of material advantage and is based on the desire to get the better of a bargain. Negative reciprocity is characteristic of both impersonal and unfriendly transactions. Tribal and peasant societies often distinguish between the insider, whom it is morally wrong to cheat, and the outsider, from whom every advantage may be gained. Anthropologist Clyde Kluckhohn did important studies of the Navajo in the 1940s and 1950s. He reported that, among the Navajo, the rules for interaction vary with the situation; to deceive when trading with outsiders is a morally accepted practice. Even witchcraft techniques are considered permissible in trading with members of foreign tribes (Kluckhohn 1959).

Negative reciprocity helps explain some of the findings from the ultimatum game described in the opening of this chapter. Recall that in ultimatum, one person splits a quantity of money, offering a portion to another. If the second person accepts the split, they divide the money. If the second person rejects the offer, neither gets any money. Researchers found that the results of the game vary from society to society. In many kin-based societies, the first person was likely to offer only a small percentage of the money and the second person usually accepted it, whereas in market-based societies, the first person offered much larger percentages and the second was likely to reject small offers (Chibnik 2005; Henrich et al. 2004).

A key aspect of the ultimatum game is that the players are anonymous. The results are explained because, in kin-based societies, negative reciprocity often characterizes anonymous transactions. For players from such societies, offering little or nothing to an anonymous partner is both expected and proper. Since the second player does not expect to receive much from an anonymous person, the second player is likely to accept very small offers.

Redistribution

In **redistribution**, goods are collected from or contributed by members of a group and then given out to the group in a new pattern. Thus, redistribution involves a social center to which goods are brought and from which they are distributed. Redistribution occurs in many different contexts. In household food sharing, pooled resources are reallocated among family members. In state societies, redistribution is achieved through taxation.

redistribution Exchange in which goods are collected from or contributed by members of a group and then given out to the group in a new pattern.

Redistribution can be especially important in horticultural societies where political organization includes bigmen, self-made leaders who gain power and authority through personal achievement. Such individuals collect goods and food from their supporters. Often these items are redistributed back in communal feasts, which the bigman sponsors to sustain his political power and raise his prestige. Redistribution also occurred in some chiefdoms. In these cases, however, a distinct hierarchy is involved. Chiefs collected goods and staple foods from many communities to support their households and attendants as well as to finance large public feasts that helped solidify their power (Earle 1987).

Potlatch feasting among Native American groups of the Pacific Northwest, including the Kwakiutl and Tlingit, is a good example of redistribution. In these groups, potlatches were held to honor and to validate the rank of chiefs and other notables, usually in connection with births,

potlatch A form of redistribution involving competitive feasting practiced among Northwest Coast Native Americans.

Potlatches are competitive feasts held among Native Americans of the Northwest Pacific Coast. In this picture, taken around 1900, Tlingit people, their canoes heavily laden with trade goods and decorated with American flags arrive at Sitka, Alaska for a Potlatch.

Alaska State Library, ASL-Sitka Harbor-24

deaths, and marriages (Rosman and Rubel 1971). A leader holding a potlatch called on his followers to supply food and other goods to be consumed and distributed during a feast to which he invited group members and rivals. The number of guests present and the amount of goods given away or destroyed revealed the wealth and prestige of the host chief. At a potlatch, the host publicly traced his line of descent and claimed the right to certain titles and privileges. Each of these claims was accompanied by the giving away, and sometimes the destruction, of large quantities of food and goods, such as blankets and carved wooden boxes. As these goods were given or destroyed, the individual and his supporters boasted of their wealth and power. In the early 20th century, Franz Boas collected speeches given at potlatches, such as:

> I am Yaqatlentlis. . . . I am Great Inviter. . . . Therefore I feel like laughing at what the lower chiefs say, for they try in vain to down me by talking against my name. Who approaches what was done by my ancestors, the chiefs? Therefore I am known by all the tribes over all the world. Only the chief my ancestor gave away property in a great feast, and all the rest can only try to imitate me. . . . (in Benedict 1961/1934:191).

The feasting and gifts given at a potlatch demonstrated the host's right to the titles and rights he claimed and created prestige for him and his followers. Guests either acknowledged the host's claims or refuted them by staging an even larger potlatch. Thus, potlatching involved friendship but also competition and rivalry.

From an economic perspective, the drive for prestige encouraged people to produce much more than they would otherwise. This increased the amount of work they did but also the amount of food and goods they produced and consumed. Since this wealth was given to people who traveled substantial distances to come to a potlatch, it was distributed to a fairly large population and ecological area.

In the late 19th century and early 20th century, Canadian government authorities saw the potlatch as a symbol of native irrationality. They believed that investment was the key to economic success and, to them, the potlatch focus on consumption and destruction of goods was both disturbing and wasteful. The result was that potlatching was outlawed between 1884 and 1951 (Bracken 1997). Since then, the potlatch has been revived but primarily as a symbol of tribal identity rather than a major element in tribal economy. Simeone (1995) and Stearns (1975), for example, report that the Tanacross and Haida people consider the potlatch a central symbol of cooperation and respect that separates native from nonnative peoples.

Although the term *potlatch* refers specifically to the feasting of Northwest Coast people, Rosman and Rubel (1971:xii) report that rivalrous, competitive feasting is found among many peoples. It is common, for example, throughout the Pacific Islands. We may even see some elements of it in our own society. There may be competition within families or within communities to throw the largest and most elaborate holiday parties, weddings, or coming-of-age celebrations (such as confirmation, bar or bat mitzvah, and quinceañera). In all of these cases, the prestige that accrues to the people who give the party is a critical factor. This reminds us that there is much more to giving a gift than simply trying to determine what another person desires.

leveling mechanism A practice, value, or form of social organization that evens out wealth within a society.

Redistribution may either increase or decrease inequality within a society. A **leveling mechanism** is a form of redistribution that tends to decrease social inequality. Leveling mechanisms force accumulated resources or capital to be used in ways that ensure social goals are considered along with economic ones. Leveling mechanisms take many different forms. For example, if generosity rather than the accumulation of wealth is the basis for prestige, those who desire power and prestige will distribute much of their wealth. Sometimes, as with the potlatch, this is accomplished through feasting. However, there are numerous other possibilities.

Manning Nash (1961) and June Nash (1970) described a number of leveling mechanisms that operate

The Pacific Northwest.

in the village of Amatenango, in the Chiapas district of Mexico. One is the organization of production by households. As mentioned earlier, economic expansion and accumulation of wealth are limited where households, rather than business firms, are the productive units. A second is inheritance. Because all children share equally in the estate of a parent, large estates rarely persist over generations. Accusations of witchcraft are a third mechanism. People who accumulate more wealth than their neighbors or have wealth but are not generous may face such accusations, and those believed guilty of witchcraft may be killed.

Finally, in Amatenango, prosperous community members must hold religious and secular offices, called "cargos." Cargos are held for a year at a time and require their holders to perform civic duties and to pay for feasts and celebrations. Cargos are ranked, and those held by older, wealthier community members are more prestigious and more expensive. Such customs are common in southern Mexico and Central America and are referred to as **cargo systems**.

cargo system A ritual system common in Central and South America in which wealthy people are required to hold a series of costly ceremonial offices.

Anthropologists have shown that community obligations such as cargos help to limit the economic gap between the relatively rich and the poor, but they do not eliminate it. In fact, they may help to preserve social hierarchies (Chance and Taylor 1985). Wealthy individuals take expensive cargos that increase their prestige but do not severely impact their total wealth. They remain rich throughout their lives. The poor are generally unable to take cargos and remain poor throughout their lives. Thus, although some wealth is redistributed, economic differences are reinforced rather than equalized (Cancian 1989:147).

Market Exchange

market exchange An economic system in which goods and services are bought and sold at a money price determined primarily by the forces of supply and demand.

Market exchange is the principal distribution mechanism in most of the world's societies today. Goods and services are bought and sold at a monetary price determined, at least in theory, by impersonal market forces.

The market involves cultural and moral assumptions that are well illustrated by the results of the ultimatum game. As we noted earlier, ultimatum players from market economies tended to offer relatively large shares of their money to their partners, and these partners tended to reject low offers, even though this penalized both players. They played this way because they shared a culturally based understanding of the market. For an impersonal market to run smoothly, most participants must believe that they will usually be treated fairly by people they do not know. People who take advantage of anonymity to enrich themselves at others' expense spoil the market and must be punished. Thus, ultimatum players from market economies are often willing to reject low offers, taking a loss to show the other player that anonymous partners must bargain and exchange fairly.

© Getty Images

Of course, the ideal of fair and impersonal exchange is just that—an ideal. Real markets are full of conflicts, inequities, and outright cheats. In our own society, there are clearly areas of commerce where people anticipate a certain amount of deceit. For example, merchants of used goods, particularly cars and machinery, often have reputations for shady practice. The continued importance of social connections among market participants is well illustrated by electronic marketplaces such as eBay, where buyers and sellers come close to true anonymity. In these cases, a sophisticated system of ratings simulates social connections and knowledge. This gives trading partners a degree of certainty that the terms of trade will be fair. But, eBay participants know that the fewer and worse the ratings of their trading partners, the greater the risk of a hostile exchange. The phrase *caveat emptor* (let the buyer beware) neatly captures the notion that the rules of even trade are not always in force.

In principle, the primary factors that set prices and wages in a market are related to supply and demand, and individuals participate freely in a market, choosing what they buy and sell. However, the market is almost never truly free. Most markets occur in social and cultural contexts that limit or forbid certain kinds of transactions. As we have seen, people in many societies gain access to land, labor, and some goods through ties of kinship or obligations of reciprocity and redistribution. In such places, markets, if they exist at all, are limited to a small number of goods. In our own society, although much is available on the market, governments limit trade in certain goods for moral, social, and political reasons. For example, there are restrictions on the sale of drugs, guns, children, and college degrees. Many other factors interfere with the market in almost all societies. In some cases, wealthy and powerful individuals, organizations, and industries fix prices or wages, forcing people into wage labor or the market at disadvantageous terms. In other cases, monopolies, secret knowledge, private deals, and hidden connections may distort the market. In yet other cases, cultural ideas about the proper or "just" price of a good or service are more important than supply and demand. Sometimes, governments control or influence the prices of commodities such as grain, setting them either high (to encourage farmers) or low (to feed often rebellious city dwellers cheaply).

Capitalism

In the past 300 years, capitalism has become the world's predominant economic system. Capitalism expanded from northern Europe, North America, and Japan and has transformed economies worldwide, connecting them in a complex integrated international economy (Wallerstein 1995). We describe this historic process in Chapter 12, and we examine and analyze the problems and promises of the global economy in Chapter 13. Here we focus on describing capitalism and pointing out some of its most salient features.

In noncapitalist societies, most people produce goods to consume them, to trade them for other goods, or to pay rents and taxes. In capitalist societies, a **firm** produces goods as a means to create wealth. For example, General Motors is not really in business to make cars. General Motors is in business to increase the wealth of its shareholders. Manufacturing automobiles is one (but only one) of the ways it achieves that end. GM is also heavily involved in banking and was historically involved in aviation, military contracting, and the production of consumer products such as refrigerators.

Productive resources become **capital** when they are used with the primary goal of increasing their owner's financial wealth. In capitalism, this becomes the most common (but not the only) use of such resources. **Capitalism** is further characterized by three fundamental attributes. First, most productive resources are owned by a small portion of the population. Banks, corporations, and wealthy individuals own the vast majority of farms, factories, and business of all kinds. Although many Americans invest in business through ownership of stocks, mutual funds, and retirement plans, ownership of substantial wealth is highly concentrated. For example, in the United States in 2002, almost half of all households owned some stocks or mutual funds (and thus owned some share of a business). However, the median value of these investments was $65,000. Fewer than 4 percent of American households had stocks and mutual funds valued

firm An institution composed of kin and/or nonkin that is organized primarily for financial gain.

capital Productive resources that are used with the primary goal of increasing their owner's financial wealth.

capitalism An economic system in which people work for wages, land and capital goods are privately owned, and capital is invested for profit.

at more than a half million dollars (Investment Company Institute 2005). Thus, although a great many people held some ownership of business, the vast majority was held by a comparatively few.

The second attribute of capitalism is that most individuals' primary resource is their labor. To survive, people sell their labor for a salary or an hourly wage.

The third attribute is that the value of workers' contribution to production is always intended to be greater than the wages they receive. The difference between these two is the profit that accrues to those who own the productive resources, generally the shareholders of a corporation (Plattner 1989:382–384). The extremely high wages of some professional athletes and entertainers provide a good illustration of this principle. For example, Los Angeles Lakers player Kobe Bryant earned $23 million in the 2009–2010 season. For the team owners, his high salary was easily justified. They believed that his presence would enable them to earn substantially more than they paid him. This proved a good guess. With Bryant, the team won 92 percent more games than the average NBA team per dollar spent on player salary. Team owners Jerry Buss and Philip Anschutz saw the value of their investment rise from $288 million to over $600 million (Forbes 2009a). Because a good deal of this appreciation was due to Byrant's skill and popularity, the value of his labor was substantially greater than the wages he received. Because of his success, Bryant has been able to supplement his Lakers income with another $25 million in product endorsements (Forbes 2010). Although Bryant is undoubtedly very rich, his wealth pales before that of team owners Buss and Anschutz whose combined wealth is well over $7 billion (most belonging to Anschutz, America's 37th richest person) (Forbes 2009b).

In general, workers wish to receive as close to the full value of their labor as possible, whereas owners wish to pay as small a portion of labor's value as possible. This frequently results in conflict between the two groups.

Modern capitalist economies are dominated by market exchange, but this does not mean that people always experience their economy in terms of buying and selling at whatever price the market will bear. Capitalism always occurs within the context of other social relationships, and sometimes these provide a mask behind which it can hide. In other words, capitalist relationships are sometimes camouflaged by family ties or social obligations. When this happens, entrepreneurs may be able to extract extra profits. The production of knitted sweaters in Turkey is a good example of this.

Turkey produces many goods and services used in wealthy capitalist nations. Most of the inhabitants of Istanbul, its largest city, are part of a capitalist economy selling their labor in enterprises aimed at generating a profit. However, as Jenny B. White (1994) reports, many of them, particularly women, understand their work in terms of reciprocity and kin obligations rather than capitalism and the marketplace.

Turkey is a patrilineal and patriarchal society. Turkish women live in complex social networks characterized by social obligations and relations of reciprocity. To a great degree, they measure their worth by the work they do for family members, including parents, in-laws, husbands, and children. Being a good woman means laboring for relatives.

Married women live with their husband's family and are expected to manage the household and to keep their hands busy with knitting and other skilled tasks. Such tasks are not considered work (in the sense of work outside of the home) but are rather understood as necessary obligations of married life.

Business in Turkey is often patterned on social life, and this can be seen clearly in women's piecework. Women produce garments that are sold in the United States and other Western nations. The materials they use are generally supplied to them by an organizer, who also finds a buyer for the finished product. The organizers often are relatives, neighbors, and friends of the women who do the work.

In the neighborhood White (1994:13) investigated, almost everyone believed that women should not work for money, yet about two-thirds of women are involved in piecework. How is this contradiction explained? The women who do it see piecework as a way for them to keep their hands busy and thus part of their duty as wives rather than a form of paid labor. Their work forms part of their obligation to their husband's family and to organizers with whom they have social connections, and they consider it a gift of labor. They understand the payments they receive as gifts from someone with whom they have an established social relationship.

Because the women's work is set within a context of global capitalism, work organizers may be friends and neighbors, but they are also capitalist entrepreneurs hoping to make money. In the end, women produce goods for the capitalist marketplace, and their wages ultimately derive from that market. However, these capitalist relationships are masked by social relations of balanced or generalized reciprocity with the labor organizer. Because they understand their work in terms of a social obligation, they rarely think about how much they are earning per hour or how they might use their time and talents to make more money. Thus, they are willing to accept far lower wages than might otherwise be the case.

In some ways, the system serves the women well. They are able to fill their roles as wives and in-laws, and their social connections with labor organizers may give them some degree of security from the ravages of the marketplace. This is important in a country such as Turkey, where most people have little money and social services are few. However, it is clear that the greatest beneficiaries of this system are firms and consumers in wealthy nations. The fact that reciprocity masks capitalism for poor women in Turkey allows rich consumers in Europe and America to buy

Turkey.

hand-knitted sweaters at very low prices and the firms based in these nations to make windfall profits.

It would be difficult to find any people in the world today not affected by capitalist markets. For the most part, members of traditional societies enter the market as low-wage laborers. The wealth they produce accrues to elites within poor nations as well as to owners and consumers in wealthy nations (Wolf 1982). The case of the Turkish women illustrates some of the ways in which this process takes place. Not all societies are able to make such accommodations, however, and the expansion of capitalism and political power has been accompanied by the wide-scale destruction of traditional societies. Chapter 12 examines this process in some detail.

Resistance to Capitalism

Capitalism is a powerful economic system. It undoubtedly provides a greater number of goods and services to larger populations than do other ways of organizing an economy, but at a cost. When some individuals or groups own or control basic resources, others must inevitably be denied access to them. This results in permanently differentiated economic and social classes. Capitalism dictates that there will always be rich and poor. Often, part of the population lives in extreme poverty, without access to basic resources. In American society, this includes the homeless, the landless rural poor, and the permanently unemployed.

Although there are probably some individuals who act as capitalists in most monetized economies, societies organized primarily by capitalism

Garage sales, gardening, raising livestock, and doing odd jobs help many Americans avoid full participation in the capitalist economy.

© Catherine Li, 2008

are a late development in the history of humankind. Such societies were not a natural and inevitable outcome of economic evolution. Rather, they owe their origin to the specific conditions of the Industrial Revolution in Europe in the 18th and 19th centuries and have become increasingly prevalent in the world in the past 150 years.

Although the capitalist economy has expanded in every part of the world, there probably are no countries where all of the population is directly involved in it. Noncapitalist groups remain in many areas, although they are often pushed to geographically marginal areas, such as the border between Pakistan and Afghanistan or the jungles of Brazil. In other places, issues of race, gender, and ethnicity prevent people from fully participating in the capitalist economy. However, mass-produced goods, media, and fashions from capitalist societies are easily found, even in these locations.

Individuals join the capitalist economy by selling their labor for wages. Alternatively, they might own productive resources and operate them with hired labor, reinvesting any profits to increase the value and size of their operation. Although most Americans probably think of themselves as being in favor of capitalism, many do not wish to actively engage in it.

Consider the inhabitants of Putnam County, New York (Hansen 1995). Located about 50 miles north of New York City, Putnam County has been poor since the time of the American Revolution. Even in the preindustrial era, its farms were unable to compete successfully with surrounding areas. Today, its people follow two fundamentally different strategies for survival and belong to two different but related economic systems.

Many of Putnam County's inhabitants are new residents who commute to jobs in New York City. They work for union-scale wages as police officers, firefighters, and schoolteachers, using their wages to buy houses, food, and so on. They are deeply in debt to mortgage and credit card companies but believe that higher future earnings will permit them to accommodate this financial burden. They are committed to economic and social advancement, and many hope eventually to move to more prosperous suburbs closer to the city. Members of this group are deeply committed to capitalism. They own few productive resources, sell their labor for wages, and conduct the economic aspect of their lives almost entirely through the capitalist market.

Putnam County's other residents have lived there for generations. Members of this group very rarely have full-time wage employment. They almost never visit New York City, which to them has become "a metaphor for all the world's evils" (Hansen 1995:146). Instead they follow what Halperin (1990) called a *multiple-livelihood strategy*. They acquire their land through inheritance and generally own it outright. Their lands include both forest and gardens that provide almost all of the vegetables they consume. While women work in the gardens, men hunt year-round, taking deer, rabbits, guinea fowl, and pheasants. They fish in ponds and streams and chop wood for fuel. In addition to these subsistence activities, members of this group do carpentry, electrical repair, masonry, plumbing, and other jobs. They barter these skills among themselves and sell them for cash to the commuters. They may work temporarily for wages at construction jobs. Although Putnam County's traditional residents do depend on markets for goods they cannot produce themselves or get through barter, only a small part of their total subsistence comes from the market.

Through such strategies, these residents avoid participation in the capitalist economy. Their financial goals are not to make money or to move to a higher level of consumption. They are concerned with stability rather than mobility, and they wish to live as independently as possible. Although they own productive resources such as land and equipment, these do not become capital because they are used to increase the security of their self-sufficiency rather than to accumulate wealth.

The self-sufficient residents of Putnam County remind us that culture counts. For most of us, capitalism seems both natural and inevitable, the way that society must be organized to make sense. However, the ways in which we organize our economy are the result of history, politics, economics, and individual choices—a creation of culture, not natural law.

BRINGING IT BACK HOME:
PRODUCT ANTHROPOLOGY

In *Creating Breakthrough Products*, Jonathan Cagan and Craig M. Vogel (2002) write that the most promising area of research is "new product ethnography." They argue that anthropologists can offer vital services to business, turning the techniques and theoretical perspectives of anthropology into a resource for the corporate world. Those who promote it argue that anthropologists can and should provide vital information that helps corporations design and market products in ways that maximize their profits.

One of the most successful examples of new product ethnography was the creation of Yoplait's Go-Gurt. In focus groups, mothers reported that they always wanted to provide complex, healthy breakfasts for their children. However, ethnographic fieldwork by anthropologist Susan Squires (Squires and Byrne 2002) showed that working parents, complicated schedules, and different notions about what constitutes a "good" breakfast meant that mothers had difficulties producing breakfasts and kids frequently did not eat them. The solution, Go-Gurt, was portable, sweet, brightly colored, and made claims to be nutritious.

In many ways, product anthropology and other uses of anthropology in business and government are promising breakthroughs. Since the founding days of the discipline, anthropologists have wanted their voices heard by people outside the university. Now they are increasingly employed in different capacities in consumer research, product design, and marketing. On the one hand, this results in a better fit between products and consumers as well as higher profits for corporations. From the PT Cruiser (partially designed by French anthropologist G. Clotaire Rapaille) to computer software, toothbrushes, cookware, and ethnobanking (developing banking services for ethnic target groups), anthropologists have made products more friendly and businesses more money. As companies create products for markets around the globe, anthropologists have valuable contributions to make to design, production, and marketing. On the other hand, the involvement of anthropologists in these fields raises difficult ethical problems. For example, anthropologists mine information from their informants. If corporations then profit from this information, is payment owed to the informants? Historically, the introduction of mass-produced products has destabilized craft production and destabilized local economies. Should anthropologists sell their services to corporations to promote this process? Should anthropology be a way to help corporations make more money?

▮▮▮ YOU DECIDE

1. Historically, the introduction of cheap, mass-produced manufactured goods has undercut existing economies and drawn people into the capitalist economy, generally as consumers of low-quality merchandise and low-paid wage earners. Given this, should anthropologists be involved in the design and marketing of products to groups about which they have expertise?

2. The advance of capitalism into all areas of the world has been relentless. With the aid of anthropologists, corporations can produce products that meet local needs and are marketed in culturally appropriate ways. The alternative often is inappropriate, poorly designed and poorly marketed products. Given this, can anthropologists justifiably refuse to work with corporations?

3. Perhaps the previous two questions present a false dichotomy. What are some positions that anthropologists might take between these two? Are they practicable in the real world without the security of a university appointment?

▌▌▌ CHAPTER SUMMARY

1. Experiments in which the ultimatum and dictator games have been played in many cultures show that people's economic behavior differs from culture to culture. Some of this variation is systematic. People from market-oriented societies tend to play differently than those from societies with other forms of economic organization.

2. Economics is the study of the ways in which the choices people make combine to determine how their societies use their scarce resources to produce and distribute goods and services. People, and hence societies, make such choices differently because they value and are motivated by different goods and different principles.

3. In every society, certain goods are productive resources. Such resources generally include land, labor, and knowledge. Societies have systems by which such resources are allocated to their members. As social complexity increases, access to productive resources becomes increasingly more restricted.

4. Labor must be organized in specific ways to produce goods. In most preindustrial and peasant economies, labor is organized by the household or kin group. Work that people both perform and receive locates them with respect in their social network and often is integral to their identity.

5. As societies become more populous, the number of specialized jobs found in them increases. Current-day wealthy societies have extremely high degrees of specialization. This creates great efficiency but involves changing notions of identity and often has heavy human costs.

6. In all societies, there are systems for distributing and consuming goods and services. Every society uses some combination of reciprocity, redistribution, and the market to redistribute goods and services and to provide patterns and standards for their consumption.

7. Exchange among people of similar status is characterized by reciprocity. As social distance among individuals increases, the characteristic form of reciprocity tends to change from generalized, to balanced, and, sometimes, to negative. The kula trade in the South Pacific provides an example of balanced reciprocity.

8. Redistribution is characteristic of exchange in chiefdoms as well as parts of state-level economy. Goods are collected by a central individual or office and then distributed. Potlatch among Pacific Northwest coastal Native Americans provides an example of redistribution.

9. In market exchange, goods and services are bought and sold at a money price determined, at least in theory, by the impersonal forces of supply and demand.

10. In capitalism, the owners of productive resources use them to increase their financial wealth. In capitalist societies, productive resources are held primarily by a small percentage of the population, most people sell their labor for wages, and the value of people's labor is always more than the wages they receive. Capitalism can be masked by other relationships such as reciprocity.

11. Although capitalism is ubiquitous around the world, many people resist it, avoiding wage labor and, to some degree, participation in the market. Some residents of Putnam County, New York, provide an example.

▌ KEY TERMS

Balanced reciprocity
Capital
Capitalism
Cargo system
Division of labor
Economic system
Economics
Firm
Generalized reciprocity
Household

Kula ring
Leveling mechanism
Market exchange
Negative reciprocity
Potlatch
Prestige
Productive resources
Reciprocity
Redistribution

In almost all societies, marriage is a central structure in the formation of families and the linkages between wider relations. This photo of India shows a marriage ritual that contains many symbolic elements, such as the color red, which symbolizes fertility.

Chander Dembla

CHAPTER 7

MARRIAGE, FAMILY, AND KINSHIP

A SOCIETY WITHOUT MARRIAGE: THE NA OF CHINA

"OVE and marriage . . . go together like a horse and carriage." But perhaps not in all cultures (Blumenfield 2004:15, Hua Cai 2001, Harrell 2001, Shih 2001, Walsh 2004). Among the Na and some other societies of southwest China, the culturally normative institution that joins men and women in sexual and reproductive partnerships is called *sese*. Except historically, among the elites, the Na do not practice marriage, and do not even have a word for it. In the sese relationship, a man passes a night in a lover's household and returns to his own family in the morning. All sexual (and potentially reproductive) activity takes place during this concealed visit of a Na male to the house of a woman who has agreed beforehand to lie with him. As lovers, their relationship involves affection, respect, and intimacy, but does not include notions of fidelity, permanence, or paternal responsibility for children. There is no coercion in the sese relationship: Either party may offer, accept, or decline an invitation for a visit. To spare the other's feelings, one may say: "Tonight is not possible. I already have one for tonight," and a woman may even turn away an invited lover at the door if she chooses. But although either the woman or the man may initiate the visit, it is always the man who comes secretly to the woman's household. Concealment is necessary because of a Na taboo forbidding a household's male members from hearing or seeing any sexual talk or activities involving household females. Males will never answer the door after dark lest they encounter a woman's lover, and the lover himself makes every effort to avoid detection, often bringing food to prevent the guard dog's barking, speaking only in whispers during intercourse, and leaving quietly before daybreak.

The matrilineal family, which centers on a core of women, and includes brothers and sons, but not husbands and fathers, is the most important kinship group among the Na and allied ethnic groups in China.

© Sara Gouveia/photographersdirect.com

Both women and men have multiple partners, serially or simultaneously, and no records are kept of visits to ascertain the paternity of children. The Na do not have a word for incest, illegitimate child, infidelity, or promiscuity. The Na are matrilineal, and children by a variety of fathers stay with the mother's household for their entire lives. When a generation lacks females, a household may adopt a relative's child or encourage a son to bring his lover into the household. Where males are in short supply in a family, a woman may bring her lover home. The only males in a Na household are relatives of different generations, who are brothers, uncles, and granduncles. There are no husbands or fathers.

The Na visit, which has been part of Na culture for more than a thousand years, is treated as a mutually enjoyable but singular occurrence that entails no future conditions. The Chinese state has periodically tried to change what they call a "barbarous practice," but without success so far. As the Na adapt to the new conditions of the nation-state and the globalizing economy, however, they are increasingly subjected to state-sponsored public school education and media, which reflect mainstream Han mores and lifestyles and stigmatize Na practices. This, as well as their inability to name a father on official documents, may spell the end of Na visits, eliminating yet one more example of the rich diversity of human adaptive strategies.

Location of the Na.

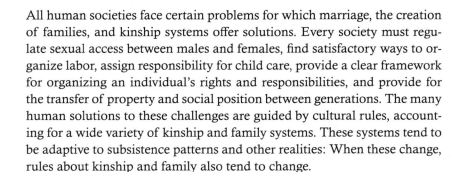

All human societies face certain problems for which marriage, the creation of families, and kinship systems offer solutions. Every society must regulate sexual access between males and females, find satisfactory ways to organize labor, assign responsibility for child care, provide a clear framework for organizing an individual's rights and responsibilities, and provide for the transfer of property and social position between generations. The many human solutions to these challenges are guided by cultural rules, accounting for a wide variety of kinship and family systems. These systems tend to be adaptive to subsistence patterns and other realities: When these change, rules about kinship and family also tend to change.

FORMS AND FUNCTIONS OF MARRIAGE

The need to regulate sexual access stems from the potentially continuous receptivity of human males and females to sexual activity. If sexual competition was not regulated and channeled into stable relationships that were given social approval, it could cause societal conflict. These relationships

marriage The customs, rules, and obligations that establish a socially endorsed relationship between adults and children, and between the kin groups of the married partners.

need not be permanent, though they are relatively stable in most (but not all) societies. We refer to these relationships as marriage. **Marriage**, which refers to the customs, rules, and obligations that establish a socially endorsed relationship between adults and children, and between the married couple's kin groups, is a very widespread social institution. However, it is not universal, as the Na illustrate. But in the absence of safe and dependable contraception throughout most of human history and with the near certainty that children would be born, marriage, as a relatively stable union between a male and female that involves responsibility for children as well as economic exchange, became the basis for most human adaptations.

In addition to forming bonds between a couple, marriage extends social alliances by linking together different families and kin groups, leading to cooperation among groups of people larger than the married couple. This expansion of the social group within which people can work together and share resources is of great advantage for the survival of the human species.

Although marriage and the subsequent formation of families in most societies rest on the biological complementarity of males and females in reproduction, both marriage and family are cultural patterns. Thus, they differ in form and function both among and within human societies and change over time with changing political and economic circumstances and the life stages of individuals.

Heterosexual, monogamous marriage, dominant in the United States, is only one of many culturally acceptable kinds of marriages. Marriages involving plural spouses or same-sex relationships also fulfill the functions of marriage in satisfactory ways. Because of this cultural variation, it is difficult to find any *one* definition of marriage that will fit all cultural situations.

Among some African societies, for example, in addition to marriage between a man and a woman, there are also woman–woman marriages. These allow a barren woman to divorce her husband, take another woman as her wife, and arrange for a surrogate to impregnate this woman. Children born from this arrangement, which does not involve sexual relations between the wives, become members of the barren woman's natal lineage and refer to her as their father (Kilbride 2004:17).

Like marriage, the concept of the family also varies among cultures. In many societies, the most important family bond is between lineal blood relations (father and children or mother and children) or between brothers and sisters rather than between husband and wife. In these societies, the lineage or the clan (see p. 168) rather than the immediate family confers legitimacy on children. Even in the United States, the definition of the family as a unit ideally defined by heterosexual marriage and the couple's biological children is changing to accommodate the new realities of a high divorce rate, same-sex commitments and domestic partnerships, the increasing number of working mothers and single-parent households, the growing number of unmarried couples living together in long-term relationships, surrogate reproduction, the growing number of childless couples, the greater number of people who never marry, and the increasing number of people who remarry after divorce or widowhood.

MARRIAGE RULES

Every society has culturally defined rules concerning sexual relations and marriage. These rules may limit marriage to certain groups, dictate the number of spouses, allow for dissolving marriages, determine rules for remarriage, specify the kinds of exchanges and rituals that legitimate marriage, and determine the rights and obligations established by marriage. Among the most universal of these rules is the incest taboo.

Incest Taboos

An **incest taboo** categorically prohibits certain kin from having sex with each other. The most widespread taboo is on mating between mother and son, father and daughter, and sister and brother. The taboos on mating between kin (or people classified as kin) always extend beyond the immediate family, however. Because marriage implies the right of sexual access, incest taboos effectively prohibit marriage as well as mating among certain kin; again, this varies among cultures.

incest taboo A prohibition on sexual relations between relatives.

Anthropologists continue to debate the origins, universality, and persistence of the incest taboo, particularly as it applies to primary (or nuclear) family relationships. The origins of the taboo, its functions in contemporary societies, and the motives of individuals in respecting or violating the taboo may all have different explanations.

One popular theory is that incest taboos arose because, as contemporary population genetics demonstrates, mating between close kin is genetically harmful to human populations. However, the sophisticated statistical techniques necessary to measure the negative influence of inbreeding were unavailable to most human cultures. It is thus unlikely that preindustrial and early industrial peoples, who have high infant mortality rates, would have discovered and understood the connection between close inbreeding and biological disadvantage.

Preventing Family Disruption

Bronislaw Malinowski and Sigmund Freud held that the desire for sexual relations within the family is very strong. Thus, they viewed the most important function of the incest taboo as preventing disruption within the nuclear family by directing sexual desires outside it. Malinowski argued that as children grow into adolescence, their natural attempts to satisfy their developing sexual urges within their families would increase the potential for family conflict and the disruption of role relationships, as fathers and sons, and mothers and daughters, competed for sexual partners.

Whereas unregulated sexual competition within the family undoubtedly would be disruptive, however, regulation of sexual competition among family members could be an alternative to the incest taboo. Furthermore, whereas Malinowski's theory suggests why the incest taboo exists between parents and children, it does not explain the prohibition of sexual relations between brothers and sisters.

Forming Wider Alliances

The alliance theory of the incest taboo (Lévi-Strauss 1969/1949) stresses the adaptive value of cooperation among groups larger than the nuclear family. The taboo on sex within the immediate family forces people to marry outside its members. This leads families to join others in a larger social community, a clearly adaptive cultural pattern. Alliance theory can also account for the extension of the incest taboo to groups other than the nuclear family, as occurs in many societies.

Thus, the incest taboo within families seems to be an effective means of promoting genetic variability, family harmony, and community cooperation. These advantages help explain the spread and persistence of the taboo, if not its origins (Aberle et al. 1963).

Exogamy

exogamy A rule specifying that a person must marry outside a particular group.

Exogamy and endogamy are marriage rules that define the acceptable range of marriage partners. **Exogamy** specifies that a person must marry outside particular groups. The incest taboo is a rule of exogamy regarding the nuclear family, but rules of exogamy also extend to wider kinship groups.

Exogamy functions much like the incest taboo. It reduces conflicts over sex within the cooperating group and forges useful alliances between groups larger than the primary family. These rights and obligations between groups linked by marriage are fundamental in most societies. The Arapesh, a horticultural society in New Guinea, clearly express the importance of exchanging women among different groups. For them, not exchanging women between families would be as unthinkable as not sharing food. When anthropologist Margaret Mead (1963/1935:92) asked an Arapesh man about marrying his own sister, he responded, "What, you would like to marry your sister? What is the matter with you? Don't you want a brother-in-law? Don't you realize that if you marry another man's sister and another man marries your sister, you will have at least two brothers-in-law, while if you marry your own sister you will have none? With whom will you hunt, with whom will you garden, with whom will you visit?"

Endogamy

Endogamy rules require people to marry within their own group, however that group is defined. To keep privileges and wealth of a group intact, blood relations may be encouraged or required to marry each other. Among royalty in ancient Egypt, Peru, and Hawai'i, for example, brother–sister marriage was encouraged as a way of limiting rivalries for the throne. In India, castes and subcastes are endogamous; in the United States, although there are no named endogamous groups, so-called racial groups and social classes tend to be endogamous, based on opportunities to meet, cultural norms, and similarities in lifestyle. Endogamy is also an important rule for some religious groups in the United States, such as the Amish.

endogamy A rule prescribing that a person must marry within a particular group.

Preferential Marriages

In some societies, marriage rules involve a preference for cousins to marry each other. In **cross-cousin marriage**, the preferred partners are the children of one's parents' siblings of the opposite sex—mother's brother or father's sister. Preferred cross-cousin marriage reinforces ties between kin groups established in the preceding generation, preserving the relationship between two intermarrying kin groups across generations. **Parallel-cousin marriage** involves children of the parents' same-sex siblings—mother's sister or father's brother—and is found in some Arab and North African Muslim societies. Because descent and inheritance are in the male line in Muslim Arab societies, parallel-cousin marriage helps prevent the fragmentation of family property and keeps economic resources within the family. Parallel-cousin marriage also reinforces the solidarity of brothers, but by socially isolating groups of brothers from one another, it adds to factional disputes and disunity within the larger social system (see Figure 7.1).

cross-cousin marriage Marriage between the children of a parent's siblings of the opposite sex (mother's brothers, father's sisters).

parallel-cousin marriage Marriage between the children of a parent's same-sex siblings (mother's sisters, father's brothers).

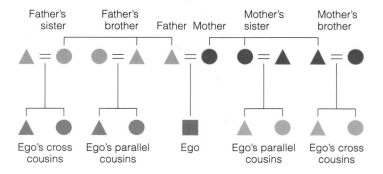

| Father's sister | Father's brother | Father | Mother | Mother's sister | Mother's brother |

Ego's cross cousins   Ego's parallel cousins   Ego   Ego's parallel cousins   Ego's cross cousins

Figure 7.1

This diagram indicates the relationships of cross-cousins and parallel cousins. In many cultures, these relationships determine rules of exogamy and endogamy and preferences for marriage partners.

Because cross-cousin and parallel-cousin marriage distinguish between kin who are equally biologically close, preferred cousin marriage rules demonstrate the important point that kinship rules are rooted in biological relationships but are based on culture. Each system of marriage and family formation has elements that contribute to solidarity and stability at one level of society but may be socially disruptive at another level.

The **levirate** and the **sororate** are two types of marriage rules that demonstrate the importance of marriage as an alliance between two groups rather than between individuals. These rules allow a marriage to survive the death of one of the partners with the continuance of group alliances and fulfillment of the marriage contract.

Under the levirate, a man marries the widow of his dead brother, and in some cases, the children born to this union are considered children of the deceased man. Thus, the levirate enables the children to remain within the dead husband's descent group and it keeps them from being separated from their mother. In the sororate, when a woman dies, her kin group supplies a sister as a wife for the widower. The sororate also means that the husband of a barren woman can marry her sister, and at least some of the children of this marriage are considered those of the first wife. If no qualifying relative is available to fulfill the levirate or the sororate, other appropriately classified kin may be substituted, or the levirate or sororate may not take place.

Number of Spouses

All societies have rules about how many spouses a person may have at one time. **Monogamy**, which permits only one man to be married to one woman at any given time, is the rule in Europe and North America, but not in most of the world's cultures. **Polygamy**, or plural marriage, includes **polygyny**, the marriage of one man to several women, and **polyandry**, the marriage of one woman to several men. About 75 percent of the world's cultures permit (and prefer) polygyny (Murdock 1949:28), but even in these cultures, the male/female ratio and the requirements of a bride price, which many men cannot afford, inhibit its actual occurrence.

Polygyny

Polygyny has important economic and political functions in some societies. Where women are economically important, polygyny increases a man's wealth and therefore his social position. Because marriage links groups together, having several wives from different groups within a society extends a man's alliances. Thus, chiefs, headmen, and state leaders may take wives from many different groups or villages to increase their political power.

levirate The custom whereby a man marries the widow of a deceased brother.

sororate The custom whereby, when a man's wife dies, her sister is given to him as a wife.

monogamy A rule that permits a person to be married to only one spouse at a time.

polygamy A rule allowing more than one spouse at a time.

polygyny A rule permitting a man to have more than one wife at a time.

polyandry A rule permitting a woman to have more than one husband at a time.

Polygyny is found primarily in societies where plural wives—and their children—increase both a family's labor supply and its productivity. For example, among the Tiwi of Australia, a foraging group, women's food collecting makes a very important contribution to the food supply. Thus, the more wives a man has, the better his family's standard of living (Goodale 1971).

Although Western cultural stereotypes criticize polygyny as oppressing women, the status of females in polygynous societies is not uniformly low and may even, as among the Tiwi, be relatively high and accord women a high degree of sexual and economic freedom (Goodale 1971). Where women's work is hard and monotonous, as it often is, women may welcome the addition of a co-wife because it eases their own workload and provides daily companionship. Conflict among co-wives does occur in polygynous societies and sometimes is mitigated by a preference for a man to marry sisters. In many polygynous societies, co-wives live in separate dwellings. Cultural norms requiring a man to distribute his economic resources and sexual attentions evenly among his wives as well as for each wife also mitigate family conflict. Like all other cultural patterns, polygyny changes with changing economic and social circumstances. In spite of the favorable view of polygyny in many African societies, changing economic conditions, such as a declining amount of available agricultural land, increasing expenses in educating children, and the social pressures of Western and Christian condemnation of polygyny, have to some extent changed its frequency or driven it underground (Kilbride 2006).

Polyandry

Polyandry is relatively rare, found mainly in Tibet, Nepal, and some indigenous groups, like the Toda, in India. Most polyandry is fraternal: Brothers marry a single wife. In Tibet, as in other polyandrous societies, polyandry is related to a shortage of land. If brothers marry a single wife, their father's land can be kept intact within the family rather than fragmented over the generations. Polyandry may be an adaptation to a shortage of females, created by female infanticide. It is functional in societies where men are away from home for long periods of time, in that a woman has more than one husband to provide for her.

Choosing a Mate

In most societies, kin group interests, rather than individual desires, are the basis of mate selection, and the families of the bride and groom take an important, even determinative, role in selecting their children's spouses. This practice of **arranged marriage** strongly contrasts with marriage in the United States, where individuals ideally select their own mates on the

arranged marriage The process by which senior family members exercise a great degree of control over the choice of their children's spouses.

Among the Wodaabe of Niger, marriages are both arranged and based on romantic attachment. At the annual Gerewol celebration, young men apply makeup, dance, and make facial expressions that best display their charms in order to capture the hearts of young women.

© Judith Pearson

basis of sexual compatibility, emotional needs, physical attractiveness, and personality, a cluster of patterns called "romantic love."

In most societies, the economic potential of the groom is of great importance; for brides, reproductive potential, health, and physical attractiveness are important criteria. In addition, each culture has its own special qualities that it emphasizes in a bride or groom. In India, where a woman is ideally expected to live with her husband's joint family, she must be—or at least act—submissive and modest, repressing behavior suggesting assertiveness or an independent nature (Nanda 2000a; Nanda and Gregg 2009). Although the "Matrimonial" section of any Indian newspaper in America today indicates that globalization and westernization have expanded the personal criteria for a "good match" to include a preference for a professional woman, and some advertisements indicate that caste affiliation is not important, the traditional expectations for arranging an Indian marriage continue to apply.

THE EXCHANGE OF GOODS AND RIGHTS IN MARRIAGE

Because the sanctity of marriage results from its public acknowledgment, marriage involves public rituals and ceremony, almost everywhere. The presence of guests at these ceremonies bears witness to the lawfulness of the transaction and distinguishes marriage from other kinds of unions that resemble it. Marriage involves the transfer of certain rights and obligations, primarily involving sexual access of the partners to each other, rights over any children born to the marriage, obligations by one or both parents to care for children born to the union, and rights of the marriage partners to the economic services of the other.

In almost all societies, marriage also gives the families or kin groups of the bride and groom certain rights to goods or services from each other. These may be voluntary "gifts," given perhaps as a way of winning the goodwill of those with the power to transfer marital rights, but in many cultures, such exchanges are a required part of the transfer of marital rights. Thus, even when called "gifts," if these exchanges are not completed, the rights in marriage can be forfeited.

Bride Service and Bridewealth

Bride service, bridewealth, and dowry are three kinds of exchanges in marriage. In **bride service**, most commonly found in foraging societies where few material goods are accumulated, the husband must work for a specified number of years for his wife's family in exchange for his marital rights (Marlowe 2004). Among the Ju/'hoansi of the Kalahari Desert in Africa, this may be as long as 15 years or until the birth of the third child.

The most common form of marriage exchange is **bridewealth**, where cash or goods are given by the groom's kin to the bride's kin to seal the marriage. Bridewealth previously was called *bride price,* but this falsely conveys the idea that the marriage is merely an economic exchange (Ogbu 1978) and that women's status in such societies is devalued. In fact, in these societies, daughters are valuable to their families because their bridewealth finances males' marriages.

In societies with customary bridewealth, a person can claim compensation for a violation of conjugal rights only if the bridewealth has been paid. Furthermore, bridewealth paid at marriage is returned (subject to specified conditions) if a marriage is terminated.

Although many studies of bridewealth emphasize its role in entitling the husband to domestic, economic, sexual, and reproductive rights, bridewealth also confers rights on the wife. By publicly validating a marriage, bridewealth allows wives to hold their husbands accountable for violations of conjugal rights. In sanctioning these mutual rights and obligations, bridewealth stabilizes marriage by giving both families a vested interest in keeping the couple together. Nevertheless, divorce does occur in societies with bridewealth.

Although globally widespread, bridewealth transactions are particularly characteristic of Africa. Among the Kipsigis, a pastoralist/horticultural

bride service The cultural rule that a man must work for his bride's family for a variable length of time either before or after the marriage.

bridewealth Goods presented by the groom's kin to the bride's kin to legitimize a marriage (formerly called "bride price").

Bridewealth is the most common form of gift exchange at marriage. Among the Medlpa of New Guinea, the family of the groom gives gifts to the family of the bride to formalize a marriage. The bigman of the groom's family (left) praises the gifts while the bigman of the bride's family denigrates them. Cash and pig grease have replaced pigs and shells as the most important marriage gifts.

Jean Zorn

society of East Africa, the traditional bridewealth payment was livestock, but it now includes cash. First marriages are paid for by the groom's father and subsequent marriages by the groom himself, although grooms working for wages may help with the first payment (Borgerhoff Mulder 1995:576). Formerly, when agricultural land was available and crop prices were high, bridewealth was high because of the importance of women's labor in cultivation. However, bridewealth payments have declined recently because now land is scarce, crop prices are low, and women's agricultural labor has lost value. On the other hand, Kipsigis parents of girls educated beyond elementary school often demand high bridewealth, both as compensation for the high school fees they have spent on their daughters and because their increased earning potential will benefit their marital home.

Dowry

dowry Presentation of goods by the bride's kin to the family of the groom or to the couple.

A **dowry**, which consists of goods given by the bride's family to the groom's family, is associated with private ownership of property. Among the European peasantry the dowry accompanied the bride and belonged to the newly married couple, often constituting the basic household items for their new home. This contrasts with bridewealth, which does not belong to the married couple but rather is distributed through a wider kin network.

Giving a dowry occurs in fewer societies than does the bridewealth exchange. Although it is constitutionally outlawed, dowry is especially important in India, both historically and today. One interpretation of Indian dowry is that it is a voluntary gift, symbolizing affection for a beloved daughter leaving home and compensating her for the fact that she could not traditionally inherit land or property. Dowry also has been interpreted as a source of security for a woman because the jewelry given as part of her dowry is theoretically hers to keep (in practice, her husband's family usually keeps control of it). Another theory holds that dowry is a compensatory payment given by the bride's family to the groom's family as acknowledgment of their taking on an economic burden, because women in India ideally do not work outside the home. In contemporary India, with its new emphasis on consumerism and social class mobility, dowry has increasingly become a payment to the husband and his family that improves their financial and social standing. As such, insufficient dowry can be the basis of emotional blackmail of a woman's family and has been linked to wife abuse and even murder (Stone and James 2005; Nanda and Gregg 2009).

▮▮ FAMILY STRUCTURES, HOUSEHOLDS, AND RULES OF RESIDENCE

Two basic types of families are the elementary, or nuclear, family and the extended family. A **nuclear family** is organized around the **conjugal tie**, that is, the relationship between husband and wife. The **extended family** is based on **consanguineal**, or blood, relations extending over three or more generations.

A household, or domestic group, is not the same as a family. Although most households contain people related by blood or marriage, nonkin may be included; conversely, members of a family may be spread out over several households. Household composition is affected by the cultural rules about residence after marriage. Under **neolocal residence** rules, married couples create their own households. Under **patrilocal residence** rules (sometimes called *virilocality*), the newly married couple lives with the husband's family, whereas under **matrilocal residence** rules (also called *uxorilocal residence*), the couple lives with the wife's family. Two other rules are **avunculocal residence**, in which the couple lives with the husband's mother's brother, and **bilocal residence**, in which a couple can choose between living with the wife's family or the husband's family. Each of these residence rules is associated with different types of kinship systems. For example, avunculocal residence permits the geographical concentration of male lineage mates and the preservation of male-controlled lineage wealth in a matrilineal system.

nuclear family A family organized around the conjugal tie (the relationship between husband and wife) and consisting of a husband, a wife, and their children.

conjugal tie The relationship between a husband and wife formed by marriage.

extended family Family based on blood relations extending over three or more generations.

consanguineal Related by blood.

neolocal residence System under which a couple establishes an independent household after marriage.

patrilocal residence System under which a bride lives with her husband's family after marriage.

matrilocal residence System under which a husband lives with his wife's family after marriage.

avunculocal residence System under which a married couple lives with the husband's mother's brother.

bilocal residence System under which a married couple has the choice of living with the husband's or the wife's family.

Nuclear Families

A nuclear family, consisting of a married couple and their children, is most often associated with neolocal residence. Only 5 percent of the world's societies (which includes the United States) are traditionally neolocal. The nuclear family is adapted to making a living in a capitalist society where jobs do not generally depend on family connections and where employment and promotion often require geographical mobility. Independence and flexibility are also requirements of foraging lifestyles, and more than three-quarters of all foraging groups live in nuclear families.

The Changing American Family

The idealistic picture of the independent nuclear family as typical of the United States must be modified to reflect some new (and some not-so-new) realities. One of these is the high rates of divorce and remarriage that enmesh nuclear families in larger and more complicated kinship networks. Sometimes called blended families, these networks include previously divorced spouses and their new marriage partners, children from previous marriages, and multiple sets of grandparents and other similar relations.

surrogate motherhood A variety of reproductive technologies in which a woman helps a couple to have a child by acting as a biological surrogate, carrying an embryo to term.

© Jonathan Nourak/PhotoEdit

A significant change in the American family over the past 50 years is the increasing number of women who work outside the home. In most families, however, women still are responsible for child care and managing the home.

Although "blended families" do sometimes provide the kind of support provided in two-parent families, the facts are that only one child in six averages a weekly visit with a divorced father, and only one in four sees him once a month. Almost half of the children of divorced parents have not seen their biological fathers for more than a year, and more than two-thirds have lost contact with him ten years later (Hacker 2002a:22). Another change in the American family is the growing number of multigenerational families, which has increased substantially since 1970, caused both by the increase of immigrants who live in such families and an increase in the number of adult children moving back to their parental home because they can't find employment (Roberts 2010).

The availability of new technologies, particularly those involving the possibility of **surrogate motherhood**, which involves the participation of a third party to assist a couple in "having" a child, is also changing the American family. Surrogate motherhood involves the willingness of some women to conceive, gestate, and part with a child. As anthropologist Helena Ragoné illustrates in her ethnography, *Surrogate Motherhood: Conception in the Heart* (1994), surrogacy is both in opposition to and also consistent with American cultural assumptions and ideals about the importance of family, motherhood, fatherhood, and kinship. American laws surround surrogacy with many restrictions, reflecting fears of abuse of this technology for commercial purposes, and it has received much negative representation in the media. In some surrogacy programs, the surrogates and the couples are introduced to each other and interact closely throughout the process, from insemination to delivery; in other programs, the couple sees only the biography and photograph of the surrogate and meets only for finalizing the stepparent adoption and the pro forma court suit for paternity brought after the child is born.

Many anthropologists predicted that the increase in surrogate births would change the pattern of American kinship, but Ragoné found the opposite to be true, illustrating once again the powerful hold of culture. Ragoné found that participants in surrogacy programs universally used reinterpreted traditional American kinship ideology and definitions of motherhood to "re-create" the conventional cultural norms that surround "traditional" American parental roles, reproduction, birth, the importance of the family, and the biogenetic essence of kinship. Because the mother is not biogenetically related to the child, the participants redefined motherhood as consisting of two parts: biological motherhood and social motherhood (a view many cultures hold with regard to fathers).

Part of this redefinition is achieved by de-emphasizing the biological ties of the surrogate to both the father and to the child, though again, in fact, the child is related biologically to the father. Regardless of the mechanics of surrogacy, the couples involved all emphasized the biological relationship of the child to the father, demonstrating the continued importance of the blood tie at the core of traditional Euro-American kinship ideology. The determination of childless couples to pursue surrogacy, in spite of the many difficulties, is also a testimony to the American cultural ideology that a "family is two adults with a child or children" (Ragoné 1994:115), despite the expansion of alternative family structures.

Composite Families

Composite (compound) families are aggregates of nuclear families linked by a common spouse, most often the husband. The typical composite family is a polygynist household, consisting of one man with several wives and their respective children, with each wife and her children normally occupying a separate residence. In composite families, the tie between a mother and her children is particularly strong. The dynamics of the composite family typically involve the interaction of the husband with several wives, interaction between co-wives, and competition among the children of different wives over inheritance and succession.

Extended Families

The extended (consanguineal) family consists of two or more generations of male or female kin and their spouses and offspring, occupying a single household under the authority of a household head. An extended family is not just a collection of nuclear families; in an extended family system, lineal ties—the blood ties between generations (such as father and son)—are more important than the ties of marriage.

Extended families are particularly adaptive among cultivators as they provide more workers than in nuclear families. This is adaptive both in food production and in the production and marketing of handicrafts. In peasant agricultural societies where landownership is important for both prestige and power, the extended family helps keep land intact over generations rather than parceling it out into ever smaller and more unproductive pieces among male descendants. Although the extended family is the ideal in more than half of the world's societies, it is found most often among the landlord and prosperous merchant classes.

A patrilineal extended family is organized around the male line: a man, his sons, and the sons' wives and children. Societies with patrilineal extended families also tend to have patrilocal residence rules. A matrilineal family is organized around the female line: a woman, her daughters, and the daughters' husbands and children. Matrilineal families may have matrilocal residence rules or avunculocal residence rules.

Rules of residence as well as family type are economically adaptive. Thus, patrilocality is functional in hunting and agricultural societies where men must work cooperatively. It also may be adaptive in societies where males cooperate in warfare (Ember and Ember 1971). Where fighting between different groups or villages within a society is common, it is useful for men who will fight together to live together. Otherwise, they might wind up having to choose between defending their wife's local group, the one with whom they live, or the families into which they were born.

KINSHIP SYSTEMS: RELATIONSHIPS THROUGH BLOOD AND MARRIAGE

kinship A culturally defined relationship established on the basis of blood ties or through marriage.

Kinship includes relationships established through blood, described through the idiom of blood, and relationships through marriage. Kinship determines the formation of social groups (like families), is the basis for classification of people in relation to one another, structures individual rights and obligations, and regulates behavior. Because all of these elements of social life are entwined, anthropologists refer to kinship as a system. Although a **kinship system** always rests on some kind of biological relationship, kinship systems are cultural phenomena, as indicated earlier by the differential classification of parallel and cross-cousins. Kinship classification may or may not reflect a scientifically accurate assessment of biological ties.

kinship system The totality of kin relations, kin groups, and terms for classifying kin in a society.

In small-scale, nonindustrial societies, kinship is the most important social bond. It is the basis of group formation, and norms of kinship govern the most important relationships, rights, and responsibilities between individuals and groups. The extension of kinship ties is the main way of linking groups to one another and of incorporating strangers into a group. Even in modern industrialized societies, where citizenship is an important basis of rights and obligations, kinship has many important functions. It is the major context within which wealth is inherited. Kinship is important on many ritual occasions, and there is a strong sentiment that "blood is thicker than water."

Kinship systems have several functions necessary to the continuation of a society: They provide continuity between generations and provide for the orderly transmission of property **(inheritance)** and social position **(succession)** between generations. Kinship systems define a universe of others on whom a person can depend for aid. The adaptiveness of social groups larger than the nuclear family accounts for the fact that expanded kin groups are found in so many human societies.

inheritance The transfer of property between generations.

succession The transfer of office or social position between generations.

Kinship systems grow out of a group's history as well as its relationship to the environment and its subsistence strategies. Once in place, however, kinship systems take on a life of their own, although as economic and historical circumstances change, kinship ideologies may be manipulated and negotiated to fit the new realities.

Rules of Descent and the Formation of Descent Groups

In anthropological terminology, **descent** is a culturally established affiliation with one or both parents. Descent is an important basis of social group formation in many societies. A **descent group** is a group of consanguineal (blood-related) kin who are lineal descendants of a common ancestor extending beyond two generations. In nonindustrial societies, descent groups organize domestic life, enculturate children, determine the use and transfer of property and political and ritual offices, carry out religious ritual, settle disputes, engage in warfare, and structure the use of political power.

descent The culturally established affiliation between a child and one or both parents.

descent group A group of kin who are descendants of a common ancestor, extending beyond two generations.

▓▓ Unilineal Descent

unilineal descent A rule specifying that membership in a descent group is based on links through either the maternal line or the paternal line, but not both.

The rules for establishing descent may be unilineal or bilateral. Under **unilineal descent**, descent group membership is based on links through *either* the paternal line or the maternal line, but not both. Unilineal descent rules are either patrilineal, where a person belongs to the descent group of the father, *or* matrilineal, where a person belongs to the descent group of the mother. One important adaptive advantage of unilineal descent systems is that kin groups do not overlap, thus binding their members more tightly to one another. Also, unilineal descent rules provide a clearly defined group membership for everyone in the society. This allows people to more easily understand their rights of ownership, social duties, and social roles and allows them to relate to a large number of known and unknown people in the society.

corporate descent groups Permanent kinship groups that have an existence beyond the individuals who are members at any given time.

Unilineal descent groups can perpetuate themselves over time, even though their membership changes. Like modern corporations, **corporate descent groups** are permanent units that have an existence beyond the individuals who are members at any given time. Old members die and new ones are admitted through birth, but the integrity of the corporate group persists. Such groups can own property and manage resources, also like modern corporations.

▓▓ Types of Unilineal Descent Groups

lineage A group of kin whose members trace descent from a known common ancestor.

patrilineage A lineage formed by descent in the male line.

matrilineage A lineage formed by descent in the female line.

clan A unilineal kinship group whose members believe themselves to be descended from a common ancestor but who cannot trace this link through known relatives.

A **lineage** is a kin group whose members trace descent from a common ancestor and who can demonstrate those genealogical links among themselves. A **patrilineage** is a lineage formed by descent through the male line; a **matrilineage** is formed by descent through the female line. Lineages may vary in size, from three generations upward. Related lineages may form a **clan**. The common clan ancestor may be a mythological figure; sometimes, no specific ancestor is known or named.

Clans and lineages have different functions in different societies. The lineage often is a local residential or domestic group whose members cooperate on a daily basis. Clans are generally not residential units but tend to spread out over many villages. Therefore, clans often have political and religious functions rather than primarily domestic and economic ones. Clans are important in regulating marriage. In most societies, clans are exogamous, which strengthens their unilineal character. If a person married within the clan, his or her children would find it difficult to make sharp distinctions between maternal and paternal relatives. This person would not know how to act toward others, and others would not know how to act toward him or her. Clan exogamy also extends the network of peaceful social relations within a society as different clans are allied through marriage.

Patrilineal Descent Groups

In societies with **patrilineal descent** groups, both males and females belong to the descent group of the father, the father's father, and so on (see Figure 7.2). Thus, a man, his sisters and brothers, his own children, his brother's children (but not his sister's children), and his son's children (but not his daughter's children) all belong to the same descent group. Inheritance and succession to office move from father to son.

Whereas the status of women varies in patrilineal systems, in general, the husband is guaranteed rights and control over his wife (or wives) and children because the continuity of the descent group depends on this. Patrilineal systems most often have patrilocal rules of residence, so a wife may find herself living among strangers, which tends to undermine female solidarity and support.

The Nuer, an East African pastoral people, are a patrilineal society. All rights, privileges, obligations, and interpersonal relationships are regulated by kinship. A man, his father, his brothers, and their children are considered the closest kin. Patrilineal membership confers rights to land, requires participation in certain religious ceremonies, and determines political and judicial obligations, such as making alliances in feuds and warfare.

Lineage membership may spread over several villages, thus helping to create alliances between members of otherwise independent villages that contain members of several different lineages. Each Nuer clan, which is viewed as composed of related lineages, not individuals, is also spread over several villages. A person cannot marry someone from within his or her own lineage or clan, or from the lineage of the mother, so kinship relations extend widely throughout the tribe. In the absence of a centralized system of political control, these kinship-based alliances are an important mechanism of governance. Because the Nuer believe that close kin should not fight with one another, disputes within the lineage or clan tend to be kept small and settled rapidly (Evans-Pritchard 1968/1940). Those who are not kin are perceived as potential enemies, so an attack by outsiders on one lineage segment may cause all members of a clan to coalesce against a common enemy and their clan brothers (Sahlins 1961). Thus, the coalescence of the whole clan results from closer kin joining together against more distant kin.

Matrilineal Descent Groups

In matrilineal societies, the most important ties are between a woman, her mother, and her siblings. Children

patrilineal descent A rule that affiliates a person to kin of both sexes related through males only.

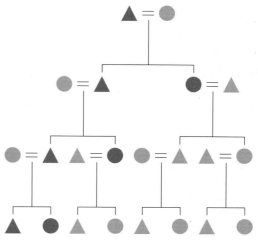

Figure 7.2

Membership in a patrilineal descent group is based on links through the father only. Sons and daughters belong to their father's descent group (shown in dark green), as do the children of sons but not of daughters.

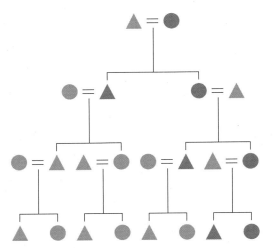

Figure 7.3

Membership in a matrilineal descent group is defined by links through the mother. Sons and daughters are members of their mother's descent group (shown in dark green), as are the children of daughters but not of sons.

matrilineal descent A rule that affiliates a person to kin of both sexes related through females only.

Location of the Hopi.

belong to the mother's descent group, not the father's. Thus, the membership of a **matrilineal descent** group (see Figure 7.3) consists of a woman, her brothers and sisters, her sisters' (but not her brothers') children, her own children, and the children of her daughters (but not of her sons).

In matrilineal societies, the rights and responsibilities of the father in a patrilineal society fall to a woman's brother rather than her husband. A man gains sexual and economic rights over a woman when he marries her, but he does not gain rights over her children. After marriage, a man usually goes to live with or near his wife's kin, which means that he is an outsider in the household, whereas his wife is surrounded by her kin. Because a husband's role in a matrilineal society is less important than in a patrilineal one, marriages in matrilineal societies tend to be less stable. Nevertheless, a man's position in a matrilineal society is less vulnerable than that of a woman in a patrilineal society.

In a matrilineal society, a father's relationship with his son is free of the problems of authority and control that exist between fathers and sons in a patrilineal society, as rights and responsibilities vested in male elders fall to a woman's brother rather than her husband. Although this may lessen conflict between fathers and sons, it also means that a man is committed to pass on his knowledge, property, and offices to the sons of his sister, not his own sons. This may engender conflicts between a man and his nephews, who are subject to his control. Thus, in a matrilineal system, a man's loyalties are split between his own sons and the sons of his sister. In a patrilineal system, this tension does not occur as part of the kinship structure.

The Hopi, a Puebloan group in the American Southwest, are matrilineal. Hopi matrilineages are contained within matrilineal clans. The Hopi household revolves around a central and continuing core of women. The mother–daughter relationship is exceedingly close, based on blood ties, common activities, and lifelong residence together. A mother is responsible for the economic and ritual training of her daughters. Daughters normally live with their mother and their mother's sisters after marriage. The strongest tie is between sisters, whose relationship to each other and to their mother is the foundation of the household group; if one sister dies, another looks after her children. Sisters cooperate in all domestic tasks, and the few quarrels that may occur are settled by the mother's brother or by their own brothers.

The Hopi are matrilocal and men are peripheral in their wife's household. They consider their mother's place as their home, to which they return for many ritual and ceremonial occasions and upon separation or divorce. A son belongs to his mother's lineage, keeps his personal and ritual property in her home, and consults his mother for all important decisions.

As in all matrilineal societies, a Hopi man has authority and control over his sister's sons and has the primary responsibility for transmitting the lineage and clan's ritual heritage. He helps decide on his nephews' marriages and formally welcomes his niece's husband into the household. A man usually selects his most capable nephew as his successor and trains him in his ceremonial duties.

A boy's relationship with his maternal uncle is characterized by reserve, respect, and even fear, whereas his relationship with his father is affectionate and involves little discipline. His obligations to his father's family involve some ritual and economic obligations, but little direct cooperation or authority. A Hopi man teaches his sons the main economic tasks of farming and sheepherding and sons support their father in his old age. A man has an affectionate but not close relationship with his daughters, and he has few specific duties regarding their upbringing.

Hopi matrilineal clans extend over many different villages. A Hopi man cannot marry within his own clan or within the clan of his father or his mother's father. Through membership in his mother's clan and through marriage, a Hopi man acquires a wide range of relatives, all of whom are called by kinship terms. This relates a Hopi man to almost everyone in his village and in other villages, and also to similar clans in other Pueblo societies (Eggan 1950).

About 5 percent of the world's cultures practice **double descent**. In this system, a person belongs both to the patrilineal group of the father and to the matrilineal group of the mother. However, these descent groups operate in different areas of life. Among the Yako of Nigeria, for example, rights to farmland, forest products, as well as some religious offices derive from membership in a patrilineal group, whereas the transfer of accumulated wealth, such as currency, livestock, tools, weapons, and household goods, is governed by matrilineal relations.

The Hopi family is matrilineal and revolves around a core of women. A husband moves to his wife's household, in which he has important economic responsibilities but few ritual obligations. The most important male role in Hopi society, as in other matrilineal societies, is a man's relation to his sister's son, and a man retains authority and leadership in his natal household even after he marries.

double descent The tracing of descent through both matrilineal and patrilineal links, each of which is used for different purposes.

Bilateral Kinship Systems

nonunilineal (cognatic) descent Any system of descent in which both father's and mother's lineages have equal claim to the individual.

bilateral descent System of descent under which individuals are equally affiliated with their mother's and their father's descent group.

kindred A unique kin network made up of all the people related to a specific individual in a bilateral kinship system.

kinship terminology The words used to identify different categories of kin in a particular culture.

ambilineal descent A form of bilateral descent in which an individual may choose to affiliate with either the father's or mother's descent group.

About 40 percent of the world's societies are **nonunilineal (cognatic)**. Most nonunilineal systems are bilateral; the rest are ambilineal (discussed later). Under rules of **bilateral descent**, both maternal and paternal lines are used equally as the basis for reckoning descent and for establishing the rights and obligations of kinship. Bilateral systems do not have clear-cut descent groups. Rather, they have a network of kin, called a **kindred**, that is defined only in its relation to a particular individual. Except for brothers and sisters, every individual's kindred is unique. Kindreds actually are overlapping categories of kin, rather than social groups, and thus are more difficult to organize as cooperative, kin-based collectivities. For example, because a kindred is an ego-centered network, not a social group, it cannot own land or have continuity over time.

Bilateral kinship systems seem particularly adaptive in societies where mobility and independence are important. They are basic to Western culture, including the United States, and predominate among foraging societies as well, such as the Inupiat speakers of Alaska. The flexibility of bilateral kinship systems is expressed in their **kinship terminology**, the words they use to identify different categories of kin.

The second type of cognatic system, found mainly in Pacific Island societies, is **ambilineal**. In these societies, individuals may choose to affiliate with either their mother's or with their father's descent group, but not simultaneously with both. Upon marriage, the new couple can live with either spouse's descent group, a decision most often based on access to land, although friendship and politics also play a role.

THE CLASSIFICATION OF KIN

In all societies, kin are referred to by special terms. The total system of kinship terms and the rules for using these terms make up a *kinship classification system*. Every kinship classification system classes some relatives together (referred to by the same kinship term) and differentiates them from other relatives (called by different terms). Some kinship systems have only a small number of kinship terms, whereas others have a different term for almost every relative.

ego (in kinship studies) The person from whose perspective a kinship chart is viewed.

The classification of kin is related to the roles they play in society. In a kinship diagram, **ego** is the person from whose perspective the chart is drawn and viewed. If, for example, ego refers to his father and his father's brothers by the same term, his relationship with them tends to be similar. By the same token, if ego's father and father's brothers are referred to by different terms, it is expected that ego will act differently toward each of them and that they will act differently toward him. These ideals, of course, are modified (within limits) by the relationships and personalities of particular individuals.

Kinship classification is one of the most important regulators of behavior in most societies. It denotes each person's rights and obligations—how he or she must act toward others and how they must act toward him or her. Kinship classification systems are related to other aspects of culture, such as the types of social groups that are formed and the systems of marriage and inheritance.

Understanding the variety of kinship systems makes a crucial anthropological point: Although people in every society consider their own kinship classification system natural and normal, the logic underlying all kinship systems is cultural, not biological. For example, in the United States, the brothers and sisters of one's parents and their spouses are called "aunt" and "uncle," and the children of these relatives are called "cousin." Have you ever asked yourself why the same term is used for mother's sister, a relative by blood, and mother's brother's wife, a relative by marriage? Or why there are no separate terms for male and female cousins, but gender does differentiate nieces from nephews?

Principles for the Classification of Kin

Societies use a combination of some, but not all, of seven important principles of kinship classification in their kinship terminology: (1) *Generation* distinguishes ascending and descending generations from ego. (2) *Relative age,* where seniority counts, for example, distinguishes older and younger brother. (3) *Lineality* refers to where lineal kin are related in a single line, such as grandfather–father–son, whereas **collateral kin** are descended from a common ancestor with ego but are not ego's direct ascendants or descendants (for example, siblings or cousins). (4) *Gender* differentiates relatives according to whether they are male or female; in English, for example, gender distinguishes between aunt and uncle, but not cousins. (5) The principle of *consanguineal* versus **affinal** kin differentiates relatives by blood in contrast to relatives by marriage. (6) In contrast, the principle of the *sex of linking relative* operates, for example, in differentiating between cross-cousins and parallel cousins (see p. 157). (7) Yet another principle, which distinguishes relatives from the mother's side of the family from those from the father's side, is called **bifurcation**, such as is used by societies that distinguish the mother's brother from the father's brother. These seven principles combine in different ways to form different types of kinship systems.

In making sense out of kinship systems, anthropologists attempt to understand the relationship of terminologies, rules of descent, and kinship groups to the ecological, economic, and political conditions under which different kinship systems emerge.

collateral kin Kin descended from a common ancestor but not in a direct ascendant or descendant line, such as siblings and cousins.

affinal Relatives by marriage; in-laws.

bifurcation A principle of classifying kin under which different kinship terms are used for the mother's side of the family and the father's side of the family.

BRINGING IT BACK HOME:
POLYGAMY IN THE UNITED STATES

The Mormons have had a long history of conflict with the United States. In the 19th century, opposition from non-Mormons and local governments forced them to move from New York to Ohio, Missouri, Illinois, and finally Utah. Following the revelations of Latter-day Saints founder Joseph Smith, Mormons permitted the practice of plural marriage from the late 1830s, until they disavowed the practice in 1890. In that year, in a U.S. Supreme Court case, the court held that Mormon polygamy is "a crime against the laws, and abhorrent to the sentiments and feelings of the civilized world" (Norgren and Nanda 2006:94).

However, since that time and up until today, in defiance of federal courts, state statutes, mainstream cultural values, and excommunication by the Church of Jesus Christ of Latter-day Saints, the organization that represents the vast majority of Mormons, polygamy continues among the Mormon sect that calls itself Fundamentalist Latter-day Saints (FLDS). FLDS church members consider polygamy the sacred marriage pattern of the biblical prophets and hold that its restoration is critical to the entrance of the faithful into the celestial kingdom of God.

In the face of some sensationalist murder and sexual abuse cases that involved Mormon fundamentalism (Krakauer 2003) and that reinforced the already negative opinion most Americans have of polygamy, fundamentalist Mormons have campaigned to win public acceptance of their religion-based marriage practice. Those tolerant of polygamy point to the many variations in marriage and the family now existing in America as a reason to look the other way. The appearance in 2006 of a national television program called *Big Love,* about a polygamous family, might indicate increasing tolerance. In his provocative book *Plural Marriage for Our Times,* anthropologist Philip Kilbride (1994) proposes that polygamy could be a solution to some of the problems of contemporary American society. For example, he argues that infidelity in marriage often leads to divorce and that polygamy might be a better alternative because of the very damaging effects of divorce on children. Other arguments in support of polygamy include the following: Limiting sex to several wives might halt the epidemic spread of sexually transmitted disease; women who wish to both have a career and to provide a loving home for children would have access to a co-parent and therefore have greater autonomy; a legal, stable marital relationship would be available for women who might otherwise remain single; and older women might benefit because of the chronic shortage of men in the oldest age categories.

Opponents of polygamy cite evidence of incest, child abuse, violence against women, rape, and the coerced marriage and sexual relations between teenage girls and much older men as reasons to continue to hold polygamy illegal. In addition to these cases, they cite the hundreds of teenaged boys who have been expelled or felt forced to leave fundamentalist Mormon polygamous families, supposedly for disobedience to religious precepts. Some former sect members and state officials argue that, in fact, such boys are forced out of the community to make more young girls available to marry older men (Eckholm 2007). With the increasing conflict in the United States over the purposes and meanings of marriage, polygamy has once again moved front and center as a subject for debate.

YOU DECIDE

1. Consider the possible advantages and disadvantages of polygamy as a form of marriage in the contemporary United States. In what ways might it be adaptive? Maladaptive?
2. In spite of the freedom of religious practice guaranteed by the U.S. Constitution, polygamy is illegal in the United States. How would you build a case either for or against the continued criminalization of this religion-based form of marriage?
3. Many of the attacks on Mormon polygamy stress its oppression of women. Consider the different possible perceptions of polygamy in the United States today from a male and from a female point of view.

CHAPTER SUMMARY

1. Three major functions of marriage and the family are regulating sexual access between males and females, arranging for the exchange of services between males and females, and assigning responsibility for child care.
2. Incest taboos are prohibitions on mating between people classified as relatives. Various theories of the adaptiveness of the incest taboo are that it prevents disruption based on sexual competition within the family and that it forces people to marry out of their immediate families, extending their alliances to a larger social community.
3. All societies have marriage rules: which groups a person may marry within (endogamy); which groups they must marry outside of (exogamy); whether cousins are permitted, preferred, or prohibited from marrying; the number of spouses; the exchanges of goods and services validating a marriage; and the degree of control a family or kin group has over a child's choice of spouse.

4. Two basic family types are the nuclear family, found mainly in contemporary industrial and foraging societies, and the extended family, found predominantly among cultivators.

5. A household (domestic group) usually contains members of a family but may also include others. Household composition is shaped by a society's postmarital residence rules. The most common, patrilocality, requires a wife to live with her husband's family. Matrilocality, which requires a husband to live with his wife's family, is found primarily in horticultural societies. Neolocality, in which the married couple lives independently, is found in a small number of societies, including the United States.

6. Kinship systems are cultural creations that define and organize relatives by blood and marriage. A kinship system includes the kinds of groups based on kinship and the system of terms used to classify different kin, such as lineages and clans. Kinship systems provide continuity between generations and define a group of people who can depend on one another for mutual aid. In traditional societies, kinship is the most important basis of social organization.

7. In many societies, descent is the basis of the formation of corporate social groups. In societies with a unilineal rule of descent, descent group membership is based on either the male or the female line. Unilineal systems are found among pastoral and cultivating societies. In bilateral systems, the individual is equally related to mother's kin and father's kin. Bilateral systems result in the formation of kindreds, which are overlapping kinship networks, rather than a permanent group of kin. Bilateral kinship is found predominantly among foragers and in modern industrialized states.

8. A lineage is a group of kin whose members can trace their descent from a common ancestor. A clan is a group whose members believe they have a common ancestor but cannot trace the relationship genealogically. Lineages tend to have domestic functions; clans tend to have political and religious functions. Both lineages and clans are important in regulating marriage.

9. In patrilineal systems, a man's children and his sons' children, but not his daughters' children, belong to his lineage. In matrilineal systems, as exist, for example, among the Hopi, a woman's children belong to her lineage, not that of their father. The mother's brother has authority over his sisters' children, and relations between husband and wife are more fragile than in patrilineal societies.

10. Kinship terminology groups together or distinguishes relatives according to various principles, such as generation, relative age, lineality or collaterality, gender, consanguinity or affinity, bifurcation, and sex of the linking relative. Different societies may use all or some of these principles in classifying kin. Each type of kinship classification system reflects the particular kinship group that is most important in the society.

▚▚ KEY TERMS

Affinal
Ambilineal descent
Arranged marriage
Avunculocal residence
Bifurcation
Bilateral descent
Bilocal residence
Bride service
Bridewealth
Clan
Collateral kin
Composite (compound) family
Conjugal tie
Consanguineal
Corporate descent groups
Cross-cousin marriage
Descent
Descent group
Double descent
Dowry
Ego
Endogamy
Exogamy
Extended family
Incest taboo
Inheritance

Kindred
Kinship
Kinship system
Kinship terminology
Levirate
Lineage
Marriage
Matrilineage
Matrilineal descent
Matrilocal residence
Monogamy
Neolocal residence
Nonunilineal (cognatic)
  descent
Nuclear family
Parallel-cousin marriage
Patrilineage
Patrilineal descent
Patrilocal residence
Polyandry
Polygamy
Polygyny
Sororate
Succession
Surrogate motherhood
Unilineal descent

The hijras of India are an alternative gender, neither man nor woman. They exhibit exaggerated female gestures, wear women's clothing, keep their hair long, and are called to celebrate a marriage or the birth of a child.

© Serena Nanda

CHAPTER 8

SEX AND GENDER

NEITHER MAN NOR WOMAN: THE HIJRAS OF INDIA

ALIMA, born intersexed, is a real hijra. Accepting that Salima was "neither one thing nor the other," Salima's mother sent her to join the hijras when Salima was about 12 years old. In her early teens, Salima, along with a group of her "sister" hijras, began to beg and perform the traditional hijra *badhai.* They would seek out families where a wedding was taking place or where a child had been born. Salima played the *dholak,* the two-sided drum that accompanies every hijra performance. Salima told me she doesn't remember much about her childhood, but she does know that her mother was very sad about her birth, that she was born "neither here nor there." "But from my childhood, I am like this," Salima said. "From my birth my [male sex] organ was very small. My mother took me to doctors but they told her it was no good, your child is not a man and not a woman. This is God's gift. So when I came to the age of knowing, they gave me to the hijras. And I have been living with them ever since, as you see me now."

A **hijra** is an ambiguous gender role in India. Although born male, hijras are considered neither man nor woman. Hijras undergo an operation in which their genitals are surgically removed. This "operation" accounts for the popular designation of hijras as eunuchs. Hijras consider this operation a rebirth, and it is carried out as an act of devotion to the Hindu Mother Goddess. After the operation, hijras are believed to incorporate the goddess's powers of procreation. Thus, their presence is required at weddings and at the birth of a child.

Hijra performances involve clapping, drumming, and the tinkle of ankle bells, which announce their arrival. Tossing their spangled scarves, flashing their heavy jewelry, and beating their drums, the hijras sing and dance, making comic, ribald gestures and striking sexually suggestive feminine poses, causing laughter by the men and more discreet embarrassed giggling behind their hands by the women. In celebrating the birth of a male child, the dancers take the infant from his mother's arms and bless him with wishes for prosperity and virility. Meanwhile examining his genitals to confirm that he is a fully formed male infant. At the end of their performance, the hijras are given their traditional payment of money, cloth, and sweets, satisfied with having once again confirmed their importance in Indian society.

Because they are born male, hijras are mainly perceived as "not man," but they are also thought of as "man plus woman." They adopt women's clothing, gestures, and behaviors. They must wear their hair long, like women, and they have a special language that includes feminine expressions, intonations, and female kinship terms. But hijras are also "not woman," mainly because they cannot bear children.

hijra An alternative gender role in India conceptualized as neither man nor woman.

As neither man nor woman, hijras identify with the many ambiguous **gender roles** and figures in Hindu mythology and Indian culture: male deities who change into or disguise themselves as females temporarily, deities who have both male and female characteristics, male religious devotees who dress and act as women in religious ceremonies, eunuchs who served in the Muslim courts, and the ascetics, or holy men of India, whose renunciation of all sexuality paradoxically becomes the source of their power to bless others with fertility. Indian culture thus not only accommodates such androgynous figures as the hijras but views them as meaningful, sacred, and even powerful (Nanda 1999).

gender role The cultural expectations of men and women in a particular society, including the division of labor.

India is only one of the many societies throughout the world where cultural support is given to individuals who transcend or bridge the differences between male and female (Herdt 1996; Nanda 2000b). Among these are the **mahu** of Polynesia (Besnier 1996; Matzner 2001), the **xanith** of Oman on the Saudi Arabian peninsula (Wikan 1977), the **two-spirit** found in many Native American tribes (Roscoe 1991, 1995; Whitehead 1981; Williams 1986), the *travesti* of Brazil (Kulick 1998), the *kathoey* of Thailand (Costa and Matzner 2007), and the *waria* of Indonesia (Boellstorff 2004; Graham 2006), just to name a few. Most of these roles involve males who adopt women's work, dress, and behavior, but there are female alternative gender roles as well (Blackwood 1998).

mahu An alternative gender role in Tahiti.

xanith An alternative gender role in Oman on the Saudi Arabian peninsula.

two-spirit An alternative gender role in native North America (formerly called berdache).

Among some subarctic groups, for example, people depended on sons to feed the family through big game hunting. A family that had daughters and no sons would select a daughter to "be like a man." When the youngest daughter was about 5 years old, the parents performed a transformation ceremony in which they tied the dried ovaries of a bear to a belt the child always wore. This was believed to prevent menstruation, protect her from pregnancy, and give her luck on the hunt. From then on, she dressed like a male, trained like a male, and often developed great strength and became an outstanding hunter (Williams 1996:202). For these native peoples, being male or female included both biological elements, such as menstruation and the ability to become pregnant, and cultural features, such as the ability to hunt.

You might wonder why anthropologists study such esoteric topics as alternative genders and what we can learn from them. After all, the division of humans into two opposite sexes—male and female—appears to be a basic characteristic of human biology, a natural and inevitable aspect of human life. Sex assignment, which takes place at birth, is assumed to be permanent over a person's lifetime. Most of us take for granted that sex is the same as gender and that people come in two opposing and unchangeable categories. Although it is true that every culture acknowledges the biological differences between male and female, there is great cultural variety in both the number of sexes and genders a society constructs and the ways in which sex and gender are defined.

■ SEX AND GENDER AS CULTURAL CONSTRUCTIONS

A basic anthropological concept is the distinction between the biological and cultural aspects of being male or female. **Sex** refers to the biological differences between male and female, particularly the visible differences in external genitalia and the related difference in the role each sex plays in the reproductive process. **Gender** is the cultural and social classification of masculine and feminine. In other words, gender is the social, cultural, and psychological constructs that different societies superimpose on the biological differences of sex (Worthman 1995:598). Every culture recognizes distinctions between male and female, but cultures differ in the meanings attached to these categories, the supposed sources of the differences between them, and the relationship of these categories to other cultural and social facts. And, as we saw in the opening of this chapter, genders are not limited to masculine and feminine in many cultures.

Gender and gender relations are among the basic building blocks of culture and society, central to social relations of power, individual and group identities, formation of kinship and other groups, and attribution of meaning and value. This makes gender a central interest of contemporary anthropology. Understanding that gender roles are not biologically determined but rather are culturally constructed raises new questions about the culturally patterned nature of women's and men's lives in all cultures, including our own.

Cross-cultural ethnography demonstrates that not only do different cultures incorporate different genders beyond those of man and woman, but that concepts of masculine and feminine also vary among cultures. Thus, to grasp the potential and the limits of diversity in human life, we must look at the full range of human societies—particularly those outside Western historical, cultural, and economic traditions. When we broaden our perspective on sex and gender beyond our own society, we see that culture counts. Gender is culturally constructed and extraordinarily diverse, as are the relationships between sex and gender.

The work of anthropologist Margaret Mead was essential in developing the now-central anthropological principle that gender is a cultural construction. In the 1930s, Mead (1963/1935) began to question the biologically determined nature of gender. She organized her ethnographic

sex The biological difference between male and female.

gender A cultural construction that makes biological and physical differences into socially meaningful categories.

research around the question of whether the characteristics defined as masculine and feminine in Western culture, specifically the United States, were universal. In her studies of three groups in New Guinea—the Arapesh, the Mundugamor, and the Tchambuli—Mead found that culture patterns the whole repertoire of behaviors, emotions, and roles that go into being masculine and feminine. Among the Arapesh, men and women both were expected to act in ways that Americans considered "naturally" feminine. Both sexes were concerned with taking care of children and nurturing. Neither sex was expected to be aggressive. In Mundugamor society, both sexes were what American culture would call "masculine": aggressive, violent, and with little interest in children. Among the Tchambuli, the personalities of men and women were different from each other but opposite to American conceptions of masculine and feminine. Women had the major economic role and showed common sense and business shrewdness. Men were more interested in esthetics. They spent much time decorating themselves and gossiping. Their feelings were easily hurt, and they sulked a lot.

Although Mead's ethnographic descriptions of these societies were later criticized and superseded (di Leonardo 1998:213–215, 2003; Roscoe 2003), her work made a lasting contribution by raising the issue of the great diversity in cultural definitions of masculine and feminine and by calling attention to the ways in which gender and gender relations are a **cultural construction**. A society's **gender ideology**, that is, its totality of ideas about sex, gender, the natures of men and women, including their sexuality, and the relations between the genders, is significant not only in its own right but because it is a core element in a society's gender stratification system, a subject discussed later in this chapter.

Location of the Arapesh, the Mundugamor, and the Tchambuli.

cultural construction of gender The idea that gender characteristics are the result of historical, economic, and political forces acting within each culture.

gender ideology The totality of ideas about sex, gender, the natures of men and women, including their sexuality, and the relations between the genders.

Gender, Culture, and Art

Art and a wide variety of cultural performances are important ways of displaying both conscious and unconscious cultural themes relating to gender ideology and personal gender identity. Games and sports such as football in the United States, cockfighting in Bali, or bullfighting in Spain are all ways of reinforcing culturally constructed gender values. Clifford Geertz calls these activities "deep play" (Geertz 1973a). Like the arts, deep play is an expressive form of culture that heightens emotions, displays compelling aspects of social structure and culture, and reinforces culturally constructed gender identities.

Bullfighting in Spain

For cultural outsiders, bullfighting is a cruel assault on animals, but from an emic viewpoint, bullfighting is an aesthetic ritual expressing culturally significant gender values (Eller 2006:104). In Spanish culture, the bullfight is not viewed as violence or cruelty. Despite his violent acts, the bullfighter is culturally compelled to restrain any sign of anger or aggression; indeed, such signs contradict the essence of the ritual of running the bulls. In Spanish culture, bullfights involve a complex and elaborate process of ritualized violence that makes it not only acceptable, but beautiful.

Within the Spanish cultural context, the point of a bullfight is not simply to kill a bull: That would be easy and would lack any cultural meaning. Rather, it is the skill, grace, and courage of the bullfighter that is critical. In some ways similar to cockfighting, the bullfight embodies the values of male competition in defense of the male self-image of honor. For the audience, the maximum vindication of honor is in the physical showdown, in public, between two men. The matador symbolizes the role of the honorable male; he is not a fighter or a man with a reputation for violence, nor is he an athlete, nor personally aggressive, nor necessarily big or muscular. In a bullfight, the matador does not initiate violence, nor does he act against the bull in self-defense. It is the bull that is angry and ferocious whereas the matador is skilled, self-controlled, and calm—he is able to master the violent situation without becoming violent himself.

For the matador and the spectators, it is not the suffering of the bull but the style and aesthetic performance of the matador that is the central element in this aesthetic ritual. At the kill, the most dangerous part of the performance for the matador, the matador cannot use his sword to weaken the bull or defend himself. Any prolonged suffering of the bull is vociferously disapproved of by the spectators, and a matador who performs a "sloppy" kill is called a "murderer." For the Spanish, a bullfight is not an example of indulging in man's animal nature (which is how they view a North American boxing match), but a performance that allows a man to transcend his animal nature of violence and aggression and to display all of the elegance, poise, and self-control that distinguishes a man of honor from a man of anger. The aspect of honor in masculine identity is central in Spanish—and indeed much of Mediterranean—culture (Gilmore 1996). The art of the bullfight is one of the ways in which this cultural value is expressed, both for the performers and the audience.

Art and Gender Identity: Frida Kahlo

One of the more obvious functions of the arts, especially in European-based cultures, is the expression of personal identity, in which gender plays a central role. Indeed, identity is assumed to be deeply connected to an artist's body of work, and art critics and historians often try to link the artist's personal and gender identity with his or her art.

The work of Frida Kahlo, a 20th-century Mexican painter, illustrates how art expresses elements of personality and gender-related experiences and identity. Born in 1907, Frida Kahlo caught polio in her childhood, and a subsequent bus accident left her leg deformed and her body in great pain. Her marriage to the great Mexican muralist Diego Rivera was filled with conflict, and her attempts to have a child ended in a miscarriage. All of these cultural and personal gender issues are reflected in her paintings, which deal with issues of illness and health and, particularly, female sexuality and gender identity.

Frida Kahlo was profoundly influenced by the Mexican culture, like many other artists of the time, and incorporated pre-Columbian Mexican art and indigenous Mexican clothing in her art. One of her significant artistic themes was the Mexican folkloric image of La Llorona, the archetypical, sexually voracious predator and evil woman who stands in contrast to the saintly wife and mother; this is a gender theme found in much of Christian theology and art as well. Kahlo also expressed her politics in her art, using the indigenous Mexican Tehuana costume, with its long embroidered skirts and blouses, in her paintings, expressing her solidarity with the peasants and poor of Mexico.

Frida Kahlo was well known in Mexico, but in the 1990s, she emerged as an international feminist cult figure. Her art particularly speaks to women, especially women's experiences of physical pain, of childbirth, and of the emotional pain of love, which is symbolized by the many broken hearts in her self-portraits. In Frida Kahlo's art, we clearly see the important role of art in expressing the many strands—cultural, political, physical, familial, and gender—that make up an artist's personal identity. Through their expression in art, they speak to a world wider than their own.

Art is often an expression of gender and political identities. Frida Kahlo incorporated Mexican cultural elements in her self-portraits as well as frequently dealing with female sexuality, gender identity, and power and pain.

CULTURAL VARIATION IN SEXUAL BEHAVIOR

Understanding gender systems as culturally constructed also helps explain the cultural variations in definitions of appropriate sexual behavior. Although sexual activity is most often viewed as "doing what comes naturally," a cross-cultural perspective demonstrates that human sexual activity is patterned by a culture's gender ideology and influenced by learning.

Culture patterns the habitual responses of different peoples to different parts of the body. What is erotic in some cultures is considered disgusting in others. Kissing, for example, is not universal. The Tahitians learned to kiss from the Europeans; before this cultural contact, Tahitians began sexual intimacy by sniffing. Among the Alaskan Inuit, sniffing the hollow in another's cheek can be a pattern of sexual as well as nonsexual behavior. When an adult asks a child to do this, it is affectionate and innocent, whereas among adults it is considered quite erotic. Like a kiss in our own culture, it is the social construction of behavior that counts.

Sexual foreplay is also culturally diverse. In the Trobriand Islands, a couple expresses affection by inspecting each other's hair for lice, a practice Westerners may find disgusting. To the Trobrianders, however, the European habit of a couple going on a picnic with a knapsack of prepared food is equally disgusting, although it is perfectly acceptable for a Trobriand boy and girl to gather wild foods together as a prelude to sexual activity (Malinowski 1929b:327, 335).

Who is considered an appropriate sexual partner also differs among cultures. In some societies, like the United States, homosexual activity is generally considered shameful or abnormal, but elsewhere it is a matter of indifference or approval.

Among the Sambia of New Guinea, what Americans call homosexual practice is culturally central in the sex/gender system, not as an aspect of sexual orientation but as a core ritual in male initiation considered essential for the development of adult masculinity. In Sambian culture, women are viewed as dangerous creatures that pollute men, deplete them of their masculinity substance, and are inferior in every way except for reproduction capabilities. The Sambia believe that women are naturally fertile and mature naturally without external aid, whereas males do not naturally mature as fast or as competently as females. The Sambia believe that males cannot attain puberty or become "strong men" without semen. They further believe that male bodies do not naturally produce semen, so it must be externally and artificially introduced into the body. This they do by magical ritual treatments, which include homosexual fellatio during the boys' initiations, as a way of the boys consuming semen from adult men. Only repeated inseminations of this kind are considered capable of conferring on young boys the reproductive competence that results in manliness, necessary to become a vigorous warrior and a father. As adults, these men are expected to make heterosexual marriages (Herdt 1981, 1996:431–436). Among ancient Greeks, homosexual relationships were considered to be superior to those between men and women, whereas in many cultures, the male who takes the dominant role in same-sex relationships is not considered homosexual. The many cultures in which same-sex relationships are viewed as normal variants of human sexuality strongly contrast with the varied and constantly changing ways that homosexuality has been seen in modern Europe and within the dominant cultural ideology in the United States, where consistent heterosexuality is considered essential to masculine identity.

The ages at which sexual response is believed to begin and end, the ways in which people make themselves attractive, the importance of sexual activity in human life, and its variation according to gender—all these are patterned and regulated by culture and affect sexual response and behavior. A comparison of the cultures of the Irish of Inis Beag and the Polynesians of Mangaia makes clear the role of culture in sexuality.

Anthropologist John Messenger (1971:15) describes Inis Beag as "one of the most sexually naive of the world's societies." Sex is never discussed at home when children are near, and parents provide practically no sexual instruction to children. Adults believe that "after marriage nature takes its course." (As we shall see, "nature" takes a very different course in Inis Beag than it does in Polynesia!) Women are expected to endure but not enjoy sexual relations; to refuse to have intercourse is considered a mortal sin among this Roman Catholic people. There appears to be widespread ignorance in Inis Beag of the female capacity for orgasm, which is considered deviant behavior in any case. Nudity is abhorred, and there is no tradition of "dirty jokes." The main style of dancing allows little bodily contact among the participants; even so, some girls refuse to dance because it means touching a boy. The separation of the sexes begins very early in Inis Beag and lasts into adulthood. Other cultural patterns related to sexual repression here are the virtual absence of sexual foreplay, the belief that sexual activity weakens a man, the absence of premarital sex, the high percentage of celibate males, and the extraordinarily late age of marriage. According to a female informant, "Men can wait a long time before wanting 'it' but we [women] can wait a lot longer" (Messenger 1971:16).

Although the idea of total sexual freedom in the South Sea Islands is a Western myth, Mangaia, as described by Donald Marshall (1971), presents a strong contrast to Inis Beag. In this Polynesian culture, sexual intercourse is one of the major interests of life. Although sex is not discussed at home, the elders of the group teach sexual information to boys and girls at puberty. For adolescent boys, a two-week period of formal instruction about the techniques of intercourse is followed by a culturally approved experience with a mature woman in the village. After this, the boy is considered a man. This contrasts with Inis Beag, where a man is considered a "lad" until he is about 40. In Mangaia, there is continual public reference to sexual activity; sexual jokes, expressions, and references are expected as part of the preliminaries to public meetings. And yet, in public, sex segregation is the norm. Boys and girls should not be seen together in public, but practically every girl and boy has had intercourse before marriage. The act of sexual intercourse itself is the focus of sexual activity. What Westerners call sexual foreplay generally follows intercourse in Mangaia. Both men and women are expected to take pleasure in the sexual act and to have an orgasm. Female frigidity and male celibacy are practically unknown. The contrast between Inis Beag and Mangaia indicates clearly that societies' different attitudes pattern the sexual responsiveness of males and females in each society.

Gender Ideology and Women's Sexuality

A culture's gender ideology always includes ideas about sexuality, and most societies view males and females as different in this respect. These differences are often used to justify men's control over women's sexuality, and they become a basis for gender stratification, constraints on women's lives, and discrimination against women. This control may take forms such as seclusion of women (Hale 1989) and male control—institutionalized in law and organized religion—over dress codes for women, marriage, divorce, adultery, concepts and treatment of rape (Sanday 1992), and abortion. Society's control of female sexuality is often inscribed on female bodies, as in female circumcision in some African societies (Barnes-Dean 1989), Chinese foot binding (Anagnost 1989), and *sati* (now outlawed in India), the traditional Hindu practice of a woman burning herself on her husband's funeral pyre (Narasimhan 1990).

In many cultures, male control of female sexuality is central to notions of honor and shame, and thus to cultural understandings of masculinity (Gilmore 1996). This pattern, which is central in many circum-Mediterranean cultures, may have its roots in religious beliefs, for example, medieval Christianity and Islam (Brandes (1981).

Although Islam is a global religion, Muslim gender ideologies and practices regarding women, especially as related to their sexuality and requirements for modest dress, vary in different Islamic cultures, shaped by varying interpretations of the Qur'an and by local histories and politics. Much of the debate on the correct roles and attire for Muslim women centers on the hijab, or head covering. For some Muslims as well

The hijab, or headscarf, worn by these Malaysian girls is one means by which some Muslims accommodate the Islamic requirement for women to dress modestly. Wearing the headscarf has become a political issue in Turkey and in many European countries, which have large numbers of Muslim immigrants.

© Joan Gregg

as non-Muslims, the hijab is a sign of the oppression of women, making them invisible and restricting their freedom of choice. Others, however, especially young Muslim women, view the hijab as a liberating garment that forces the world to see them as more than sexual objects and establishes their identity as Muslims (Bowen 2007).

Muslims base their commitment to modest dress for women on the Qur'an (24:30–31), which says "And say to the believing women that they should lower their gaze and guard their modesty; . . . [and] that they should draw their veils over their bosoms and not display their beauty except to their husbands." The Qur'an also speaks of the need to erect a "curtain" (hijab, which means to hide from view or conceal) between women and men. Some Muslims interpret this as requiring separations of men and women within a house, others that it requires that women wear clothes that conceal their bodies (Bowen 2007). Although the Qur'an specifically requires face covering only for Muhammad's wife, some Muslims interpret this command as requiring all women to cover their head, hair, neck, and bosom (Center for Muslim-Jewish Engagement, 2007). Thus, although female modesty is a central tenet in Islam, the Qur'an does not command any specific styles, nor specifically mention hijab, making room for much local variation.

Varying practices regarding female modesty are shaped by history and culture, particularly the degree of male dominance in a society and the commitment to secularism of governments in largely Muslim societies. These practices also vary among religious sects, social classes, between rural and urban populations, and among generations. In some societies, most Muslim women only wear a hijab that loosely covers their hair and neck; in others, like Yemen, women wear full head and body coverings as well as a face veil. In the airlines of the United Arab Emirates, a compromise is reached between fashion and religion as air hostesses wear "jaunty little caps with attached gauzy scarves that hint at hijab" (Zoepf 2008). In Saudi Arabia, women must wear a face veil, whereas in Afghanistan, under Taliban rule, women were required to wear a burka, or full body and face covering. In all of these countries, some women resist these laws and customs (Ali 2006; Manji 2003; The Revolutionary Association of the Women of Afghanistan, www.rawa.org). Wearing the veil is discouraged in Tunisia, and both veil and hijab are not generally worn by Muslim Bedouin women (see p. 197). In Egypt, conflict over what constitutes women's modest dress is an important political issue between religious parties and the government. Today, almost 90 percent of Egyptian women wear a headscarf, and many Egyptians believe the Qur'an explicitly requires it. At the same time, some Egyptian government officials publicly oppose the Islamist call for women to cover themselves entirely, including their faces. One official called the hijab "a step backward for Egyptian women" (Slackman 2007). In Turkey, women commonly wear the headscarf in public, though they were previously not permitted to wear it in government offices or universities, and the hijab is part of a heated public debate about the secular versus the religious character of this largely Muslim state (Tavernise 2008).

In Europe and the United States, the headscarf has also become a source of controversy and conflict. In France, the growing number of Muslim immigrants led to a law banning headscarfs (and other religious symbols) in public institutions, specifically public schools (Bowen 2007). In the United States, some discrimination cases have been filed by Muslim women denied the right to wear the headscarf while, for example, teaching in public schools. However, the American commitment to individual freedom of religious practice has made Islamic dress less of an issue here (Moore 1998).

In the Islamic Republic of Iran, women are required to wear a hijab, and wearing a chador (outer garment or cloak) is increasingly common due to government and some public pressure. At the same time, however, anthropologist Pardis Mahdavi, in her new ethnography of sexuality in Iran (2009), describes the widespread breach of many Muslim sexual restrictions, such as premarital chastity, marital fidelity, and the wearing of modest dress among educated, upper-class Iranians. Dating, fashion, nail polish, and immodest dress are outlawed in Iran, and although these restrictions are policed in public spaces, girls wear layers of makeup in private. Women's more modern headscarfs are often so transparent and fashionable that they actually look sexy.

Gender ideologies, such as a focus on honor and shame as it relates to female sexuality, as well as other aspects of gender roles are taught in all cultures, in both explicit and indirect ways. One of the most important cultural institutions that pass on gender roles is rites of passage.

MALE AND FEMALE RITES OF PASSAGE

In all cultures, the role expectations of individuals change at different points in life and the individual must learn what is necessary for these new roles. In many societies, the transition from one social status to another is formalized by a special **rite of passage**, which moves individuals publicly and ceremonially from one stage of life to the next (see pp. 264–265). One widespread rite of passage signals the transition from childhood to adult gender roles (van Gennep 1960).

rite of passage A ritual that moves an individual from one social status to another.

Male Rites of Passage

Male rites of passage have important psychological and sociological functions. They reinforce the social order by dramatizing cultural values in a public context; they express and affirm male relationships, male solidarity, and, sometimes, male dominance; they publicly validate a change of status from child to adult; and they transmit the cultural knowledge necessary to being a responsible adult male in the society.

Male rites of passage often involve an extended period during which boys are separated from the larger society, which emphasizes the importance of an individual's responsibility to his kinship group as well as the larger community (Hart 1967). These rites often include painful practices such as scarification or circumcision that symbolize the formal transition from child to adult. Such rites may also include difficult and dangerous tasks, such as killing a large animal, which test a boy's preparation for the obligations of male adulthood.

Male rites of passage have been interpreted as a means of psychologically separating boys from identification with their mothers (Whiting, Kluckhohn, and Anthony 1967), as the symbolic appropriation of the fertility related to female reproductive capacities, and as a fertility cult in which men celebrate and ritually reproduce their control over the fertility of crops, animals, and humans.

Although masculinity does take different forms in different cultures (Conway-Long 1994; Gutmann 1996), a very widespread cultural pattern is one in which men must *prove* themselves to be virile, successful in competition with other men, daring, heroic, and aggressive, "proving their manhood" in formal rites, or more informally, on the streets, in bars, or in warfare (Gilmore 1990). In Chuuk, Micronesia (formerly the U.S. territory of Truk), for example, male adolescents engage in excessive drinking and violent brawling as an expression of a cultural concept of masculinity that is defined by competitiveness, assertiveness, risk taking in the face of danger, physical strength, and physical violence (Marshall 1979).

Anthropologist David Gilmore calls the widespread male need to publicly test and prove one's manhood, the **manhood puzzle**. To the question of why manhood needs to be proved, why it is regarded as so uncertain or precarious that manhood requires trials of skill or endurance, or special rituals, Gilmore suggests that cultural patterns of "proving manhood" help ensure that men will fulfill their roles as procreators, providers, and protectors of their families. This essential contribution to society, he argues, is at the heart of the "*macho*" masculine role and accounts for its intensity, near universality, and persistence.

Female Rites of Passage

Female rites of passage are more widespread than male rites, although generally less spectacular and intense. Female initiation into adulthood often is performed at **menarche** (first menstruation), but there is

manhood puzzle The question of why in almost all cultures masculinity is viewed not as a natural state but as a problematic status to be won through overcoming obstacles.

menarche A woman's first menstruation.

much cross-cultural variability (Lutkehaus and Roscoe 1995). Sometimes the initiate is isolated from society; sometimes she is the center of attention. Some rituals are elaborate and take years to perform; others are performed with little ceremony.

As with male rites, female initiation rites also have multiple interpretations. In matrilocal societies where the young girl continues her childhood tasks in her mother's home, an important function of the rites is to publicly announce a girl's status change, as she will now carry out these tasks as a responsible adult (Brown 1965), and to teach her what she needs to know to be an effective adult. Female rites of passage also channel sexuality into adult reproduction, and in some rituals, the rites emphasize the connections between beauty, sexuality, and power. These rites, in New Guinea, for example, motivate girls to bear and rear children, strengthen their fortitude, and provide them with the capacity for the hard work necessary to assist their husbands in gathering wealth.

▇ POWER AND PRESTIGE: GENDER STRATIFICATION

gender stratification The ways in which gendered activities and attributes are differentially valued and related to the distribution of resources, prestige, and power in a society.

A central concern in anthropology is **gender stratification**. Anthropologists have long debated whether male dominance is universal and, if so, why it is so. In the interest of addressing these questions, anthropologists look at (1) the social and cultural significance of women's roles as mothers, sisters, wives, and daughters; (2) women's economic contributions in different types of societies; (3) informal as well as formal sources of women's power and influence; (4) development of women's identities; and (5) changes in all these dimensions as a result of historical factors, particularly colonialism, technological and economic change, and globalization.

private/public dichotomy A gender system in which women's status is lowered by their almost exclusive cultural identification with the home and children, whereas men are identified with public, prestigious economic, and political roles.

One early anthropological theory that addresses the widespread, some say universal, subordination of women to men is called the **private/public dichotomy**. This theory holds that female subordination is based on women's universal role as mothers and homemakers, occupying a domestic (private) world that is less prestigious than the public world dominated by men (Rosaldo and Lamphere 1974). But a closer look indicates that the private/public dichotomy is not universal but rather characterizes the highly gender-stratified 19th-century capitalist societies, such as those of Victorian Europe and the United States: In these societies, productive relationships moved out of the household and middle-class women (but not working-class women) retreated into the home, where they were supposed to concern themselves solely with domestic affairs, repress their sexuality, bear children, and accept a subordinate and dependent role (Martin 1987; see also Lamphere 2005 for a reevaluation of this theory). The private/public dichotomy seems less applicable to smaller-scale, non-Western societies where home and family and economics and politics were not so easily separated, and where women played an important, though perhaps a less observable, role in economic production and distribution (Friedl 1975). With increasing Western influence on these societies, through capitalism, Christian missionaries, and colonialism, the public/private dichotomy became a more relevant context for gender stratification (Leacock 1981; Lockwood 2005:504).

Other anthropologists have used controlled cross-cultural comparisons to understand male dominance. Peggy Sanday (1981), for example, concluded that male dominance was *not* universal but occurred in connection with ecological stress and warfare. Where the survival of the group rests more on male actions, such as warfare, women accept male dominance for the sake of social and cultural survival.

GENDER RELATIONS: COMPLEX AND VARIABLE

Anthropological debates in earlier gender studies focused on which gender dominated a society. Male dominance, called **patriarchy**, was considered universal, or nearly so, although **matriarchy**, or female dominance, was held to exist in some societies. Although anthropologists generally do not find matriarchies where women hold power equal to that of men in patriarchies, there is more recognition today that female power does find a place in many societies. With a greater understanding of the complexity and variability in gender stratification systems, anthropologists today have moved from the question of whether male dominance is universal to explanations of gender stratification in particular societies. This has led to a closer examination of the sexual division of labor in different types of societies and an examination of the informal as well as formal bases of female power.

patriarchy A male-dominated society in which all important public and private power is held by men.

matriarchy A female-dominated society in which women hold all important public and private power.

Gender Relations in Foraging Societies

Earlier anthropological descriptions of foraging societies viewed male hunting as the major source of the food supply, providing the basis of male dominance in these societies. Contemporary ethnographic studies have modified this view. In many foraging societies, such as the Tiwi of Australia and the Ju'/hoansi of the Kalahari Desert in Namibia (Africa), women make very significant contributions to the food supply by gathering vegetable foods (Hart and Pilling 1960; Lee 2003). In other societies, like the Agta of the Philippines, women also substantially contributed to

The Tlingit, on the Northwest Coast of North America.

the food supply by hunting (Estioko-Griffin 1986), although in different ways and for different kinds of animals than men hunted. These contributions by women to the society's food supply were an important source of female power.

The Tlingit of the Northwest Coast of North America is a foraging society in which women traditionally have had equal power and prestige with men. Important Tlingit social roles are based on individual ability, training, and personality rather than on gender (Klein 1995). Both Tlingit women and men achieve prestige through their own efforts and their own kin relationships. Women may be heads of clans or tribes, and Tlingit aristocrats are both male and female. Titles of high rank are used for both men and women, and the ideal marriage is between a man and woman of equal rank. The prestige the Tlingit achieved through extensive trade with other coastal societies is open to both men and women. Although long-distance trade centered on men in the past, women often accompanied the men, acting as negotiators and handling the money, and both girls and boys were—and are today—expected to "work, save, get wealth and goods" (Klein 1995:35).

Gender egalitarianism continues to be a core Tlingit cultural value. Today, women occupy the highest offices of the native corporations administering Tlingit land and are employed in government, social action groups, business and cultural organizations, and voluntary associations (Klein 1976). Tlingit women take advantage of educational opportunities and easily enter modern professions. Unlike in many non-Western societies where European contact diminished women's economic roles and influence, modernization expanded Tlingit women's roles, and modern gender egalitarianism is not experienced as diminishing men, who encourage their wives and daughters to go into public life.

Gender Relations in Horticultural Societies

Generally speaking, women have more autonomy and power in egalitarian foraging societies, such as those in native North America (Klein and Ackerman 1995), some tribal populations in Southeast Asia (Ong 1989), and some hunters and gatherers in Africa (Shostak 1983), than in horticultural, pastoral, or agricultural societies, but again, there is great cross-cultural variation. For example, the Iroquois of the eastern United States are highly egalitarian (Brown 1975), whereas the Yanomamo of Venezuela and Brazil are highly sex segregated and male dominated (Chagnon 1997), as are most societies in highland New Guinea (Strathern 1995, but see Lepowsky 1993).

A high degree of sex segregation, paralleled by the importance of males in ritual, is associated with male dominance in some horticultural societies. Among the Mundurucu of South America, for example, adolescent boys are initiated into the men's cult and thereafter spend most of their lives in the men's house, only visiting their wives, who live with the children in their own huts in the village. The men's cults exclude women and are surrounded by great secrecy. The men's house itself usually is the most imposing structure in the village and houses the cult paraphernalia and sacred musical instruments, which, flutelike in shape (like male genitals), are the symbolic expressions of male dominance and solidarity (Murphy and Murphy 1974).

The solidarity of women in horticultural societies usually is not formalized in cults or associations but is based on the cooperation of domestic life and strong interpersonal bonds among female kin. In sub-Saharan Africa, for example, the most important economic and emotional ties for both men and women are more likely to be between generations (consanguineal ties) than between spouses (conjugal ties). Women's most important ties are with their children, particularly their sons, on whom women depend for emotional support and security in old age (Potash 1989:199). Women, like men, also use kinship ties with their natal groups to gain access to land, gain support in marital disputes, and participate in ritual activities (Sacks 1982). In many parts of West Africa, women's power is expressed through political office (Kaplan 1997) and also formally organized secret societies, such as the Sande society of Sierra Leone (MacCormack 1974). Contemporary ethnography demonstrates that women's power and influence sometimes go beyond their economic contributions, their significant roles within households and families, and even beyond formal political offices women sometimes occupy. An important dimension of female power may rest on female alliances and participation in networks and groups outside the household that provide arenas for entertainment, prestige, influence, and self-esteem. Anthropologist Annette Weiner (1976), for example, demonstrated the important exchanges among women in the Trobriand Islands, where the emphasis on male kula exchanges had excluded any anthropological attention to women's participation in exchange networks.

In some societies, like the Yoruba of West Africa, there is a concept of power as a vital force that is in all living things. Personal power may be projected through certain body parts, for example, the eyes, mouth,

© Judith Pearson

An emphasis on male dominance and aggression in horticultural societies overlooks the elements of affection and nurturance that males display as fathers, as in the Iban society of Indonesia.

hands and fingers, and genitals. Power associated with sexuality and reproduction is especially strong and potentially dangerous and polluting, especially female genital power. Indeed, the universal covering of the female genitals may well be related to the power of these body parts (Stevens, Jr. 2006).

The impact of European expansion on women in horticultural societies varied. Generally, women's roles declined as indigenous economies shifted from subsistence horticulture to cash crops sold in the world market. Among the Nukumanu, a Pacific Island society, women's primary responsibilities were domestic, whereas men contributed food acquired at longer distances from the home through fishing, collecting shellfish, and collecting and husking coconuts. Men also made canoes and constructed new buildings, whereas women cooked food and collected and prepared leaves for thatch. Both women's and men's roles were highly valued in traditional Nukumanu society. Women exclusively controlled and cultivated swamp taro lands, which were inherited matrilineally. Matrilocality added to women's status, whereas men's power came from their economic contribution and their exclusive occupation of formal positions of power in the chiefly hierarchy.

With the advent of German colonial occupation in the 1880s, most of Nukumanu was turned over to the production of copra (dried coconut meat). Wage laborers were brought in from nearby islands, commercially marketed foods such as wheat flour and rice supplanted taro, and men's wages were needed to buy coffee, tea, and sugar (once luxury items). As a result, women's traditional sphere of influence and their status declined, whereas men's spheres of power expanded (Feinberg 1986). The traditional segregation of men's and women's activities also intensified. Kareve (a potent alcoholic beverage made from fermented coconut sap) was introduced in the 1950s, and men's economic activities, such as canoe building, took on a social aspect involving drinking. Because kareve production and consumption takes up much of men's leisure time and excludes women, sexual segregation increased.

As taro declined in importance, women's collective activities became more individualized, leaving them more isolated and dependent on their husbands and brothers than previously. Male–female tensions also increased partly as a result of kareve drinking, which many women vehemently oppose. The traditional tendency for men to travel off the island more than women also lowered women's status, and even today, men primarily go overseas for wage labor and higher education. More recently, however, more women have been leaving the island to take advantage of opening educational and career opportunities, and the prestige, money, and social influence of such women may move Nukumanu back toward its tradition of sexual egalitarianism.

◼◼ Gender Relations in Pastoral and Agricultural Societies

Pastoral and agricultural societies tend to be male dominated, although there is some variation. In pastoral societies, women's status depends on the degree to which the society combines herding with cultivation, its specific historical situation, and the diffusion of cultural ideas, such as Islam. Generally speaking, women's contribution to the food supply in pastoral societies is small (Martin and Voorhies 1975). Men do almost all the herding and most of the dairy work as well. Male dominance in pastoral society is partly based on the required strength to handle large animals, but females sometimes do handle smaller animals, engage in dairy work, carry water, and process animal by-products such as milk, wool, and hides (O'Kelly and Carney 1986). Pastoral societies generally do not have the rigid distinction between public and domestic roles of agricultural societies. Herders' camps typically are divided into male and female spaces, but both men and women work in public, somewhat blurring the private/public dichotomy.

In pastoral societies, men predominantly own and have control over the disposition of livestock, which is an important source of power and prestige. However, the disposition of herds is always subject to kinship rules and responsibilities, and animals may be jointly held by men and by women. Still, the male economic dominance in pastoral societies seems to give rise to general social and cultural male dominance, reinforced by patricentric kinship systems and the need for defense through warfare (Sanday 1981).

Again, this generalization is subject to variation. Among the Tuareg of the central Sahara, for example, which is a matrilineal society, women generally have high prestige and substantial influence (Rasmussen 2005). Tuareg women do not veil their faces, they have freedom of movement, and they have social and economic independence and can own property, including herd animals. There is minimal sex segregation, and women are singers and musicians and organize many social events. Although the traditionally high status of Tuareg women, and matrilineality itself, is undermined today by the migration of men to cities, where they work for wages, and the incorporation of the Tuareg into larger nation-states, with their patrilineal cultures, cities may also provide increasing opportunities and freedom for Tuareg women.

In agricultural societies, with the use of plows, the direct female contribution in food production generally drops drastically, though this varies. Women, for example, play important productive roles in wet rice agriculture. As women's economic contribution declines, they lose status and this is also generally accompanied by their increasing isolation in domestic work in the home and increasing numbers of children (Ember 1983). Machine technology reduces the overall labor force, and this too particularly affects women, who are disproportionately excluded from the mechanized agriculture. Women are also paid lower wages as agricultural laborers and are concentrated in such labor-intensive agricultural tasks as weeding, transplanting, and harvesting. Also, as men more easily enter a cash economy, selling crops and animals, transition to this economic system in most cases also lowers women's status and makes them more dependent on men.

Gender Relations in the Global Economy

As with colonialism, foreign aid and development programs often ignore women while increasing male productivity, and often fail because they do not address the economic role of women (Kristoff and Wudunn 2009). Indeed, development programs may actually increase gender inequality (Moser 1993; Warren and Bourque 1989). Where anthropologists are involved in development projects, however, more attention may be paid to women's roles. Ann Dunham, an anthropologist, craftsperson, and weaver, did her fieldwork in Indonesia, and was particularly interested in craft marketing, an important potential source of income for village Indonesians (Dunham et al. 2009; Remnick 2010:84–87).[1] Dunham became particularly interested in the economic possibilities of marketing and later worked for the Ford Foundation and USAID development projects in Indonesia and Pakistan. Her fieldwork findings challenged the then-common notion that the roots of poverty were the poor themselves. Rather, she observed, underdevelopment in these village communities largely resulted from a scarcity of capital. As a development anthropologist, Dunham set up credit cooperatives for Indonesian women to be street food sellers, factory workers, hand-loom weavers, shopgirls, and scavengers (Dewey and White 2008). As Dunham pointed out, with the exception of iron tools, which have a religious connection to blacksmithing and are only handled by men, women mainly work in Indonesian markets and form an essential part of the economy and the family. The success of the Grameen Bank project of microlending for women, which results in their increasing prestige, income, and autonomy, confirmed Dunham's anthropological insights about the potential of village woman (Dove 2009). The global marketing of women's textiles and pottery from Mexico and Guatemala has also proven economically successful, although here it has sometimes led to greater tension and even violence between men

---

[1] Ann Dunham-Soetoro is the mother of President Barack Obama.

and women (Nash 1993, 1994:15). As anthropologists increasingly point out, the impact of development projects on women is a result of the interplay of specific material and cultural conditions in a particular society (Lockwood 2005).

Women's status in modern, stratified societies varies greatly and is affected by economic development, political ideology, and globalization. Women have been highly involved in the global economy, primarily through the expansion of industrial production by multinational corporations in Latin America, Asia, and Africa (see Chapter 13, pp. 311–313). As rural lifestyles and agriculture are replaced by urban lifestyles and industrial production, women may even benefit relative to men. For example, in Mata Chico, Peru, in the 1930s, the only way for women to get land, a critical resource, was to marry. By the 1980s, however, as Peru became increasingly urban, many occupations were available to both men and women. Because women could support themselves and their children through employment in urban areas, they began to remain single longer and chose to not marry at all in some cases (Vincent 1998).

Even in the developed nations of Europe, Japan, and the United States, the status of women is not equal to men. In the United States, for example, the view that women should be excluded from all but domestic and child-rearing roles has historically been culturally dominant and remains so among many Americans today (Norgren and Nanda 2006). Although American women have made great strides in professions such as law, medicine, and academe, there is still much stereotyping and discrimination. More women than men may go to medical school, but they tend to take on less prestigious medical specializations after graduation. Even in academic anthropology, where women like Margaret Mead and Ruth Benedict are among our most influential and celebrated elders, women's rates of promotion to full professor lag behind the rates of men. Although legal restrictions on public roles for women, such as jury duty, no longer apply today, the number of women in Congress is decidedly small, and, as of this writing, there has yet to be a female president or vice president. Domestic violence and sexual harassment of women are other significant problems, again based on an American cultural pattern that values masculine aggression and control over women. But it is perhaps in the struggle for reproductive autonomy, in the right to choose whether or not to end a pregnancy, that cultural patterns defining women's roles as domestic and reproductive emerge most strongly. The American debate over abortion is really a cultural debate about the meaning of life, the nature of women, and the limits of gender equality (Ginsburg 1989).

In all societies, gender stratification is a complex issue. It has social, economic, and political dimensions, it is embedded in culture, and it affects both men and women and the relationships between them.

BRINGING IT BACK HOME:
FEMALE GENITAL OPERATIONS AND INTERNATIONAL HUMAN RIGHTS

During female initiation, elders impart important information to girls that allows them to participate as responsible adults in their society. Where initiation involves circumcision, as among the Kikuyu of Kenya, elder women give the girls the necessary emotional support to help them get through this very painful ritual.

Approximately 100 million females in the world today, mainly in Africa and the Middle East, undergo some form of female genital operations, the ritual cutting of a girl's genitals. These practices vary in intensity from a ritualized drawing of blood to infibulation, the removal of almost all of the genitals, stitching together the wound, and leaving only a small opening for passing urine and menstrual flow. Where practiced, female genital operations are viewed as essential gender rites. They are intended to preserve a girl's virginity before marriage, to symbolize her role as a marriageable member of society, and to emphasize her moral and economic value to her patrilineage (Barnes and Boddy 1995; Walley 1997).

Scientific evidence demonstrates that female genital cutting substantially raises the likelihood of a woman's death in childbirth. The name of the rites themselves is a subject of debate. Many anthropologists, feminists, and international health and children's organizations condemn the more extreme forms of female genital operations, which they call *genital mutilation,* as a violation of the human rights of women and children (Seddon 1993). Sometimes the rite is called *female circumcision,* a label that seems to make it parallel to male circumcision, when in fact female genital cutting is much more invasive and painful and has more frequent debilitating effects on health than does cutting the male foreskin.

Another point of view, held by some anthropologists and some members of cultures that practice this ritual, urge that the practice not be condemned outright but rather examined carefully in its cultural context, both for greater understanding of its variety as well as the positive values it has in connection with marriage within particular societies (Gruenbaum 2001). Indeed, from the perspective of some women in some African societies, female genital cutting is an affirmation of the value of women in traditional society

(Walley 1997). Today, many women from societies where female genital rituals are practiced are migrating to Europe and the United States, giving this once local cultural pattern a global dimension. Although some women have fled their countries for fear of being forced to undergo some form of genital cutting, others wish to preserve this practice in their new countries. As a result of the diffusion of female genital cutting, these practices now are outlawed by several European countries and by the United States.

Female genital operations reveal the difficulty of steering a just course between the demands of multiculturalism and cultural relativity, which emphasize respect or at least understanding of local cultural patterns in their cultural context, and the concept of universal rights, incorporated into the United Nations Universal Declaration of Human Rights, which specifically includes the protection of women against gender-specific violence.

Although some women from societies that practice female genital operations defend them as affirming a woman's value and enhancing traditional cultural cohesion, others from those cultures speak out against them (el Saadawi 1980). Even for many African women who oppose female circumcision, however, denunciation of the practice by outsiders is resented as yet another Eurocentric assault on African cultural integrity by former colonial powers. Some anthropologists also decry this as a form of cultural imperialism and, more importantly, as an obstacle to reforming the practice or finding more effective ways to eliminate it (Gruenbaum 2001).

YOU DECIDE

1. Should female circumcision be outlawed globally as a violation of women's and children's rights, even if it is a valued cultural tradition in many societies?
2. Because female circumcision is most often associated with religious belief, does outlawing the practice in the United States impermissibly violate our Constitution's freedom of religion clause?
3. What can anthropologists contribute to the debate over female genital operations and other debates that pit universal human rights, especially regarding women, against local cultural patterns? What does the example of female genital operations suggest about the possible limits of the anthropological principle of cultural relativism?

CHAPTER SUMMARY

1. *Sex* refers to biological differences between male and female; *gender* refers to the social classification of masculine and feminine and the roles that people assume.

2. An important anthropological principle is that gender, including sexuality, is not biologically determined but is culturally constructed. This is demonstrated by the presence of alternative genders in different societies and by the culturally variable definitions of femininity and masculinity in different cultures.

3. Views about the nature of male and female sexuality are part of gender ideologies. Attempts to control female sexuality, for example, in constraints on women's dress in Islam, are embedded in gender hierarchies and culture.

4. Many societies have rites of passage for males and females, in which boys and girls are transformed into adult men and women. These rites have many social and psychological functions, such as the transmission of cultural knowledge, the public acceptance of the obligations of adulthood, and the reaffirmation of cultural values, including gender hierarchies.

5. A male-dominated gender stratification system is one in which men are dominant, reap most of the social and material rewards of society, and control the autonomy of women.

6. Gender stratification systems differ in foraging, horticultural, agricultural, and industrial societies. These have changed through the impact of European colonialism on non-European societies and as a result of contemporary globalization.

▮▮ KEY TERMS

Cultural construction of gender
Gender
Gender ideology
Gender role
Gender stratification
Hijra
Mahu
Manhood puzzle

Matriarchy
Menarche
Patriarchy
Private/public dichotomy
Rite of passage
Sex
Two-spirit
Xanith

As societies become more complex, specialized positions of authority, such as kings and chiefs, develop as centers of power and control, as in many states of West Africa. The state controls wealth, and symbols of wealth surround the Asante king to enhance his authority.

CHAPTER 9

POLITICAL ORGANIZATION

NATIONALISM AND ETHNIC CONFLICT: TURKEY AND THE ARMENIANS

N defending the Nazi extermination of the Jews during World War II, Adolph Hitler said, "After all, who today speaks of the massacre of the Armenians?" Who indeed! The massacre of the Armenians in Turkey—and other ethnic minorities—during and after World War I, was related to the attempts of the newly created Turkish state to foster Turkish nationalism by eliminating from the country large parts of its population who were religiously and culturally different from the Turkic-speaking, Muslim majority. The old Ottoman Empire, like many empires, had no concept of nationalism and treated its non-Muslim populations as inferiors. At the same time, the empire enabled its Christian Greek and Armenian populations, as well as its Jews, to thrive, particularly in commerce. The empire's slow decline in the 19th century led to the rise of Turkish, Armenian, and other nationalist movements. Although the Turkish revolutionaries were initially allied with Armenian reformers in hoping to establish a modern, multicultural Ottoman state, this movement soon broke down into a Turkish national movement in which Armenians, as non-Turks, would have no place. In 1908, when the "Young Turks" completed a political takeover, the government began violent harassment of Armenians. With the beginning of World War I, as the Russian armies were threatening Turkey, some Armenian nationalists took up arms against the Turks. Turkish leaders decided to deport the Armenians from the militarily threatened provinces to the Syrian desert. Much cruelty accompanied this process: The Armenians were beaten, robbed, raped, and deprived of food, water, and shelter. Although the Turkish authorities organized these atrocities, many of the participants were themselves members of non-Turkish minorities, such as the Kurds and the Circassians.

Unless you are Turkish or Armenian, you may be wondering: Why am I reading all this ancient history? The point is, it is not ancient history but has repercussions in contemporary society, both internationally and nationally. Turkish treatment of the Armenians is a subject of intense debate today. How many Armenians were killed in the deportations? The figures range from 800,000 to one and a half million, depending whether the source is Turkish or Armenian. Was the Turkish treatment of the Armenians ethnic cleansing? Intentional massacre? Genocide? Were the Armenians innocent victims of ethnic conflict or was their treatment justified by their attempts to undermine the new Turkish state? Again, you may ask, who cares? It happened one hundred years ago.

But again, people today care very much. The Armenians care because their history under the Turks is a source of great suffering and trauma that even now has not lost its power and figures centrally in Armenian identity in the diaspora (Chelala 2009). Only recently, a Turkish journalist was killed for refusing to let go of the subject, while some Turkish writers and historians are challenging the decades-old Turkish denial of this ethnic violence (Akcam 2006; Tavernise 2008). The Turks care, because today Turkey is a modern nation with a strong interest in joining the European Union and playing an important role in international diplomacy. Many European nations, who characterize Turkish treatment of the Armenians as genocide, will not vote for Turkish membership until the Turks admit to their genocide and alter their constitutions so that open discussion of the Armenian massacres is no longer "an insult to Turkishness" (Tavernise 2008).

In the United States and other countries, politicians from districts with large Armenian populations have introduced national resolutions, calling the Turkish treatment of the Armenians a genocide and demanding an apology. This has created tension between Turkey and its allies. And in Turkey itself, the treatment of the Armenians has led to acrimonious political debate. The secular parties that have dominated Turkey in the 20th century support repression of open conversations on the issue, while the conservative, Islamic parties argue for an expansion of free speech (de Ballaigue 2007).

This ongoing story of Turkey and the Armenians emphasizes a major theme in this chapter: Political organization and political process can only be understood in their specific cultural, historical, economic, and political contexts. Political organization and the uses of power grow out of specific situations and change as those situations change. The conflict between Turkey and the Armenians is but one of the many ethnic conflicts that have assumed great importance with the rise of the nation-state in the 20th and 21st centuries.

POLITICAL ORGANIZATION

Political organization is about how societies use power to address a universal problem of human societies: how to maintain themselves over time with a minimum of social disorder and social discontent. This means that every society must make and implement decisions affecting the whole society; provide a means of managing conflicts, dissent, and deviance; and generally regulate behavior so that it is consistent with social order. **Political organization** refers to the ways in which power is used in all societies so that they can maintain themselves collectively over time.

political organization The patterned ways in which power is legitimately used in a society to regulate behavior, maintain social order, make collective decisions, and deal with social disorder.

Power and Authority

Anthropologists examine the uses and sources of power and analyze how political organization is related to other cultural patterns and social institutions in a society. **Power** is the ability to exercise one's will over others. The source of power is ultimately based on the control of resources that people need or desire.

Power differs from **authority**, which is the socially approved use of power. Authority may be based on personal characteristics such as honor, status, knowledge, ability, respect, and/or the holding of formal public office. Political leaders have authority based on their occupation of public office, but may also wield power through their control of resources and/or control over the use of force or knowledge. Power can exist without authority: An armed robber certainly has power, but is denied authority.

The shared values and beliefs that legitimate the distribution and uses of power and authority in a particular society are called its **political ideology**. A political ideology may be widely, though not universally, shared throughout a society. The sources of power may be coercive (based on force or the threat of force) or consensual, or more likely, both. One difference among types of political organization is the degree to which they rely on coercion or consensus to achieve social order.

Political Process

Political process refers to how groups and individuals use power and authority to achieve various public goals—for example, building a road or increasing a society's goods through trade—that may benefit the larger society, or may benefit only smaller groups or individuals. Decisions and activities by groups and individuals may be motivated by material profit, prestige, altruism, survival, or any combination of these, but are usually justified by reference to the public good.

Formal political institutions and informal systems of alliance are both sources of power and authority. In many West African societies, for example, both men and women exercise power through their membership in secret societies, while power in many societies is wielded through kinship groups or religious institutions. The study of political process emphasizes how power changes hands and how new kinds of political organization and ideologies develop. Different kinds of power and authority may be used to stabilize a social order, avoid or resolve conflicts, and promote the general welfare, but they may also contest prevailing political ideologies and change or even destroy existing political systems. Groups or **factions**, informal alliances within a group or society, as well as governments, use diverse means to gain their ends. These may include violence and terror as well as

power The ability to impose one's will on others.

authority The ability to cause others to act based on characteristics such as honor, status, knowledge, ability, respect, or the holding of formal public office.

political ideology The shared beliefs and values that legitimize the distribution and use of power in a particular society.

political process The ways in which individuals and groups use power to achieve public goals.

factions Informal alliances within well-defined political units such as lineages, villages, or organizations.

© Diane Greene Lent

Political processes are the ways in which different, often conflicting groups in society mobilize to achieve their goals. This peaceful protest is directed against the American invasion of Iraq.

behind-the-scenes manipulation, peaceful protest, the ballot box, and political lobbying, and even such a seemingly mundane activity as gossip.

Rebellion, which is the attempt of one group to reallocate power and resources within an existing political structure, and **revolution**, which is an attempt to overthrow the existing political structure and put another type of political structure in its place, are both examples of political process. The 2005 riots of Africans and Arabs in France are referred to as a rebellion; their participants were not seeking to overthrow the French society but to gain a larger presence in it. Rebellion and revolution are sometimes related: the American Revolution, for example, started out as a rebellion but ended up as a revolution.

rebellion The attempt of a group within society to force a redistribution of resources and power.

revolution An attempt to overthrow the existing political structure and put another type of political structure in its place.

SOCIAL CONTROL AND CONFLICT MANAGEMENT

Because all societies contain conflict, they must also manage conflict and persuade individuals to conform to (at least most of) society's norms to maintain themselves. In small-scale societies, organized through kinship, conformity mainly results from the internalization of norms and values as part of the enculturation process, and from many informal processes and sanctions. Internalization of norms also regulates behavior in complex, socially stratified state societies, but the control of the state over many social institutions and regulatory processes, including the mobilization of force, also becomes very important.

deviants Those who transgress society's rules.

Deviants, or those who transgress society's rules, are handled differently in different types of societies. In small-scale societies, informal mechanisms of social interaction, such as ridicule, avoidance, or gossip, are effective means of social control because most people value the esteem of (at least some) others and because marginalized people may also be restricted from access to resources. In writing about the importance of gossip in the small central Pacific atoll of Nukulaelae, anthropologist Niko Besnier (2009) suggests that **gossip**, although difficult to define, is probably universal and plays an important role in studying political action beyond the structured political institutions of parliaments, bureaucracies, street protests, and other formal contexts (see Chapter 14).

gossip A generally negative and morally laden verbal exchange taking place in a private setting concerning the conduct of absent third parties.

Informal sanctions, such as gossip, avoidance, and ridicule, may also be effective in industrialized societies in long-term forms of associations such as housing developments, the workplace, or local voluntary associations (Merry 1981). Fear of witchcraft accusations or other supernatural interventions are other effective social control mechanisms (Evans-Pritchard 1958; Lemert 1997; Seitlyn 1993). These are often directed at people who stand above the group, are malicious, have a nasty temper, or refuse to share according to group norms. Avoidance works in small-scale groups and societies because, where cooperative action is necessary, a person shunned by others is at a great psychological and economic disadvantage.

law A means of social control and dispute management through the systematic application of force by a politically constituted authority.

Law refers to the systematic application of force by a constituted authority in society (S. Moore 1978:220). Law is applied when a social norm is so important that its violation authorizes the community, or some part of it, to punish an offender, resolve a conflict, or redress a wrong. In every society, some offenses are considered so disruptive that force or the threat of force is applied. In this sense, law is universal, although in small-scale societies it is most often embedded in other social institutions, such as the kinship system or religion, and is most often directed at maintaining existing social relationships. In more complex, stratified societies, law's functions belong to separate legal institutions, such as a police force, courts, or a prison system. Punishment is aimed at asserting society's control over an individual, rather than repairing damaged social relationships.

TYPES OF POLITICAL ORGANIZATION

social complexity The number of groups and their interrelationships in a society.

Societies vary in their systems of political organization, which is related to a society's **social complexity**. Social complexity refers to the degree to which political roles, institutions, and processes are centralized and differentiated from other aspects of social organization or embedded within other social institutions. Anthropologists have identified four main types of societies: the band, tribe, chiefdom, and state. Each of these types of societies is associated with a characteristic way in which people make a living, their dominant principle of economic exchange (see Chapter 6), their characteristic forms of leadership and social control, and different systems of social differentiation (Service 1962). In smaller-scale nonindustrial societies such as bands, tribes, and chiefdoms, the uses of power and authority, decision making, and the coordination and regulation of human behavior are highly integrated. In these societies, power and authority do not operate independently but are embedded in other social institutions such as kinship, economics, and religion. In many of these societies, **leadership**, the ability to direct an enterprise, may be a function of political office or an individual's authority. On the other hand, it may also be based on an individual's position as the head of a kinship group, on supernatural connections and interventions, or on control over the production and distribution of goods.

> **leadership** The ability to direct an enterprise or action.

    Social differentiation, another way to characterize these types of societies, refers to the relative access individuals and groups have to basic material resources, wealth, power, and prestige. Anthropologists define three ideal types of social differentiation: egalitarian societies, rank societies, and stratified societies. In an **egalitarian society**, individual differences, such as age and gender distinctions, are recognized, but no individual or group is barred from access to material resources or has power over others. There are no rules of inheritance by which some individuals accumulate material goods or prestige passed down over generations. Unlike egalitarian societies, a **rank society** recognizes formal differences among individuals and groups in prestige and symbolic resources, and these may be passed on through inheritance. However, there are no important restrictions on access to basic resources. All individuals can obtain the material necessities for survival through their membership in kinship groups.

> **social differentiation** The relative access individuals and groups have to basic material resources, wealth, power, and prestige.

> **egalitarian society** A society in which no individual or group has more privileged access to resources, power, or prestige than any other.

> **rank society** A society characterized by institutionalized differences in prestige but no important restrictions on access to basic resources.

    In a **stratified society**, there are formal and permanent social and economic inequalities. Wealth, prestige, and office are frequently passed down over generations, establishing relatively permanent elites. **Elites** are those who have maximum access to all culturally valued resources, whether power, wealth, or prestige, and possessively protect their control over these resources. In stratified societies, some individuals and groups are also systemically denied access to the basic material resources needed to survive. Thus, stratified societies are characterized by permanent and wide differences among groups and individuals in their standard of living, security, prestige, political power, and the opportunity to fulfill their potential. Contemporary industrialized nations, such as the United States, are all stratified societies.

> **stratified society** A society characterized by formal, permanent social and economic inequality in which some people are denied access to basic resources.

> **elites** The social strata that has differential access to all culturally valued resources, whether power, wealth, or prestige, and possessively protects its control over these resources.

Although political organization, social differentiation, and social complexity can be analyzed separately, in reality these intersect with one another in significant ways. Within each type of society, history, geography, culture, and other factors lead to cross-cultural diversity. Although many anthropologists reject any evolutionary implications of this typology (the idea that societies develop from simpler bands to more complex states), the typology is useful in grasping some of the varieties of political organization.

Band Societies

band A small group of people related by blood or marriage, who live together and are loosely associated with a territory in which they forage.

A **band** is a small group of people (usually 20 to 50) belonging to extended families who live together and are loosely associated to a territory in which they make a living. Foragers are primarily organized into bands, which tend to be egalitarian and mainly use generalized or balanced reciprocity as mechanisms of exchange (see pp. 135–137). Band societies have minimal role specialization and few differences of wealth, prestige, or power. Bands are fairly independent of one another, with few higher levels of social integration or centralized mechanisms of leadership. Bands tend to be exogamous, with ties between them established mainly by marriage. Bilateral kinship systems link individuals to many different bands through ties of blood and marriage. Trading relations also link individuals to other band members. Membership in bands is flexible, and people may change their residence from one band to another fairly easily. The flexibility of band organization is particularly adaptive for a foraging way of life and low population density.

Band societies have no formal leadership; decision making is by consensus. Leaders in foraging bands are usually older men and women whose experience, knowledge of group traditions, special skills or success in foraging, and generosity are a source of prestige. Leaders cannot enforce their decisions; they can only persuade and attract others to their leadership on the basis of past performance. Thus, among some Inuit, the local leader is called "The One to Whom All Listen," "He Who Thinks," or "He Who Knows Everything Best."

Social order in band societies is primarily maintained informally through gossip, ridicule, and avoidance, or in some cases, as among the Inuit, supernatural interventions and sanctions, such as public confession directed by a shaman (Balikci 1970). This practice leads to an interesting example of culture clash: When Inuit people go before American courts, they may freely admit guilt, but this is contrary to what is required (and what lawyers advise their clients) in the adversary legal system of the United States. In Inuit bands, disputes are sometimes resolved through public contests that involve physical action, such as head butting or boxing, or verbal contests like song duels, where the weapons are words—"little, sharp words like the wooden splinters which I hack off with my ax" (Hoebel 1974:93). These traditional and highly esteemed means of resolving conflict are now publicly performed as part of the annual World Eskimo-Indian Olympic Games held in Alaska and connected in the minds of their participants to the survival of Inuit culture (personal communication).

Individual violence, such as the frequent fights over women among the Ju'hoansi hunters of the Kalahari Desert in Africa, does occur in band societies, but because of the low level of technology, lack of formal leadership, and other ecological factors, warfare is largely absent. Bands have no formal organization or production for war, and no warriors and no cultural or social support for sustained armed conflict (Lee 2003). When conflict gets too disruptive, bands may break up into smaller units, which separates people in extended conflict and prevents prolonged hostilities (Turnbull 1968).

Tribal Societies

A **tribe** is a culturally distinct population whose members think of themselves as descended from the same ancestor or as part of the same "people." Tribes are mainly found among pastoralists and horticulturalists. Tribes tend to be egalitarian and exchange goods through reciprocity and redistribution (see pp. 135–140). Like bands, most tribes do not have distinct or centralized political institutions or roles, and power and social control are embedded in other institutions, such as kinship or religion.

Tribes are usually organized into unilineal kin groups (see p. 168), who "own" the basic economic resources and are the units of political activity. These large unilineal kin groups are consistent with the larger populations in horticultural and pastoral societies, compared to foraging band societies.

The effective political unit in tribal societies is a shifting one. Most of the time, the local units of a tribe operate independently; in some societies, the local units may be in a state of ongoing violent conflict among themselves. A higher-level unity among tribal segments most often occurs in response to the threat of attack from another society or the opportunity to attack another society, as among the Nuer of East Africa, where lineages at different levels (from minimal to maximal) will join one another to attack a common enemy (see p. 169) (Evans-Pritchard 1968/1940). This coalescing of lineages directs the energies of the society away from competition between close kin to an outside enemy. This kind of tribal integration works particularly well when stronger tribes want to expand into nearby territories held by weaker tribes.

Other types of groups that help integrate tribal societies beyond kinship are **age sets** and **age grades**, groups organized on the basis of age,

tribe A culturally distinct population whose members consider themselves descended from the same ancestor.

age set A group of people of similar age and sex who move through some or all of life's stages together.

age grades Specialized associations, based on age, that stratify a society by seniority.

who move through some or all of life's stages together in an organized progression. Age sets are mainly male, and have political and military functions. Because their members come from different kinship groups, they are an important basis for wider social integration throughout a tribal society. Other kinds of associations, such as the military societies among some Plains Indian tribes in North America, and the **secret societies**, such as the Poro male society and Sande female society found in West Africa, also help integrate tribal societies (Sahlins 1961).

secret societies West African societies whose membership is secret or whose rituals are known only to society members. Their most significant function is the initiation of boys and girls into adulthood.

Tribal societies have leaders but no centralized government and few positions of authority. In Melanesia and New Guinea, a characteristic form of leadership is the **bigman**—a self-made leader who gains power and authority through personal achievements rather than through holding office. A bigman starts out as the leader of a small, localized kin group. He builds up his capital, mainly in the form of pigs, and attracts followers through generous loans, sponsoring feasts, purchasing high ranks in secret societies, helping his military allies, paying bridewealth for young men seeking wives, and other initiatives. These actions increase his reputation and put other people under obligation to him, thus further extending his alliances and influence.

bigman A self-made leader who gains power through personal achievements rather than through political office.

compensation A payment demanded by an aggrieved party to compensate for damage.

As a form of tribal leadership above the local level, the bigman is a fragile mechanism of tribal integration because it does not create a permanent office but rather depends on the personality and constant striving of an individual. Bigmen rise and fall, and with their deaths their support disperses. Bigmen are vulnerable because they must spur their local group on to ever-greater production if they are to hold their own against other bigmen in the tribe. To maintain prestige, a bigman must give his competitors more than they can give him. Excessive giving to competitors means the bigman must begin to withhold gifts to his followers. The resulting discontent may lead to defection among his followers, or even murder of the bigman. As bigman status cannot be inherited, each aspiring bigman must begin anew to amass the wealth and forge the internal and external social relationships on which bigman status depends (Sahlins 1971).

© Irven DeVore/AnthroPhoto, Inc.

The bigman is an informal leader in many Melanesian cultures. Much of his influence is based on his ability to distribute resources, of which pigs are the most important.

Tribes have a variety of (mainly) informal and some formal mechanisms for controlling deviant behavior and settling conflicts. **Compensation**—a payment demanded by an aggrieved party to compensate for damage—is important in New Guinea, among other places. The amount of compensation is based on the severity of the act that precipitated the dispute, and the individual's kin group shares in the payment. Payment of compensation implies acceptance of responsibility by the donors, and acceptance of compensation implies a willingness to terminate the dispute by the recipients (Scaglion 1981). Demands for excessive compensation, however, may not resolve conflicts, but rather become the basis for further disputes (Ottley and Zorn 1983).

Mediation, a common form of tribal conflict management, is particularly effective between parties with ongoing social relationships. Mediation aims to resolve disputes through consensus rather than adversarial interactions, so that the prior social relationship between the disputants is maintained and harmony is restored to the social order. Mediation involves a third party, either a go-between or even the whole community, to resolve conflict between the disputants. Through the work of anthropologist James Gibbs (1988), the mediation of the Kpelle of West Africa became widely known and served as a model for the emerging mediation movement in the United States (Fry and Bjorkqvist 1997).

mediation A form of managing disputes that uses the offices of a third party to achieve voluntary agreement between the disputing parties.

Warfare in Tribal Societies

Despite the wide variety of nonviolent methods of conflict resolution, tribal societies seem prone to a high degree of **warfare**. Anthropologists have suggested that in the absence of strong mechanisms for tribal integration through peaceful means and the absence of strong motivations to produce food beyond immediate needs, warfare may regulate the balance between population and resources in tribal societies. With slash-and-burn horticulture, for example, it is much harder to clear forest for cultivation than to work land that has already been used. Thus, a local group may prefer to take land from other groups, by force if necessary, rather than expand into virgin forest (Vayda 1976). Tribal warfare may also be linked to patrilineality and patrilocality, which promote male solidarity, enabling the use of force in resolving both local conflicts and warfare carried out over long distances, as occurred among the Iroquois (Ember and Ember 1971). Although anthropologists may not agree about the specific causes of warfare, they do generally agree that warfare is grounded in historical, material, cultural, social, and ecological conditions, and not in any biologically based human instinct for aggression.

warfare (war) A formally organized and culturally recognized pattern of collective violence directed toward other societies, or between segments within a larger society.

The Yanomamo of the Amazon areas of Venezuela and Brazil experience high degrees of both warfare and personal violence. This violence is directed by men against women, occurs among men within the same village, and takes the form of warfare between villages (Chagnon 1997). Anthropologist Napoleon Chagnon explains ongoing Yanomamo warfare and their military ideology as a way of preserving village autonomy. The high degree of violent conflict between men within villages leads to the division of villages

The Yanomamo.

into hostile camps. To survive as an independent unit in an environment of constant warfare, a village adopts a hostile and aggressive stance toward other villages, perpetuating intervillage warfare in an endless cycle.

William Divale and Marvin Harris (1976) challenge Chagnon's explanation of Yanomamo violence, arguing that tribal warfare in horticultural societies like the Yanomamo regulates population—not by causing deaths in battles, but indirectly through female infanticide. In societies with constant warfare, there is a cultural preference for fierce and aggressive males who can become warriors. Because male children are preferred over females, female infants are often killed. The shortage of women that results from female infanticide among the Yanomamo provides a strong conscious motivation for warfare—when asked, the Yanomamo say they fight for women, not for land—and a continuing "reason" to keep fighting among themselves. In a Yanomamo raid on another village, as many women as possible are captured.

Yanomamo warfare may also have resulted from European contact. Anthropologist Brian Ferguson (1992) notes that the extreme Yanomamo violence documented by Napoleon Chagnon in the 1960s was precipitated in the 1940s, as a result of severe depopulation due to European disease epidemics, fatal malnutrition, and intensified competition over European goods. The high death rate led to disruption of Yanomamo family life, and negotiating marriages became particularly difficult due to the deaths of adult males. In addition, the Yanomamo desire for European manufactured goods—particularly metal machetes, axes, and knives, which are very useful for horticulturalists—increased competition among Yanomamo males, and firearms substantially increased the number of fatalities in warfare. Whereas previously such goods were traded into even remote Yanomamo villages, by the 1960s, the desire to acquire these goods led to the increasing settlement of Yanomamo around European outposts such as missionary stations. This led to the depletion of game, a highly desired food for Yanomamo cultivators who were also hunters. With the depletion of game, cultural norms of reciprocity broke down, meat was less likely to be shared, and conflict within villages increased. This, in turn, led to enmity between villages. The increasing intervillage warfare reinforced the low status of Yanomamo women and helped further male violence against them, perpetuating the cycle of female infanticide, shortage of women, and raids for women described by Divale and Harris as well as Chagnon. Thus, historical factors complement other explanations of Yanomamo "fierceness" and indeed raise the question about how fierce the Yanomamo actually are.

chiefdom A society with social ranking in which political integration is achieved through an office of centralized leadership called the chief.

Chiefdoms

Although there is a great diversity among chiefdoms (Earle 1987), a **chiefdom** may be defined as "an autonomous political unit comprising a number of villages or communities under the permanent control of a paramount chief" (Carneiro 1981:45). Two main characteristics distinguish chiefdoms from tribes. First, unlike tribes, in which all social segments are structurally and functionally similar, chiefdoms are made up of social parts that are structurally and functionally different from one another. Chiefdoms have been called the first step in integrating villages as units within a multicommunity political organization (Carneiro 1981).

Second, chiefdoms have centralized leadership. Chiefdoms vary greatly in their social complexity (Peoples 1990), ranging from simpler tribal structures to those with elaborate systems of social stratification and large settlements that function as administrative centers, surrounded by smaller villages. Each geographical unit within a chiefdom may also have its own chief or council.

Chiefdoms, like tribes, are organized through kinship ties. However, although tribes tend to be **acephalous**, that is, without centralized government, chiefdoms have centralized leadership vested in the political office of the chief. Chiefs are born to the office and often are sustained in it by religious authority and genealogical records.

acephalous Lacking a government head or chief.

Rank societies are normally based on highly productive horticulture or pastoralism (highly productive foragers such as the Kwakiutl and other foraging groups on the Northwest Coast of North America are exceptions), both of which permit sufficient accumulation of food so that chiefs can appropriate a surplus and redistribute throughout the society. Redistribution is the characteristic mode of exchange in rank societies, though balanced reciprocity is also important.

Anthropologists generally agree that the rise of a centralized governing center (that is, a chief with political authority) is related to redistributive exchange and the ability to deploy labor. Goods are appropriated by the chief and then redistributed to the rest of society in feasts and rituals. Although this redistribution is a primary support of the chief's power and prestige, chiefs may also control their communities by coercion or despotism (Earle 1987). Internal violence within chiefdoms is lower than in tribes because the chief has authority to make judgments, punish deviant individuals, and resolve disputes.

Complex chiefdoms are characteristic of Polynesia. In Tahiti, society was divided into the Ariki, the immediate families of the chiefs of the most important lineages in the larger districts; the Raatira, who were the heads of less important lineages and their families; and the Manahune, or the remainder of the population. Social rank in Tahiti had economic, political, and religious aspects. Mana, a spiritual power, was possessed by all people, but in different degrees depending on rank (see Chapter 11, p. 263). The Ariki had the most mana because they were closest to the ancestral gods from which mana comes. An elaborate body of taboos separated those with more mana from those with less and also regulated social relations among the three ranks. Higher-ranked people could not eat with those of lower rank, and because men had higher rank than women and children, they could not eat with them. The highest-ranking Ariki was so sacred that anything he touched became poison for those below him. In some Polynesian islands, the highest chief was kept completely away from other people and even used a special vocabulary that no one else was allowed to use.

Although a chief's authority is backed by his control of symbolic, supernatural, administrative, economic, and military power, violent competition for the office of chief does sometimes occur. Chiefdoms may also be rendered unstable if the burdens the chief imposes on the people greatly exceed the services they receive from him. Chiefs generally suppress any attempt at rebellion or threats from competitors and deal harshly with those who try to take their power. To emphasize the importance of this office for the society, offenses against a chief are often punished by death.

State Societies

A **state** is a hierarchical (socially stratified), centralized form of political organization in which a central government has a legal monopoly over the use of force. Generally speaking, states are based on agriculture and industrialism, but some are also based on horticulture. In states, **citizenship** rather than kinship regulates social relations between the different social strata and defines a person's rights and duties. Units based on territory are central to state organization, and individuals belong to states through virtue of being born in a specific locale (or of parents from that locale). The state can incorporate a variety of political units, classes, and ethnic groups without disintegrating, making them more populous, heterogeneous, and powerful than any other kind of political organization.

States are characterized by **government**: an interrelated set of status roles that become separate from other aspects of social organization, such as kinship. **Bureaucracy**, an administrative hierarchy characterized by specialization of function and fixed rules, is essential to the functioning of government. The administrative divisions of a state are territorial units—cities, districts, and so on. Each unit has its own government specifically concerned with making and enforcing public policy, although these governments are not independent of the central government.

State organization helps maintain a society in many ways. Through taxation, for example, the state redistributes wealth and can stimulate or discourage various sorts of production. It can order people to work on roads and buildings and to serve in armies, thus affecting the workforce available for other occupations. The state protects the exchange and distribution of goods by making travel safe for traders as they move from

state A hierarchical, centralized form of political organization in which a central government has a legal monopoly over the use of force.

citizenship Those people invested by the state with rights and duties, based on criteria such as residence or other group affiliations.

government An interrelated set of status roles that become separate from other aspects of social organization, such as kinship, in exercising control over a population.

bureaucracy Administrative hierarchy characterized by specialization of function and fixed rules.

one place to another and by keeping peace in the marketplace. The many economic, coordinating, and controlling functions of states, in peace and war, require extensive record keeping, and gave rise to writing and systems of weights and measures. In some states, cities arose as administrative, religious, and economic centers. These centers then stimulated important cultural achievements in science, art, architecture, and philosophy.

A key characteristic of state societies is the government's monopoly over the use of force. Most modern states use a code of law to make clear how and when force will be used and to forbid individuals or groups to use force except under its authorization. Laws (usually written) are passed by authorized legislative bodies and enforced by formal and specialized institutions. Courts and police forces, for example, have the authority to impose all kinds of punishments on deviants: fines, confiscation of property, imprisonment, and even death. In practice, a ruler in an authoritarian state may "become the law," implementing and enforcing those laws that suit his or her own purposes.

States frequently engage in warfare that both increases and centralizes their power. In warfare, states may attempt to regulate daily life and internal conflict and take control over information and channels of communication. This strengthens both the war effort and the power of the state.

Anthropologists explain the origin of the state, one of humankind's most significant cultural achievements, in a variety of ways. States evolve in different ways in different historical and ecological circumstances, as societies respond to internal and external situations. They may change some of their internal structures, subdue a competing group, or through trade, for example, establish their dominance in a region. These initial shifts set off a chain reaction that may eventually lead to state formation.

Anthropologist Robert Carneiro (1970) emphasizes ecological factors in the emergence of the Inca Empire. In this area, independent, dispersed farming villages were confined to narrow valleys bounded by the sea, the desert, or mountains. As the population grew, villages split and populations dispersed until all the available land was used up. At this point, more intensive methods of agriculture were applied to land already being farmed, and previously unusable land was brought under cultivation by terracing and irrigation. As population continued to increase, pressure for land intensified, resulting in war. Because of the constraints of the environment, villages that lost wars had nowhere to go. To remain on their land, they had to accept a politically subordinate role. As more villages were defeated, the political organization of the area became more complex, and chiefdoms developed. The warring units were now larger, and as conquest of larger areas continued, centralization of authority increased. Finally, the entire area was brought under the control of one chief. The next step was the conquest of weaker valley chiefdoms by stronger ones until powerful empires emerged, most notably that of the Inca.

Anthropologist Keith Otterbein (2010), in his studies of primary states in Mesopotamia, China, Mexico, and Peru, concludes that, after several periods of internal peace, these states emerged out of violent rivalry between kinship groups, and the "winners become the rulers," leading to early state formation. The rulers controlled the population by repressive sanction and waged war through their control of elite military organizations. In the next phase of state development, repression and war decline; mature states do not wage war against each other but may wage defensive war against other, early state aggressors.

The State and Social Stratification

The productivity of intensive cultivation enables a state's government to appropriate an economic surplus through taxation. This surplus supports the development of cities, economic and occupational specialization, and extensive trade. As specialized, non-food-producing elites emerge, economic and social inequalities become a key element in social structure. In state societies, unlike most chiefdoms, only a part of the surplus goes back to the people directly. The rest is used to support the activities of the state itself such as maintaining administrative bureaucracies; sustaining standing armies, artists, and a priesthood; and supporting the ruling class in a luxurious lifestyle that differs substantially from that of ordinary people.

In state societies, elites are almost always a numerical minority, so the question arises: How do they manage to dominate? One means is through **hegemony** (Gramsci 1971), a process whereby the state achieves dominance through promoting the internalization of elite values by ordinary people in the larger society. As Karl Marx said, "The ideas of the ruling class are . . . the ruling ideas" (in Durrenberger and Doukas 2008:214). While serving elite interests, hegemonic cultural ideologies explain the existing social order as being in the interest of the greater good. For example, the American cultural ideology of the individual as responsible for his or her own economic failure or success is an example of how hegemony contributes to the continued dominance of elites by repressing the corporate interest underlying our political and economic system (Durrenberger and Doukas 2008:214).

Hegemony, however, must be constantly reinforced. Elite interests cannot count on permanent stability as the inequalities inherent in state societies continually pose substantial challenges to the status quo. Political and economic elites are thus constantly alert to ward off threats to depose the government, outbreaks of violence that might result in civil war, or the disruption of the privileges of vested interests. As we see later,

hegemony The (usually elite) construction of ideologies, beliefs, and values that attempt to justify the stratification system in a state society.

elites use various economic, political, and symbolic means to ensure their continued control. To the extent that elites maintain hegemonic dominance and reasonably effective protection of some basic economic and political rights, the constant use of force is not necessary. It is always there in the background, however, as a potential instrument of social control (Nagengast 1994:116).

Anthropological theories of the rise of the state tend to emphasize either conflict (Fried 1967) or integration (Service 1971). Integration theories emphasize the benefits of the state to its members: its ability to provide stability for growth and technological development, protection of the rights of its citizens, effective mechanisms for the peaceful settlement of disputes, protection of trade and financial arrangements, defense against external enemies, and the ability to expand. Conflict theories emphasize the emergence of the state as centrally related to protecting the power and privileges of an elite class through management of political ideology and force, when necessary.

THE EMERGENCE OF THE NATION-STATE

Although an empire is a state that expands to incorporate a wide variety of ethnic groups and cultures, a **nation-state** is a government and territory that is identified with (relatively) culturally homogeneous populations and national histories. A nation is popularly felt by its members to be a natural entity based on bonds of common descent, language, culture, history, and territory. However, all modern nation-states are composed of many ethnic (and other) groups. Benedict Anderson (1991) calls nation-states "imagined communities" because an act of imagination is needed to weld the many disparate groups that actually make up the state into a coherent national community. Anthropologists are interested in the historical circumstances under which nation-states evolve, the processes by which they are constructed and maintained, and the circumstances under which they are challenged and destabilized (Stolcke 1995).

Nation-states construct national identities partly by drawing boundaries between spatially defined insiders and outsiders (Bornstein 2002; Handler 1988). Regardless of some cultural differences, people who live within these boundaries are viewed as having an essential natural identity, based on a common language and a shared culture; those outside the national boundary are viewed as essentially different. The importance of the spatial dimension of the nation-state is reinforced by colorful world maps, which visually represent the world of nations as a discrete spatial partitioning of territory (Alonso 1994:382).

nation-state A sovereign, geographically based state that identifies itself as having a distinctive national culture and historical experience.

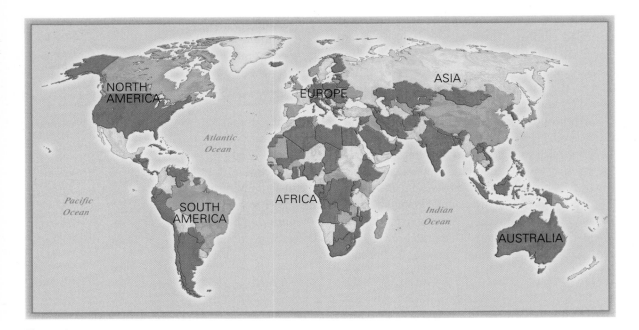

Figure 9.1

World maps reinforce the importance of the nation-state as a territorial unit.

Nations also erect physical boundaries, such as the Great Wall of China, to define their territory and to protect citizens from outsiders (see the Bringing It Back Home feature on pp. 224).

Nation-states are further constructed by attaching people to time as well as to space. A common interpretation of the past is essential in creating national identities. As we see in the chapter opening story of Turkey and the Armenians, however, because different groups within a nation may have different interpretations of its history, the creation of national histories often is marked by struggles over which version of history will prevail (Friedman 1992; Deák 2002). "Tradition," "the past," "history," and "social memory" all are actively invented and reinvented in accordance with contemporary national interests and reproduced through rituals, symbols, ceremonies, memorials, and representations in museums and other cultural institutions (Hobsbawm and Ranger 1983; Nanda 2005; White 1997).

The "cultural politics" of nation-states include coronations, inaugurations, publicly pledging allegiance to the flag, singing the national anthems, and building monuments and museums of history—constructions that link the nation's dead to its living and thus the past to the present. All these are essential to maintaining the nation-state. Nation-states may also outlaw, as currently in Turkey, the public presentations of alternative histories.

Constructing national identities has been particularly problematic for postcolonial states, whose artificial colonial boundaries encompassed many different ethnic groups (see Chapter 12), but it also is true in older nations. After World War I and World War II, the ethnic homogeneity of many nation-states, not just Turkey, was achieved by the coerced migration of ethnic minorities (Judt 2005), and ethnic cleansing and genocide were both widely used to make nations culturally homogenous (Naimark 2001; Levine and Roberts 1999; Kaufman 2001). In Canada, because of the dual influence of English and French culture, the search for Canadian national identity is ongoing, occasionally flaring up in demands for French-speaking Quebecois separatism (Handler 1988). In 2006, Quebec officially became "a nation within Canada."

The nation-state always seeks to repress the invented or imagined nature of national unity (Foster 1991:238), and it has many sources of power in fostering some group identities and marginalizing or disparaging others. States use media, politics, educational institutions, and the law, among others, to create a national culture and identity that become the only authorized representations of society and to suppress subcultural variations.

The Nation-State and Ethnicity

Ethnicity, like the nation, is a social construction, which refers to *perceived* differences—such as culture, religion, language, national origin—by which groups of people distinguish themselves and are distinguished from others in the same social environment. **Ethnic groups** are categories of people who view themselves as sharing an **ethnic identity** that differentiates them from other groups or from the larger society as a whole. **Ethnic boundaries** are the claimed cultural attributes by which ethnic groups distinguish themselves from others.

Ethnicity, like the nation, is popularly viewed as a "bedrock" of "natural" ties based on "common blood, language, attachment to a place, or culture" passed down largely unchanged from generation to generation (Meier and Ribera 1993; Geertz 1973b:277). But although ethnicity does have cultural content, ethnic group identity is constructed by groups to differentiate themselves from other similar groups, even when the cultural differences among them are small. The perception that one belongs to a particular ethnic group, and the emergence of particular ethnic groups and identities, evolves from the *interaction* of a group with other groups and with the larger society, significantly shaped by competition and conflict over resources (Barth 1969/1998). This view that ethnicity is primarily significant in defining group *relationships* leads anthropologists to ask questions about

© Serena Nanda

Nation-states intensify national identities by presenting history in emotionally intense ways, such as this sculpture of the capture of Iwo Jima in World War II by the United States Marines.

ethnic groups Categories of people who see themselves as sharing an ethnic identity that differentiates them from other groups or the larger society.

ethnic identity The sense of self a person experiences as a member of an ethnic group.

ethnic boundaries The perceived cultural attributes by which ethnic groups distinguish themselves from others.

how ethnic groups and ethnic identities emerge, change, and disappear in responses to economic and social environments, especially as related to political and economic inequality (De Vos and Romanucci-Ross 1995).

Ethnic Conflict and Political Instability

Political instability and violent confrontation are nothing new in our world. Traditional societies often fought with one another. Western expansion, colonial and otherwise, was accompanied by great loss of life and culture. The trenches of World War I, the death camps of World War II, nuclear weapons, the purges under Stalin and Mao, and the growth of nationalism, political instability, and ethnic conflict make the past one hundred years appear to be a particularly brutal time in human history.

Poor nations were deeply affected by Europe's wars, and for many, the devastation continued long afterward. In French Indochina (later Vietnam), World War II faded into wars of independence that persisted until the 1970s. In many cases, traditional peoples became involved in networks of warfare that drew them into the competition between the United States and the Soviet Union, who furnished guerilla movements, impoverished governments, and rebel armies with vast amounts of weaponry.

Although the end of the Cold War brought relief to some poor nations, other violent conflicts emerged as the strong, centralized, and frequently repressive governments that the United States and the Soviet Union had supported fell apart. Nations containing multiple ethnic and religious groups, such as Yugoslavia, Somalia, Liberia, Sudan, and others, disintegrated as these smaller groups openly fought for wealth, power, and control.

The popular media often explain intranational conflict and violence, including genocide—between Hutu and Tutsi in Rwanda, between Hindus and Muslims in India, between Tamils and Sinhalese in Sri Lanka, between Kurds, Shi'a, and Sunni Muslims in Iraq, between Basques and Spanish in Spain—as natural eruptions of age-old ethnic hatreds and culture clashes between different ethnic groups within nation-states. In fact, some of these conflicts may be better explained as contemporary struggles for political and economic power, now finding its main expression in nationalism (Stolcke 1995). Ambitious politicians may promote ethnic identities in opposition to the state, building constituencies from groups that hope to gain increased access to economic and political power. Such individuals mobilize a rhetoric of historical abuses and inequities, arousing fears of victimization among members of different groups who then become openly in conflict with one another or with their governments, as happened in the former Yugoslavia. Authoritarian governments may also repress ethnic groups as disruptive to government, as in the case of China's conflicts with Tibet and its Muslim Uighur minority, or even repress historical memory of certain ethnic groups in the interest of fostering national solidarity, as we see in the chapter opening story of Turkey.

The Nation-State and Indigenous Peoples

In much of the world today, particularly in North and South America, Africa, and parts of Asia, indigenous peoples are an important part of the multicultural landscape in nation-states. **Indigenous peoples** are those small-scale societies designated as bands, tribes, and chiefdoms that occupied their land prior to European contact. Generally, indigenous people are closely identified with their land, are relatively egalitarian, manage resources at the community level, and (previously) had high levels of economic self-sufficiency. They consider themselves distinct from other sectors of society now living in their territories and today function as nondominant sectors of the larger nation-states of which they are a part. Indigenous societies today are determined to preserve and transmit their lands and culture to future generations to continue their existence as a people, which frequently brings them into conflict with the nation-state (Lee 2000).

Indigenous peoples Small-scale societies designated as bands, tribes, or chiefdoms that occupied their land prior to European contact.

As a result of European expansion to Asia, Africa, and the New World beginning in the 15th century, many indigenous societies completely disappeared, or survived only as remnants in marginal geographic areas (see Chapter 12). The destruction of indigenous peoples intensified rapidly by the mid-19th century as new frontiers were opened up in nations such as the United States, Australia, and Brazil. Although there was much resistance, indigenous peoples in most places were no match for the military and economic power of nation-states. After World War II, many indigenous peoples were incorporated into new postcolonial states, such as in Indonesia, Malaysia, and India, and few independent, self-sufficient indigenous societies remained (Maybury-Lewis 1997).

The incorporation of indigenous peoples into modern nation-states involved at least partial destruction of their political and economic autonomy. Because indigenous peoples must maintain control over their land base and subsistence resources to remain self-sufficient and politically autonomous, their political defeat was usually accompanied by their economic marginalization. Europeans appropriated their land, and, without their land base, indigenous peoples were forced to give up their traditional livelihoods and participate in the global market economy or were pulled into national economies by their desire for Western goods. The colonial agenda was also imposed on indigenous peoples through the imposition and enforcement of Western law.

After World War II, the United Nations provided an international framework within which the concepts of human rights and self-determination were expanded to include indigenous peoples. Because the United Nations policy worked within the framework of the nation-state, however, it did little to support indigenous rights in any substantial way. Some of this changed with the passage of the Declaration on the Rights of Indigenous Peoples (2007), although several industrialized societies, such as Canada, fearful of indigenous land claims, did not sign the declaration.

National policies of neglect or hostility toward indigenous peoples were often based on the expectation that indigenous peoples eventually would disappear as they were assimilated into national cultures. International financial organizations, such as the World Bank and the International Monetary Fund, whose lending practices supported economic "development" programs that adversely affected the subsistence economies of indigenous peoples (Bodley 2000:378), were also founded on this assumption.

National policies of cultural assimilation, designed to foster a national identity, also contributed to cultural loss among indigenous peoples. In many Central and South American countries, indigenous Indian cultures may not be totally repressed, but Indians may be identified with a fossilized past as a folkloric irrelevance, a tourist commodity, or a backward culture standing in the way of national development (Alonso 1994:398). Only a few nations, most recently Bolivia, with the election of President Evo Morales, have raised indigenous Indian ethnicity to a central place in national identity and political leadership (Guillermorprieto 2006).

BRINGING IT BACK HOME:
DO GOOD FENCES MAKE GOOD NEIGHBORS?

Contemporary states view a fixed and secure border as essential to sovereignty and national security. They accept the notion that states have a right and responsibility to restrict and control immigration. The most passionate debate about immigration today concerns the U.S. border with Mexico, which has become increasingly militarized in an effort to keep out undocumented workers.

Politicians often justify the militarization of the border through the rhetoric of protecting domestic labor markets, and since 9/11, protecting the nation from terrorism. In spite of fencing, lighting, infrared scopes, underground sensors, increased law enforcement, and vigilante groups, hundreds of thousands of undocumented Mexicans continue to cross the border in search of work. They are encouraged by employers who use them as a source of cheap labor. Although there are supposedly penalties for employers who exploit undocumented workers in this way, in fact, there are far too few law enforcement officers to make such penalties meaningful. And so, although the debate over undocumented immigration generates much heat, most of it is aimed at the undocumented immigrants themselves, rather than the employers of such workers who are subject to much less vigilance.

The latest proposal to control undocumented migration is the erection of a double-layered 700-mile-long border fence. Thus far, measures such as the fence have only succeeded in directing immigration to more difficult and dangerous terrain, making the immigrants even more vulnerable to exploitation (Chavez 1998:196; Holthouse 2005).

The border fence is a controversial project and highlights the clash of interests and cultures in the American Southwest. Seventy-five miles of the border, at one of its most vulnerable points, is located on the Tohono O'odham (Indian) Reservation, not far from Tucson, Arizona. The Tohono O'odham oppose the wall, claiming a need to freely cross the border to visit friends and relatives in Mexico, take their children to school, gather traditional foods, and visit religious sites to perform rituals, all of which they have been doing for years. Their cultural concerns also focus on the wall's restricting the free range of deer, wild horses, coyotes, jackrabbits, and other animals they revere and regard as kin. "In our tradition we are taught to be concerned about every living thing as if they were people. We don't want that wall," said one tribal council member.

The Tohono O'odham cooperate extensively with the U.S. Border Patrol and the Department of Homeland Security in patrolling the border. As the federal government is the trustee of all Indian lands, it could build the fence through the reservation without tribal permission, but that would jeopardize the valuable help the Tohono O'odham now give the government (Archibold 2006).

Protecting borders is an urgent concern for nation-states as they try to hold back refugees, undocumented immigrants, and terrorists, who are increasingly crossing borders for economic and political purposes.

YOU DECIDE

1. Do you think human movement between states should be free and unrestricted? Why or why not? If you believe that there should be restriction of immigration, what criteria would you use for admitting immigrants?

2. What kinds of solutions would you suggest to the problem of undocumented immigration? Do you think that the construction of the border fence will make a substantial contribution in addressing this problem? Why or why not?

3. Decisions made by states often pit groups in society against one another. In this case, do you think the need to prevent undocumented immigrants crossing the border justifies overriding the cultural values of the Tohono O'odham? How would you mediate the conflict between the United States government and the Tohono O'odham over the building of a wall on their reservation?

CHAPTER SUMMARY

1. Anthropologists try to understand political organization by focusing on power: who has it, what are its sources, how is it related to other aspects of culture, especially political ideology, and how is it used in achieving public goals.

2. Social control in all societies is effected through formal sanctions such as exile, death, and punishments meted out by courts, judges, police, and other institutionalized forms of regulation. Conformity is also achieved through informal means such as gossip, ridicule, and ostracism.

3. Political organization is closely related to social differentiation, which is in turn related to the dominant pattern of making a living and exchanging goods and services. Band societies, which are characteristic of foragers, are egalitarian and dominated by generalized reciprocity.

4. Tribal societies, found among pastoralists and horticulturalists, also tend to be egalitarian and operate through generalized reciprocity as well as balanced reciprocity. Though tribal societies have many different nonviolent means of resolving conflicts within the society, they also have a high degree of warfare.

5. Chiefdoms, which are found in highly productive horticultural societies and among pastoralists, are called rank societies. Though kinship integrates the society, social units are socially ranked, and social position may be inherited. The chief is a central office, supported by his position as one who redistributes goods within the society.

6. The most complex form of political organization is the state, found mainly in agricultural and industrial societies, and associated with social stratification. Social, political, and economic inequality are institutionalized and maintained through a combination of internalized controls (hegemony) and force. Kinship ties between the upper and lower classes no longer serve to integrate the society, and there is a wide gap in standards of living.

7. The nation-state is a state that identifies itself with a culturally homogenous group and a shared history and geographic territory, and uses various social and cultural institutions to foster nationalism.
8. Many nation-states are in fact multicultural, incorporating ethnic groups who also define themselves as culturally homogenous. Sometimes ethnic conflict occurs between various ethnic groups within a nation, or as in China, between ethnic groups and the nation iself.
9. Many nation-states today incorporate indigenous peoples, whose cultures, economies, and social institutions are constrained by the need to live within these complex societies and their regulatory systems.

KEY TERMS

acephalous
age grades
age set
authority
band
bigman
bureaucracy
chiefdom
citizenship
compensation
deviants
egalitarian society
elites
ethnic groups
ethnic identity
ethnic boundaries
factions
gossip
government
hegemony

indigenous peoples
law
leadership
mediation
nation-state
political ideology
political organization
political process
power
rank society
rebellion
revolution
secret societies
social complexity
social differentiation
state
stratified society
tribe
warfare (war)

© AFP/Getty Images

The first African American president, Barack Obama, and his appointment of the first Hispanic Supreme Court Justice, Sonia Sotomayor, represent a historic moment in the intersection of race, class, and ethnicity in the United States.

CHAPTER **10**

STRATIFICATION: CLASS, RACE, ETHNICITY, AND CASTE

CHAPTER OUTLINE

TROUBLE IN PARADISE

NE early Sunday morning in September 1931, in Honolulu, Hawai'i, an elegantly dressed woman walking alone waved down a car. As the driver lowered his window, the woman, whose face was bruised, peered inside and asked, "Are you white people?" When the driver said yes, she said, "Thank God," climbed in the car, and directed them to drive her home. Within 24 hours, everyone in Honolulu heard the shocking story of a young navy officer's wife, Thalia Massie, who claimed she was gang-raped by a carload of native Hawaiians (Stannard 2005:7–8). The ensuing rape trial and subsequent events, known as the Massie case, were a national media sensation, playing on the obsessive fears in America, and particularly the South, over the assault of white womanhood by blacks and other "people of color."

As the rape investigation proceeded, five young men identified by Thalia Massie were arrested: two Native Hawaiians, two Japanese, and one Chinese. The prosecutor explicitly played on white fears regarding the vulnerability of "white womanhood" attacked by "lust-sodden beasts," as he called the defendants, urging the jury to "protect its women" and justify their manhood by voting guilty. In the face of the lies, contradictions, distortions, and suppression of evidence by the prosecution, the racially and ethnically mixed jury was deadlocked after deliberating 97 hours. The judge called a mistrial, allowing the defendants to go free on bail. A storm of outrage followed, with prominent whites, including high-level naval officers, claiming that Thalia Massie was another victim of Hawai'i's "half-breed natives" who had voted along racial lines. As a result of the verdict, in January 1932, Thalia Massie's mother and husband and two sailors kidnapped and killed Joe Kahahawai, one of the Hawaiian defendants. On their way to dump Joe's dead body into the ocean, the four were stopped and arrested for murder by a passing policeman. The national media went wild with headlines such as "Honor Killing in Honolulu Threatens Race War," focusing on Hawai'i as an unsafe place for white women. In the South, many called for the original defendants to be lynched. (p. 274).

The four whites accused of the murder were defended by Clarence Darrow, who reminded the jury that it was a widely shared American belief—an unwritten law—that a man has a right to kill another man who has assaulted his wife, especially when the rape victim was white and the rapist was not (p. 376). This time, the ethnically mixed jury found the four defendants guilty of manslaughter and, though they were sentenced to ten years of hard labor, Hawai'i's governor, under political pressure from whites, pardoned the defendants, who then secretly took a navy ship to San Francisco (p. 390).

But the Massie case was not quite over. Under pressure from a different direction, the governor ordered the Pinkerton Agency to investigate

Thalia Massie's original rape charges. The Pinkerton report overwhelming demonstrated that the defendants were not guilty and indeed questioned whether Thalia Massie was raped at all. As a result, the judge dropped the charges against the original defendants (Stannard 2005:398–99).

The Massie case officially ended here, but its impact permanently transformed the ethnic, racial, political, and class structure of Hawai'i. At the top of this structure were the minority of whites, or *haoles,* who owned most of the land and who dominated business, the media, the territorial government, and the navy establishment at Pearl Harbor. Most of Hawai'i's population—immigrants of Portuguese, Filipino, Chinese, and Japanese descent—were plantation workers or slum dwellers who occupied the lowest rungs of society. Despite their common class interests, these immigrant groups had little social interaction and no class solidarity. The native Hawaiians were viewed by whites more favorably than the immigrants, but were little better off economically and were also feared as racial "others."

As a result of the murder of Joe Kahahawai and the Massie trial, however, the beginnings of solidarity appeared among the various immigrant populations and the native Hawaiians, along with a new, inclusive concept of racial/ethnic identity. The term *local,* previously used for any longtime resident of the islands, now was used only for native Hawaiians and longtime Pacific Islander and Asian residents. *Haoles*—whites—whatever their character, could never be "local."

Hawaiian, Japanese, Chinese, Filipino, and Portuguese community leaders also began finding common political ground, as Hawai'i (along with the rest of the nation) turned overwhelmingly Democratic in the 1932 elections; this included native Hawaiians, who previously voted Republican, partly out of a fear of political dominance by the Japanese. The new ethnic solidarity was also reflected in the increasing success of the labor movement. Although earlier ethnic separatism had undermined the success of labor protests, now strikes by combined ethnic groups of workers succeeded both on the plantations and on the docks.

The impact of the Massie case in transforming the racial, ethnic, and class configuration in Hawai'i illustrates the important role of culture and history in constructing categories of race and ethnicity. It demonstrates how these identities interact in different systems of social inequality and how they change over time, within specific economic and historical contexts. . . As our opening story indicates, class, race, ethnicity, and caste are culturally constructed and intersect in our own and other socially stratified societies. We need to hold this concept in mind as we examine the various issues involved in social stratification.

EXPLAINING SOCIAL STRATIFICATION

social stratification A social hierarchy resulting from the relatively permanent unequal distribution of goods and services in a society.

Social stratification is the structure that results from unequal access to and distribution of goods and services in a society. Social stratification is related to social complexity and is one of the criteria by which states, the most socially complex type of society, are defined. No society has ever successfully organized a large and diverse population without stratification and inequalities.

Two basic perspectives on social stratification are functionalism and conflict theory. **Functionalism** holds that social stratification generally benefits the whole society, by rewarding people socially and economically for working harder, taking risks, doing difficult jobs, or spending more time in school or occupational training. For example, the rewards of prestige and high income motivate some people to become medical doctors, a profession that requires more than ten years of higher education and is difficult to achieve but necessary for the well-being of the whole society.

functionalism (functionalist perspective) The anthropological theory that specific cultural institutions function to support the structure of a society or serve the needs of its people.

Functional theory has several flaws: The inequality characteristic of social stratification is not always functional for the larger society, and not all of society's most difficult jobs are well rewarded. In the United States, for example, schoolteachers, nurses, and many others do difficult jobs that may require substantial training, yet are not that well compensated financially. In addition, many low-prestige "dirty jobs" that are nevertheless essential to the functioning of society are not well paid. Nor does social stratification necessarily result in recruiting the most able people to the most demanding positions. In addition, though wealth is a powerful motivating force in many contemporary societies, money's ability to motivate a person may have limits, and other considerations also count (see Chapter 6). Furthermore, although inequality seems inevitable in large-scale social systems, even in the most open class systems, resentment, sometimes simmering, sometimes openly expressed, always seems to accompany substantial inequalities (Scott 1992), leading to conflict or violence. This is especially true when the inequalities are based on ascribed factors—family background, social connections, gender, ethnicity, race, inherited wealth, and so on—that an individual is born with and cannot change (Berreman 1988).

conflict theory A perspective on social stratification that focuses on economic inequality as a source of conflict and change.

In contrast to functionalism, **conflict theory** holds that social stratification results from the constant struggle for scarce goods and services in stratified societies. Inequalities exist because those individuals and groups who have acquired power, wealth, and prestige use their assets and their power to maintain control over the system of production and the apparatus of the state. When these attempts to establish dominance falter or are challenged, elites may fall back on the threat or use of force to maintain the status quo. Conflict and change are essential dimensions in understanding social stratification.

Conflict theory is central to the work of Karl Marx and his followers, who focus on the economic system in explaining social stratification. According to Marx, the relationship of individuals to the means of production is critical in determining how much power and prestige they have. Marx differentiated two main social classes in capitalist society: the capitalists, who own the means of production, and the workers, who must sell their labor to survive. Marx predicted that the conflict between the workers and the owners of the means of production, a central feature of capitalism, would eventually lead to its downfall. Although Marxist predictions have not been fully realized, conflict theory has been useful in exploring some aspects of social stratification in different kinds of societies. However, just as the functional view of inequality may lead theorists to ignore the possibility of structural conflict, conflict theorists may sometimes ignore the social mechanisms that promote solidarity across class, racial, ethnic, and caste lines.

Criteria of Stratification: Power, Wealth, and Prestige

The social stratification system of any society depends on the complex interaction of the three main dimensions of stratification: power, wealth, and prestige. Anthropologists analyze **power** (the ability to control resources in one's own interest) by examining its sources, the channels through which it is exercised, and the goals for which it is deployed to achieve (see Chapter 9). For example, in the United States, we might analyze the different sources, uses, and goals of power among corporate presidents, elected public officials, entertainment celebrities, or heads of organized crime families. From a cross-cultural perspective, we might compare the sources and uses of power of an American president, the prime minister of France, the general secretary of the Communist Party of China, and the ruling royal family of Saudi Arabia.

power The ability to impose one's will on others.

Wealth is the accumulation of material resources or access to the means of producing these resources. Although wealth is not the sole criterion of social status even in capitalist societies, it can eventually translate into high social position and power. Wealth enables people to send their children to the most prestigious schools, buy homes in the best neighborhoods, and to join the right social clubs. It further enables people to gain access to political power by giving large campaign contributions to politicians. It may also allow people to run for political office themselves.

wealth The accumulation of material resources or access to the means of producing these resources.

Prestige, or social honor, is the third dimension of social stratification. The cultural bases of prestige vary cross-culturally: Prestige may be related to race and ethnicity, income, accumulated wealth, power, personal characteristics such as integrity, family history, and the display of material

prestige Social honor or respect.

Occupation, as both a source of income and social status, is probably the most prevalent class marker in the United States. Here, Americans protest increasing inequality, as the loss of jobs, with its related decline in income, has most affected the working and middle classes.

© Joan Gregg

goods. Not all wealth, in and of itself, is a source of prestige. For example, people who earn their incomes illegally generally have less prestige than do those whose incomes are legally earned. The head of an illegal gambling syndicate, a drug kingpin, or a Somali pirate may make hundreds of millions of dollars but have little prestige. On the other hand, few winners of the Nobel Peace Prize make much money but they surely have great prestige. And committing oneself to poverty, as India's great leader Mahatma Gandhi did, may paradoxically be a source of greater prestige than the display of wealth.

A key source of prestige in all societies is occupation, both for its relation to income and the cultural values attached to it, though different societies rank occupations differently. In the Hindu caste system (discussed further later), occupations are ranked according to their level of spiritual purity or pollution, a concept formally absent from occupational rankings in the United States. Americans do, however, connect prestige—or lack of it—and the "dirt" involved in various occupations, though this is not always voiced aloud. Dirty jobs are generally not prestigious jobs.

As socioeconomic conditions change, the cultural value system that supports a particular system of ranking occupational prestige may also change. In 18th-century Europe, surgery was performed by barbers and was a lower-class occupation; in contemporary North America, surgeons rank very high in prestige, both because they make a great deal of money and because surgery requires great skill and training. In the People's Republic of China, the prestige and power associated with different occupations has almost completely reversed itself from traditional Chinese society. Before the communist revolution, China followed a Confucian value system, in which scholars had the highest honor. After the revolution, workers were honored and scholars often explicitly ridiculed and despised. Today, with China's growing free market practices and increasing economic role in globalization, businesspeople, previously a target of socialist contempt and even violence, are highly regarded, or at least highly rewarded financially.

Social scientists have long debated whether prestige or economic factors are more important in explaining the behavior of people in complex, stratified societies. Karl Marx argued for the primacy of economic or class interests whereas Max Weber, a German sociologist of the late 19th century, argued for the importance of status rather than economic interests. Although Marx thought that people were (or should be) most conscious of their class membership (their economic status), Weber believed that people may value prestige and the symbolic aspects of status even more than their economic position. Weber further argued that political action can be motivated by a group's desire to defend its social position as well as, or even in opposition to, its economic self-interest, a position Marx called "false consciousness." In the American South, for example, poor whites did not join poor blacks in working to improve their common economic position because they were more committed to maintaining the prestige value based on color or race.

CLASS SYSTEMS

In comparing social stratification systems, anthropologists differentiate between "open systems" where social position is based on **achieved status** (a person's individual efforts) and "closed systems," where social position is based on **ascribed status** (based on characteristics from birth, such as race, ethnicity, family of origin, or biological sex). In fact, in most modern complex societies, both achievement and ascription play roles in the social stratification system, though to different degrees.

A **class** is a category of people who all have about the same opportunity to obtain economic resources, power, and prestige and who are ranked high and low in relation to other class categories. In a **class system**, there are possibilities for **social mobility**, or movement between the classes or social strata, which are (ideally) based on individual achievement rather than

achieved status A social position that a person chooses or achieves on his or her own.

ascribed status A social position into which a person is born.

class A category of people who all have about the same opportunity to obtain economic resources, power, and prestige and who are ranked relative to other categories.

class system A form of social stratification in which the different strata form a continuum and social mobility is possible.

social mobility Movement from one social stratum to another.

ascribed status. Even in the most open class systems, however, ascribed statuses always play a role in moving from one class to another. Closed stratification systems, in which there is little or no possibility of social mobility, are called caste systems and are discussed later in the chapter.

In class systems, the different strata (classes) are not sharply separated from one another but form a continuum. Social mobility (upward) from one class to another—through means such as education, marriage, good luck, hard work, and taking risks—is theoretically possible for all of society's members. In the United States, we call this opportunity for upward social mobility for all "the American Dream," and it is a central cultural value. Although belief in the American Dream and an open society is strong among all the diverse racial and ethnic groups in the United States (*New York Times* 2005), evidence indicates that educational achievement, levels of indebtedness, income, and wealth accumulation, including home ownership and home foreclosures, are significantly correlated (Haskins, Isaacs, and Sawhill 2008; Bialostok 2009).

◼️ The American Class System

Gloria Castillo, 22, a child of undocumented immigrants, was married, with two children, from a tough neighborhood in Dallas, Texas. She worked the night shift at the drive-through window at a highway Burger King, from 10:30 PM to 6:30 AM, for $252 a week before taxes, and received no health care benefits. To help make ends meet, she worked a second job, earning $150 a night for the 1 ½ hours it took her to clean three bathrooms in a local bar. Her husband worked at an auto parts place during the day, so Gloria took the children, ages 7 and 8, for a fast-food breakfast before dropping them at school, returned home, slept till 2:00, picked up the kids, prepared their frozen food dinners, put them to bed at 7:00, spent a few hours with her husband, and left for work. On Saturdays, she attended a community college, working toward a degree as a paralegal. "I got dreams," she said (LeDuff 2006b).

The American Dream, as expressed in the life of Gloria Castillo, is closely tied to other core American values such as individualism, meritocracy, the work ethic, optimism, pragmatism, progress, and a belief in the ability of individuals to control the circumstances of their lives. One corollary of the American Dream is that economic failure and downward social mobility is largely viewed as a result of the individual failings as well as the behaviors, attitudes, and cultures of members of the lower classes, rather than as a systemic aspect of social structure (see Durrenberger and Doukas 2008 for a different view). Until the recent recession, downward mobility was almost invisible in the media and in the culture. As anthropologist Katherine Newman observed, "Downward mobility is a hidden dimension of our society's experience because it . . . does not fit into our cultural universe" (1999).

Currently, downward mobility has become a highly visible dimension of the American class system, increasingly making media headlines (Greenhouse 2008). It has now become clearer to many Americans that systemic aspects of our economic system outweigh individual factors in explaining economic failure and class inequality. Instead of reading stories like those about Gloria Castillo, we read about people like Mark Cooper who lost his $70,000 a year job as a security manager for a Fortune 500 company and is now working as a janitor for $12 an hour and feels lucky to have the job (Luo 2009). As we see in the Bringing It Back Home feature at the end of this chapter, the cultural emphasis on individualism central to the American Dream also leads many to underestimate the important role that government programs and policies have played in creating a growing middle class since World War II.

The Material Basis of Class in the United States

There is no complete cultural consensus in the United States on the social class structure, how the social classes are defined, or even whether there are social classes at all. American optimism and the economic growth post-World War II enhanced the perception that the American stratification system was not one of deep divides but rather it was like a ladder with lots of rungs, which could be climbed with ingenuity and hard work (Durrenberger 2001).

Recent—and growing—statistical and ethnographic evidence contests this image, however. Although materially, middle-class Americans typically have a sturdy roof over their heads, television sets, computers, cell phones, air conditioners, and cars (even if all financed by debt), they are also struggling with growing unemployment, loss of wealth in the form of stocks, lack of access to medical care that often accompanies unemployment, inability to pay the mortgage and subsequent home foreclosures, the rising cost of college tuition and the high cost of student loans, and many other criteria that define middle-class status.

The culturally defined view of America as a middle-class nation is also challenged by the growing income inequality between the huge incomes of the very rich, and the declining opportunities and stagnant or declining incomes of ordinary people. But despite ambiguities about the definitions of the American class system, most Americans would agree that the rungs on the ladder of social mobility are most significantly defined by income. Income is the gateway to a middle-class lifestyle or subculture and serves as the basis for family economic security. Over the long term, sufficient and steady income is essential toward saving and accumulating assets, especially home ownership, and in supporting a consumer-oriented middle-class lifestyle.

The widely held perception of America as an equal society for all has become unhinged from reality over the past 30 years, which have seen an extraordinary jump in income inequality. During this period, the after-tax income of the top 1 percent of American households jumped 139 percent to more than $700,000; the income of the middle fifth of households rose only 17 percent, to $43,700, and the income of the poorest fifth rose only 9 percent. In 2004, the chief executives at the 100 largest companies in California took home a collective $1.1 billion, an increase of nearly 20 percent during these three decades. For most workers, only during the speculative bubble of the 1990s, did income rise above inflation. Reductions in pensions have also increased the prospect of financial insecurity in retirement. Tax cuts for the wealthy under President George W. Bush greatly exacerbated this inequality: The 400 taxpayers with the highest incomes—over $87 million a year each—now pay income tax and Medicare and Social Security taxes amounting to the same percentage of their incomes as people making $50,000 to $75,000 a year. As Warren Buffett, one of the richest men in the world has repeatedly emphasized, his 2006 tax rate on his $46 million income was 17.7 percent, while his secretary's tax rate was 30 percent (Brown 2009).

Income and accumulated wealth are correlated with good health, quality health care in illness, and the life span itself (J. Scott 2005). People with higher education and income are less likely to have and die of heart disease, strokes, diabetes, and many types of cancer (Scott 2005). They are also more likely to benefit from advances in medicine, have more useful information about medicine, and be covered by health insurance. They are also less likely to smoke, are less obese, exercise more, and eat healthier food than people in the lower classes. Sufficient and steady family income is also the essential gateway to increasing **life chances** (realizing opportunities for success) and social mobility. Insufficient and irregular income negatively affects not only one's own life chances and social mobility but also those of one's children (Bowles, Gintis, and Groves 2005; Corak 2004; Frank and Cook 1996; Lareau 2003; Neckerman 2004).

life chances The opportunities that people have to fulfill their potential in society.

Social Classes as Subcultures

In addition to material differences, social classes also differ in attitudes, behavior, consumption patterns, lifestyle, values, and social connections. The members of a social class tend to share similar life experiences, occupational roles, values, educational backgrounds, affiliations, leisure activities, buying habits, religious and social affiliations, and political views. Not merely income, but how that income is spent, is an important dimension of class status.

On the surface, the cultural aspects of social class in America seem to be blurring because, while income and wealth inequalities rise, class-related lifestyles expressed in consumer purchasing are growing more similar. This is partly because globalization and easy credit make cheaper consumer goods more easily available; in addition, more people within a household are working, contributing to slightly increasing median household incomes (*New York Times* 2005:135).

However, although surface lifestyle similarities between classes increase, income does make a difference. As what were once luxury goods have gone down with the market, the market produces ever more expensive luxury goods that are only affordable for those with great incomes and wealth: $4,000 handbags, a $100,000 Porsche 911, and $12,000 mother/baby diamond bracelet sets. Even more than material goods, class differences are expressed in personal services and exclusive experiences: personal chefs and personal trainers, face-lifts and other cosmetic surgery, private school for children, and private jet tours of the seven most wonderful sights in the world costing $50,000 (Newman and Chen 2007). But perhaps the most important lifestyle difference related to income is the ability of the wealthy to buy homes in residential areas restricted to those with a great deal of money. Where people live reflects the American class structure in one of its most permanent aspects, and impacts many other dimensions of life, such as safety, availability of high-quality schools, and the chances of being affected by environmental pollution and disasters (Checker 2005, see Chapter 14, pp. 340–341).

Class differences also significantly affect such things as family structure and educational achievement. The upper classes are more likely to be married before they have children, they have fewer children, and they have them later in life. All these factors impinge on the possibilities of upward social mobility (*New York Times* 2005:125). As Katherine Newman notes, family circumstances are among the most important factors determining whether those in the category she calls the "near poor," who have household incomes between $20,000 and $40,000 a year for a family of four, can make it into the middle class (Newman and Chen 2006). "Women with children and no one to help them with those kids [are] much more likely to get trapped—they [can't] get more education which limit[s] their job options [and] their contact with the labor market [is] more fragile and episodic" (Newman quoted in Press 2007:23).

In addition to a shared culture, members of a social class also tend to associate more with one another than with people in other classes,

© Nubar Alexanian/Stock, Boston, Inc.

Consumption of material goods has been a central marker of the American middle class. This consumption has largely been built on credit card debt and the availability of cheap, Asian-imported goods. This system collapsed in the recession of 2008, as Americans began to cut back on nonessential consumer purchases.

reinforcing a common lifestyle. Through interaction based on common residence and schooling, religious participation, voluntary associations, and other social institutions, people learn the lifestyle of their social class. Because lifestyle is an important part of sociability, informal and intimate social relationships, such as friendship and marriage, also tend to bring together people from the same social class. This partly explains why social classes tend to be largely endogamous.

▌RACE: A CULTURAL CONSTRUCTION

When traveling in Malaysia, Nanda asked a friend to explain the exceptionally diverse society. He began by saying, "The Indians are the black people," referring to the dark skin color of the Indians in Malaysia who are mainly from South India. Joking with him a little, Nanda asked, "If the Indians are the black people, who are the white people?" "Oh," he answered, without missing a beat, "the Portuguese used to be the white people but now the Chinese are the white people."

This conversation, and our chapter opening story about Hawai'i, emphasize the anthropological view that "race" is a cultural construction, based on specific histories and social structures. To make sense of the conversation about Malaysia, we need to know that what has changed in Malaysia is the economic position of Malaysia's main ethnic groups: the Chinese, the Indians, the indigenous Malays, and the small population of Portuguese descended from 16th-century traders who politically dominated Malay society for 100 years. The Portuguese were later defeated by the British, who colonized Malaysia (then called Malaya), and replaced the Portuguese in the most important political and economic positions. When the British left, after Malaysia's independence, the Chinese moved into many commercial and professional positions and now dominate the Malaysian economy. Having taken over the economic position formerly occupied by the Portuguese and then the British, the Chinese are now defined as having taken over their racial category ("white people") as well.

race A culturally constructed category based on *perceived* physical differences.

The term **race** is used to define people based on *perceived* physical differences that imply hereditary differences. But although anthropologists emphasize that race is not a natural category, it can and does become a significant cultural and social fact: It is used to justify differential treatment and discrimination and affects the lives of both the racial majority and racial minorities.

Even when there are no objective physical differences between groups of people, such as skin color, other differences, such as class, ethnicity, and caste, are often conceptualized in racial terms. The 19th-century English theologian Charles Kingsley described the Irish as "human chimpanzees . . .

a race of utter savages, truly barbarous and brutish . . . ," noting unhappily, that "[their] skins are as white as ours" (in Curtis 1968:84). The idea of a "degenerate Irish race," differing from the British by class and religion, was used by the British to justify their control over Ireland. As the Irish migrated to the United States, the notion of their cultural and biological inferiority was also commonly expressed in the language of race (Shanklin 1994:3–7).

Such differences, when discussed in racial terms, are then associated with traits of culture, character, morality, intelligence, personality, and purity that are seen as natural, inherited, and unalterable—in a word, ascribed. Although it is socially easier to distinguish a race when individuals differ in obvious physical characteristics, the English perceptions of the Irish and, as we will see later, the racial designation of many European immigrants demonstrate that a lack of observable physical differences does not prohibit the invention of racial categories or the emergence of racial stratification.

Racial stratification occurs in societies with different culturally constructed views of race. For example, in Brazil, race is viewed as a continuum, with multiple racial categories, no laws against interracial marriage, and a comparatively high degree of interracial sexual intimacy (Goldstein 1999; Sheriff 2001). However, racial stratification is still an important aspect of Brazilian social structure. In the United States, race is largely defined as a binary opposition between black and white, although a new idea of "mixed-race" identity is becoming more important. Under **apartheid** in South Africa, multiple exclusive racial classifications—black, white, colored, and Asian—were formally recognized, treated differently in law and life, and occupied different and almost exclusive statuses within the society (A. Marx 1995; Frederickson 2009). Although apartheid was dismantled in the 1990s, and blacks enormously increased their political power, economic racial stratification remains a dominant feature of South African society.

apartheid The South African system of multiple exclusive racial groups—black, white, colored, and Asian—that were formally recognized, segregated, treated differently in law and life, and occupied different and almost exclusive statuses within the society.

Race and Racial Stratification in the United States

As noted earlier, race in the United States is culturally constructed largely on the basis of a few observable traits such as skin color and hair texture and presumed ancestry. Apart from a few regional variations on race—for example, the Anglo-Hispanic distinction in the American Southwest, the complex racial/ethnic system in Hawai'i, and the place of Native Americans—historically, the North American system of racial stratification has primarily divided people into blacks and whites. This dichotomy ignores the reality that skin color actually forms a continuum and that widespread racial mixing occurred historically and continues in the present (Basson 2008). Recent trends show, however, that a cultural view of race that includes a mixed racial identity is increasing. For the first time, the 2000 U.S. Census permitted people to self-identify as more than one race, and seven million people, almost half of whom were under 18, chose to do so (Boynton 2006; Nobles 2000). Indeed, some scholars suggest that as multiraciality undermines the American "binary race" construction (Daniel 2006), the cultural construction of race in the United States may be becoming more like Brazil's, where race is viewed as a continuum, rather than discrete categories.

Furthermore, although we in the United States think of race mainly in terms of African Americans, Hispanic/Latino Americans, Asian Americans, or Native Americans (that is, minority races), anthropologists point out that white is also a racial identity. Because white is a cultural norm in the United States, however, the privileges and advantages that go with it are unconsciously assumed and largely invisible (T. Allen 1997; Frankenberg 1993; Hartigan 1997; J. Hill 1998). For whites, ordinary experiences such as shopping, buying or renting a place to live, finding a hairdresser, or using a credit card, do not generally involve a reflection on their racial identity. But for Hispanic/Latino Americans, Asian Americans, Native Americans, and particularly African Americans, these everyday activities cannot be taken for granted (McIntosh 1999).

The binary form of American racial classification and its accompanying racial stratification grew out of historical conditions of slavery. The racial stereotypes that were used to justify slavery and later segregation were, shamefully, supported by the then-emerging biological and social sciences, including anthropology, which legitimized races as hierarchically arranged natural categories characterized by physical, cultural, intellectual, and moral differences (Smedley 1998). These hypotheses today are roundly critiqued by anthropologists (Nisbett 2007).

The Intersection of Race and Class

Although academics debate whether social class or race is more important in explaining the American stratification system, both these factors, along with ethnicity, interact in complex ways to produce the particular social stratification system of the United States. Race is misguided as a scientific concept, but race as a social fact is centrally implicated in the American social stratification system. The intersection of race with class impacts every aspect of life; indeed, it impacts the potential of life itself. This is demonstrated by statistics on the higher mortality rate for both infants and mothers among African Americans (Stolberg 1999; Chelala 2006), access to health care, and health care outcomes. Cancer survival rates, death rates for heart disease and HIV/AIDS, and complications from diseases like diabetes, such as loss of a limb or kidney disease, are all substantially higher for African Americans than for whites. The causes of these and many other health disparities are clearly linked to unequal treatment and health care. And these are linked significantly to medical insurance. In New York City, for example, 30 percent of African Americans, Latinos, and members of other minority groups are uninsured, compared to 17 percent of whites. Where people are covered by Medicaid, they are also treated differently by health care institutions, more likely, for example, to be seen by rotating medical students and interns and thus less likely to receive coordinated medical care (Calman et al. 2005:25).

Race and racism are also highly correlated with industrial pollution (Akom 2008; and see Checker 2005) and in the experience of natural disasters, as tragically demonstrated by Hurricane Katrina. In New Orleans, death came most often for the poor—those who had no private transportation, no credit cards, no wealthy relatives to rely on, no home insurance, and no resources to evacuate the young and the aged. As anthropologist Neil Smith notes, not just the effect of the hurricane, but the government's response to it, deepened the social grooves of class and race already built into New Orleans society (Paredes 2006; Smith 2005:9). In a sad confirmation of this view, a white vigilante caught shooting African Americans during the Katrina aftermath justified his action as defense of his property and neighborhood, saying, "I'm not a racist. . . . I'm a classist. I want to live around people who want the same things as me" (Thompson 2009). Thus do race and class intersect!

Racial stratification also affects job and educational opportunities open to racial minorities; access to fair credit, salary levels, and accumulation of wealth, all of which affect social mobility; home ownership, mortgage rates, and housing foreclosures; use of public spaces; levels and types of violence; and interactions with law enforcement and the criminal justice system (Bajaj and Nixon 2006; *New York Times* 2005; Reed, Jr. 2006). As anthropologist Faye Harrison points out (2009), in spite of the election of the first African American U.S. president, racism as a system is still embedded in American society, particularly in the forms of mass unemployment, mass incarceration, and mass disenfranchisement. Although African Americans and Latinos comprise only 25 percent of the national population, they are more than 60 percent of those in prison. Black women, too, are overrepresented in prison, convicted at rates 10 to 35 times higher than white women. The effect of these disparities on minority communities is also reflected in many state laws that disqualify ex-felons from employment, public housing, welfare benefits, college student loans, and voting.

The importance of the intersection of race with class is indicated by long-standing inequalities in income and wealth between blacks and whites: In 2005, the median per capita income was $16,629 for blacks and $28,946 for whites. This economic gap is even more obvious in asset accumulation: In 2004, African American families' median net worth was $20,600, and that of Latinos was $18,600, only 14.6 percent and 13.2 percent, respectively, of the $140,700 median net worth for whites (Muhammad 2008). The current recession has made this gap even wider. The meltdown in Detroit particularly impacted African Americans: The auto industry was one of their most important routes to upward mobility into the middle class, and the chances for new employment among African Americans is reduced by the lack of college education compared to other groups (Chapman 2008).

Educational achievement also reflects the stratified nature of class, race, ethnicity, and indigenous status in the United States, though anthropologists differ in explaining this variation. Some anthropologists and other social scientists (for example, Patterson 2006) argue that variation in educational achievement reflects cultural differences among racial and ethnic minorities. "Involuntary minorities," as anthropologist John Ogbu categorizes African Americans, Mexican Americans, and Native Americans, view social stratification in the United States as unfair, permanent, and systemically discriminatory, and develop cultural traits that hinder their success. In contrast, "voluntary minorities," or immigrants, put more emphasis on education as the main route to economic success and accordingly exhibit higher degrees of educational achievement (Gibson and Ogbu 1991).

Other anthropologists acknowledge the negative effect of these "oppositional cultures" of involuntary minorities. However, they also emphasize that these cultural patterns have their source in the poverty of inner-city neighborhoods, discriminatory educational policies, overcrowded and underfunded schools, and less qualified teachers (Gibson 1997; Mateu-Gelabert and Lune 2007; Bourgois 1993), and that most involuntary minorities do view educational achievement as a major route to upward social mobility (Anderson 1999). Thus, where an oppositional cultural model puts the burden on involuntary minorities to change their culture, other anthropologists emphasize the need for a fairer distribution of resources, more equitable educational policies, and the transformation of schools into safer, more disciplined environments.

ETHNICITY

As noted in Chapter 9, ethnicity, like the nation, is a constructed narrative that focuses on cultural rather than racial differences, though it may incorporate these. Nation-states may be characterized by ethnic stratification, as different ethnic groups have differential access to political and economic resources, and different symbolic roles in the national narrative.

Ethnicity in the United States

In the United States, the dominant narrative of ethnicity is that of America as a nation of immigrants, who come to this country to pursue freedom from fear and the vision of the American Dream. This takes place simultaneously with the ongoing project of creating an American national identity—a process that began with the American Revolution (A. Wallace 1999), based on a common culture and language. In contrast to this idealistic vision, ethnicity has always been implicated in America's system of social stratification. The earliest visions of America as a land of economic opportunity, upward mobility, and political freedom were largely restricted to immigrants from northern and western Europe. The American Constitution limited citizenship to those who were "free and white [and male]," which excluded Native Americans, Mexican Americans, and African Americans. By the 1920s, immigration was also restricted for Asians, Latin Americans, and people from southern and eastern Europe, and the Middle East. These restrictions were based on a widely shared view that these people were racially inferior, or came from cultures that would prevent their assimilation into the larger American culture.

Race remains a salient category in the definition of Native Americans and African Americans. Latinos, including Mexican Americans, however, are more likely to identify themselves—and be identified by others— in terms of their ethnicity (see Strum 2010). For many ethnic groups of European ancestry, the most obvious cultural differences, particularly language, have faded, but more subtle ethnic patterns continue to exist, such as food preferences; verbal and nonverbal means of communication; the experience of health, illness, and pain; occupational choices; and voting patterns (Cerroni-Long 1993; Schensul 1997).

Simultaneously with the American cultural narrative that the United States is "a nation of immigrants," contentious debates over immigration have a long history, growing out of both economic and political considerations. Earlier economic concerns that immigration results in lowering wages for American workers, or that immigrants are subject to political manipulation, continue to be passionately argued today.

Until the mid-20th century, the dominant American ideology regarding immigrants was **assimilation**, a process through which immigrants were expected to abandon their distinctive cultures and become "mainstream" Americans. Settlement houses, public schools, and citizenship classes were formed to teach immigrants "American" ways and to motivate them to assimilate. The famous "melting pot" analogy compared American society to a stew in which all ethnicities were blended to produce an American identity (see Glazer and Moynihan 1970). This was true to some extent, and by the 1950s, much of the cultural distinctiveness of many ethnic groups had been lost in the so-called melting pot. However, the melting pot analogy referred primarily to ethnic groups descended from European populations. It excluded Mexican, African, and Native Americans, and people from Asia or the Middle East, although they too (particularly Native Americans)

assimilation The process by which immigrants abandon their cultural distinctiveness and become mainstream Americans.

Multiculturalism highlights the cultural contributions that different immigrant groups make to the American nation. One element of highlighting ethnic diversity is through ethnically focused parades, as in this St. Patrick's Day parade in New York City.

multiculturalism The view that cultural diversity is a positive value and makes an important contribution to contemporary societies.

were subject to assimilationist policies (Wallace 1999; Norgren 1996). And indeed, although European ethnic groups did lose much of their cultural identity, group identities persisted as ethnic groups organized around political and economic goals (Glazer and Moynihan 1970).

After the civil rights movement of the 1960s, concepts of ethnicity and its relation to American nationhood changed. **Multiculturalism**, which embraces cultural diversity as a positive value that adds richness to the whole society, emerged to contest older, assimilationist views and to challenge the theory of the melting pot. Most importantly, a new Immigration and Nationality Act, passed in 1965, was explicitly aimed at reversing the discriminatory basis of earlier immigration laws. This act greatly expanded the number of people permitted to immigrate from nations previously discriminated against, abolished immigration quotas, gave high priority to the social goal of family unification, and put refugee immigration on a more structured basis (Lamphere 1992:Introduction; Fix and Passel 1994). As a significant result of this law, immigration increased substantially, particularly from areas like the Middle East, the Indian subcontinent, China, Korea, the Caribbean, parts of Central and South America, and Africa, which had previously been restricted by earlier immigration laws.

As anthropologists study these new immigrants, they take into account the variety of changing contexts of immigration as they are shaped by changes in local, national, and global economies and political conditions (Brettell 2003; di Leonardo 1984; Lamphere 1992). Such conditions include the events of 9/11 (Nguyen 2005), especially as they affect Muslim immigrants; the rise of international terrorism; the cyclical nature of global, national, and regional economies; the increase of illegal immigration and issues of the American border with Mexico; transnationalism (Glick-Schiller, Basch, and Szanton-Blanc 1992); and the changing nature of immigrant social networks in the United States (Wong 2008) and globally.

Although little ethnographic attention had previously been paid to Muslim immigrants to the United States, this has changed (see Ewing 2008). From an early construction of a common "Arab" ethnic identity, which included both Christian and Muslim immigrants from the Middle East, Muslim identity has increased and diversified since 1965. Muslims are now more ethnically diverse, and the younger generation, particularly, is more oriented toward religion as a strong factor in their identity. This is partly reflected in a more public presence of all things Islamic, with expanded construction of mosques and Islamic schools (Abdo 2006), the expansion of an acceptable banking system that rejects charging interest on loans (*New York Times* 2009), and the emergence of Muslim institutions providing information about Islam to the American public, particularly after 9/11.

Despite increased hostility toward Muslim immigrants (Strum 2005; Strum and Tarantolo 2003; Strum 2006) and concerns about the compatibility of Islam with American values, recent surveys indicate that American Muslims express almost as much satisfaction with their lives as other Americans, and on many socioeconomic indicators, such as annual income, compare favorably with non-Muslims (Pew Research 2007). The report also concludes that most American Muslims are highly assimilated and believe in adopting American customs.

In many ways, this picture contrasts with the experiences of Muslims in European countries (Goodstein 2009). Although young American Muslims increasingly express feelings of alienation from other Americans since 9/11, with the exception of some highly publicized cases such as the proposed building of an Islamic community center in lower Manhattan, the threats of an evangelical preacher in Florida to publicly burn the Qur'an, and a number of American Muslims leaving the country to seek training from al Qaeda, the Muslim presence in America has engendered little of the extreme conflict and violence that has occurred in Europe, over, for example, the wearing of headscarfs and Muslim dress for women (Buruma 2006; Bowen 2007). This is partly because European nations tend to be far more culturally homogenous than the United States, and their Muslim populations make up a far greater percentage of their populations; in France, for example, Muslims are 10 percent of the population (Ireland 2005). European Muslims are also far less economically integrated into their societies: Their widespread poverty, discrimination in employment, and spatial segregation in huge housing projects at the margins of big cities have been causes of much conflict and frequent violent interaction with the police.

CASTE

In contrast to open class systems, characterized, at least theoretically, by individual social mobility, a **caste system** is based on birth, or ascribed status. Individual movement between castes or marriage between individuals from different castes is not possible. Castes are ranked in relation to one another and are characteristically associated with traditional occupations. A caste system, then, consists of ranked, culturally distinct, interdependent, endogamous groups, with rigidly maintained boundaries between the castes. The caste system exists in various cultures, but is mainly identified with India, where it is deeply culturally and historically embedded and plays a central role in social stratification.

caste system Social stratification based on birth or ascribed status in which social mobility between castes is not possible.

The Caste System in India

The unique elements of the Indian caste system are its complexity, its relation to Hindu religious beliefs and rituals, and the degree to which the castes (or, more accurately, subcastes) are cohesive and self-regulating groups. The Hindu caste system contains four main categories, called *varna,* ranked according to their ritual purity, which is largely based on traditional occupations. The highest ranked varna, the Brahmins, are priests and scholars; next highest are the Kshatriyas, the ruling and warrior caste; third ranked are the Vaisyas, or merchants; and fourth are the Shudras, or menial workers and artisans. Below these four varnas is a fifth group, previously called untouchables, now called Dalits, who perform spiritually polluting work such as cleaning latrines or tanning leather. They are considered so ritually impure that their mere touch, or even shadow, contaminates the purity of the higher castes. A person's birth into any one of these caste categories is believed to be a reward or punishment for his or her actions in a previous life. Strict social rules maintain caste boundaries: Intercaste marriage and eating together is prohibited, and a higher-caste person will not accept most kinds of food or drink from a lower-caste person. In Indian villages, the lowest castes are spatially and socially segregated, and prohibited from using high-caste wells and temples.

In its rural setting, the Indian caste system involves traditional exchanges of goods and services between higher and lower castes. Families of various artisan and serving castes—carpenters, potters, blacksmiths, water carriers, and leather workers—perform their services for high-caste landowning families and receive food, grain, clothing, fodder for animals, butter, milk, small amounts of cash, and many other things in return. These relationships, which may continue over several generations, are viewed by the higher castes as of social benefit to all: Landowners have a steady supply of available workers while the serving castes gain a relatively reliable

India.

source of subsistence. The lower castes, however, emphasize their exploitation in the system rather than its mutual benefits.

Although Indian castes are ranked on the basis of prestige rather than wealth, the gains of high caste position are not merely symbolic. The higher castes benefit materially as well as symbolically from their higher status; they use their considerable political power to maintain these material benefits and resist lower castes' attempts to change the system. Although the lower castes appear to accept their low position on the surface, their conformity largely hinges on their awareness that economic sanctions and physical force will be used against them if they try to resist the system or rise above it. And indeed, in both local and regional arenas, violent conflict between castes has been frequent in rural India.

The traditional Hindu religious belief that individuals occupy a social position based on the virtue of their actions in a previous life is used to justify elite caste hegemony: The upper castes benefit from the widely shared Hindu belief that social position reflects an individual's spiritual achievement. Just as in the American class system, political and economic power further the interests of some social strata over others, a conflict obscured by widespread cultural consensus.

Changes in the Caste System

The caste system in India, like any social stratification system, is not static. An important change occurred at Indian independence when "untouchability" was outlawed by the new constitution and affirmative action programs in education and government jobs for lower castes and untouchables were initiated. In addition to government action, groups may try to change their own caste status. Unlike a class system, change in the Indian caste system relies primarily on group rather than individual mobility. A caste that has been economically successful in some new occupation may try to raise its prestige by adopting the customs of a higher caste, claiming a new rank for itself. These new behavior patterns are formulated by caste councils, and nonconforming members will be publicly censured or even cast out of the group, a serious sanction when caste membership controls so much of a person's life. As part of its attempt to increase its caste ranking, a lower caste may also invent a new origin myth, claiming it originally belonged to a higher-ranked varna than it is presently assigned. Some previously untouchable castes, led by B. R. Ambedkar, a Western-trained lawyer, converted to Buddhism to put themselves outside the caste system entirely.

In addition to legal sanctions against caste, partly as a result of increasing differentiation of wealth and power within castes, caste ranking appears to be less sharply defined than formerly, both in rural and urban areas, especially within the higher caste categories. There has also been a significant weakening of the traditional connection between caste and occupation. New occupations, such as factory work, government service, information technology, and the professions, which are not caste-related, have opened opportunities, especially for the middle- and lower-level castes. Still, a connection between caste status and economic success continues, as the higher castes have primarily benefited by new economic opportunities through their previous accumulation of capital, their higher education, their business and social contacts, and their ability to speak English (Beteille 1998).

In public, also, caste boundaries such as inter-dining have weakened; however, in private and in rural areas, many caste-related boundaries remain, particularly regarding arranged marriages. Affirmative action in education and employment, based on (low) caste status, which is incorporated into the Indian constitution, keeps caste alive for more pragmatic reasons. Even with the rise of a new Indian class system, caste remains an important structural element in Indian society and is unlikely to disappear in the near future.

Although systems of social stratification, based on culturally specific intersections of class, race, ethnicity, gender, or caste, are always changing, anthropologists also look for the obstacles in culture, economics, or politics that help maintain the status quo, in which those at the top have such a vested interest.

▆▆▆BRINGING IT BACK HOME:
GOVERNMENT RESPONSIBILITY VERSUS THE GOSPEL OF WEALTH

For many people, the American Dream of social mobility continues to be a core value of American culture. But statistical and ethnographic evidence shows growing income inequalities and declining opportunity for economic advancement for many Americans. Members of the lower and middle classes are increasingly leading a precarious existence.

The expansion of the American middle class from the 1940s to the 1970s was to a large extent based on government policies and programs including the GI Bill, Social Security, Medicare, unemployment insurance, a progressive income tax, and federal mortgage assistance programs. It involved a cultural vision that held that government should attempt to improve citizens' economic security and increase their economic opportunities. The argument for a government obligation to provide basic security was also the guiding philosophy of the health care reform bills passed in 2010. Those who support this view hold that these policies have a moral basis to put government to work for the larger society, and also an economic basis: Putting more money in the hands of consumers will lead to an increased demand for goods, a growing economy, and a more just and equitable distribution of wealth. Further, they argue that as people experience improvement in their economic life, they will become more invested in the core values of our democratic society and more willing to participate to keep these values alive.

Competing with this view is the vision sometimes called the "gospel of wealth," a phrase coined by 19th-century capitalist Andrew Carnegie. Carnegie and others like him claim that the best government is the least government. They argue that government regulations stifle entrepreneurial initiative, that progressive taxation and policies like a minimum wage undermine investment in the economy by small businesses and large corporations, and that government entitlement programs—like Social Security, welfare, and health care—lead to laziness and a declining sense of individual responsibility. Proponents of this view hold that policies that increase corporate profits lead to higher rates of economic growth, and will "trickle down" to the society, providing opportunities and jobs that will ultimately benefit the most people. Privatization—whether in the form of individual savings accounts, privately insured health care, or school vouchers—is sound economic doctrine and will give people responsibility for their actions and their future.

▨▨▨ YOU DECIDE

1. What is your American Dream? Do you believe that education, hard work, and high personal character will be rewarded with a higher material standard of living for yourself and your children—or not? What evidence do you use for your view as it affects your own life or those of other people you know?

2. How do you think government policies (for example, regarding child care or family leave, availability of credit, health care reform, home ownership, business or college loans, and so on) have affected or will affect your own success in life and the achievement of your American Dream?

3. If you ran the world, what kind of social stratification system would you design? What would be its goals? What role would government play in this system?

▌▌ CHAPTER SUMMARY

1. Functionalist theory holds that social stratification benefits the whole society because it motivates people to undertake all the jobs necessary for the society to survive. Conflict theory emphasizes the conflicts within stratified societies as different social strata, with opposing interests, clash with one another over goals and resources.

2. The major dimensions of social stratification are power, wealth, and prestige, which are closely tied to occupation, which is closely tied to income. The particular value system of a culture shapes how these factors interact to determine where a person is placed in the stratification system.

3. In a class system, social position is ideally achieved, rather than ascribed, although class status is also ascribed in reality. People can move between the social classes. Classes are largely based on differences of income and wealth, but also characterized by different lifestyles and cultural differences.

4. The culture of the United States emphasizes "the American Dream," the idea that one can and should improve one's life chances and material wealth. Although many Americans dismiss the importance of class in the United States, there are important material and life change differences in the different social classes. Inequality between social classes is increasing, as is downward mobility.

5. The major cultural construction of race in the United States is the dichotomy between white and black. This is changing as the idea of mixed race becomes more important in self-identity.

6. The cultural diversity of the United States has largely been framed in terms of ethnicity based on the national origins of immigrants, largely ignoring the presence of African Americans, Native Americans, and Mexican Americans. Previously committed to the assimilation of cultural minorities, multiculturalism has now supplanted the concept of the melting pot, and cultural differences among immigrants and other minorities are now viewed in a more positive light.

7. In the Indian caste system, based on Hindu ideas of ritual purity, social position (caste) is largely ascribed (based on birth). Caste boundaries are sharply defined by prohibitions on intercaste marriage and intercaste sharing of food, as well as by some cultural differences. Although caste boundaries may weaken, especially in cities, the Indian caste system is partly maintained by low-caste benefits of affirmative action. As economic and occupational opportunities expand, the relationship between caste and class becomes less strong, especially in urban India.

▐▐▌ KEY TERMS

achieved status
apartheid
ascribed status
assimilation
caste (system)
class (system)
conflict theory
functionalism

life chances
multiculturalism
prestige
race
social mobility
social stratification
wealth

On Vanuatu, the John Frum movement is a classic example of what anthropologists call a cargo cult. Here, John Frum worshippers celebrate by marching in military formation. The letters USA are painted in red on their chests.

© Steve Axford

CHAPTER 11

RELIGION

CARGO CULTS

IGH on a mountaintop in New Guinea, a group of men are performing a ritual around the body of a small plane that crashed there years ago. Their ritual is aimed at ensuring the arrival of *cargo*, their word for the trade goods of Western culture that are the focus of their desires, stimulated by the encounters with Europeans, Americans, and Japanese over the past hundred years. Outsiders frequently promised wealth and political equality, but members of these groups soon realized that their words did not match reality. Not only did Melanesians fail to gain riches and power, but, in many cases, they grew poorer and were more deeply oppressed under colonial rule.

Melanesians observed that whites did not seem to work but instead made "secret signs" on scraps of paper, built strange structures, and behaved in strange ways. For example, they built airports and seaports with towers and wires, and they drilled soldiers to march in formation. When they did these things, planes and ships arrived, disgorging a seemingly endless supply of material goods. Melanesians, who did so much hard physical labor, got nothing.

In Melanesian culture, secret knowledge was the source of power and wealth. Plainly, the whites knew the secrets of cargo and were keeping it from the islanders. If Melanesians could learn the secret knowledge and rituals of cargo, they believed they could rid their societies of oppressive colonial governments and gain access to this immense wealth for themselves.

Cargo cults usually began with a local prophet who announced that the world was about to end in a terrible catastrophe, after which God (or the ancestors, or a local culture hero) would appear, and a paradise on earth would begin. The end of the world could be caused or hastened by the performance of rituals that copied what they had observed the whites doing. In some places, the faithful sat around tables dressed in European clothes, making signs on paper. In others, they drilled with wooden rifles and built wharves, storehouses, airfields, and lookout towers in the hope that such ritual would cause planes to land or ships to dock and disgorge cargo.

Cargo cults are not limited to Melanesia. In the United States and Latin America, millions of followers of prosperity theology or the Word-Faith movement believe that God wants Christians to be wealthy (Van Biema and Chu 2006). Promoted by Oral Roberts and other televangelists, the movement teaches their adherents that if they give money (the more the better) to movement churches and pray with sincerity, devotion, and frequency, God will reward them with cash and other material wealth, such as cars and houses. In other words, if they perform the correct rituals, they will receive cargo. If they remain poor, it is because they failed to properly ask God for wealth.

But perhaps cargo is not merely a cult in the United States but is central to our culture. Westerners do seem obsessed with cargo: an endless desire for consumer goods and the belief that buying specific brands of cars, drinks, or clothing will make them forever young, sexy, and powerful (Lindstrom 1993). Some might say that this is as likely to happen as it is for cargo to descend from the skies in Melanesia.

DEFINING RELIGION

Recent research links religious experience to specific capacities of the right temporal and right parietal lobes of the brain (Chan et al. 2009, Johnstone and Glass 2008). Since religiosity is a biologically based capacity of humans, it is unsurprising that all societies have spiritual beliefs and practices that anthropologists refer to as *religion*. Yet because of the great diversity of these beliefs and practices, defining religion is surprisingly difficult. Most definitions focus on the supernatural. Because Westerners make a clear distinction between natural and supernatural, this seems logical. But some religions explicitly deny that supernatural beings exist, whereas others do not distinguish them from what Westerners call the natural.

The phenomena that anthropologists identify as religion share five common characteristics. First, religions are composed of sacred stories that members believe are important. Second, religions make extensive use of symbols and symbolism. Third, religions propose the existence of beings, powers, states, places, and qualities that cannot be measured by any agreed-upon scientific means—they are nonempirical (for convenience, we refer to the nonempirical as supernatural, even though, as previously noted, this term is problematic). Fourth, religions include rituals and specific means of addressing the supernatural. Fifth, all societies include individuals who are particularly expert in the practice of religion. Thus, we might define **religion** as a social institution characterized by sacred stories; symbols and symbolism; the proposed existence of supernatural beings, powers, states, places, and qualities; rituals and means of addressing the supernatural; and specific practitioners.

Early anthropologists were primarily interested in the development of religion. They argued that religion had evolved from **animism**, the belief that all living and nonliving objects are imbued with spirit, passed through a stage of polytheism and finally arrived at monotheism. They held that this evolutionary process was characterized by increasing levels of logic and rationality. However, this view has been discredited. Today anthropologists understand that there is no orderly process of religious evolution and

religion A social institution characterized by sacred stories, symbols, and symbolism; the proposed existence of immeasurable beings, powers, states, places, and qualities; rituals and means of addressing the supernatural; specific practitioners; and change.

animism The notion that all objects, living and nonliving, are imbued with spirit.

that no religion can be considered any more logical or evolved than any other. Anthropologists today are interested in exploring religion in terms of its functions, its symbolism, and its relation to both social stability and change.

SOME FUNCTIONS OF RELIGION

Religion has many and varied functions in society. It may provide meaning and order in people's lives. It may reduce social anxiety and give people a sense of control over their destinies. It may promote and reinforce the status quo. But, it does not always do these things. In some cases, religion may make people profoundly disquiet or fearful. It may be an important force resisting the status quo and it may catalyze radical politics and, on occasion, even murderous violence.

The Search for Order and Meaning

A basic function of religion is to explain important aspects of the physical and social environment. Thus, religions provide a **cosmology** or framework for interpreting events and experiences. Cosmologies may include sets of principles or beliefs about the nature of life and death, the creation of the universe, the origin of society, the relationship of individuals and groups to one another, and the relationship of humankind to nature.

cosmology A system of beliefs that deals with fundamental questions in the religious and social order.

Religions provide a sense of order and meaning in a world that often seems chaotic. Here in the village of Kościelisko, Poland, a priest leads a procession on the Feast of Corpus Christi.

© Jialiang Gao

Cosmologies give meaning to the lives of believers. By defining the place of the individual in society and through the establishment of moral codes, they provide people with a sense of personal identity, a sense of belonging, and a standard of behavior. When people suffer a profound personal loss or when life loses meaning because of radically changed circumstances or catastrophic events, religion can supply a new identity or new responses that become the basis for personal and cultural survival.

Reducing Anxiety and Increasing Control

Many religious practices are aimed at ensuring success in human activities. Prayers, sacrifice, and magic are often used in the hope that they will aid a particular person or community. The practice of these rituals is frequently related to risk. The less predictable an outcome is, the greater the likelihood they will be used. For example, if you have studied for a test and know the material well, you are unlikely to spend much time praying for success. You are more likely to pray if you have not studied, and you may even bring your lucky pencil or another charm to the test.

Praying or doing magic to help or hurt an individual seems to have no effect, if that person does not know about your prayers or magical activities (see Flamm 2002, Tessman and Tessman 2000). However, when such attempts are known, they may have profound effect, altering the emotional state of the individuals involved. Bringing your lucky pencil to the exam may give you added confidence and improve your performance. Anthropologists in many parts of the world have observed cases in which sorcery is used to increase anxiety, and even cause death. In a study of such reports, Walter Cannon (1942) argued that an individual who was aware that he or she was being attacked by sorcery could exhibit an extreme stress reaction that might lead to death. Much work in biomedicine in the past 60 years confirms Cannon's ideas and details the specific biochemical pathways through which such reactions may occur (Sternberg 2002).

Reinforcing or Challenging the Social Order

Religion, culture, and society tend to reinforce one another, and religion generally works to preserve the social order. Through religion, dominant cultural beliefs about good and evil are reinforced by supernatural means of social control. Sacred stories and rituals provide a rationale for the present social order and give social values religious authority. Religious ritual intensifies social solidarity by creating an atmosphere in which people experience their common identity in emotionally moving ways. Finally, religion is an important institution for transmitting cultural values and knowledge.

In reinforcing the social order, religion generally serves the needs of the powerful. However, it may also serve the needs of the powerless. At times, religion may provide an escape from a grim political reality. Through religious belief in a glorious future or the coming of a savior, powerless people who live in harsh and deprived circumstances can create an illusion of power. In these circumstances, religion may provide an outlet for individual frustration, resentment, and anger, thus deflecting opposition to the state. However, religion can also focus this same frustration, resentment, and anger against political or social targets, thus catalyzing rebellion and revolution. The American civil rights movement, the Iranian revolution, the rise of the Taliban government in Afghanistan, and the rise of the Tea Party movement in the United States are all examples of this (see Warner 2010).

CHARACTERISTICS OF RELIGION

As previously noted, all religious traditions share certain similarities. They involve stories—sacred narratives and myths. They have symbols. They are characterized by nonempirical or supernatural beings and states. There are rituals, and there are practitioners who perform the rituals. We explore each of these characteristics in this section.

Sacred Narratives

At a fundamental level, all religions consist of a series of stories told by members of a group. These **sacred narratives** are powerful ways of communicating ideas. Sometimes, such stories are held to have a sacred power that is evoked when they are told. Sacred narratives may recall historic events, although these are often clothed in poetic language.

myths (sacred narratives) Stories of historical events, heroes, gods, spirits, and creation that members of a religious tradition hold to be holy and true.

Sacred narratives are often called **myths** and, in some ways, this is appropriate as they often include stories of heroes, explanations of origins, and distortions of reality. However, we frequently use the word *myth* to denote a false belief (or one we do not share). Clearly we should apply the same terminology to others' religious beliefs that we apply to our own.

By explaining that things came to be the way they are through the activities of sacred beings, sacred narratives legitimize beliefs, values, and customs. Malinowski (1992/1954:146) noted that myths "are not merely idle tales, but a hard-worked active force [that functions] to strengthen tradition and endow it with a greater value. . . ."

The origin narrative of the Hopi, an agricultural people of Arizona and New Mexico, provides a clear example of what Malinowski meant.

The Hopi subsist mainly on blue corn, a variety that is more difficult to grow than other varieties of corn but is stronger and more resistant to damage. According to Hopi belief, before their ancestors appeared on the earth's surface, they were given their choice of subsistence activities. The ancestors chose blue corn and were taught the techniques for growing it by the god Maasaw. The Hopi believe that in growing blue corn, they recreate the feelings of humility and harmony their ancestors experienced when they first chose this form of agriculture. Thus, the Hopi live their religious understanding of the world as they grow blue corn. The stories that accompany this action reinforce social traditions and enhance solidarity.

Symbols and Symbolism

Religious stories depend on symbolism, which may be expressed in words, in material objects such as masks and statues, in body decorations, by objects in the physical environment, or through performance. The use of symbolism connects the realms of religion and art. Indeed, art is very often used to express religious ideas. Some religious symbols may have supernatural power in and of themselves, such as the masks used in African ceremonies or the wafers used in Catholic communion.

Part of the power of religious symbols (like art) is that they pack many different and sometimes contradictory meanings into a single word, idea, object, or performance. Consider the Christian cross. Among its meanings are death, love, sacrifice, identity, history, power, weakness, wealth, poverty, and many more.

Because they carry so many meanings, religious symbols often have great emotional and intellectual power. As a result, they can be used in leadership. For example, since the first centuries of Christianity, the cross has been used as a military symbol and to rally people to political causes. Desecration of the cross may inflame passions and provoke very strong reactions as well.

Symbolic representation allows people to grasp the often complex and abstract ideas of a religion without much concern or knowledge of the underlying theology. The Christian ritual of communion, for example, symbolizes the New Testament story of the Last Supper, which communicates the abstract idea of communion with God. In Hinduism, this idea is represented in plays, paintings, and sculptures as the love between the divine Krishna, in the form of a cowherd, and the milkmaids, particularly Radha, who are devoted to him. The dramatic reenactments and devotional singing about the love of Krishna and Radha offer paths to communion with God that ordinary people can understand and participate in.

© Bob Burch/Bruce Coleman, Inc./Photo shot

In religious ritual, humans may be transformed into supernatural beings. This masked dancer from Cote d'Ivoire is not just a person wearing a mask, but a person who has become a supernatural being.

god (deity) A named spirit who is believed to have created or to have control of some aspect of the world.

polytheism Belief in many gods.

monotheism Belief in a single god.

Supernatural Beings, Powers, States, and Qualities

Although many religions do not separate the natural from the supernatural, all religions propose that there are important beings, powers, emotional states, or qualities that exist apart from human beings. These are nonempirical in that there is no scientifically agreed-upon way to measure them. For example, although many people claim to see proof of God's existence, there is nothing that members of all religions, as well as those who do not believe in any religion, could agree to measure that would demonstrate the existence of God. Thus, science, which depends upon such empirical measurement, can neither prove nor disprove the existence of God.

Most religions populate the world with nonempirical beings and spirits. These can be happy or unhappy, stingy or generous, or can experience any other human emotion. The understanding of spirits and souls of animals among the Netsilik Inuit provides a good example. The Netsilik depend upon hunting and believe that if the soul of an animal they kill receives the proper religious attention, it will be pleased. Such an animal will reincarnate in another animal body and let itself be killed again. An animal soul that does not receive the proper attention, however, will be angered and will not let itself be killed a second time. Particularly offended animal souls might become bloodthirsty monsters and terrorize people (Balikci 1970:200–01).

The term **god (or deity)** is generally used for a named spirit believed to have created or to have control of some aspect of the world. Gods, who are the creators of the world and the ultimate powers in it, are present in only about half of all societies (Levinson 1996:229).

Polytheism refers to belief in many gods, and **monotheism** to a belief in a single god. However, the difference between these two is sometimes small. In polytheistic religions, the many gods may be different aspects of one god. For example, India has millions of gods, yet Indians understand these are all aspects of one divine essence. Conversely, in monotheistic religions, the one god may have several aspects. For most Christians, God the Father, God the Son, and God the Holy Spirit are all part of a single, unitary God.

In addition to supernatural beings, religions posit the existence of supernatural states, qualities, or powers, such as the enlightenment of Buddhist tradition, the saintliness of Catholicism, or the nirvana of the Hindus. Religious beliefs often include the notion of a spiritual force that anthropologists call **mana** (a term of Polynesian origin). Mana may be concentrated in individuals (for example, the Tahitian chiefs discussed in Chapter 9), in objects, or in places. Mana is like electricity: It is powerful, but dangerous if it is not approached with caution. That is why a belief in mana often is associated with an elaborate system of taboos, or prohibitions.

mana Religious power or energy that is concentrated in individuals or objects.

Rituals and Ways of Addressing the Supernatural

People enact their religion through **ritual**, a ceremonial act or a repeated stylized gesture used for specific occasions involving the use of religious symbols (Cunningham et al. 1995). Religious rituals may involve the telling or acting out of sacred stories; the use of music, dance, drugs, or pain to move worshippers to a state of trance; or the use of ritual objects to convey religious messages.

ritual A ceremonial act or a repeated stylized gesture used for specific occasions involving the use of religious symbols.

The stories, symbols, and objects of worship that make up the content of religious rituals are exceedingly diverse, yet there are commonalities. Most religious rituals involve a combination of prayer, sacrifices, and magic to contact and control supernatural spirits and powers. Further, despite great diversity, some types of rituals, including rites of passage and rites of intensification, are extremely widespread, if not universal.

The Power of the Liminal

The word **liminal** refers to those objects, places, people, and statuses that are understood as existing in an indeterminate state, between clear-cut categories. Objects that are liminal often play important roles in religious ritual.

liminal The stage of a ritual, particularly a rite of passage, in which one has passed out of an old status but has not yet entered a new one.

Anthropologist Victor Turner (1969) wrote that rituals frequently generate liminal states in which the structured and hierarchical classifications that normally separate people into groups such as caste or class are dissolved. Because of this, in ritual, people can behave in ways that would be clearly unacceptable under other circumstances. In some cases, this includes role reversals. For example, many Japanese festivals included ritual transvestism, where community members dance in the clothing of the opposite sex (Norbeck 1974:51). In the Wubwang'u ritual among the Ndembu of Zambia, men and women publicly insult each other's sexual abilities and extol their own, but no one is allowed to take offense

(V. Turner 1969:78–79). Ritual role reversals include class as well as gender. In Holi, the Hindu harvest festival, members of the lower class and castes throw colored powder (and in the old days, excrement and urine) at males of the middle and upper classes.

More controversially, Turner argued that in liminal states people experience a state of equality and oneness he called **communitas**. In communitas, the wealthy and the poor, the powerful and the powerless are, for a short time, all equals. In the United States, one example of communitas is the incredibly diverse crowd of over a million people who gather on New Year's Eve to watch the falling of the illuminated ball in the center of Times Square.

In state-level societies, institutionalized liminal statuses sometimes emerge. Organizations such as monasteries and convents where people live permanently as members of a religious community embody liminality.

Anthropologists often refer to rituals and statuses involving liminality as **antistructure**. Although all societies must be structured to provide order and meaning, according to Turner (1969:131), antistructure—the temporary ritual dissolution of the established order—is also important, helping people to more fully realize the oneness of the self and the other.

Turner's ideas are provocative, but people in higher statuses may experience the unity of communitas more than the powerless. The powerless may use liminal symbols and rituals of reversal to subvert the social order (even if temporarily), expressing feelings not of oneness, but of conflict with the powerful. Further, where liminal groups exist, either temporarily, during rituals or religious festivals, or permanently, associated with certain occupations, they frequently have low status and an ambiguous nature. This, paradoxically, is the source of their supernatural power and their perceived subversion of the social order, as illustrated by the hijras of India (see pp. 180–181), whose sexual ambiguity contains the power both to bless and to curse.

Rites of Passage

Rites of passage are public events that mark the transition of a person from one social status to another. Rites of passage almost always mark birth, puberty, marriage, and death and may include many other transitions as well. Rites of passage involve three phases (van Gennep 1960/1909). The first phase is separation, in which the person or group is detached from a former status. The second phase is transition and is often characterized by liminality. The individuals in this phase have been detached from their old statuses but not yet attached to a new one. The third stage is reincorporation, in which the passage from one status to another is symbolically completed. After reincorporation, the person takes on the rights and obligations of his or her new social status.

---

communitas A state of perceived solidarity, equality, and unity among people sharing a religious ritual, often characterized by intense emotion.

antistructure The socially sanctioned use of behavior that radically violates social norms; frequently found in religious ritual.

rite of passage A ritual that moves an individual from one social status to another.

The rites of initiation for boys and girls described in Chapter 8 are good examples of rites of passage. Before these rituals, the boys and girls have the public status of children. Afterward, they have the public status of grown men and women. Other rites of passage affect similar changes of status. Baptisms and other ceremonies around birth move the new child from the status of not-a-community-member to membership in the community. Quinceañeras mediate between the status of childhood and that of young womanhood, eligible for dating. Marriages mediate between single and couple status. Funerals mediate between the living and the dead.

Basic training for military service is an example of a rite of passage with which many Americans are familiar. In basic training, recruits are separated from their friends and families and are taken to a military post where they are given identical haircuts and identical uniforms. All signs of differences among them are minimized; no matter their position in life before joining the military, ideally they are treated identically during training. Training itself involves a wide variety of rigorous exercises and tasks designed to impart knowledge and build trust and camaraderie. In this state, they experience communitas, a shared identity along with the breaking down of barriers between individuals. Training ends with a large ceremony that reintegrates the recruits, now soldiers, into society with a new identity.

Rites of Intensification

Rites of intensification are rituals directed toward reinforcing the values and norms of the community and strengthening group identity and well-being. Through these rituals, the community maintains continuity with the past, enhances the feeling of social unity in the present, and renews the sentiments on which social cohesion depends (Elkin 1967).

In some groups, rites of intensification are connected with totems. A **totem** is an object, an animal species, or a feature of the natural world that is associated with a particular descent group. Totemism is a prominent feature of the religions of the Australian aborigines. In aboriginal Australia, groups of related individuals are linked with particular totemic species which, usually, they are prohibited from eating (see Verdon and Jorion 1981).

In their religious rituals, members of each group assemble to celebrate their totem. The ceremonies explain the origin of the totem (and hence, of the group) and reenact the time of the ancestors. Through singing and dancing, both performers and onlookers are transported to an ecstatic state in which they no longer recognize themselves and feel as though they are being carried away to a special world (Durkheim 1961/1915:247–251).

Emile Durkheim, a pioneer in the anthropological study of religion, believed that totems were symbols of common social identity. When people

rite of intensification A ritual structured to reinforce the values and norms of a community and to strengthen group identity.

totem An object, an animal species, or a feature of the natural world that is associated with a particular descent group.

worshipped totems, they were worshipping that common identity and at the same time reinforcing the moral and social order of their society. The ecstatic religious experience of their shared identity helped to bind them together.

The religious rituals of the Australian aborigines may seem exotic, but Americans participate in similar observances, some religious but many secular, to the same effect. The rallies associated with college football games are a good example. If the game is "good" or the school has "spirit," these gatherings produce enormous excitement among their fans and transport them to "a special world," increasing collective identity and intensifying loyalty to the school (and hopefully motivating financial donations from them as alumni). Schools, like Australian descent groups, also have totems (animal mascots).

Prayer, Sacrifice, and Magic

Prayer, sacrifice, and magic are found in most religious traditions. Although theoretically differentiated by the degree of control that humans believe they exert over the spirit world, the distinctions between them are more a matter of degree than of exclusive classification.

prayer Any conversation held with spirits and gods in which people petition, invoke, praise, give thanks, dedicate, supplicate, intercede, confess, repent, and bless.

Prayer is any conversation held with spirits and gods in which people petition, invoke, praise, give thanks, dedicate, supplicate, intercede, confess, repent, and bless (Levinson 1996). A defining feature of prayer is that people believe the results depend on the will of the spirit world rather than on actions performed by humans. When prayer involves requests, the failure of a spirit to respond to a request is understood as resulting from its disinclination rather than from improper human action. Prayer may be done without any expectation of a particular response from the beings or forces prayed to. There are many forms of prayer. In the West, prayer mainly involves words recited aloud or silently, but in Buddhist tradition, people may pray by hoisting flags or spinning wheels with prayers written inside them.

sacrifice An offering made to increase the efficacy of a prayer or the religious purity of an individual.

Sacrifice occurs when people make offerings to gods or spirits to increase their spiritual purity or the efficacy of their prayers. People may sacrifice the first fruits of a harvest, animal lives, or, on occasion, human lives. Changes in behavior are often offered as sacrifices, as in the Muslim practice of fasting for Ramadan or the Christian practice of giving up something for Lent, a sacrifice intended to help the worshipper identify with Jesus, show devotion, and increase purity. In many religions, people make a vow to carry out a certain kind of behavior, such as going on a pilgrimage or building a place of worship, if a prayer is answered.

Among many East African cattle pastoralists, such as the Nuer or Pokot, cattle sacrifices are central to religion, and cattle are killed and eaten only in the context of religious ritual. This is clearly adaptive. In the absence of refrigeration, animals must be consumed rapidly after they are slaughtered. One family could not consume a whole steer by itself, but

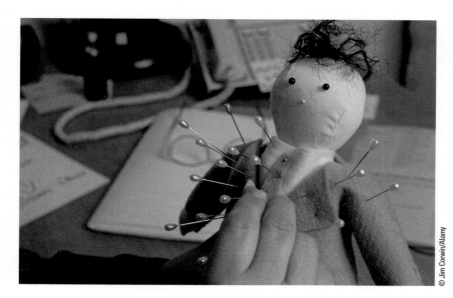

© Jim Corwin/Alamy

A voodoo doll is an example of both imitative and contagious magic.

offering it to the community in a ceremonial setting solves this problem. Cattle sacrifices happen in community feasts that occur about once a week. In addition, the religious taboo that a person who eats ritually slaughtered meat may not take milk on the same day results in making milk more available to those who have no meat (Schneider 1973).

Magic is an attempt to mechanistically control supernatural forces. When people do magic, they believe that their words and actions *compel* the spirit world to behave in certain ways. Failure of a magical request is understood to result from incorrect performance of the ritual rather than the refusal of spirits to act, as in prayer.

Imitation and contagion are two of the most common magical practices. In **imitative magic**, the procedure performed resembles the result desired. A voodoo doll is a form of imitative magic based on the principle that mistreatment of a doll-like image of a person will cause injury to that person. **Contagious magic** is based on the idea that an object that has been in contact with a person retains a magical connection with that person. For example, one might attempt to increase the effectiveness of a voodoo doll by attaching a piece of clothing, hair, or other object belonging to the person he or she wishes to injure. People in the United States often attribute special power and meaning to objects that have come in contact with famous or notorious people. Signed baseballs, bits of costumes worn by movie stars, and pens used to sign famous documents all become collector's items and are imbued with special power and importance.

In many cultures, magical practices accompany most human activities. Among the people who live along the upper Asaro River in Papua

magic A religious ritual believed to produce a mechanical effect by supernatural means. When magic is done correctly, believers think it must have the desired effect.

imitative magic The belief that imitating an action in a religious ritual will cause the action to happen in the material world.

contagious magic The belief that things once in contact with a person or object retain an invisible connection with that person or object.

New Guinea, when a child is born, its umbilical cord is buried so that it cannot later be used by a sorcerer to cause harm. To prevent an infant from crying at night, a bundle of sweet-smelling grass is placed on the mother's head, and her wish for uninterrupted sleep is blown into the grass. The grass then is crushed over the head of the child who, in breathing its aroma, also breathes in the mother's command not to cry (Newman 1977:413). In cultures where magic is not universally used, it may accompany risky activities. Professional baseball players in the United States are more likely to use magic for hitting and pitching, the least predictable aspects of the game. Few magical practices are invoked in outfielding, which has little uncertainty. For example, after each pitch, one major league pitcher would reach into his back pocket to touch a crucifix and then straighten his cap. Detroit Tigers infielder Tim Maring wore the same clothes and put them on exactly in the same order each day during a batting streak. One baseball myth is that eating certain foods will give the ball "eyes," that is, the ball will seek the gaps between fielders, so eating certain foods on the day of a game is another example of baseball magic (Gmelch 2000).

divination A religious ritual performed to find hidden objects or information.

Divination is a widespread ritual practice directed toward obtaining useful, hidden, or unknown information from a supernatural authority. Divination may be used to predict the future, diagnose disease, find hidden objects, or discover something about the past. In many cultures, divination is used to discover who committed a crime. Many Americans are familiar with divination techniques such as tarot cards, palmistry, flipping coins, and reading auras.

Divination makes people more confident in their choices when they do not have all the information they need or when several alternative courses of action appear equal. It may be practiced when a group must make a decision about which there is disagreement. If the choice is made by divination, no member of the group feels rejected.

Religious Practitioners

Every society includes people who are believed to have a special relationship with the religious world and who organize and lead major ritual events. There are many kinds of religious practitioners but anthropologists generally organize them into two broad categories: shamans and priests.

Shamans

shaman An individual socially recognized as being able to mediate between the world of humanity and the world of gods or spirits but who is not a recognized official of any religious organization.

A **shaman** is a part-time practitioner who otherwise works like an average member of his or her community. The activities of shamans are reserved for specific ceremonies, times of illness, or crises. Learning to be a shaman may involve arduous training, but such study is never sufficient. The distinctive characteristic of shamans is that they have direct personal

© Judith Pearson

Among the Mentawai of Indonesia, shamans read the entrails of chickens and pigs to diagnose and cure illness.

experiences of the supernatural that other members of the community accept as authentic. Shamans use prayer, meditation, song, dance, pain, drugs, or any combination of techniques to achieve trance states in which they understand themselves (and are understood by their followers) as able to enter into the real world of the supernatural. They may use such contact to search for guidance for themselves or for their group, to heal the sick, or to divine the future. Almost all societies have some shamans, but in foraging and tribal societies shamans are likely to be the only religious practitioners.

In some cultures, almost every adult is expected to achieve direct contact with the supernatural. In some Native American societies, this was achieved through a vision quest in which individuals developed a special relationship with a particular spirit from whom they received special kinds of power and knowledge and who acted as a personal protector or guardian. The vision seeker might fast, might isolate himself or herself at a lonely spot, or might use self-mutilation to intensify his or her emotional state to receive the vision.

Particularly before the advent of modern medicine, many societies treated illness by means that today would be considered primarily spiritual rather than medical. Illnesses were thought to be caused by broken taboos, sorcery, witchcraft, or spiritual imbalance, and shamans had an important role in curing. The shaman, usually in a trance, would travel into the supernatural world to discover the source of illness and how to cure it.

In the modern world, shamanic curing often exists alongside modern technological medicine. People go to shamans for healing when they have diseases that are not recognized by modern medicine, they lack money to pay for modern medical treatment, or they have tried such treatment and it has failed. Shamanistic curing can have important therapeutic effects. Shamans frequently treat their patients with drugs from the culture's traditional pharmacopoeia, and some (but not all) of these have been shown scientifically to be effective (Fábrega 1997:144). Shamanic curing ritual also uses symbolism and dramatic action to bring together cultural beliefs and religious practices in a way that enables patients to understand the source of their illness. Such rituals present a coherent model of sickness and health, explaining how patients got ill and how they may become well again, and these models can exert a powerful curative force (Roberts et al. 1993).

Priests

priest One who is formally elected, appointed, or hired to a full-time religious office.

In most state societies, religion is a formally established institution consisting of a series of ranked offices that exist independently of the people who fill them (a bureaucracy). Anthropologically, a **priest** is a person who is formally elected, appointed, or hired to a full-time religious office. Priests are responsible for performing certain rituals on behalf of individuals, groups, or the entire community. Jewish rabbis, Muslim imams, Christian ministers, and Hindu *purohits* all fit the definition of priests. Priests are most often associated with powerful gods and, where they exist, there is a division between the lay and priestly roles. Laypeople participate in ritual largely as passive respondents or as an audience rather than as managers or performers.

People generally become priests through training and apprenticeship and are certified by their religious hierarchy. Although in mainstream religious denominations in the United States, priests need not have ecstatic religious experiences, this is not the case in all priestly religions. Ultimately, the priest's authority derives from a priestly office. However, in some cultures, like the ancient Maya, such office may also give a person the right to seek direct ecstatic contact with gods and spirits.

State societies generally attempt to suppress independent shamans or bring them under bureaucratic control. Shamans claim the ability to directly contact the supernatural without certification by any institutionalized religion, and this challenges the authority of church and state.

Witches and Sorcerers

witchcraft The ability to harm others by harboring malevolent thoughts about them; the practice of sorcery.

Belief in the existence of witches and sorcerers is widespread but not universal. In some societies, **witchcraft** is understood as a physical aspect of a person. People are witches because their bodies contain a magical witchcraft substance, generally acquired through inheritance. If a person's body contains the witchcraft substance, his or her malevolent thoughts will result in misfortune among those around him or her.

The Azande of East Africa, a classic example, believe that witches' bodies contain a substance called *mangu,* which allows them to cause misfortune and death to others (Evans-Pritchard 1958/1937). People who have the witchcraft substance may not be aware that they are witches and are believed to be unable to prevent themselves from causing evil. They are suspected of witchcraft when evil befalls those around them, particularly family members.

Sorcery is the conscious manipulation of words and ritual objects with the intent of magically causing either harm or good. For example, in Melanesia, a sorcerer may make a magical arrow of a pointed object. He then catches sight of his victim and viciously stabs the air as if to wound the individual and twist the point in the wound (Malinowski 1984/1922:75). A similar technique was employed among the Nez Perce, a Native American group (Walker 1967:74).

sorcery The conscious and intentional use of magic.

Although people do actually practice witchcraft and sorcery, their main effects on society are through witchcraft accusations. Leveling witchcraft accusations against friends and neighbors is common in many cultures and serves various purposes. The most common form of witchcraft accusation serves to stigmatize differences. People who do not fit into conventional social categories are often suspected of witchcraft, exemplified by the Western image of the witch as an evil old hag dressed in black. In traditional Western European society, social norms dictated that women should have husbands and children (or alternatively become nuns). Impoverished women who remained in the community yet were unmarried or widowed without children violated this social convention and might be subject to witchcraft accusations (Brain 1989; Horsley 1979). Although such witches were sometimes killed, they were usually allowed to remain in a community, serving as valuable negative role models, examples of what not to be. The lesson that a young girl might have derived from the witch is that you should get married and have children or you might end up accused of being a witch.

Witchcraft and sorcery accusations may be used to scapegoat. In times of great social change when war, disease, calamity, or technological change undermines the social order, people's lives lose meaning. Under such circumstances, a community may turn to witchcraft accusations, blaming their misfortunes on the presence of evildoers—witches and sorcerers who must be found and destroyed to reassert normality.

In Europe, for example, the witch craze, which resulted in the death of thousands of men and women, occurred primarily in the 16th and 17th centuries, a time of great artistic and technological achievement but also of great social disasters (Hester 1988). Plague swept repeatedly through Europe, and the medieval social and religious order collapsed in war and chaos. Where governments and religious institutions remained strong, witchcraft accusations were relatively scarce. However, where these institutions collapsed, accusations were frequent (Behringer 2004). Under these circumstances, people were willing to believe that witches were the cause of their misery and to pursue reprisals against people they suspected of witchcraft.

Recent times in Europe and the United States have seen the emergence of religious worshippers who call themselves witches, Wiccans, or neo-pagans. Such individuals have little connection with the types of witchcraft and sorcery previously described. Many Wiccans say they practice an ancient religion of nature worship. The "threefold law" is a basic principle of most Wiccan belief and states that whatever good or ill people do in the world returns to them threefold. Wiccans are no more likely to commit evil acts than are members of more mainstream religious groups.

RELIGION AND CHANGE

As we have seen, religion is generally a force that preserves the social order. This may be particularly evident in stratified societies where the elite invoke religious authority to control the poor. In such situations, religion acts as a way of maintaining social, economic, and political inequality. However, even when religion does not support oppression, it is usually a conservative force, promoting the idea that the way that society has historically been ordered is right and proper.

Most religions contain implicit or explicit visions of the ideal society— images of the way a correct, just social order should look. No society actually achieves its vision; people never live exactly the way they are supposed to. However, most of the time religion validates society. As a result, most people feel that the society they live in is reasonably good.

However, if societies change very rapidly (as a result of colonization, disease, or technological change) or if groups are systematically enslaved and oppressed, the vision of the ideal world painted by people's religious beliefs may move far from their daily experience. People may feel that they are lost, that their vision of the ideal cannot be attained, or that it is simply wrong. Under these conditions, prophets may emerge, and new religions may be created. Religious movements vary in the effectiveness with which they bring social and political change. Even those that fail in these respects may create powerful new identities among their members.

In the United States, rapid cultural and economic change, economic oppression, and powerlessness have frequently led to new religious movements, sometimes with dire results. The prophecies of People's Temple leader Jim Jones and the Branch Davidian David Koresh provided new lives for their followers, giving them consistent and meaningful (if, in others' view, misguided) ways of understanding the world. However, these prophecies also led to the deaths of Jones, Koresh, and most of their followers.

Religion offers a series of principles, encapsulated in story, symbol, and interpretation. Thus, it can be a powerful force for social change, providing people with the rationale and motivation for political involvement and personal renewal. From the Iranian Revolution and the Taliban to the Christian Coalition and the 700 Club, religious leaders can have a powerful political impact. However, prophets may also give their followers convincing models that cannot exist in our material, social, and political world. When that happens, the results may be explosive.

Varieties of Religious Prophecies

To begin a new religion or substantially modify an existing one, prophets must identify what is wrong with the world, present a vision of what a better world looks like, and describe a method of transition from the existing world to the better world. Religious movements can, to some degree, be characterized by what they believe about this better world and the ways to achieve it.

Many religious movements are either nativistic or vitalistic. A nativistic movement aims to restore what its followers believe is a golden age of the past. The nativistic message is generally that things in the past were far better than at present. The reason things have degenerated is because the people have fallen away from the ways of the ancestors. The glorious past may be regained if certain practices are followed.

The Ghost Dance is a good example of a nativistic religious movement. It arose in the late 19th century among the Plains Indians of the United States and was a response to the disastrous effects of European invasion. Disease, warfare, and technological change had undermined native cultures. As a result, prophets emerged whose visions were directly related to the expansion of Euro-American power (Wallace 1970). In 1889, the prophet Wovoka had a vision in which "he saw God, with all the people who had died long ago engaged in their old time sports and occupations, all happy and forever young" (Mooney 1973/1896:771). Wovoka taught that the arrival of paradise could be hastened if Indians returned to their traditional practices and performed specific rituals, including dances, songs, and the wearing of specially designed "ghost shirts." Some of Wovoka's followers believed these had the power to protect them from bullets. Although Wovoka called for peace with the whites, he also taught that the whites either would be carried away by high winds or would become Indians (Lesser 1933).

The Ghost Dance prophecy spread widely among Native Americans, especially the Sioux, for whom the conditions of conquest and reservation life were particularly oppressive. After their defeat of Custer in 1876, they had been restricted to agriculture on nonproductive reservations and nearly starved to death. Thus, Wovoka's vision of the disappearance of their oppressors and the return of traditional ways was compelling. U.S. government agents became increasingly frightened that the Ghost Dance movement would lead to a Sioux war against the whites and ordered the Sioux to stop the dance. Some Sioux did, but others fled into the Badlands and continued to perform the Ghost Dance and to await the cataclysm that would sweep their oppressors from the Plains. In December 1890, the 7th Cavalry captured the last remaining band of Ghost Dancers at Wounded Knee. In the ensuing battle, about 350 Sioux Ghost Dancers, including many women and children, were killed. This battle effectively ended the Ghost Dance, although it continued among small groups up until the 1960s.

A vitalistic prophecy looks to the future rather than the past. For the vitalist, the past is either evil or neutral. The golden age is in the future and can be achieved following the teachings of the prophet. Though it is not specifically religious, an example of a vitalism with which most Americans are familiar is Martin Luther King Jr.'s "I Have a Dream" speech. In that speech, King describes a future where "the sons of former slaves and the sons of former slave owners will be able to sit down together at the table of brotherhood" and where children "will not be judged by the color of their skin but by the content of their character." King thus looks ahead to a future then unprecedented in American history.

Often, the poor and powerless in a society create religions that challenge those of the mainstream. Such religions may rationalize their lower social position and emphasize an afterlife in which their suffering will be rewarded. In some cases, these religions have a **messianic** outlook; they focus on the coming of a special individual who will usher in a utopian world. Other religions are **millenarian**; they look to a future disaster that will destroy the current world and establish a world characterized by their version of justice. In many messianic and millenarian religions, members participate in rituals that give individuals direct access to supernatural power. They experience states of ecstasy heightened by singing, dancing, handling dangerous objects such as snakes, or using drugs.

The holiness churches common among coal miners and the rural poor in Appalachia are a good example of a religion that has emerged in response to poverty and hardship. In church services, loud music, singing, and dancing cause some members to experience "being filled with the

messianic Focusing on the coming of an individual who will usher in a utopian world.

millenarian Belief that a coming catastrophe will signal the beginning of a new age and the eventual establishment of paradise.

© Associated Press

In states of religious ecstasy, members of holiness churches in Appalachia handle poisonous snakes. They believe they are instructed to do so by a passage in the Gospel of Mark. For church members, such practices demonstrate their ability to gain access to God's power.

Holy Spirit." In this ecstatic state, they handle poisonous snakes. Snake handlers are frequently bit and sometimes die. However, for members, snake handling proves that "Jesus has the power to deliver them from death here and now" (Daugherty 1976:344). For them, such ecstatic practices demonstrate their ability to gain access to God's power. The fact that social elites are rarely members of such groups is proof that holiness members have access to forms of power that social elites lack (Covington 1995; Burton 1993).

Religious **syncretism** is often found among deeply oppressed people. In syncretism, people merge two or more religious traditions, hiding the beliefs, symbols, and practices of one behind similar attributes of the other. Santeria, an African-based religion originating in Cuba, is a good example (Murphy 1989). Santeria emerged from slave society. Europeans attempted to suppress African religions, but the slaves resisted by combining African religion, Catholicism, and French spiritualism to create a new religion (Lefever 1996). They identified African deities, called orichas, with Catholic saints and used them for traditional purposes such as curing and casting spells, and influencing other aspects of the worshipper's life. In this

syncretism The merging of elements of two or more religious traditions to produce a new religion.

way, they could appear to practice Catholicism as they continued to practice their own religions.

Fundamentalism and Religious Change

fundamentalism A proclamation of reclaimed authority over a sacred tradition that is to be reinstated as an antidote for a society that is believed to have strayed from its cultural moorings.

In the past two decades, there has been an increase in religious **fundamentalism**. Islamic fundamentalism is implicated in numerous conflicts around the world. Membership in American Christian denominations that describe themselves as fundamentalist has ballooned. Jewish ultraorthodox groups such as the Lubavitch Hasidim have also been growing. Fundamentalism is well known in the United States, but other countries have seen fundamentalism grow as well. For example, in India, there are numerous Hindu fundamentalist organizations including the Bharatiya Janata Party (BJP), which plays a very important role in national politics.

Although members of fundamentalist groups sometimes see their religious beliefs as unchanging, the rise of fundamentalism is an important religious change. Further, fundamentalist movements tend to have specific founders and locations of origin. For example, much of the American fundamentalist movement began with the publication of *The Fundamentals: A Testimony to the Truth*, a series of books published between 1910 and 1915. Modern Islamic fundamentalism is associated with the work of Sayyid Qutb (born in the Egyptian village of Musha described in Chapter 5) and the Muslim Brotherhood.

The rise of fundamentalism raises important questions for anthropologists. First, it is clear that the people we call fundamentalist have greatly varying beliefs, but do fundamentalist groups have commonalities despite these differences? Second, have these groups emerged in response to purely local forces or are there global forces at work that have encouraged the development of fundamentalism in so many different locations? Finally, is fundamentalism a problem and, if so, what should be done about it? None of these questions can be answered easily or definitively but we can propose some partial explanations.

Scholars have shown that fundamentalisms have similar properties. Fundamentalists tend to see religion as the basis for both personal and communal identity. They tend to believe that there is a single unified truth that they can possess and understand. They tend to envision themselves as fighting in a cosmic struggle of good against evil. In this battle, demonizing the opposition is a perfectly appropriate tactic. Fundamentalists tend to perceive themselves as a persecuted minority even when this is not the case. They are selective about which parts of their tradition they emphasize and which parts of modernity they accept and reject (Hadden and Shupe 1989; Almond, Sivan, and Appleby 1995).

Determining the reasons for the surge in the popularity of fundamentalism is difficult. To some degree, the pattern of emergence fits the model described in this chapter. In the past 50 years, the world has faced truly revolutionary changes. The forces of technology and global capitalism have permeated societies and brought people of disparate cultures together in a vast global network. However, this process has not been peaceful and has not produced equity. Traditional livelihoods, from cloth dyeing in West Africa to family farming in the Midwestern United States, have been undermined. The gap between the wealthy and the poor has grown. Governments have been discredited. Faced with profound change, people look for stability and certainty. For some, fundamentalism seems to offer a solution. Much (but not all) fundamentalism is nativistic; it presents a call to return to the society and values of an earlier time, a time that believers understand as better than the current era. However, specific local histories also play an extremely important role in the emergence of fundamentalisms. It would be impossible, for example, to explain the appearance of the fundamentalist group Hamas without reference to the Israeli-Palestinian conflict. Similarly, the development of the Taliban is directly related to the events surrounding the Russian invasion of Afghanistan.

The forces that create rich ground for fundamentalism do not seem likely to abate any time soon. In fact, continual political and technological change seems likely to create even more extreme dislocations in the future. Various fundamentalisms will probably continue to experience strong growth. This poses an extraordinarily difficult problem. On the one hand, people are surely entitled to their religious beliefs. The vast majority of people who might be classified as fundamentalist are innocent of any wrongdoing; they neither promote nor condone violence. They live peacefully with neighbors of different religious beliefs. On the other hand, fundamentalist beliefs have been repeatedly implicated in murderous violence: from the bombings of abortion clinics and the Olympic Games in Atlanta to the 9/11 attacks on the United States to the repeated anti-Muslim and anti-Sikh violence perpetrated by Hindu fundamentalists in India.

There is no doubt that much violence is enflamed by the harsh political and economic conditions of life and by the subversion of long-standing cultural practices. Promoting prosperity, more equitable distribution of resources, greater cultural sensitivity, and more responsive and honest government will certainly reduce popular support for violence. However, a small percentage of believers in all fundamentalist traditions understand the world in absolutist terms and see violence as a divinely ordained response.

◼BRINGING IT BACK HOME:
RELIGION, ART, AND CENSORSHIP

". . . [T]his show is disgusting," said New York City's then (1999) Mayor Rudolph Giuliani, commenting on an art exhibit called "Sensation," at the Brooklyn Museum of Art. He was referring specifically to a painting by the African artist Chris Ofili called "The Holy Virgin Mary." The painting depicted a black Madonna in a colorful flowing robe, dabbed with a clump of elephant dung and surrounded with images of women's buttocks and genitals clipped from pornographic magazines (Steiner 2002).

In 2009, Sony released the video game *Hanuman: Boy Warrior* to worldwide protest by Hindu groups (Hanuman is a Hindu deity and a central figure in one of the epics of Hinduism).

Rajan Zed, a leader of the protest and president of the Nevada-based Universal Society of Hinduism, said that controlling Hanuman with a joystick was denigrating. "Lord Hanuman was not meant to be reduced to such a 'character' in a video game and be in the company of *America's 10 Most Wanted, Bad Boys, Jackass,* and *Killer7*" (Das 2009).

In spring 2010, an episode of *South Park* depicted Muhammad as being inside a bear suit (presumably to avoid showing his image). Following the airing of the episode, a radical Islamic website warned the show's creators that they could be killed. In the following episode, Muhammad was replaced by Santa Claus, and Comedy Central, which airs the show, censored numerous scenes (Pilkington 2010).

In the United States, religious freedom and freedom of speech are both deeply held cultural values. Yet, Americans also believe, as Supreme Court Justice Oliver Wendell Holmes Jr. (1841–1935) said, "the right to swing my fist ends where the other man's nose begins" (Trachtman 2009:87). In an age of complexity, diversity, and instant global communication, someone's nose seems always to be in the way.

◼ YOU DECIDE

1. Have you experienced portrayals of your own beliefs that you found offensive? If so, did you think they should be censored? What role did your culture play in your opinion?
2. If the majority in a community finds a religious representation offensive, should it be censored? Why or why not? Does it make a difference if censorship comes from the government or from a corporation like Sony or Viacom (the company that owns Comedy Central)?

3. Art offensive to religion has sometimes led to violence and death (consider deaths resulting from protests over the Danish cartoon depictions of Muhammad or the Nazis' use of anti-Semitic art). Is fear of violence sufficient justification for censorship?

▌ CHAPTER SUMMARY

1. Although the great diversity in beliefs and practices worldwide makes religion difficult to define, all religions include sacred stories, ideas about the supernatural (or nonempirical), rituals, and specialized practitioners.
2. Through religion, societies create meaning and order in the world, explain aspects of the physical and social environment, and reduce anxiety in risky situations. Religions generally reinforce the social order but may sometimes challenge it.
3. All religions have sacred narratives, sometimes called myths, that legitimize beliefs, values, and customs.
4. Religious ideas are often expressed in symbols that have multiple meanings and emotional power. Symbols allow people to grasp the complexities of religion without much knowledge of the underlying theology.
5. Religions assume that there are nonmeasurable beings, powers, emotional states, and qualities that exist apart from humans but are important to them.
6. All religions use ritual. One important aspect of ritual is liminality, a state of betweenness in which people may experience radical equality or role reversals. Rites of passage and rites of intensification are two important types of ritual.
7. Shamans and priests are two kinds of religious practitioners. Shamans receive power through claims of direct contact with the supernatural and are found in almost all societies. Priests are members of bureaucracies and are appointed, elected, or hired to their positions. They are most common in state-level societies. Witches and sorcerers are those believed to be able to harm people through magical means.
8. Under conditions of rapid social, economic, technological, and political change, prophets emerge who call for religious change.
9. Religious prophecy may be nativistic, calling for a return to a past golden age, or vitalistic, looking to a future golden age. It may emphasize the coming of a savior or a period of destruction after which a new world will emerge.
10. Fundamentalism tends to occur in times of rapid change. Fundamentalists often view religion as a basis of identity, believe in a single

truth, understand life as a battle between good and evil, and believe they are a persecuted minority. They are selective in their acceptance of modernity.

▮▮▮ KEY TERMS

Animism
Antistructure
Communitas
Contagious magic
Cosmology
Divination
Fundamentalism
God (deity)
Imitative magic
Liminal
Magic
Mana
Messianic
Millenarian
Monotheism

Myths (sacred narratives)
Polytheism
Prayer
Priest
Religion
Rite of intensification
Rite of passage
Ritual
Sacrifice
Shaman
Sorcery
Syncretism
Totem
Witchcraft

A man sits next to a picture of his father, a combat veteran of the Tirailleurs Senegalais. The Tirailleurs Senegalais was an army the French drafted and recruited from their colonial possessions in West Africa between the 1850s and 1960.

© Richard Warms

CHAPTER 12

POWER, CONQUEST, AND A WORLD SYSTEM

VETERANS OF COLONIAL ARMIES

WHEN I (Rich Warms) was young, I was a Peace Corps Volunteer. I lived in a town called Ouahigouya in a country that was then called Upper Volta (now Burkina Faso) in West Africa. I spent most of my time working in small villages, but I'd also wander around the town. Frequently on my wanderings, I'd be stopped by a grizzled-looking old man who would start yelling at me in German. Then in French (the language of government and education in Upper Volta), he'd inform me that he'd been a prisoner of the Germans in World War II. At first I took him to be a drunk and a crazy person (where he stopped me was always near a bar). But, as I got to know him and other residents of the town better, I learned that what he told me was, indeed, true. He had been a German prisoner. That, of course, left me wondering how it was possible. After all, I didn't think that this particular individual could have been visiting Europe when the war broke out.

As I spoke to him and to many others like him over the 15 years that followed, I learned a story that had been left out of my high school and college history lessons. I learned that, starting in the second half of the 19th century, France began to create a black African army called the Tirailleurs Senegalais or Senegalese Riflemen. In the early years, the French bought slaves to fill the army ranks. But as time progressed, they turned to levying a draft on their colonies and then, finally, after World War II, to a volunteer force. First they used this army to conquer the areas that became French colonies in Africa. Later, they used these troops to fight in the trenches in World War I and to suppress rebellion in various colonial possessions. In World War II, African troops were essential to the conquest of North Africa and Italy and to taking back France itself. When people think of Charles De Gaulle's Free French forces of that war, they generally summon up a Hollywood image of a white guy in a beret. In fact, before the last phase of the liberation of France in 1944, most Free French forces were black Africans and were more likely to be called Mahamadou than Pierre. In the late years of French colonialism, it was African troops, among others, who fought at the Battle of Dien Bien Phu that ended the French colonial venture in Vietnam in 1954.

In the 1990s, I interviewed more than 50 surviving members of the Tirailleurs Senegalais. The stories they told were fantastic, even unbelievable. Dragged out of small African villages and sent to fight in Europe and elsewhere around the globe, they faced horrors and culture shock that nothing could have prepared them for. Some cracked under the strain, responding with violent outbursts and, when they made it home, with drunkenness and insanity. However, most learned to adapt. When they got home, they sometimes put their language skills, organizational skills, and bravery to new uses, playing important roles in their communities. But many are also deeply aggrieved. They feel neglected by history and by France. In 1991, Mory Samake, a veteran of World War II, told me:

> Look, when you work for someone, he's got to recognize your efforts. They treat us like their dogs. They are white, we are black but we are all equal. If someone cuts my hand and someone cuts one of their hands, the blood is just the same. When we were there fighting the war, no one said "this one is white, this one is black." We didn't go to fight with ill will. We gave our blood and our bodies so that France could be liberated. But now, since they have their freedom, they have thrown us away, forgotten us. If you eat the meat, you throw away the bone. France has done just that to us.

The story of the Tirailleurs Senegalais and Mory Samake's anger with the French reminds us of several extremely important points. A cliché has it that history is written by the winners. It might be more accurate to say that history is written by the powerful and usually presented as a narrative of their inevitable triumph. But such a history ignores inconvenient truths or relegates them to footnotes and appendices. The relation between wealth and poverty and between the powerful and the powerless, or, in this case, between the colonized and the colonizer, is among the most important of these truths.

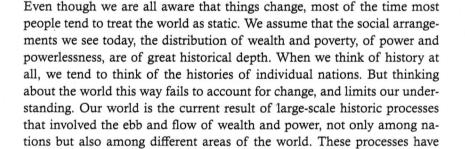

Even though we are all aware that things change, most of the time most people tend to treat the world as static. We assume that the social arrangements we see today, the distribution of wealth and poverty, of power and powerlessness, are of great historical depth. When we think of history at all, we tend to think of the histories of individual nations. But thinking about the world this way fails to account for change, and limits our understanding. Our world is the current result of large-scale historic processes that involved the ebb and flow of wealth and power, not only among nations but also among different areas of the world. These processes have had a particularly important impact on the kinds of small-scale, seemingly isolated societies that anthropologists often study.

We all know that the pace of change has been extremely rapid in the past several centuries. We know less about the patterns of change and their effects on cultures around the world. The story of these patterns is complex and diverse; it is a story of contact between cultures. A significant part of the story concerns the expansion of the affluence and power of places that are now wealthy. This expansion of power occurred in thousands of locations and had many different effects. Sometimes cultural contact was accidentally genocidal, sometimes intentionally so. Many traditional cultures have been destroyed, but others have prospered, although in altered forms. Members of different cultures often confronted each other through a veil of ignorance, suspicion, and accusations of savagery. But sometimes, common interests, common enemies, mutual curiosity, and occasional friendships among people overrode their differences.

In this chapter, we describe the overall pattern of change during the past several hundred years. In the broadest sense, this involved the incorporation of relatively separate cultures and economies into a vast, chaotic, yet integrated world economic system. The formation of this system resulted in enormous inequality both within and among nations as wealth and labor flowed from one area of the world to another. It created the financial accumulation necessary for the industrial revolution and the development of capitalism. In this era, empires rose and fell as powers competed for dominance within their own borders and with each other. The Ottoman Empire as well as the growth of Russia and of Japan played critical roles in the story. However, the expanding influence and power of western European states and the colonies settled by their subjects and citizens probably had the greatest impact worldwide. For that reason, we begin with a bird's-eye view of Europe and the rest of the world as it might have appeared in 1400.

▇▇MAKING THE MODERN WORLD

As surprising as it may seem now, a visitor touring the world on the eve of European expansion in 1400 might well have been amused by the notion that European societies would soon become enormously wealthy and powerful. Other areas of the globe would have seemed much more likely prospects for power. Europeans had devised oceangoing vessels, but Arab and Chinese ships regularly made much longer voyages. The cities of India and China made those of Europe look like mere villages. Almost no European states could effectively administer more than a few hundred square kilometers. Certainly there was nothing that could compare to China's vast wealth and centralized bureaucracy. Europeans were masters of cathedral and castle construction, but other than that, their technology was backward. War, plague, and economic depression were the order of the day (Scammell 1989). Moreover, other areas of the world seemed to be growing in wealth and power. Despite occasional setbacks, the Islamic powers had expanded steadily in the five centuries leading up to 1400, and Muslim societies stretched from Spain to Indonesia. Not only had these empires preserved the scholarship of India and the ancient Mediterranean civilizations, but they also had greatly increased knowledge in astronomy, mathematics, medicine, chemistry, zoology, mineralogy, and meteorology (Lapidus 1988:96, 241–52).

China had an extraordinarily ancient and powerful civilization. As late as 1793, Emperor Ch'ien Lung, believing China to be the most powerful state in the world (or perhaps showing bravado in the face of foreign traders), responded to a British delegation's attempt to open trade by writing to King George III: "Our dynasty's majestic virtue has penetrated into every country under heaven and kings of all nations have offered their costly tribute by land and sea. As your Ambassador can see for himself, we possess all things. . . . [W]e have never valued ingenious articles, nor do we have the slightest need of your country's manufacturers" (Peyrefitte 1992:288–92). Unfortunately for the Chinese, by the time the emperor wrote this letter, it was no longer accurate. Within a half century, at the end of the First Opium War, Britain virtually controlled China.

EUROPEAN EXPANSION: MOTIVES AND METHODS

From slow beginnings in the 15th century, European power grew rapidly from the 16th to the 20th centuries. Many theories have been suggested to account for the causes and motives of European expansion. Although it was often a cover for more worldly aims, the desire of the pious to Christianize the world was certainly a motivating factor. The archives of the Jesuit order include more than 15,000 letters, written between 1550 and 1771, from people who wanted to be missionaries (Scammell 1989:60). The desire to find a wide variety of wonders, both real and imagined, was also important. The Portuguese looked for routes to the very real wealth of Eastern empires, such as China, but also for the mythical kingdom of Prester John, a powerful but hidden Christian monarch, the fountain of youth, and the seven cities of Cibola.

Beyond this, there was always the desire for wealth. Nations and nobles quickly invested in exploration as gold and diamonds were discovered. The poor and oppressed of Europe saw opportunities for wealth and respect in the colonies. There, they sometimes fulfilled their dreams of wealth by recreating the very social order they had fled.

Various social and technological developments aided European expansion. These included the rise of a banking and merchant class, a growing population, and the development of the caravel, a new ship that was better at sailing into the wind. Two other developments, the **monoculture plantation** and the **joint stock company**, were to have critical impacts on the world's people.

In many cases, however, the key advantage Europeans had over other people was the diseases they carried. Almost every time Europeans

monoculture plantation An agricultural plantation specializing in the large-scale production of a single crop to be sold on the market.

joint stock company A firm that is managed by a centralized board of directors but is owned by shareholders.

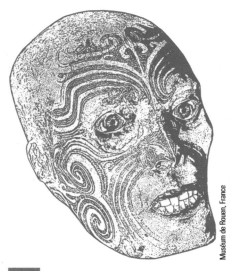

Muséum de Rouen, France

Drawing of a mummified Maori head. This head has been in the collection of the Museum of Natural History at Rouen, France. In 2007, the mayor of Rouen offered to return the head to New Zealand in "atonement" for the trafficking of human remains that occurred in the colonial era. However, the French government prevented the return of the head.

pillage To strip an area of money, goods, or raw materials through the threat or use of physical violence.

encountered populations in the Americas or on islands, they brought death and cultural destruction in the form of microbes.

The European search for wealth depended on tactics that, in their basic form, were ancient. Two of the quickest ways to accumulate wealth are to steal it from others and to get other people to work for you for free. State societies have always practiced these methods. War, slavery, exploitation, and inequality were present in most of the world before European contact, so there was nothing fundamentally new about their use by Europeans. However, no earlier empire had been able to practice these tactics on the scale that the European nations would. All previous empires, however large, were regional affairs. European expansion, for the first time in history, linked the entire world into an economic system. This system created much wealth but made impoverishment and slavery possible on a scale never seen before.

Pillage

One of the most important means of wealth transfer was **pillage**. In the early years of expansion, Europeans were driven by the search for precious metals, particularly gold and silver. When they found such valuables, they moved quickly to seize them. Metals belonging to indigenous peoples were soon dispatched back to Europe, and mines were placed under European control. The profits of these enterprises were enormous. For example, in 1531, Pizarro captured the Inca emperor Atahuallpa and received between 11 and 24 tons of silver and gold as his ransom. A gang of Indian smiths worked nine forges day and night to melt down this treasure, which was then shipped back to Spain (Duncan 1995:158). In the early 17th century, 58,000 Indian workers were forced into silver mining in the town of Potosí in the Peruvian Andes (Wolf 1982:136). Between 1500 and 1660, Spanish colonies in the Americas exported 300 tons of gold and 25,000 tons of silver (Scammell 1989:133).

Such looting was not limited to the New World. After the British East India Company came to power in India, it plundered the treasury of Bengal, sending wealth back to investors in England (Wolf 1982:244). In addition, art, artifacts, curiosities, and occasionally human bodies were stolen around the world and sent to museums and private collections in Europe.

Forced Labor

Forced labor was another key element of European expansion. Although Europeans acquired forced labor through debt servitude—the pawning of adults and children—as well as by simply oppressing people, the most notorious example of forced labor was African slavery. Europeans did not invent slavery in general or African slavery in particular. Slavery had long been practiced in both Europe and Africa. Non-Europeans probably exported more than seven million African slaves to the Islamic world between 650 and 1600 (Lovejoy 1983). However, Europeans did practice African slavery on a larger scale than any people before them. Between the end of the 15th century and the end of the 19th century, approximately 11.7 million slaves were exported from Africa to the Americas. More than six million left Africa in the 19th century alone (Coquery-Vidrovitch 1988). No one really knows how many died in the process of capturing and transferring slaves within Africa. Estimates vary from one to five individuals dead for every slave successfully landed in the Americas.

The massive transport of people had two important economic effects. First, the use of slave labor was extremely profitable for both slave shippers and plantation owners. Second, slave labor created continuous warfare and impoverishment in the areas from which slaves were drawn. Although some undoubtedly grew rich on the profits of slavery, the loss of so many people and the violence and political instability resulting from the capture and transport of slaves radically altered African societies (Coquery-Vidrovitch 1988).

The demand for slaves was created by monoculture plantations—farms devoted to the production of a single crop for sale to distant consumers. Sugar and cotton produced in the Americas and spices produced in Asia were sold to consumers located primarily in Europe. Through the 19th century, sugar was the most important monoculture crop. British consumption of sugar increased some 2,500 percent between 1650 and 1800. Between 1800 and 1890, sugar production grew another 2,500 percent, from 245,000 tons to more than six million tons per year (Mintz 1985:73). The massive amount of labor required for the growing and processing of sugar was largely provided by slaves. Between 1701 and 1810, for example, Barbados, a small island given over almost entirely to sugar production, imported 252,500 slaves, almost all of whom were involved in growing and processing sugar (Mintz 1985:53).

Joint Stock Companies

The joint stock company was another innovation that allowed extremely rapid European expansion and led to enormous abuses of power. Most early European exploration was financed and supported by aristocratic governments or small private firms. By the turn of the 17th century, however, the British and Dutch had established joint stock companies. The French, Swedes, Danes, Germans, and Portuguese followed by midcentury. The best known of these companies include the Dutch East India

Company (founded 1602), the British East India Company (founded 1600), the Massachusetts Bay Company (founded 1628), and the Hudson's Bay Company (founded in 1670).

Joint stock companies were the predecessors of today's publicly held corporations. The idea was simple. To raise the capital necessary for large-scale ventures, companies would sell shares. Each share entitled its purchaser to a portion of the profits (or losses) from the company's business. Exploration and trade by joint stock companies had critical advantages over earlier forms. First, a great deal of capital could be raised rapidly, so business ventures could be much larger than previously possible. Second, although the motives of aristocratic government often included the search for prestige and missionary zeal, joint stock companies existed to provide profits to their shareholders and were relatively single-minded in pursuit of that goal. Since they frequently were empowered to raise armies and conduct wars, they could have devastating effects on the societies they penetrated.

The **Dutch East India Company (VOC**, after its initials in Dutch) is a model example of a joint stock company. Based on money raised from the sale of shares, the VOC was chartered by the Dutch government to hold the monopoly on all Dutch trade with the societies of the Indian and Pacific Oceans. Shares in the VOC were available on reasonable terms and were held by a wide cross-section of Dutch society (Scammell 1989:101). In many ways, the company functioned as a government. Led by a board of directors called the **Heeren XVII** (the Lords Seventeen), it was empowered to make treaties with local rulers in the name of the Dutch Republic, occupy lands, levy taxes, raise armies, and declare war. Thus, the VOC acted like a government. However, governments are to some degree beholden to those they govern, whereas the VOC was interested solely in returning dividends to its shareholders. This it did very successfully. Through the 17th and early 18th centuries, the VOC distributed annual dividends of 15.5 to 50 percent. It returned dividends of 40 percent per year for six consecutive years from 1715 to 1720 (Boxer 1965:46). By comparison, the average annual dividend paid by a Standard and Poor's 500 stock index between 1960 and 2007 was between 2 and 5 percent.

Through the 17th century, the VOC used its powers to seize control of many of the Indian Ocean islands. Among these were Java, including the port of Jakarta (which became their headquarters, renamed Batavia), Sri Lanka (Ceylon), and Malacca. In addition, the VOC acquired the right to control the production and trade of the most valuable spices of the area (cloves, nutmeg, and mace) and took brutal steps to maintain this monopoly. For example, during the 1620s, virtually the entire population of the nutmeg-producing island of Banda was deported, driven away, starved to death, or massacred. They were replaced with Dutch colonists using slave

Dutch East India Company (VOC) A joint stock company chartered by the Dutch government to control all Dutch trade in the Indian and Pacific Oceans. Also known by its Dutch initials VOC for Verenigde Oostendische Compagnie.

Heeren XVII The Lords Seventeen, members of the board of directors of the Dutch East India Company.

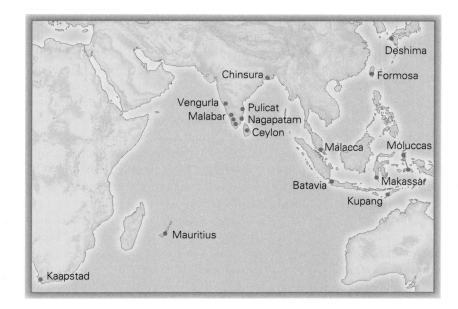

Principal holdings of the Dutch East India Company in the Pacific in the 1660s.

labor (Ricklefs 1993:30). By the 1670s, the Dutch had gained complete control of all spice production in what is now Indonesia (Wolf 1982).

Natives did not submit passively to VOC control, and the company did not have a clear-cut military advantage. Instead, the VOC rapidly (and ultimately disastrously) became embroiled in the area's wars. For example, in the 17th century, the Mataram Dynasty controlled most of central Java. In 1677, when the dynasty faced rebellion, the VOC intervened on its behalf in hopes of cash payments and trade concessions. In a bloody campaign, the combined VOC and dynasty forces crushed the rebellion and established Emperor Amangkurat II on the throne. Trouble ensued when the VOC received neither payments nor concessions. An armed force that the VOC sent to make its demands was defeated by Amangkurat II in 1686. The company was unable to recoup its losses or to claim its trading privileges (Ricklefs 1990). This was just the beginning of a series of extremely brutal wars pitting different factions of Javanese kingdoms against each other and against the VOC. Kingdoms alternately allied with and fought against the VOC as their interests dictated. These conflicts lasted until 1757.

The company often acted with extraordinary violence. The treatment of the Chinese in Batavia is a good example. The Chinese had come to Batavia as traders, skilled artisans, sugar millers, and shopkeepers. Despite harsh measures against them, roughly 15,000 lived there by 1740. VOC officials believed they were plotting rebellion, and after an incident in which several Europeans were killed, VOC governor general Adriaan Valckenier hinted that a massacre would not be unwelcome. In the melee that followed,

Europeans and their slaves killed 10,000 Chinese. The Chinese quarter of the city burned for several days, and the VOC was able to stop the looting only by paying its soldiers a premium to return to duty (Ricklefs 1993:90).

The burden of continual warfare, as well as corruption and inefficiency, forced the VOC into serious financial difficulties. By the last quarter of the 18th century, large areas of coastal Java had been depopulated by years of warfare, but the VOC had not succeeded in controlling the principal kingdoms of the island. The Heeren XVII were dismissed by the Netherlands government in 1796, after an investigation revealed corruption and mismanagement in all quarters. On December 31, 1799, the VOC was formally dissolved, and its possessions were turned over to the Batavian Republic, a Dutch client state of France.

The story of the VOC was, in large measure, repeated by other mercantilist trading firms organized by the British, French, Germans, Portuguese, Danes, and Swedes. In each case, companies generated enormous profits but eventually fell into disarray and either were dissolved or were taken over by their national governments. Despite their eventual failure, the trading companies placed fantastic riches in the hands of European elites. Europeans invested this wealth in many different ways: in the arts, in luxury goods, in architecture, but also in science and industry. This supply of wealth became one of the sources for the Industrial Revolution and the rise of capitalism itself.

The effects were far less pleasant for the regions in which the trading companies operated. The VOC and other trading companies left poverty and chaos in their wake. In every case, Europeans fundamentally altered the communities with which they came into contact. Frequently, brutal policies and disease destroyed entire cultures. However, in most cases, societies were not simply overrun. Before the 19th century, Europeans did not have a truly decisive technological advantage over others. Instead, Europeans collaborated with local elites, which often were able to use their contact with the foreigners to increase their own wealth and power. However, as a whole, their societies suffered.

■■■THE ERA OF COLONIALISM

colonialism The active possession of a foreign territory and the maintenance of political domination over that territory.

colony A territory under the immediate political control of a nation-state.

Colonialism differs in important ways from the earlier expansion of European power. Whereas much of the initial phase of European expansion was carried out by private companies and often took the form of raid and pillage, colonialism involved the active possession of foreign territory by European governments. **Colonies** were created when nations established and maintained political domination over geographically separate areas and political units (Kohn 1958).

There were several different types of European colonies. Some, as in Africa, existed primarily to exploit native people and resources. In other areas, such as North America and Australia, the key goal was the settlement of surplus European population. Still other locales, such as Yemen, which borders on the Red Sea and thus controlled shipping through the Suez Canal, were seized because they occupied key strategic locations.

At one time or another, much of the world came under direct European colonization, but the timing of colonialism varied from place to place. The Americas were colonized in the 1500s and 1600s, but most other areas of the world did not come under colonial control until the 19th century. As long as Europeans confronted others with broadly similar weaponry and military tactics, the result was indecisive, and local governments were able to retain autonomy and power. By the 19th century, however, the Industrial Revolution gave Europeans (and their North American descendants) decisive advantages in both technological sophistication and quantity of arms. Although European colonizers faced frequent rebellions and proved unable to entirely subdue guerrilla activity in all places, no non-European government or army could defeat them.

▌Colonization, 1500 to 1800

As we have seen, before the 1800s very little of Africa or Asia was colonized. In these places, Europeans were able to establish small coastal settlements, but these existed largely because they were profitable for both Europeans and at least some local elites. In most cases, local powers had the ability to expel Europeans or to strictly limit their activities. Relatively few Europeans settled permanently in such colonies.

In the Americas, the situation was radically different. There, Europeans quickly established colonies and immigrated in large numbers. For example, between 1492 and 1600 more than 55,000 Spaniards immigrated to the New World. In the 50 years that followed, another quarter million joined them (Boyd-Bowman 1975). By comparison, in the first half of the 19th century, the total Dutch population of Indonesia, Holland's most important colonial possession, was about 2,100 (Zeegers et al. 2004).

Although there was stiff resistance to European expansion in the Americas, and Indian wars continued until the late 19th century, Europeans were quickly victorious almost everywhere they wanted to expand. Technology aided European expansion, but the main reason for rapid European success was probably disease. In the wake of contact, up to 95 percent of the total population of the New World died. Although Europeans also died of diseases, they did so in far smaller numbers (Karlen 1995; Newson 1999; Palkovich 1994).

Although occasionally epidemics may have been caused intentionally, neither Europeans nor natives had any knowledge of contagion or germs. The vast majority of deaths were not premeditated. However, Europeans came to see the handiwork of God in the disappearance of native populations. God, they believed, clearly intended them to populate the Americas and was removing the native population to make that possible.

New World natives lacked immunity to European diseases for two principal reasons. First, the key diseases that killed indigenous populations, such as smallpox, influenza, and tuberculosis, require large reservoirs of population, in some cases up to a half-million individuals (Diamond 1992). Many North American groups were too small to sustain such crowd diseases and therefore lacked immunity to them. Second, although some Central and South American groups did have large populations, most crowd diseases originate in domesticated animals, which largely absent from the Americas.

Cortés's conquest of Mexico is a good example of the effects of disease. When Cortés first appeared in 1519, the Aztec leader Montezuma, following his tradition, gave Cortés gifts and opened the city of Tenochtitlán to the Spanish. When it became clear that the Spanish were their enemies, the Aztecs expelled them from the city in a fierce battle that cost the Spanish and their allies perhaps two-thirds of their total army. By the time Cortés returned in 1521, a smallpox epidemic had killed up to half the Aztecs. Even after such crushing losses to disease, the Spanish conquest of Tenochtitlán took more than 4 months to accomplish (Berdan 1982; Clendinnen 1991; Karlen 1995). Had the Aztecs not been devastated by disease, they might have again defeated Cortés.

The die-off of Native Americans had dire effects throughout the Americas. The increasing population of Europeans and the diminishing population of natives assured that resistance could not be very effective. When John Winthrop, the first governor of Massachusetts, declared that the settlers had fair title to the land because it was *vacuum domicilium* (empty land), he was creating a legal fiction (he was well aware of the natives and their need for agricultural and hunting land), but he also knew that the native population was declining sharply.

If not for disease, the European experience in the Americas probably would have been very similar to its experience in Asia and Africa. Rather than establishing control over vast amounts of territory, Europeans probably would have been confined to small coastal settlements and would have been involved in protracted battles with powerful local kingdoms.

Colonizing in the 19th Century

By the beginning of the 19th century, industrialization was under way in Europe and North America. This had two immediate consequences.

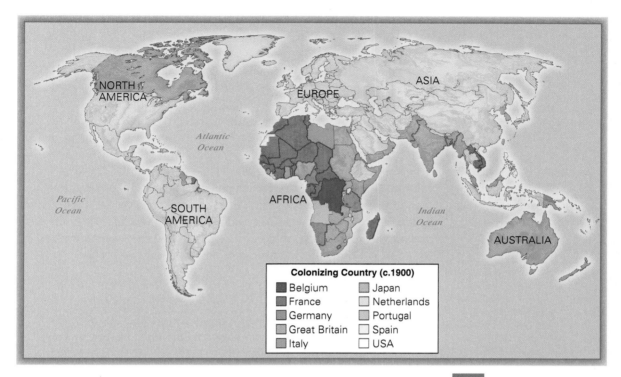

Colonizing Country (c.1900)
- Belgium
- France
- Germany
- Great Britain
- Italy
- Japan
- Netherlands
- Portugal
- Spain
- USA

First, it enabled Europeans and Americans to produce weapons in greater quantity and quality than any other people. Second, it created an enormous demand for raw materials that could not be satisfied in Europe. In addition, discoveries in medicine, particularly vaccines and antimalarial drugs, improved the odds of survival for Europeans in places previously considered pestilential. Thus, Europeans had both motives and means to colonize.

Acting in their own self-interest, Europeans and Americans generally did not move rapidly to place other areas under their colonial control. The primary goal of European expansion was the pursuit of wealth and plunder. Mercantilist firms were rapid, cost-effective ways to get them. The financial burden of establishing companies such as the VOC was borne by their shareholders. However, colonizing an area required some level of government expenditure. At the very least, this included government officials and the troops to back them, all of whom had to be equipped and paid out of government funds. In most cases, infrastructure such as roads, bridges, and railways had to be built. These were expensive undertakings, and European taxpayers and governments were generally not enthusiastic about funding them.

Most often, European governments felt forced to assume colonial control either because of the scandals surrounding the collapse of mercantile companies or out of fear that their national commercial interests were

By 1900, most nations in the Americas had achieved independence. However, much of the rest of the world was under colonial rule. Many areas not formally colonized, such as China, were dominated by European powers.

threatened, generally by other European nations. It was this fear that led to the Berlin conference partitioning Africa among European powers in the late 19th century.

After European governments had established colonies, they had to sell this fact both to their own populations and to those they colonized. They defended their actions by cloaking them in the ideology of social betterment. In Britain, citizens were encouraged, in the words of the poet Rudyard Kipling, to take up "the white man's burden" of bringing civilization to the "savage." In France, the population was told that it had a *"mission civilisatrice,"* a civilizing mission that would both help the "savages" in the colonized areas and increase French political and cultural power throughout the world. The government portrayed its colonial practices as *"rayonnement,"* lighting the way for others (Cole and Raymond 2006:158–59). In the colonies, as we will see next, subjects were taught that they were colonized for their own good and that their societies would advance as a result.

Making Colonialism Pay

Once colonies were seized, they had to be administered and they had to be made profitable. Colonizing powers hoped that tax revenues from colonial subjects would support the cost of colonial government as well as the construction of various public works. However, in many cases, taxes were insufficient, and taxpayers in the colonizing country were required to make up the difference between colonial income and expenses. Despite this situation, colonies were extremely profitable (see Bagchi 2002, for example).

Colonies gave businesses based in the colonizing country places in which they could operate free of competition. This was particularly important for Britain and France, two of the most important colonial powers. In the late 1700s, the Industrial Revolution began in Britain, but by the end of the 19th century, its factories were aging. New, more efficient industrial processes developed in the United States and Germany enabled these countries to produce cheaper manufactured goods (Allitt 2002). France came to industrialization relatively late and had a relatively weak road and rail network. As a result, France too had difficulty competing with the United States, Germany, and Britain. Colonies created a zone of protection for older British industry and newer French manufacturers, thus enabling high profits for firms in these nations.

The costs of the colonies were borne (unequally) by subject colonial populations and by colonizing country taxpayers. The windfall profits from colonialism went to shareholders of companies operating in the colonies.

Finding ways to extract taxes and create the conditions in which corporations could make money often meant the systematic undermining of indigenous ways of life. Although the newly colonized communities had traded with other communities and frequently with Europeans for centuries, trading generally accounted for only a small percentage of their economy. For the most part, their economic relations were drawn along kinship lines, and most of their production was for their own consumption. For colonialism to be profitable, these patterns had to change. Colonial subjects had to be made to produce the goods that colonizing societies wanted and to labor in ways that would be profitable to the colonizers. From the colonizers' perspective, the key problem was finding ways to cause these changes. Some of the methods they used were control of local leaders, forced labor, forced production of particular commodities, taxation, and direct propaganda through education.

Sometimes colonial powers seized direct control of the political leadership, placing their own nationals in most controlling positions, but this was expensive, and foreign colonial leaders often lacked sufficient knowledge of local language and culture. More often, colonialists ruled indirectly through native leaders. Promises of power and wealth as well as the realization that colonial governments held the reins of power and were unlikely to lose them any time soon drew colonial subjects. In some cases, colonial powers offered education, employment, and improved status to people who were oppressed or outcast in precolonial society; and these individuals were particularly attracted to support the colonizers.

A well-organized chain of command was needed for colonial powers to rule effectively. In hierarchical societies where kings or chiefs already existed, this did not pose a difficult problem. Most often, local elites sympathetic to the colonizers were able to retain a degree of power, although they became answerable to the colonial authorities. Those unsympathetic to colonial rule were rapidly replaced. Regions where precolonial relationships were largely egalitarian posed a more difficult problem. If there was no chief or there were many co-reigning chiefs, establishing colonial authority was far more difficult. Colonizers tried to solve this problem by creating new chiefly offices. Sometimes colonialists and missionaries forged entire new ethnic groups, lumping together people with different traditions and even different languages (Harries 1987). For example, the Bété, an ethnic group of the central Ivory Coast in Africa, did not exist before the era of colonialism but was created by the actions of colonial and postcolonial governments (Dozon 1985).

In the long run, policies of indirect rule created the preconditions for instability and violence. Political leaders were compromised by their close connections with colonial authorities, losing the confidence and respect of those they purported to lead. Ethnic groups created for the purposes of colonial rule tended to fragment when that rule diminished.

One of the most direct ways that European governments tried to make their colonies profitable was by requiring **corvée labor**—unpaid work demanded of native populations. Until World War II, most colonial

corvée labor Unpaid labor required by a governing authority.

governments insisted on substantial labor from their subjects. The British often compelled subjects to work for up to one month per year, two months for the Dutch. In 1926, the French enacted a law that permitted an annual draft of labor for their West African colonies. Conscripts were compelled to work for three years on bridge and road building, irrigation projects, and other public works. Mortality rates during the three years of forced labor often were very high, making it one of the most hated institutions of colonialism. Natives resisted colonial demands by concealing workers or by fleeing from authorities when such work was demanded (Evans 2000; Ishemo 1995).

Tirailleurs Senegalais Senegalese riflemen. An army that existed from 1857 to 1960, composed largely of soldiers from French African colonies led by officers from metropolitan France.

Even when subject populations were not forced into labor gangs, economic and social policies of colonial regimes required them to radically alter their cultures. For example, Portuguese colonial policy in Mozambique forced almost one million peasants to grow cotton. The colonial government controlled what these growers produced, where they lived, with whom they traded, and how they organized their labor. Although a few growers prospered, the great majority became impoverished and struggled to survive against famine and hardship (Isaacman 1996). By the 1960s, the brutality and terror used by the colonial regime resulted in a civil war that continued into the 1990s.

Anti-Slavery International Reg Charity 1039160

From 1885 to 1908, Congo was the property of King Leopold II of Belgium. Atrocities committed during that era cost the lives of four to eight million Congolese. Punishments for disobedience or failure to meet payment quotas included chopping off children's hands.

Conditions were perhaps worst in the Congo, ruled between 1885 and 1908, as the personal property of King Leopold II of Belgium. There, each native owed the government 40 hours of labor per month in exchange for a token wage (Bodley 1999:116). Failure to work sufficiently or to produce the proper quantities of goods (particularly rubber) was met with extreme measures. Leopold's subjects were held hostage, were beaten or whipped, had their hands cut off, and, in many cases, were killed outright. By the time the Belgian government stripped Leopold of his control of Congo, between four and eight million Congolese had been killed or had starved to death (Hochschild 1998).

In addition to forced labor and forced production, the British and French both drafted natives into their armed forces. They used these armies to capture and control their colonies, fight colonial wars, and augment their regular armies wherever needed. The **Tirailleurs Senegalais** were described at the opening of this chapter. Additional Tirailleurs units included groups from Algeria, Morocco, Madagascar, Vietnam, Cambodia, and other French colonial possessions. In East Africa, the British drafted and recruited the King's African Rifles. In India, the British created an entire army led by British officers but consisting almost entirely of colonial subjects drawn primarily from ethnic groups the British considered particularly warlike. About 1.3 million members of the Indian Army served in World War I, primarily on the Western Front but also in the Middle East (Nayar and Paul 2003:66).

Although particular projects might use forced labor, to make a colony truly profitable, colonial masters also used other methods to encourage the population to work for them voluntarily or to produce the goods they desired. Taxation was a key mechanism for accomplishing this goal. Taxation was needed to support the colonial government, but because colonizers knew that colonial economies were small and their tax receipts low, they rarely expected taxes to provide the full cost of governing. However, taxing colonial subjects had another purpose: to force them into the market system. Taxes generally had to be paid in colonial money, which native subjects could obtain only by working for a colonist or by producing something that the colonists wanted to buy. This participation in the market and wage labor was viewed as the essential precondition for "civilizing" the natives.

Taxation often forced colonial subjects into a vicious cycle of dependency on the market system. To raise money for taxes, subjects had to work directly for the colonizers or produce things that colonizers desired. But spending time on these tasks meant that less time could be spent making goods or raising crops for one's own consumption. This in turn meant that food and goods increasingly had to be purchased from the market, which was dominated by companies colonialists owned.

In addition to policies aimed at forcing subjects to take part in an economy centered in the industrial world, colonial governments took more direct aim at cultures through educational policies. Colonial education was often designed to convince subjects that they were the cultural, moral, and intellectual inferiors of those who ruled them. For example, education in 19th-century India encouraged children to aspire to be like the ideal Englishman (Viswanathan 1988). In France's African colonies, children were directly taught to obey their colonial masters, as illustrated in this passage from a turn-of-the-century reader designed to teach French to schoolchildren and used in the colonies:

> It is . . . an advantage for a native to work for a white man, because the Whites are better educated, more advanced in civilization than the natives, and because, thanks to them, the natives will make more rapid progress . . . and become one day really useful men. . . . You who are intelligent and industrious, my children, always help the Whites in their task (cited in Bodley 1999:104).

Education was often aimed at the children of elites. These children were taught that, although they might never reach the level of the colonists, they were considerably more advanced than their uneducated countrymen. In France's African colonies, individuals who were educated and assimilated to French culture were known both by the French and by themselves as *evolues,* or evolved people. This increased the perception of the uneducated and unassimilated as being backward and primitive. Thus, schooling both reinforced the colonizers' position and created a subservient educated class convinced of its superiority (Kelly 1986).

Colonialism and Anthropology

The origins and practice of modern anthropology are bound up with the colonial era. Both anthropology and 19th-century colonialism are products of the 18th-century age of European enlightenment, the romantic retrenchment of the 19th century, the Industrial Revolution, the birth of modern science, and other historical and philosophical forces. For example, the evolutionary theories of 19th-century anthropologists described a world in which all societies were evolving toward perfection. This idea shows elements of enlightenment rationality (they were systematizing knowledge and trying to discover laws of social development) and 19th-century romanticism (nations were moving toward perfection), and was very clearly influenced by the scientific theories of Charles Darwin and the social theories of Herbert Spencer. It was also a convenient philosophy that could be pressed into service as a rationale for colonization: Colonization could help "primitive" societies evolve (Ghosh 1991; Godelier 1993).

One of the most important impacts colonialism had on anthropology was in determining the locations of fieldwork. British Commonwealth anthropologists tended to work in British colonies, French anthropologists in their colonies, and Americans within U.S. borders, in areas "protected" by the Monroe Doctrine or in areas of American influence and control in the Pacific. In some cases, colonialism may have played a role in determining the topics of anthropological research. Studies of indigenous political systems or law were of particular interest to colonial governments. Colonialism and, more importantly, the discourse of rationalism and science also tended to promote a kind of anthropology where the anthropologist speaks as an active authority claiming to objectively describe essentially passive subjects.

In the first half of the 20th century, colonial governments faced with the practical problems of governing their possessions sometimes relied on information anthropologists provided. Anthropologists, anxious to find funding for their research, argued that their studies had practical value to colonial administrators (Malinowski 1929a, for example). However, anthropology did not come into being to promote or enable colonialism, which would have gone on with or without it (Burton 1992).

Anthropologists did not generally question the political reality of colonialism, but they often self-consciously tried to advance the interests of the people they studied. Most anthropological research was financed by private charitable organizations with reformist agendas and not by governments (Goody 1995). The result was that colonial officials generally mistrusted anthropologists, believing they were much too sympathetic to colonial subjects (Prah 1990).

DECOLONIZATION

The eras of Western expansion and colonization radically and permanently changed the world. By the time of World War II, all peoples had been affected by Western expansion and their cultures altered by this experience. Some, attempting to resist foreign influences and protect their ways of life, had moved as far away from outsiders as possible (for example, see Breusers 1999). However, most people lived in societies where the presence and influence of outsiders, their demands for goods and labor, and their attempts to change culture were fundamental facts of life.

Most of the nations of the Americas had gained their independence in the 18th and 19th centuries. In Africa and Asia, independence from European colonialism was not achieved until after World War II. Many nations that were part of the Soviet Union only received their independence in the late 1980s and early 1990s. Some colonies persist today, although

Kwame Nkrumah, Ghana's first president, proclaims independence on March 6, 1957.

National Archives Photo No. 306-RNT-57-18116

usually with the consent of the majority of their residents. For example, Britain has some 14 "overseas territories," including Bermuda, Gibraltar, and the Pitcairn Islands. French "overseas departments" include Martinique and French Guiana. U.S. "organized unincorporated territories" include American Samoa and Guam. Many consider the U.S. relationship with Puerto Rico colonial as well (Grosfoguel 2003; Melendez 1993).

There were as many reasons for the granting of independence as there were for exploration and colonialism, but three are of particular importance: civil disobedience, changing political alignments, and changing economic structures.

Governing colonies was never a simple affair, and from the beginning, there was rebellion against colonial rule. Strikes, acts of terrorism, and guerrilla warfare in some places were common throughout the colonial era. However, for several reasons, there was a substantial upsurge in these following the Second World War. One reason was the return of combat veterans. Veterans knew how to fight European-style warfare. Moreover, they and their supporters felt that colonizing countries owed them a deep debt for their service, a debt to be paid partially by increased political liberties.

In some places, resistance took the form of agitation and demonstrations, but in others, bitter anticolonial wars broke out. In Madagascar, for example, almost 90,000 died in a rebellion between 1947 and 1948. In Algeria, between 1954 and 1962, France fought a protracted war that left at least one-quarter of a million dead (Kepel 2005). Anticolonial wars also broke out in Vietnam, Mozambique, Angola, and numerous other places.

The end of World War II also created a fundamentally different balance of world power. European nations, which held the largest number of colonies, were greatly weakened, which left the United States and the Soviet Union as the dominant superpowers. They quickly engaged in a cold war that was to last for more than four decades, but neither nation had a strong interest in preserving the colonial status quo. Based on the belief that they could bring former colonies into their own economic and political orbit, both the United States and the Soviet Union promoted rapid independence for colonial possessions and supplied money and weaponry to their supporters within the colonies.

Finally, international economics was also changing. In many cases, colonies had been created to allow European corporations access to areas where they could operate free of competition from those based in other nations. However, in the wake of World War II, corporate ownership began to become multinational, and corporations were less tied to their nations of origin, a move that continues today. This process undercut an important economic rationale of colonialism.

By December 1960, when the United Nations declared that "all peoples have the right to self determination" and that "immediate steps shall be taken . . . to transfer all powers to the peoples of [countries that have not yet achieved independence] (UN Resolution 1514)," the process of decolonization was already well underway. At that time, recently decolonized nations included India and Pakistan (1947), Cambodia (1953), Vietnam (1954), Ghana (1957), Guinea (1958), and many others.

By the late 1970s, almost all colonies held by western European nations had achieved independence. With the formal end of the Soviet Union in 1991 and the collapse of South African apartheid in 1994, almost all areas of the world had some form of home rule. Colonized areas became independent under a variety of circumstances and with many different levels of preparedness. In some, like Ghana, the transition to independence was reasonably orderly, and there were a sizable (but still inadequate) number of individuals trained as administrators. In others, like Congo, the transition was profoundly violent, and very few colonial subjects had any experience with running government. But although there were great differences among colonies, all came to independence as relatively poor nations in a world that was increasingly divided into the wealthy and the poor rather than the independent and the colonized.

Formal independence was critical for former colonies. However, compelling connections between newly independent nations and their former colonial powers remained. In most cases, diplomatic and cultural ties between nations and their former colonies continued to be strong. In many cases, economic ties persisted as well. European and American corporations continued their operations, albeit frequently with new names, and newly independent nations continued to supply the raw materials for European, American, and increasingly Asian industries. In the 1960s, the word *neocolonialism* came to express the idea that although nations were no longer colonized, many of the institutions of colonialism remained intact.

The European expansion and the era of colonization were historic processes that changed the world from a collection of relatively independent economies and societies to a complex world system. Technological and political processes since the end of colonialism have only accelerated this process. In Chapter 13, we explore some of the problems faced by independent but poor nations as well as the forces of technology, finance, and politics that are weaving an increasingly dense fabric of globalization.

BRINGING IT BACK HOME:
CHARTER CITIES

According to award-winning economist and entrepreneur Paul Romer, by colonizing and maintaining Hong Kong, Britain did more to reduce poverty than all of the aid programs of the last century combined. Romer argues that the creation of similar cities around the world could be a critical step in reducing world poverty (Romer 2009).

For Romer, the rules under which people operate are a critical factor that makes the difference between wealth and poverty. He frequently uses the example of children studying under streetlights in Africa, arguing that they do so because the economic rules under which the electric companies in their countries operate provide no incentive for these companies to bring electricity to most people's houses. The technology exists, the demand exists, but the rules prevent progress.

Hong Kong, Romer argues, was successful because, by an accident of history, it had its own set of rules: essentially a charter provided by the British government that included elements such as minimal regulation and legal protection for property and contracts. Romer believes that poor nations should move to establish "charter cities" like Hong Kong. Specifically, they should create partnerships with wealthy nations in which these nations agree to create and administer new cities on now-vacant land in poor nations. For example, Romer has suggested that Cuba invite Canada to create a city near Guantanamo. He has also attempted to create partnerships (thus far unsuccessfully) with several African nations. Such

Students studying under street-lights in Guinea, West Africa.

cities would not necessarily be democratically governed but they would have clear business rules and legal protections for their residents and the firms doing business there. For Romer, only today's wealthy nations have the credibility and competence to create and administer such rules.

Would such cities constitute a return to colonialism? Romer argues that although his plan does involve nations ceding control of territory to wealthier, more powerful nations, it lacks the elements of coercion and condescension that made colonialism bad. Romer insists that people must be free to come to new cities or leave them as they see fit and that all city residents must be treated with dignity and respect as provided under the terms of the city's charter.

Romer's ideas are deeply controversial. Charter cities present difficult problems for both the poor nations that might offer land and the wealthy ones that might agree to administer it (Mallaby 2010). Thus far, no nation has agreed to accept a charter city (although Romer did come close to an agreement with Madagascar in 2008). Nevertheless, Romer has garnered a great deal of publicity. The *Harvard Business Review* has listed charter cities as one of its ten "breakthrough ideas" for 2010 (Amabile et al. 2010).

YOU DECIDE

1. Do you believe that businesses in wealthy nations would be willing to establish facilities in charter cities? What factors might prevent them from doing so?
2. Hong Kong was won from China in war and the British were willing to defend it from attack. If a wealthy nation established a charter city and it was attacked (either by the nation that originally permitted it or a third party), would the wealthy nation need to be willing to defend it?
3. To what degree do you believe that Hong Kong's success is due to its clear rules and relatively competent administration? What other factors might account for its success?

CHAPTER SUMMARY

1. Although we are aware of history, we tend to think of current world conditions as similar to past conditions. This is illusion. The world as we see it is the result of historical processes that have moved wealth and power from one area of the world to another. The rise of today's wealthy nations was connected with the emergence of modern poverty.

2. In the 15th century, Europe was neither wealthy nor technologically advanced. The centers of world power lay primarily in the Middle East and Asia. However, Europe was poised on the brink of a great expansion.

3. A combination of religious faith, greed, new social arrangements, and new technologies drove European expansion. Europeans were particularly successful in the Americas, where they were aided by the diseases they carried. They met far more resistance in Asia.

4. Plunder of precious metals, the use of slave labor, and the joint stock company as well as political and military maneuvering drew wealth from around the world into Europe. European nations became prosperous, but other areas of the world were impoverished.

5. Colonialism occurred when European governments took direct control of overseas territories. This happened very early in the Americas, but was a much later development elsewhere in the world.

6. Although European governments often justified colonialism by calling it a civilizing mission, governments colonized to increase their wealth and protect their trade. They used forced labor, taxation, and education programs designed to discredit local culture to compel natives to produce for European interests.

7. Anthropological knowledge was sometimes used in the process of colonialism, and some anthropologists wished to make themselves useful to colonial governments. However, anthropology did not come into being to promote colonialism, which would have gone on without it.

8. Most colonies gained their independence between the end of World War II and 1965. Civil unrest in the colonies, the emergence of the United States and the Soviet Union as superpowers, and changes in the structure of international economics played critical roles in the timing of independence.

▌▌▌ KEY TERMS

Colonialism	Joint stock company
Colonies	Monoculture plantation
Corvée labor	Pillage
Dutch East India Company	Tirailleurs Senegalais
Heeren XVII	VOC

© Time & Life Pictures/Getty Images

We live in a world of sharp contrasts. Individuals and cultures worldwide are affected by changes in communication, technology, and the flow of wealth and peoples among nations.

CHAPTER 13

GLOBALIZATION AND CHANGE

GLOBAL POVERTY

ONSIDER an average family in North America with four family members and a combined income of over $50,000. They live in a comfortable house or apartment and have one or two cars. Each child has a separate bedroom. They have numerous consumer goods, mostly manufactured outside North America. They have three meals a day and plenty of snacks, much of this food imported. The children are healthy and attend school. They can expect to complete their secondary education, probably go to college, choose among a variety of careers, and live to an average age of 77 years.

This sounds like a good life, but there are problems as well. Strong competitive pressures take their toll on the health of both parents. Rising costs of health care and college education, job insecurity, and debt threaten their way of life. Still, their economic status and lifestyle are the aspirations of millions of people throughout the world.

In contrast to this family is a typical "extended" family in rural Asia. The household is likely to comprise 10 or more people, including parents, children, and other relatives, with a combined annual income of less than $500. As tenant farmers, they live in a one-room house, without electricity or fresh water supply, on a large agricultural estate owned by an absentee landlord. The adults and older children work all day on the land. None of the adults can read or write. Of the five school-age children, only two attend school regularly, and they will get only a basic primary education. There is often only one meal a day and it is barely sufficient to alleviate the children's hunger pains. Illness abounds but there are very few medical practitioners. The work is hard, the sun is hot, and their aspirations for a better life are continually being snuffed out.

Shifting to a large city along the coast of South America, we are immediately struck by the sharp contrast in living conditions among neighborhoods. There is a modern stretch of tall buildings, wide boulevards, and gleaming beaches, but just a few hundred yards away there are squalid shanties. On a typical Saturday evening at dinnertime, in the apartment of a wealthy family, a servant sets the table with imported china, high-quality silverware, and fine linen. The family's eldest son is home from his university in North America, and the other two children are on vacation from their boarding schools in France and Switzerland. The father is a medical doctor with a wealthy clientele. Annual vacations abroad, imported luxuries, and fine food and clothing are commonplace amenities for this fortunate family.

And what of a poor family? New migrants from a rural area, this family lives in a dirt-floor hillside shack and the stench of open sewers fills the air. No dinner table is being set; in fact, there is no dinner — only a few scraps of stale bread. The four children spend most of their time on the streets begging, shining shoes, or trying to steal. The father has had part-time jobs but nothing permanent, and the family income is less than $1,000 a year. The children are in and out of school because they have to help out financially in any way they can. Occasionally the eldest teenage daughter seems to have some extra money, but no one asks where it comes from.

Now imagine that you are in eastern Africa, where many small clusters of tiny huts dot a dry and barren land. Each cluster contains a group of extended families, all sharing the work. There is very little money because most food, shelter, and other goods are made and consumed by the people themselves. There are few roads and no schools, hospitals, electricity, or water supply. In many respects, life is as difficult as for the poor family in Latin America, but perhaps less psychologically troubling because all share it.

Soon a road will pass near this village. It will bring more information about the outside world, more gadgets of modern civilization. Before long, exportable tropical fruits will be grown in this region. They may even end up on the dinner table of the rich South American family. Meanwhile, radios made in Southeast Asia playing music performed by African bands recorded in northern Europe will become prized possessions. Like many remote villages in Asia, Africa, and Latin America, this village is being linked with the outside world in many ways, a process of global economic interconnection that will intensify in the coming years.

The previous stories are perhaps oversimplified, but they dramatically capture some important truths (Todaro and Smith 2003). The historical processes described in Chapter 12 transformed the world, creating a process of globalization. But the world is not a global village. The global village is a pastoral metaphor suggesting a relatively small place, a place where anyone can easily visit any part, a place where differences are minimized, a world of screen doors, broad porches, and friendly neighbors. But as these stories illustrate, the world is one of privilege and exclusion, of rapid change, often dislocating change, and of shocking inequality. In our world, we inhabit accessible, wealthy, and powerful places in constant communication with each other. Other places are more difficult to reach, less in contact with the rest of the world, and some can be entered and exited only with real difficulty.

The distances created by inequality dwarf those of mere distance. Technology or financial specialists working in Manhattan can easily and frequently communicate with colleagues, relatives, and friends living and working thousands of miles away, while they may have almost no social connections with any of the urban poor living within sight of their office.

No culture has been left unchanged by history. In this chapter, we examine some of the principal challenges resulting from globalization and consider what anthropology teaches us about the effects of global forces on cultures worldwide.

ECONOMIC DEVELOPMENT

The impact of global forces has created a world that is enormously contradictory. All around us, we see increasing cultural homogeneity; a bottle of soda, a radio, a CD player, a cell phone can be found almost anywhere. The Internet lets teenagers in Houston bid on products in Hong Kong. But at the same time, it is in many ways an increasingly divided world, with great disparities in both the quality and quantity of life. More than 1.2 billion of the world's population lives on less than $1 a day, while a meal for two at a good restaurant in any American city can easily top $100. Someone born in the late 1990s in Japan had a life expectancy of 81 years, but a person born in those same years in Malawi or Mozambique could expect to live only 37 years. Moreover, although many forces of globalization foster cultural homogeneity, throughout the world there is also resistance, sometimes taking violent forms, as people assert their right to separate themselves from a global culture and maintain their traditional cultures (Friedman 2003; Hefner 2002). Despite the global integration of the economy and electronic communications that bring the world together, tribal, regional, and national cultures are on the rise as a means of resisting homogeneous global culture, particularly the widespread diffusion of American culture, an issue raised by the feature at the end of this chapter (Jenkins 2002; Kimmelman 2010a, 2010b).

The end of colonial rule brought challenges—of poverty, the presence of multinational corporations, urbanization, population growth, immigration and emigration, ecological disaster, war, and instability—to newly independent nations. Some, like Singapore (formerly a British colony), Korea (a Japanese colony from 1905 to 1945), and Malaysia, have done well, but most nations remain poor.

The **gross national income (GNI)** of a nation is the total value of all its production and provides a rough estimate of national prosperity. In the United States, in 2005, the GNI per capita was $42,000, but 80 of the 208 nations listed by the World Bank had a per capita GNI of less than $5,000; for 53 of these nations, the GNI was less than $2,500. In 2004, about one billion people were living on less than $1 a day.

Under colonialism, economic plans focused on making colonies productive for their owners, but in the postcolonial era, there were many changes, as various forces mobilized to bring a better life to the world's

gross national income (GNI) The total market value of all goods and services produced in a country.

poor. As a result of the cold war, Eastern and Western blocs both tried to spread their ideology, advance their economic systems, create political alliances, and secure sources of raw materials, by providing financial and military aid to poor nations. Some wealthy governments, international agencies, and private organizations also participated in the effort of raising the standard of living in poor countries.

Modernization Theory

The model of progress promoted by Western nations was called **modernization theory**. It started with the presumption that former colonies were poor because they had underdeveloped, backward economies. Modernization theorists held that poor nations could become rich by repeating the historical experience of the wealthy nations. To this end, foreign advice and financial aid were designed to alter the structural, cultural, and psychological features the theorists believed stood in the way of modernization. New roads and factories would bring industrialization to the countryside. New farming techniques would allow peasants to cultivate cash crops. The market would replace the old mechanisms of obligation and reciprocity. The result would be increased wealth and higher standards of living.

> **modernization theory** A model of development holding that some nations are poor because of their traditional cultures. Such nations should achieve wealth by attempting to repeat the historical experience of today's wealthy nations.

This development model was of mutual benefit to both donors and elites in poor nations. It spread the influence of wealthy nations and opened new markets for their products. In poor nations, development aid funds were often used to support an elite lifestyle and opened many possibilities for political patronage and corruption. Little improved, however, for most ordinary people in the recipient nations; indeed, in many cases, their poverty increased.

Among many reasons for the failure of development was the theory itself. Modernization theorists mistakenly ignored the roles that colonialism and exploitation had played in the history of both rich and poor nations, a history that could not be replicated.

Human Needs Approaches

The failure of economic development plans in the 1960s led to new ideas, one of which was the basic human needs approach of the 1970s and 1980s. In this period, the World Bank and other development agencies began to focus on filling the basic needs of the rural poor, aiming at the elimination of absolute poverty as a principal goal of development aid (World Bank Group Archives 2003).

Proponents of the basic human needs approach argued that development had failed because it had focused on large-scale projects and technological change and had not paid enough attention to improving the lives of the very poor and increasing their capacity to contribute effectively to the economy. So in contrast to development approaches, basic human needs projects emphasized assuring poor people access to land, improved but simple farming techniques, basic education, access to pure water, basic health and sanitation facilities, and involving people in rural communities in managing and promoting these goals. Because anthropologists often had expertise in studying such communities, they played increasingly important roles in development aid projects, and providing local perspectives is one of the important contributions anthropology makes to development (De Waal 2002).

But by the end of the 1980s, basic human needs projects lost their prominent role in development. Although the projects did benefit some communities, they failed to provide the economic growth that planners hoped for. Beyond this, donor governments disliked these projects because they had high overhead expenses and did not generate very much publicity. Recipient governments disliked them because the amount of money disbursed for them was lower than for more traditional modernization projects, and often the groups that the projects tried to help had relatively little political power. Perhaps most important, the development philosophy in wealthy nations again changed.

Structural Adjustment

neoliberalism Political and economic policies promoting free trade, individual initiative, and minimal government regulation of the economy and opposing state control or subsidies to industries and all but minimal aid to impoverished individuals.

structural adjustment A development policy promoted by Western nations, particularly the United States, that requires poor nations to pursue free market reforms in order to get new loans from the International Monetary Fund and the World Bank.

By the late 1970s, the failure of development programs and changing economic conditions left poor nations very deeply in debt to wealthy nations. This coincided with the rise of **neoliberalism** in the United States and Europe, a series of political and economic policies promoting free trade, individual initiative, and minimal government regulation of the economy. Neoliberals opposed state control of industries or government subsidies to them and opposed all but minimal aid to impoverished individuals. This political philosophy led to a new approach to development called **structural adjustment**. Following neoliberal policies, before making any additional loans or grants, wealthy nations demanded that poor nations restructure their economies. They required poor nations to sell off state-owned enterprises, reduce subsidies to local businesses and industries, reduce spending on education, health, and social programs, and open their markets to free trade. Critics charge that these policies have created a spiral of deepening impoverishment that particularly affects the poorest and most vulnerable populations (Schneider 2002). Supporters argue that although such policies do cause pain, earlier policies were unsustainable; they claim that unleashing free market forces will promote industry, investment, and entrepreneurship, which will lead to increased wealth and a better standard of living for all. Thus far, it seems clear that in fact structural adjustment policies have increased global inequality and that poverty remains an intractable problem (Greenberg 1997; Kim et al. 2000; SAPRIN 2004).

In spite of some important successes, such as raising the life expectancy and literacy rates and lowering the infant mortality rate in poor nations, and the effectiveness of some grassroots organizations, like the Grameen Bank, that have raised the standard of living among some of the world's poorest people through small loans to rural women (Kristoff and WuDunn 2000), the overall record of development projects around the world continues to be poor. Projects are plagued by poor design, inappropriate technologies, and deleterious effects on environment, culture, and political stability. For example, aid projects helped to increase the export of shrimp in Honduras by more than 1500 percent, but the price of this growth was pollution, environmental destruction, and the impoverishment of people who lived near the shrimp farms (Stonich, Murray, and Rossart 1994). Although the track record of development projects is mixed and the politics behind them controversial, they still have strong support and are likely to continue.

multinational corporation (MNC) A corporation that owns business enterprises in more than one nation, able to seek the most profitable venues to produce and market its goods and services regardless of national boundaries.

MULTINATIONAL CORPORATIONS

A **multinational corporation (MNC)** is a business that owns enterprises in more than one nation or that seeks the most profitable places to produce and market its goods and services regardless of national boundaries. MNCs create major and controversial changes in the natural, economic, social, and cultural environments.

Because MNCs control vast amounts of wealth, they are significant political forces throughout the world and can exert enormous influence on poor nations, making it extremely difficult for these nations to set and enforce policies that effectively regulate them. No corporation controls more than a small percentage of the economy of any rich nation, but many MNCs may have yearly budgets that are greater than those of poor nation governments. In 2005, each of the world's 20 largest MNCs had gross revenues larger than all but 47 of the 208 countries tracked by the World Bank (Fortune 2006; World Bank 2008).

© Joan Gregg

Multinational corporations such as McDonald's have profound economic and cultural impacts on the societies in which they produce and sell their products.

Like all capitalist corporations, the fundamental goal of multinational corporations is to profit their shareholders, the vast majority of whom live in wealthy nations. This movement of wealth from the poor to the rich perpetuates colonial-style relationships. Multinational corporations do bring employment opportunities, goods, and services to people who otherwise would not have them, but they often involve sweatshop labor and are thus a subject of much critical attention. A **sweatshop** is a factory where workers, particularly women and children, are employed for long hours under difficult conditions and at low pay. Large areas of South and East Asia including China, South Korea, Indonesia, Malaysia, India, and Bangladesh might be considered a sweatshop belt, accounting for about one-quarter of the global economy (Kristoff and WuDunn 2000). Much sweatshop production is funneled into the United States in the form of cheap consumer goods, sold at places like the Gap, Old Navy, and Banana Republic, all of which are owned by a single company. The company's own study found that between 10 percent and 25 percent of its factories in China, Taiwan, and Saipan use psychological coercion or verbal abuse on their workers and more than 50 percent of the factories in sub-Saharan Africa had inadequate safety practices (Merrick 2004).

For many people who work under terrible conditions in sweatshops, however, the alternatives are worse. Many workers are drawn from the ranks of the landless poor, and the money they earn, however small, often marks the difference between food and a roof over their head and hunger on the streets. Critics focus on the dehumanizing conditions of sweatshops and argue for international labor standards, while others point out that over time sweatshop conditions and wages tend to improve and that public protests and import restrictions can cause drops in sales, throwing people out of work and harming the very workers these actions are designed to help (Bhagwati 1996; Brown, Deardorff, and Stern 2003; Maskus 1997).

Sweatshop labor is not limited to poor nations. An estimated 175,000 people, mostly immigrant women, work in sweatshop conditions in the United States (Malveaux 2005). In many cases, sweatshop workers are the victims of labor law violations and some are victims of human trafficking, held by their employees against their will.

Anthropologists have both exposed sweatshop working conditions and advocated for sweatshop workers (see pp. 350–351). Robert Hackenberg's study of Nike footwear opens our eyes to globalization, sweatshop labor, and both the influence and limits of public opinion (2000). In its early days, Nike's manufacturing base was in New England, but today, Nike uses manufacturing facilities in more than 50 countries (Nike 2005). In the late 1980s and early 1990s, the grim picture of Nike's employment practices began to emerge. More than 75 percent of Nike workers were women who put in 10- to 13-hour days, 6 days a week. Frequently forced to work over-

sweatshop Generally a pejorative term for a factory with working conditions that may include low wages, long hours, inadequate ventilation, and physical, mental, or sexual abuse of its workers.

time, their wages were less than the subsistence level for a single adult. In some cases, workers were subject to harsh corporal punishment, including having their mouths taped shut for disobedience (Sage 1999:209).

In opposition to Nike's practices, a loose coalition of organizations was formed, including ones on American college campuses and groups in other wealthy nations concerned with labor rights. The coalition used the media and public protests to pressure Nike to change its labor policies (Rothenberg-Aalami 2004; Sage 1999). Nike first responded with advertising countering its critics but soon was forced to move toward real reform. It increased the minimum age for workers, adopted some U.S. occupational safety standards, offered its employees expanded educational programs and loan programs, and began to implement effective monitoring of the workplace. Although many problems remain, the company made significant strides toward eliminating the worst abuses. While the well-orchestrated grassroots campaign by the Anti-Nike Transnational Advocacy Network showed that such action can help to improve conditions for low-wage workers, its effectiveness was partly based on the fact that Nike's public image was central to its success, and athletic footwear is a highly competitive market. Other companies, unknown to the public, whose image is not critical to their success, would not be as vulnerable to social action.

URBANIZATION

Although many preindustrial societies had cities, their size and importance have increased dramatically in the contemporary world. From 1950 to 2000, the percent of the total population of nonindustrialized nations who lived in large cities increased from 16 percent to 40 percent, and by 2020, it is projected to reach 50 percent (United Nations 2003). In 1950, seven of the world's ten largest cities, with an average population of 6.5 million people, were located in Europe, Russia, Japan, and the United States. By 2015, eight of the world's ten largest cities are expected to be located in poor nations and the average population of these cities will be over 20 million inhabitants (Population Reference Bureau 2005). Providing basic services to such large populations will become even more difficult than is presently the case.

Rural people come to cities seeking jobs and the social, material, and cultural advantages they believe are available in urban areas. They are forced out of the countryside by high population levels, inability to acquire land, environmental degradation, and sometimes violence. When new migrants arrive in urban areas, they often find dismal living conditions. In cities such as Bogotá, Casablanca, Cairo, Kolkata (Calcutta), and Caracas, more than half of the urban population lives in slums and squatter settlements (Todaro and Smith 2003).

More than half the world's largest cities are in poor nations. These pictures of Rio de Janeiro, Brazil, show the enormous contrasts present in such cities. Although Rio has an extremely prosperous elite, most residents live in abject poverty. Modern office and apartment buildings and luxury resorts (left) exist alongside shantytowns with only minimal access to safe drinking water or sanitation.

Migration changes both the migrants themselves and the communities they left. New ideas and values as well as consumer goods enter the countryside through urban centers, through links between urban migrants, and through those who remain at home. Radio, television, and now websites located primarily in urban areas broadcast their messages and their advertisements to the countryside.

Urbanization brings with it the creation of a great variety of social groups based on voluntary membership. These associations may serve as mutual aid societies, lending money to members, providing scholarships for students, arranging funerals, and taking care of marriage arrangements for urban migrants. Some develop along kinship or ethnic lines that were relevant in the traditional culture; others, such as labor unions, are based on relationships deriving from new economic contexts and have no parallel in rural society.

Some of the difficulties of urban life for the poor are unemployment, hunger, unsafe drinking water, inadequate sanitation facilities, and substandard shelter. Disease and early death are rampant in the slums of the world's large cities. Research using a storytelling technique aimed at eliciting the perceptions about their lives of rural women in a traditional village, poor urban women, and middle-class urban women in Kenya showed that traditional women told positive stories with happy endings, middle-class nontraditional urban women told stories that emphasized their own power and competence, whereas poor urban migrant women told tragic stories that emphasized their powerlessness and vulnerability (Friedman and Todd 1994). The researchers noted that many poor urban women have "lost the security and protection of the old [traditional] system without gaining the power or rewards of the new system."

Yet the continued growth of cities indicates both their appeal and the desperate poverty of the countryside. Solutions to the problems caused by urbanization must thus focus on both rural and urban areas. Although nations must provide adequate services, including water, sewage, education, and health care to their urban populations, unless life chances and opportunities also are greatly improved for rural populations, better services in the cities will only draw more migrants who will quickly overwhelm any advances that are made.

POPULATION PRESSURE

The rate of population growth provides a dramatic index of the increasing speed of social change. About 2 million years ago, our remote ancestors numbered perhaps 100,000; by the time the first agricultural societies were developing 10,000 years ago, world population had reached 5 to 10 million. Two thousand years ago, there were about 250 million people in the world. By 1750, this number had tripled to 750 million. Then population growth really accelerated. By 1800, there were one billion people; by 1930, two billion. Since then, world population has tripled, surpassing the six billion mark in the summer of 1999 (Erickson 1995; Fetto 1999). Much of this population growth took place in poor nations where, between 1950 and 2000, the population rose by some three billion (Geographical 2005). World population continues to increase and is expected to rise to more than 10 billion by 2050, with most of the increase in the world's poor nations (see Figure 13.1).

In some cases, this population growth means that traditional subsistence strategies can no longer provide enough food. In parts of East Africa, for example, the amount of arable land per person declined 40 percent between 1965 and 1987 (World Bank

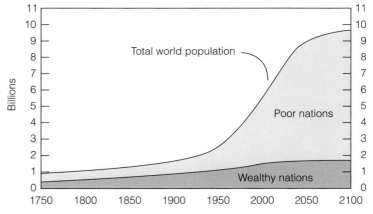

Figure 13.1

If current trends continue, world population will increase to about 10 billion by the middle of the 21st century before leveling off. The great majority of this increase will come in poor nations.

1992), and this has resulted in important cultural changes. Among the Waluguru in Tanzania, population increase resulted in land shortage, which increasingly resulted in the privatization of land. Traditionally, people gained access to land through their lineage and the lineage head was a powerful figure; now land must be purchased, and lineage leadership has completely disappeared (van Donge 1992).

In other cases, the population explosion and the search for land and wealth have pushed people onto land previously occupied only by indigenous groups. Beginning in 1955, the Agta, a foraging group in the Philippines (see Chapter 8, p. 193), were pushed off their land by loggers and migrant farmers. By 1993, the Agta had become landless migrant workers living at the lowest rung of Philippine society (Early and Headland 1998).

China's One-Child Policy

Programs to control population growth are often controversial and both affect and are affected by culture. In China, for example, in 1979, the Chinese government introduced a radical population policy limiting families to a single child (although parents were allowed to keep twins or triplets). Families faced stiff financial penalties for having additional children. This policy substantially contributed to reducing fertility in China, from about five births per women 30 years ago to fewer than two today (Gu Baochang et al. 2007). However, the cultural effects of the policy have been dramatic.

The most evident effect has been a skewing of births in favor of males, reflecting a historical cultural preference for boys. In 2000, for every 100 girls born, 120 boys were born, and in some poor regions of the country, there were twice as many male births as female births (LaFraniere 2009). This preference for male children also exists in India and other developing countries as well (Kristoff and WuDunn 2009:xiv–xv).

In China, the cultural preference for males appears to be changing somewhat. Among the newly prosperous urban Chinese, girls now are considered as good as or even preferable to boys because girls are believed to be emotionally closer to their parents and more willing than boys to support their elderly parents (Greenhalgh 2005, 2007a). Girls fare less well in poorer rural areas, however, where population control policies are less rigid and second children are more common. This continued strong preference for boys is illustrated by the fact that, in some areas, up to 90 percent of second pregnancies are aborted if the fetus is female.

The extreme sex imbalance resulting from China's policy is creating fundamental changes in society. Wealthy men have no trouble finding mates, but it is much more difficult for the rural poor. Anthropologist Susan Greenhalgh reports that 27 percent of rural men with little schooling were unmarried at age 40. The difficulty of these men finding brides has led to the importation of women from poorer countries such as Vietnam and Myanmar, informal polyandry, the sale of young women, and a trade in kidnapped girls. Because such women are essentially captives in their husband's home, physical and emotional abuse are rife.

China's limits on family size and the emphasis it places on creating "quality children" have produced a generation of single children, the most prosperous and best educated children in the nation's history. However, they also are the subjects of intense family affection and pressure to succeed. Greenhalgh (2007b) describes them as little emperors and empresses, "talented and savvy, but also spoiled and self-centered." She wonders if, when such children grow up, they will be the sort of decisive and culturally sophisticated leaders who are able to make wise decisions on behalf of their nation.

Population control is problematic in other societies as well, where a woman's value is partly measured by the number of children she bears. Religious and political authorities often inveigh against the use of birth control, and intellectuals and governments in many poor nations are deeply suspicious of population control programs coming from wealthy nations, whom they suspect are promoting their own interests by limiting population in other countries (Lichtenberg 1994).

Behind the controversy over population control programs are difficult political and economic issues. Some analysts worry that the world's population is reaching the maximum that the earth can support (its "carrying capacity"), and they argue that population must be controlled or we will face wide-scale starvation. These concerns ignore the fact that the number of people who can be supported by any given environment is critically dependent on the technologies used to support them. Estimates of carrying capacity are inaccurate because technological change is unpredictable. But, more importantly, populations must be considered in relation to their levels of consumption. The average person in an industrialized nation consumes three times as much fresh water and ten times as much energy as someone in a poor nation (Durning 1994). The number of people who can be supported living this lifestyle is far different than the number of people who could be supported if wealthy populations consumed at a lower level. Finally, the number of people who could be supported is critically dependent on assumptions we make about the value of the natural world. If we desire to preserve forestland, tropical rain forest, or other environments, we diminish the amount of land available for human population growth. Thus, the issues central to problems of population growth are primarily cultural, social, political, and moral, not scientific.

The high level of population growth and the low level of wealth and consumption in poor nations are closely related. When life expectancy at birth is low and poverty is rampant, it makes good economic sense for families to have large numbers of children. It increases the labor pool available to the family and improves the odds that some children will survive and perhaps even prosper and increase the family wealth.

As the wealth and consumption level of a population increases, the benefits of large families decline. When health conditions improve, children are more likely to survive. When jobs that pay livable salaries are available, fewer children are necessary to support a family. Increasing wealth and consumption also make raising children far more expensive, which makes large families less desirable. Clearly the best way, indeed perhaps the only way, to control population growth is to improve the life chances and increase the wealth of people in poor countries.

ENVIRONMENTAL CHANGES

Pollution

Ironically, even though the world's poor consume only a small fraction of the earth's resources, they also face some of the world's worst problems of pollution and environmental deterioration. The energy consumption of the United States alone is more than 14 times the energy consumption of the entire African continent (excluding South Africa) (Harrison and Pearce 2000). Because consumption creates pollution, one might expect that people in the United States would live in a far dirtier environment than those in Africa. But this is not the case. In Bamako, the capital city of Mali, most streets are unpaved, meaning that automobiles, trucks, carts, bicycles, and foot traffic stir up dust all day, especially in the dry season. Because most of the city lacks regular trash pickup or sewage, human and animal waste is churned into the air. As most of the city's 1.6 million people cook their evening meal, they use either charcoal or wood fires that consume about one million tons of wood a year (Cissé 2007), and the smoke from cook fires joins the dust in the air. The combined effect of smoke and dust is like a thick, hot, dry fog that easily penetrates the inside of houses, which are relatively open, lacking glass windows or doors. The total effect is an environment far dirtier and more hazardous than in any city of a comparable population in the wealthy world. And Bamako's population suffers as pollution contributes to respiratory ailments, malaria, diseases borne by sewage-contaminated water and air, and high childhood mortality.

A comparison of Bamako with San Antonio, Texas, a similarly sized American city, brings home the differential impact of pollution in our world. In San Antonio, most streets are paved; almost all homes have access to safe, publicly maintained water and sewage systems; meals are cooked on appliances powered by electricity or gas; and much of the huge numbers of cars and trucks are equipped with pollution-controlling devices. Although the population of San Antonio consumes many times the resources of the population of Bamako, its population lives in a far healthier and far less polluted environment than Bamako.

Pollution is closely related to industrialization and globalization. Poor nations desperate to provide some degree of prosperity to their citizens have limited amounts of investment capital and limited means of attracting foreign investment. Less expensive production technologies are generally more polluting than more expensive, higher-technology processes. Therefore, industry in poor nations tends to be dirtier and more polluting than similar industries in wealthy nations. China, for example, has experienced enormous economic growth but, because it has relied extensively on lower-cost, more highly polluting industries, at least 20 percent of the Chinese population lives in severely polluted areas. Ameliorating this problem by installing adequate pollution control in existing Chinese industries would cost $135 billion (Yardley 2006; Bremner 2006). In addition to industrial development, such economic activities as gold mining (Perlez and Johnson 2005; Perlez and Bergman 2005), deforestation, and oil spills also result in water, air, and ground pollution.

Multinational corporations may play an important role in pollution because their financial power allows them to circumvent national laws designed to control pollution. In oil production in the Niger delta in Nigeria, gas flaring (the burning off of the natural gas that is a by-product of oil production) releases toxins into the air as well as more carbon dioxide than the rest of Africa combined. Gas flaring has been illegal in Nigeria since the 1980s, but continues today because strong and wealthy corporations, using techniques like bribery and intimidation, are able to ignore or circumvent regulations enacted by the relatively weak government (Adetunji 2006). Gas flaring, oil spills, and other ecological problems have created an environmental disaster that has been instrumental in fomenting violence and civil unrest in the region.

Global Warming

Global warming is another important aspect of ecological change. Human activity substantially contributes to the warming of the planet (Intergovernmental Panel on Climate Change 2007; Oreskes 2004), though it is unclear what the long-term effects of this warming trend will be. In some places, global warming may even benefit some areas, like northern Europe and Russia, by extending the growing season through increased rainfall and reducing fuel consumption for heating. But global warming's major impacts will be mainly negative and will fall disproportionately on the world's poor, many of whom live in the tropics, where the effects of climate change are expected to be particularly severe. Warming in these climates may cut the growing season and reduce crop yields. The intensity of tropical storms is also expected to increase, which could have devastating effects on areas affected by them. Wealthy nations have the resources to respond to climate change that poor nations lack. Wealthy nations can build levees to control flooding, move their populations and their industries, and open new land to cultivation. Where survival is precarious today, climate change can precipitate disasters (Intergovernmental Panel on Climate Change 2007; see Chapter 5, pp. 101–102).

As we saw in Chapter 5, global warming has negatively impacted many indigenous peoples, such as the Inuit of the Arctic, and some of these groups are fighting back (Cherrington 2008). In March 2007, over 60 Inuit hunters filed a petition with the Inter-American Commission on Human Rights, charging that the United States was violating their human rights under the American Declaration of the Rights and Duties of Man and the American Convention on Human Rights. The petition alleges that the United States, as the largest global emitter of greenhouse gases and the sole nation not to sign the Kyoto Protocol, was largely responsible for global warming that violated the Inuit's rights to life, property, health, and inviolability of the home, culture, and development.

MIGRATION

Widespread political, economic, and social instability combined with relatively inexpensive air travel and economic opportunity has led to a boom in international migration, particularly of people from poor nations. Today, an estimated 200 million people, 3 percent of the world's population, live outside of the countries of their birth (Martin 2007). These migrants significantly affect both the countries they leave and those where they settle.

Out-migrants make their home communities poorer by depriving these areas of their skills and labor, leading to a "brain drain" as high-skilled workers migrate to wealthy countries where they can earn many times their local wages. But although home communities lose members, they may gain many other benefits. Migrants connect their communities of origin to the rest of the world, bringing information, ideas, products, and, perhaps most importantly, money to even the most isolated places. In 2005, migrants sent $232 billion to people in their home countries, of which $162 billion was sent to poor countries. By comparison, total U.S. humanitarian aid in 2005 was about $27 billion, almost 30 percent of which was spent in Iraq and Afghanistan (Organization for Economic Cooperation and Development 2007; World Bank 2006). In some nations, remittances from migrants constitute a substantial percentage of the national economy: 20 percent of the GNI in Honduras, 12.75 percent in the Philippines, and 21.77 percent in Lebanon.

Migrants also profoundly affect the countries where they settle. Some of these effects are cultural—immigrant cultural traditions increase the complexity and enrich the variety of the receiving nations. Immigrants provide a pool of inexpensive labor that creates large profits for businesses and low prices for consumers in wealthy countries. However, the availability of immigrant labor also suppresses wages in their host countries.

Economic immigrants come to new nations for their own profit, but they also face discrimination; they increase their wealth, but often at the price of decreasing their social status (Haines 2007:62). Discrimination resulting in isolation and alienation has led to unrest among immigrant communities in Europe, particularly among African and Muslim immigrants in England and France. This was revealed dramatically in 2005, by rioting in France and terrorist attacks in London (Ireland 2005). Illegal immigrants are in a particularly weak position as their status makes them extremely vulnerable to exploitation.

Immigrants frequently come to their new nations with an "ideology of return" (Brettell 2003, 2007), expecting their immigration will be temporary and hoping to return to their home countries. In the past, belief in return was more common than return itself because maintaining communication with those left behind was difficult, travel was expensive, and because the migrants established social ties in their new country. This is not the case today—global communication is easy and travel relatively inexpensive—but we do not yet know the effect this will have on return migration.

THE MULTIPLE IMPACTS OF GLOBAL TOURISM

Tourism is an important aspect of globalization in the transfer of information, culture, and money. A significant part of tourism involves the travel of people from wealthy countries to underdeveloped places in the non-Western world. International tourism has grown phenomenally in the last 50 years; it is the third-largest item in world trade and accounts for almost 10 percent of all world exports. One-quarter of all consumer spending in the United States is spent on domestic and international travel. Tourism is big business (Harrison 1992).

There are many varieties of tourism—ethnic tourism, ecotourism, exotica tourism, community tourism with homestays, and so on—and anthropology is particularly relevant in understanding the complex impacts of tourism on both tourists and the people they visit, particularly as this involves the role of cultural transformations (MacClancy 2002; Adams 2006). Tourism also has political and economic dimensions and, with the rise of sex tourism and drug tourism, moral dimensions as well (Harrison 1992).

Western tourists to exotic non-Western places are motivated by various desires, particularly a search for the authentic and the natural that anthropologist Colin Turnbull likens to a spiritual pilgrimage (1981). This analogy is particularly apt with the rise of ecotourism, tours of animal life in the wild, and tourism organized around "traditional" culture in formerly isolated places. But as anthropologist Jeremy MacClancy points out (2002:419), authenticity, the natural, and the traditional are just illusions in our modernizing, globalizing world. Many so-called traditional cultures, especially their art and their performances, are in fact constructed just for tourists while the "natural" world of ecotourism and wild animals are in fact not natural, but highly organized, constructed for the tourists' gaze, and sometimes even fenced in.

Although tourism does have an exploitative side, and although some communities resist tourism as "despoiling their cultures" and debasing their arts, in other cases tourism has resulted in the revitalization of traditional culture (Mullin 1995). In Bali, for example, tourist interest in traditional cultural performances provided an economic boost that enabled local troupes to buy new traditional musical instruments and new costumes. It has led to opening of institutes throughout Indonesia for training people in re-creating traditional art forms, supervised by an expert and professional group of Indonesian artists who maintain tight control over performance standards. Similarly, the development of Inuit art and its sale to tourists is an important source of income, especially with the decline of subsistence from traditional hunting.

Although tourists to "exotic" places search for the authentic, ethnographic research shows that ritually and socially significant cultural elements in indigenous societies are transformed as they are marketed to tourists. Art, particularly, because of its availability for international sale, becomes commodified as part of an international world art market (Steiner 1994). Some anthropologists now study this art as part of a global economic process, examining how it is functionally and stylistically reconceptualized to meet a global demand and how this "traffic in culture" affects the cultural identities of the people who create it (Marcus and Myers 1995, 2006; Price 1989; Steiner 1994; Venbrux et al. 2006).

Anthropologist Kathleen Adams explores the connection between the arts, tourism, cultural identity, and globalization among the Toraja, subsistence cultivators in South Sulawesi, Indonesia (Adams 2006). Two spiritually important artistic productions among the Toraja are tongkonan,

Many traditional arts have been given new life by the tourist industry. Here an artist in Bali paints traditional designs on a cloth hanging designed for sale to tourists.

© Joan Gregg

or ancestral houses, and the tau-tau, which are wooden effigies of nobles carved in connection with mortuary ritual.

Although the Toraja today are predominantly Christian, their traditional art and elaborate rituals connected with the tongkonan and the tau-tau are still a major component of contemporary Toraja cultural identity. Tourism has been essential in the maintenance of these traditional aspects of Toraja culture.

By the late 1960s, the expansion of organized tourism to the Toraja area, with a focus on viewing Toraja mortuary rituals of animal sacrifice, the spectacularly carved tongkonan, and the eerie tau-tau, was an important part of Indonesia's tourist development program, aimed at increasing the flow of Western capital (Volkman 1984:162).

Tourist interest in the tongkonan, which have upward-curving eaves resembling a boat and spectacularly carved side panels, led to the Indonesian government banning their alteration. The question was even raised whether the Toraja should be permitted to inhabit the tongkonan, lest they damage these "tourist objects" (Adams 1990:33). Reflecting the worldwide tourist demand for "portable art," the Toraja soon began carving miniature ancestral houses and selling them in souvenir shops.

The tau-tau also changed under the tourist gaze and the global art market. Traditionally, tau taus, commissioned by the family, represent the spirit of a dead person; they are the vessel of the Torajan soul (Adams 1993). When the mortuary rites are completed, the tau-tau is placed with its relatives on platforms chiseled into limestone cliffs, where it becomes a visual link between the community of the living and the community of the dead.

Today, tau-tau may incorporate Western cultural elements, such as digital watches, eyeglasses, Western clothing, Bibles, and crosses (Adams 2006). And although traditionally tau-taus were carved only for the wealthiest nobility and were therefore a symbol of aristocratic status among the Toraja, for tourists the tau-tau are symbolic of a generalized Torajan identity. Miniature tau-taus are sold in tourist markets, along with large carvings of the burial cliffs. Thus, tourism began a process by which ritually significant objects have been transformed into art objects of economic significance.

As traditional tau-taus were transformed into artistic commodities in a global art market, hundreds of them were stolen and sold to American, European, and Asian art collectors. Redesignated by Western curators and collectors as archaic Indonesian art, some effigies have also found a home in Western museums. Unlike other artistic forms such as music or dance, which if imitated or stolen can be reenacted, the tau-tau is irreplaceable. The theft of a tau-tau is tantamount to the abduction of an ancestor, and the loss must be redressed by ritual propitiation. However, legal, political, and economic obstacles stand in the way of repatriation, and tau-taus today are openly sold for thousands of dollars in international galleries. The Toraja realize that, without the tau-taus, tourism will decline, depriving them of an important source of income and prestige. The Indonesian government, more to maintain tourist interest than to address Torajan concerns, has replaced stolen tau-taus with newly made ones, but the Torajans reject these as being not only clumsily made but without spiritual significance because they were not made under ritual conditions.

Paradox and pathos thus attend the tau-tau today. Their meaning has changed from ritual to art object, and whereas the tau-tau once served as a protection for the family of the deceased, today the family of the deceased must protect the tau-tau (Adams 1993).

▎ Electronic Communication Technologies

Electronic communication technologies both affect and are affected by globalization. At the same time that they help erode national economic and cultural frontiers, they also promote local culture; they enable easy, fast communication throughout the world and also within local and national communities. Communication technologies affect our social and cultural lives through social networking, dating and arranging marriages, charitable giving, entertainment, and political activism, and by easily and quickly providing information on every conceivable subject, including anthropology (see Price 2010; Wali 2010), to people all over the world. They offer new kinds of social interactions and also extend traditional cultural patterns.

The effects of the various information technologies must be understood in their specific cultural and economic contexts (Barber 2006) and, as with all previous technologies, raise important political, ethical, economic, legal, and cultural issues (Kakutani 2010). The ease with which information can be appropriated and recycled, without adequate acknowledgment of sources, raises questions of intellectual copyright. Some critics claim that the web has created a "digital forest of mediocrity," substituting ill-informed speculation for genuine expertise (Keen 2007); others emphasize that these technologies promote the cultural ascendancy of belief over facts (Manjoo 2008). Still other critics fear that increased Internet use is impairing our ability to think deeply and creatively (Carr 2010). The hugely expanding use of social networks such as Facebook, combined with the growing use of advertising links, also raises important questions about privacy (Petersen 2010).

One of the most important—and unanswered—questions raised by the new technologies is whether they will undermine or reinforce democracy and human rights (Barber 2006; Sunstein 2006). On the one hand, the global reach of information technology may enhance local democracy. In Iran, popular political protests subsequent to elections, which many Iranians believed were fraudulent, were substantially mobilized by using social networking sites and cell phones that enabled these protests to be seen and supported by millions of people around the world. In China, the use of the Internet by dissenters to challenge the authoritarian government led to government attempts to censor Google, a primary search engine used in China (Helft and Wines 2010). In Indonesia, Facebook, Twitter, and local social networking media have also been used for organizing grassroots protests against government actions, which may result in government restrictions (Onishi 2010). Within the United States, cyber communities—email, websites, and especially social networking sites—played an essential role in mobilizing support, both fundraising and activism, in the campaign of President Obama (Petersen 2010), as well as, for example, the rise of the tea party movement. More recently, people in North Korea, one of the world's most closed nations, have been using cell phones to distribute information about their lives to South Korea and its Western allies (Sang-Hun 2010).

Although democracy may be fostered by grassroots organizations, effective democracy also requires thought, patience, and deliberation. But the Internet, some observers note, invites instant responses, which often means the venting of unfiltered prejudice, misinformation, and ill-conceived opinions. Indeed, the tendency of digital media to present information in reductive simplicity—as surveys often ask for yes/no answers—and without any mediation to ascertain its truth, may actually inhibit the meaningful exchange of ideas and thoughtful debate on which democracy depends. One result of the new technologies, with its emphasis on niche websites, is to divide and isolate individuals from others with different points of view. The virtual communities created by the Internet, although they have national and international reach, are often special-interest groups comprised of people who share common hobbies, identities, or political views. Some of these communities, like neo-Nazis, extremist Christian hate groups, and Islamic jihadist groups, also use the Internet to spread messages of fear and terror. It may well be that the intensified communication among people who already think alike contributes to the political extremism and polarization characteristic of contemporary American politics.

The speed with which the new technologies can send pictures around the globe also has a huge impact on global politics. A cell phone photograph of a young Iranian woman killed by the police for participating in the recent protests against a manipulated election outcome reached millions of people around the world and brought what might have been a contained national political issue to international attention. As with other aspects of globalization, anthropological perspectives on history, culture, politics, and economy are vital in understanding the connections between the global and the local in analyzing the complex effects of new electronic technologies.

In the following chapter, we focus on some of the ways that anthropology both contributes to our understandings of global and local issues, as well as the ways in which anthropology helps provide solutions to human problems in a local and a global context.

BRINGING IT BACK HOME:
HOW FLAT IS YOUR WORLD?

In 2005, Thomas Friedman published the best-selling book *The World Is Flat*. In it, he argues that free trade and recent technological innovations have enormously increased productivity and efficiency. The Internet, the fall of the Berlin Wall, outsourcing, the development of collaborative software, and other innovations have enabled individuals and corporations to compete and connect with one another across vast distances. Friedman claims that the result is a world that is "flat" in the sense that economic and social opportunities are increasingly available to all people, regardless of their geographical location. Friedman cites numerous examples to show how companies and individuals in India, China, and elsewhere use technology to engage effectively with the world and to build prosperity. He

Globalization and Change   **327**

interviews Bill Gates, who says that 30 years ago, the life chances of an average American were better than those of a genius born in India or China. But today, it would be better to be a genius in India or China than an average American. Friedman does see problems, including persistent poverty in some places, AIDS, and the use of technology by terrorist organizations. However, he is an optimist, perhaps even a utopian. He believes that pursuing the correct kinds of training and making the right decisions will bring us a world of peace, prosperity, and opportunity, a world in which culture is enriched and preserved as technology allows each person his or her own voice and vehicle of expression.

John Gray is a critic of Friedman. Gray (2005) notes that Friedman ignores or minimizes numerous problems in globalization. For example, Friedman contrasts the road leading to a company in India, "pockmarked" and filled with jostling "sacred cows, horse-drawn carts and motorized rickshaws," and the sedate and luxurious corporate campus. However, he does not consider the relationship between the two. The same forces of technology and globalization that open possibilities for companies and elites may foreclose them for the poor, denying them jobs, affordable food, housing, and education. Friedman believes that complex trade and communication links between nations create peace and stability, but Gray points out that these have historically created friction and warfare as well. Nationalism fueled the growth of capitalism in Europe and the United States and is doing the same in China and India. Countries promote globalization in the hopes of prosperity but also in pursuit of international power. Finally, Friedman sees a connection between globalization, the free market, and Western-style democracy. But Gray notes that the forces of globalization and technology operate effectively in both democratic nations and nondemocratic countries such as China. Gray (2005) says that globalization does make the world smaller and may make some parts of it richer, but it does not necessarily make it more peaceful, more democratic, or flat.

▗▄▄ YOU DECIDE

1. Is Bill Gates right that today it is better to be a genius in China or India than an average person in America? Do you think your opportunities would be greater if you were born in India or China? Do you think you will one day live in countries such as India and China?

2. Friedman hopes for a world in which culture is enriched because every individual has the ability to be creative and to reach other people through web technologies. Is his definition of culture the same as one you would find in anthropology? Does creating websites enrich culture?

3. Given Friedman's and Gray's positions, do you believe that global culture will be more or less homogeneous 100 years from now? What aspects of culture do you think will be homogeneous? What do you think will remain of distinctive cultural traditions?

▮▮ CHAPTER SUMMARY

1. We live in a world of extreme inequality. Although all nations suffer problems of inequality and poverty, these problems are particularly acute in poor nations and have a profound effect on many of the people that anthropologists have historically studied.

2. After World War II, development became a critical issue for former colonies and other poor nations. Economists believed that many nations were poor because they had undeveloped economies. Earlier development efforts focused on modernizing economies. More recent efforts have focused on enforcing free markets in the hope that these will create more efficient delivery of services.

3. Multinational corporations have become extremely important in poor nations. MNCs search for the most profitable places to buy, sell, and manufacture goods. Shareholders, located primarily in wealthy nations, are the primary beneficiaries of MNC activities. MNCs provide jobs but also exercise enormous influence that frequently allows them to avoid regulation.

4. More than half of the world's largest cities are located in poor nations, and urbanization has been a major force in changing traditional cultures. Providing services to poor people in large cities is beyond the financial capacity of many nations.

5. Although prosperity and population increase historically often go together, in poor nations, even high rates of economic growth have failed to keep up with rising population, and, in some cases, subsistence strategies have collapsed. The appropriate level of human population for any area is a political question involving critical assumptions about distribution of resources and the types of environment people consider desirable.

6. Even though the poor produce only a small percentage of the world's pollution, environments in poor nations frequently are more polluted than those in rich nations. Global warming is anticipated to have more dire effects in poor countries because many of these are located in ecologically fragile zones that have limited financial resources to cope with environmental change.

7. Very high levels of migration have created enormous flows of information and money between nations. Migrants change both

the societies they leave and those in which they settle, frequently enriching both. Migrants often face discrimination, alienation, and isolation.

8. Tourism and communication technology are playing ever more important roles in our increasingly globalized world. In each case, these channels of globalization must be examined in their specific cultural and political contexts and analyzed according to both their positive and negative impacts on the people involved.

■■■ KEY TERMS

Gross national income (GNI)
Modernization theory
Multinational corporation
  (MNC)

Neoliberalism
Structural adjustment
Sweatshop

Cultural Survival poster: Cultural Survival is an organization of anthropologists that helps indigenous peoples adapt to the modern world. It raises money to support its efforts through the sale of posters, such as this one, representing indigenous peoples throughout the world.

CHAPTER 14

ANTHROPOLOGY MAKES A DIFFERENCE

CHAPTER OUTLINE

THE CHAGOSSIANS AND DIEGO GARCIA

"WHAT happened to you? What happened to you?" Rita's children cried as they came running to her side. "Were you attacked?" her husband asked.

"I heard everything they said," Rita recounted, "but my voice couldn't open my mouth to say what happened. . . . We will never again return to our home! Our home has been closed." Rita relayed this story, which happened 40 years ago, to anthropologist David Vine. In his ethnography, *Island of Shame*, Vine has documented the history of the Chagossians and advocates for their right to return to their home, Diego Garcia, an island in the Chagos archipelago in the Indian Ocean. The name of Diego Garcia may ring a bell, because through the previously secret manipulations of the British and the American governments, this small island became a military base for the United States during the Cold War. It continues its military role today both as a storehouse for military weaponry and a takeoff point for United States military aircraft in its bombing in the Gulf War and the invasions of Iraq and Afghanistan. Diego Garcia is off-limits to the media, the Red Cross, and international observers. Occasionally stories about it appear in both the British and American press, and questions have been raised about its status in both the British Parliament and the American Congress.

But although you may have heard about Diego Garcia, it is almost certain that you never heard of the Chagossians, the displaced population that is the subject of David Vine's ethnography. His work is based on extensive archival research of British and American documents and fieldwork among the approximately 1,500 Chagossians evicted from the island when it was reconstituted into an American military base. Vine also "studied up," interviewing many of the military and congressional representatives who were instrumental in the island's transformation.

Vine frames the narrative of the Chagossians as a displaced people, subject to compensation under United Nations laws protecting the rights of indigenous cultures. Chagos was uninhabited until the late 18th century, when French Mauritians created coconut plantations on the islands and began importing enslaved and, later, indentured laborers from Madagascar, Mozambique, and India. Nearly all these Ilois, as the inhabitants are called, worked producing copra and coconut oil, creating a distinct culture and society. They speak a Chagos Kreol language, and their religion includes elements of Roman Catholicism and spiritual practices and beliefs from Africa and India. Until the 1960s, when it was connected by shortwave radio to Sri Lanka and the Seychelles, Diego Garcia was almost completely isolated from the rest of the world, only connected to Mauritius by boat service that ran four times a year. The people built their own houses, lived on land passed down through the generations, and subsisted on vegetables from their gardens, fish they caught themselves, and chickens and ducks. Not a luxurious life, but the island economy provided security, with universal employment and social benefits including free housing, education, pensions, and basic health care, as well as small salaries, provided by the plantation owners and the Mauritian government. Rita tells David Vine, ". . . it was a sweet life." Later the government provided schools, refuse removal, and small dirt roads, and some modern technology like motorbikes, trucks, and tractors began to appear.

But in 1965, the American and British governments decided to take complete military and political control of the islands. The British purchased the privately owned islands and plans were put into play to evacuate the Chagossians. Chagossians who were off the island were told they would not be allowed to return; public services, such as hospitals, began winding down their functions; mail service was suspended and hundreds of Chagossians found themselves stranded in Mauritius. "Life turned completely upside down," one Chagossian told Vine, "[we were] in the fire with our feet burning." By 1966, the final decision was made to remove the Chagossians from their islands. Admiral Elmo Zumwalt of the U.S. Navy signed the order: "Copra workers on Diego Garcia absolutely must go." Most Chagossians were sent to Mauritius where they were promised compensation in the form of land, housing, employment, and money. They also received some millions of (British) pounds in compensation, though not all they claimed entitlement to, and today they generally live in deep poverty.

Soon after exile, the Chagossians formed the Chagos Refugees Group, which is waging an ongoing struggle both to receive just compensation and to return to their island. They seek, in fact, to work for the U.S. military, not to remove it. By 1997, the group had brought lawsuits against the British government and planned one against the United States. They continue to fight for repatriation and more reparations, and anthropologist David Vine is helping them in this struggle.

Vine, in collaboration with several lawyers, documented the Chagossians' status as indigenous peoples, documented how they have been harmed as a result of their displacement, and helped calculate the compensation they were due as a result of these damages.

Vine's ethnography of Chagossian exiles, as well as his exposure of the military and political culture that secretly accomplished the militarizing of Diego Garcia, demonstrates the many ways that anthropology can make a difference. His ethnography is one of the many examples of anthropologists working with displaced populations, both to increase our understanding of the expansion of empire and to learn the ways that the rights of powerless populations can be restored.

░SOME CONTRIBUTIONS OF ANTHROPOLOGY IN THE CONTEMPORARY WORLD

David Vine's engagement with the Chagossians is just one example of the many different ways that anthropology engages on behalf of the many diverse populations whose human rights are abrogated. Anthropologist Walter Williams (2009), for example, advocates for gay men who are threatened by governments that take strong positions against homosexuality. Through his scholarship as an ethnographer of transgender roles among Native Americans (see Chapter 8, p. 181), Williams has become a widely known expert witness on behalf of gay defendants from China, Malaysia, and other nations who seek asylum in the United States because of persecution for their sexual orientation in their countries of origin. Williams was also instrumental in persuading the Chinese Psychiatric Association to drop homosexuality from its list of mental illnesses, as happened in the United States.

Engaged anthropologists like Walter Williams, David Vine, and the others described in this chapter and in our text (cross-list homeless, genital mutilation, industrial agriculture) demonstrate how anthropology makes a difference in the lives of individuals and communities throughout the world. But the contribution of anthropology goes beyond the commitment to advocacy on the part of many anthropologists. Anthropology emphasizes understanding the meaning and experience of people in different cultures. It teaches us about the dynamic elements of social organization and its interrelationships at both a local and global level. Anthropology's holistic, comparative approach and its emphasis on the importance of local cultures contribute to analysis of human events and solutions to human problems. Anthropology can help governments create and implement policies that are sensitive to local cultural traditions and respond to people's needs and aspirations (see Paiement 2007). And perhaps, above and beyond solving any particular problem, anthropology plays a significant role in bringing to life the ordinary, culturally shaped experiences of people's lives and ensuring that the stories of ordinary people are told and heard, and not forgotten.

In the media, for example, rhetoric about national harmony and stability on the part of political leaders often attempts to project an image of a nation that will attract tourists and foreign investment. But linguist Niko Besnier (2009) illustrates in his study of gossip on the Pacific atoll of Nukulaelae, especially malicious gossip on the character of national leaders, that these informal conversations often provide a contrasting view of local politics. Besnier's focus on anthropology "from the bottom up," through participant/observation in informal social networks, adds an important dimension to the understanding of politics in Nukulaelae and illustrates much of what is unique about anthropology as a perspective and a research methodology.

The ethnographic, comparative, and holistic dimensions of anthropololgy contribute to both the analysis of and solutions to issues in our contemporary world. As we see in this chapter, these issues range widely and involve anthropological research, engagement, and advocacy. Because of its interest in the *interaction* of culture and biology, for example, anthropological science educates people about race, as well as the many ways that racism and other forms of social stratification remain important in Western politics, foreign policy, economic development, globalization, and the defining and solving of social problems.

As anthropologists have long emphasized, understanding the relationship between biology and culture in the human species is key to understanding, and therefore changing, human behavior. The human capacity for culture rests on biological foundations embedded in our brains and bodies. But although our biology may predispose us to behave in certain ways, no aspect of human culture can be firmly tied to a gene. Anthropologists have repeatedly shown that biology is not destiny and that culture is not static but is enormously flexible, changeable, and incredibly varied. This implies that many of the problems humans face—war, poverty, pollution, so-called natural disasters, violence—and other contemporary ills are social facts, aspects of human culture and human society, not part of any inviolable human nature, and thus can be changed. Anthropology can help humans continue to invent new cultural forms and new designs for living. Thus, E. B. Tylor, often considered the founder of British anthropology, called anthropology a "reformer's science." Early- and mid-20th-century American anthropologists like Franz Boas, Edward Sapir, Ruth Benedict, and Margaret Mead also emphasized the potential public impact of anthropology and how it could address contemporary problems, and help make the world a better place.

Anthropology is once again moving in this direction. Today, an anthropological emphasis on writing for the general public, applying our knowledge to the solution of specific social problems, and engaging politically and socially with the people we study is expanding (Checker 2009; Brondo 2010). As we noted in Chapters 1 and 3, this emphasis on **public anthropology** reflects a rethinking—and some profound disagreements—on what the purpose of anthropology is and whether anthropologists have a responsibility to be active members of the larger public and intervene in the wide range of issues—domestic and foreign—that impact people's lives. As medical anthropologist Richard Nesbett (2006) has said, "anthropology is—at its core—a subversive discipline challenging the status quo and 'conventional wisdom.' The anthropologist is both witness

public anthropology Anthropology that aims to communicate with nonanthropological audiences and to have an impact on critical issues of wide social significance.

and activist, and at the same time [the discipline] incorporates objective science." In this chapter, we suggest just some of the many ways that anthropologists—through their research, writing for the general public, and active intervention in public policy making—are contributing to, and helping to change, the contemporary world.

RACE AND RACISM

Contemporary science demonstrates that human beings are more genetically alike than they are different and that no one gene, or any set of genes, supports the idea of race. With its emphasis on the role of culture in explaining human behavior and societies, anthropology makes an essential contribution to the understanding of both race and racism. The idea that "racism is not about how you look, it is about how people assign meaning to how you look" underlies the "RACE: Are We So Different Project," an exhibit the American Anthropological Association developed, aimed at educating the public about the reality—and the unreality—of race. Initiated by anthropologists Yolanda Moses and Carol Mukhopadhyay, the **RACE Project** is organized as a traveling museum exhibit, website, and program of educational materials. Its aim is to convey a comprehensive and understandable narrative about race and human variation. The three main messages of the exhibit and its associated materials are that race is a recent human invention, that understandings about race are rooted in culture, not biology, and that, despite the election of America's first African American president, racism continues to be embedded in American culture, social institutions, and everyday life (Overbey 2007).

RACE Project A traveling museum exhibition and website emphasizing race as a cultural construction and the ways in which race is assigned meanings in American culture.

The RACE Project uses the lens of history, science, and lived experience to explore the everyday experience of race; the contemporary science that is challenging commonly held ideas about race; and the history of the idea of race in the United States. Through videos, oral histories, visuals, and provocative interactive computer exercises, the RACE Project exhibit demonstrates that race is embedded in almost all areas of American life: home and neighborhood, health and medicine, and education and schools. Concepts of race and racism are not just inside our heads but are built into American laws, culture, and social institutions.

The exhibit also emphasizes that the racial and ethnic categories made by humans change over time. Race—the sorting of people by physical differences—is a recent invention, just a few hundred years old. In the United States, it is closely linked to the growth of the plantation economy, in which Africans were imported to work as slaves. Other cultural notions of race are also linked to specific political and economic histories. Notions of race and racial and cultural inferiority were built on culturally constructed ideas about primitive and civilized societies, and were often used as justifications for the expansion of empire by both Europeans and Americans. The RACE Project, which involved collaboration with many scientific institutions and scholars, is aimed at discovering what people think about race and how they talk about it. The interactive website (www.understandingRACE.org) includes a virtual tour of the exhibit with many features, including one that helps parents talk to children about race. With its four-field holistic approach, anthropology was a natural to tackle this long-standing issue in American life.

▌▌HUMAN REMAINS

Just as the RACE Project combines an analysis of human biological features in connection with the stories about race that are part of cultural constructions, so, too, the analysis of human remains, by archaeologists and forensic anthropologists, makes important contributions to understanding culture in specific contexts. Archaeology, particularly, has contributed much to our understanding of African Americans, both slave and free, in the New World (Bawaya 2010).

In 1991, while excavating a site for a new federal office building in lower Manhattan, construction workers discovered more than 100 human skeletons. The site turned out to be an 18th-century burial ground for African Americans, which had perhaps contained as many as 20,000 burials when it was closed in 1790; ultimately, 419 bodies were discovered at the site. Archaeological, cultural, biological, and historical anthropologists were called in to dig, preserve, and interpret the finds of this sensational discovery. A team led by Michael Blakely, a biological anthropologist at Howard University, translated the physical information—such as the calluses on their hands, their size, and their dental profiles—and chemical information stored in the bones into knowledge about the lives and deaths of this population. In addition to the skeletons, the 1.5 million artifacts discovered in the site point revealed knowledge about African American culture, including understanding African customs brought to the Americas as well as cultural adaptations Africans made in their new homes.

After seven years, during which Blakely's anthropological team worked on the bones, the remains were ceremonially interred in 2003. Today, the site has become the **African Burial Ground National Monument**, whose Visitor Center, tableaus, and documentary exhibits tell us something of the lives of New York's African community over a period of 200 years (Rothstein 2010). The African Burial Ground is one of the sites urban archaeologists Diana Wall and Anne-Marie Cantwell (2004)

African Burial Ground National Monument: a site in lower Manhattan in New York City where the skeletal remains and artifacts of an African American community were discovered and analyzed by anthropologists, leading to greater understanding of the role of both free and enslaved blacks in the l8th and l9th centuries.

feature in *Touring Gotham's Archaeological Past*, their guidebook to the lives and cultures of those buried beneath the surface of New York City. As Wall and Cantwell point out, prior to the discovery of the burial ground, most of what was known about enslaved people of African descent came from documents told from the perspective of the city's dominant white community. They point out that one of the many important things that the burial ground reminds us of is that although Northerners tend to associate slavery with the plantation economy of the South, there was slavery in the North as well, beginning as early as 1626, just a year after the founding of New York City, then called New Amsterdam. In their guidebook, which examines archaeological sites of Native Americans and other European settlers in New York, Wall and Cantwell contribute not only to our understanding of the history of the city and nation, but also to public anthropology by publishing in a form that makes these historical cultures widely accessible to the public beyond academe.

forensic anthropology The application of physical anthropology to identifying skeletal or badly decomposed human remains to assist in the detection of crime and the prosecution of those responsible.

Forensic anthropology is a discipline that also analyzes human remains, most often in solving crimes, but also in settling humanitarian issues, especially in discovering the identities of victims of political violence. Members of the Guatemalan Forensic Anthropology Foundation are exhuming mass graves to identify victims and examine bones to chronicle the nation's bloody 36-year civil war, during which more than 40,000 individuals disappeared. Most were the victims of government death squads who, in the late 1970s and early 1980s, kidnapped and murdered many whom they believed to be their political opponents. With the evidence anthropologists provided, Guatemalans are beginning to confront their brutal past, though the process of healing these wounds will take lots of time (Moore 1998).

Forensic anthropologists also played a key role in identifying the victims of the September 11, 2001, terrorist attack on the World Trade Center. The project of identifying these remains plays an important role in the context of American cultural views surrounding death, where the return of the body, or body parts, is central to Americans' ideas about closure. Thus, in many ways, archaeologists and forensic anthropologists, in making death come alive, make contributions to a broader understanding of contemporary cultural and political issues.

Courtesy of Chandler Prude, Texas State University

Forensic anthropologists Michelle Hamilton and Kate Spradley. Dr. Spradley collects data on U.S.–Mexico border-crossing fatalities to correctly identify remains of individuals considered Hispanic.

MUSEUM REPRESENTATIONS OF INDIGENOUS PEOPLES

As ethnographic, forensic, and archaeological studies allow local populations to articulate their own histories, anthropologists working with museums contribute to broadening the public's understanding of diverse human cultures. Early anthropological studies focused on small-scale, non-industrial, non-Western societies with cultures very different from the industrial societies of Europe and the United States. Such societies were often regarded in popular culture as "primitive" in contrast to our own "civilizations," implying inferiority and a lesser humanity. Anthropology's emphasis on "cultural relativity" and its long-term fieldwork were particularly important in changing the West's view of "the other," helping Americans and Europeans to see other peoples as equals within the human family.

Before the huge expansion of tourism, two major points of contact between Western and indigenous peoples were art museums and natural history museums. Art historians and art critics, the traditional gatekeepers of Western concepts of art, claim that great art has universal intrinsic artistic qualities. In contrast, anthropologists emphasize that art must be understood in a cultural context, in terms of how and why it is produced and the meanings it has for its makers and its audiences.

In the early 20th century, Western art underwent a modernist revolution. Pablo Picasso and other European artists began to incorporate features of African and Oceanic art into their own artistic creations. These artists and the art historians of the time had almost no interest in understanding the meanings of this art, then called "primitive art," in its original cultural context. For anthropologists, however, a cultural perspective on this art was essential. Anthropologists tried to understand what the arts, like other cultural institutions, contributed to the functioning of society. Anthropologists were particularly interested in the social or symbolic worlds in which indigenous art was originally seen or used, such as religious ritual or social relationships.

Although it took almost a half century for the anthropological approach to be widely adopted, it has made a real difference in enriching Western understandings of indigenous art and, by extension, indigenous peoples. The anthropological perspective is now incorporated into many contemporary indigenous art exhibits in ethnographic, art, and natural history museums (Cotter 2009; Nanda 2004). Ways in which the anthropological perspective is incorporated include narratives framing the exhibition of indigenous art; the labeling of objects to emphasize ethnographic context; and the collaboration of indigenous peoples in curating exhibits of their arts.

Native Americans, for example, have long contested museum exhibits of their material culture. They claim that such exhibits misleadingly represent their societies as timeless rather than dynamic; exclude Native American voices, consultation, or collaboration; neglect contemporary Native American artists; display sacred objects that should not be seen by the non-Native public; and ignore any representation of contemporary political issues involving Native Americans. As a result of anthropologists stepping in, this has changed significantly. Native American cultural revitalization, remembrance, and political struggle are now prominent in exhibitions of Native American art.

As these anthropological perspectives gained influence, many art and ethnographic museums now consider how both culture and power are implicated in displays of indigenous art (Hochschild 2005), and how these may represent the people who produced the art. The Smithsonian Institution's new National Museum of the American Indian in Washington D.C. was significantly shaped by anthropological understandings. Indeed, museum exhibits themselves have now become the subject of ethnographic inquiry (Price 2007) for what they tell us about the indigenous arts they exhibit, the culture of the people who arrange the exhibits, and the culturally influenced responses of the people who view the exhibits.

ENVIRONMENTAL POLLUTION

Although we think of the environment as "natural," it is a cultural construction. Understandings of the environment, and particularly environmental pollution, are different in different cultures. Environmental impact on human populations is intimately connected to power differences on both a local and global level, as we see in the causes of global warming in the Arctic; the establishment of factory farms in the American Midwest; the dislocation of local peoples in Kenya through the creation of national game parks (Igoe 2004); and illness resulting from environmental pollution, discussed further.

Anthropologist Melissa Checker (2005), in her ethnography of Hyde Park, a small African American community just outside Augusta, Georgia, documents both the role of racism in environmental pollution and the ways in which racial stratification shapes community response. The residents of Hyde Park, mainly sharecroppers from rural Georgia, used their savings to buy plots of land in a swampy area on the outskirts of Augusta, Georgia, after World War II. Around 1970, they began noticing environmental and health problems besetting the community: T cell lymphoma, children fainting in school, children with asthma, and fruit trees and vegetables rotting in previously healthy gardens. The community's growing awareness that local people were getting sick and dying at an alarming rate paralleled the growth of industrial plants in the area. A power plant, a ceramics factory, a junkyard, a wood treatment plant, and over 35 chemical plants were all built near black neighborhoods, including Hyde Park, under low environmental standards and ineffective enforcement of environmental laws. Residents experienced various toxic hazards. "[The] ceramic factory left white dust on cars; its smokestack penetrated the skyline; pyramids of tires from the junkyards were higher than the houses; odiferous water filled the ditches in heavy rains; and the chemical companies contaminated the air, water, and soil" (p. 64). By 1990, the community noticed residents falling ill with mysterious or uncommon forms of cancer and skin diseases, which they speculated resulted from the operation of a nearby wood-preserving factory.

The factory had been sued by a nearby white community, but because the black community was not informed about either the findings of contamination or the lawsuit, they did not participate in the lawsuit and were thus were not eligible for compensation. As Hyde Park now became identified with decline and destruction, many residents ceased investing in their homes. The neighborhood became rundown, leading to a vicious downward cycle of pollution, disease, and declining property values. For Hyde Park community residents, this was yet another example of how they suffered from racial discrimination.

Checker's ethnography illustrates that, in a racially stratified society such as the United States, race is particularly potent in predicting where hazardous waste facilities are located. Checker calls the environmentalist movement that grew out of Hyde Park's attempts to deal with contamination an environmental justice movement. It aims to redress the disproportionate incidence of environmental contamination in communities of color and communities of the poor and enable them to live unthreatened by the risks posed by environmental degradation and contamination. Ultimately, the movement achieved some successes, both by joining with mainstream environmentalists and by continuing its own culturally unique processes of political and civil rights activism. In her engaged and engaging ethnographic study of one small community, Checker illustrates the many issues at stake in the fight for **environmental justice**.

environmental justice: A movement to expose and address the problems of environmental pollution among poor, powerless, and minority communities.

DOMESTIC VIOLENCE

Anthropology has documented the many ways in which both group and individual violence grows out of particular cultural, political, and economic contexts, undermining the view that violence is the inevitable result of some biologically based human instinct for aggression. With this perspective, anthropology contributes to our understanding of the widespread practice of violence against women, whether in the context of warfare or within the home (Eller 2006:115–45), and helps shape effective responses to this worldwide problem.

Domestic violence against women occurs in Western and non-Western societies, among almost all cultures and social classes. In some cases, domestic violence may actually increase with factors associated with modernization, such as urbanization and upward social mobility. In India, for example, dowry, though outlawed, is becoming more important among India's urbanized, increasingly modern and upwardly mobile families. Sometimes, where a groom's family is dissatisfied with a bride's dowry, they may harass her to get her family to give more, or even murder her so that her son can marry again and receive another, larger dowry (Stone and James 2005; Sanghavi, Bhatta, and Das 2009; Nanda and Gregg 2009).

Domestic violence is a major problem in the United States, and though it affects all groups and classes, immigrant, poor women, and women of color are particularly vulnerable (see Sokoloff and Pratt 2005). Many of the immigrant women come from cultures with strong patriarchal values; they also often lack the language, cultural, and economically valuable skills that would provide alternatives to violent treatment within their families or access to social services. In addition, their U.S. visas are often dependent on their husbands, and this may hinder them from taking legal action.

The role of culture in domestic violence is one of great interest to anthropologists, and law enforcement authorities often seek anthropological perspectives on domestic violence (see Snajdr references in following paragraph). It is clear that, both in the United States and in other societies, cultural traditions of patriarchy and male dominance play an essential role in the widespread practices of domestic violence. Culturally based ideas, both explicit and implicit, also play an important role in responses to domestic violence, both by informal groups within local communities and by government institutions of law enforcement and courts.

Through ethnography at the local level, as well as among law enforcement personnel, anthropologists contribute to the understanding of domestic violence and can help address the issue by suggesting culturally relevant solutions. The work of anthropologist Edward Snajdr (2005, 2007) illustrates this dual contribution. At the request of the government of Kazakhstan, Snajdr carried out ethnographic research aimed at understanding domestic violence in this multicultural society that emerged as a result of the dissolution of what was formerly the Soviet Union. Snajdr's goal was to suggest and help implement more effective training for law enforcement officers to address what the Kazakh government was recognizing as a widespread and serious problem among Kazakhstan's multiethnic population which consists of approximately 50 percent Kazakhs, 30 percent Russians, and 20 percent central Asian minorities.

Snajdr's ethnography and interviews with law enforcement personnel demonstrated the important roles of ethnicity, religion, culture, and politics, both in formulating narratives of domestic violence and in implementing effective responses. Kazakh participants themselves highlighted the importance of cultural traditions in explaining domestic violence. For example, in one of Snajdr's earliest encounters, a female colonel from a domestic violence response unit told him, "From early childhood, Kazakh males are the bosses. It is normal for a husband to beat his wife" (2007:607). Male dominance in Kazakh culture is embedded in traditional practices that partly explain the high degree of domestic violence and also the difficulty of an effective state response. Families fear that if a victim of domestic violence flees her husband, she will have to return the bride price, so that women often feel they have no choice but to stay with their husbands. Divorce is also unthinkable for many wives because custody of children most often goes to the husband. Further, the Kazakh tradition of "privacy" and "family sovereignty" prevents neighbors or friends from reporting incidents of domestic violence to law enforcement or even to nongovernmental groups that provide shelter for victims.

Snajdr's ethnography documented the complex context of domestic violence: Western-oriented nongovernmental organizations had been active for a few years in Kazakhstan; these depended on outside funding and brought with them an internationalist women's rights–oriented perspective, which emphasized providing shelters for victims of domestic violence. This strategy had limited success, however: Partly for some of the previously listed reasons, women were very reluctant to make their victimization public and leave their families.

The Kazakh government, though also interested in addressing the problem of domestic violence, had a somewhat different perspective. Although on the one hand, the government saw more effective responses to domestic violence as part of its commitment to modernization, with its "rights-oriented" approach, it was also trying to create a nationalistic state, emphasizing Kazakhstan as having a unique cultural tradition. Although many Kazakhs are Muslim, the state's approach was to emphasize cultural elements, such as language, rather than Islam per se, in its nationalistic approach.

Still another, more locally oriented perspective was initiated by a nongovernmental Muslim women's group. This group emphasized elements of Russian culture, particularly widespread alcoholism, as the most important cause of domestic violence. This women's group is part of an Islamic revivalist movement in Kazakhstan. It uses Qur'anic principles to address the problems of domestic violence, focusing on counseling and mediation interventions. The group also promotes gender roles that are part of traditional Islam, including emphasizing some of the bases of female autonomy in the Qur'an, and puts pressure on women victims of domestic violence to maintain their commitment to their families as part of a valuable contribution of women to society.

These three understandings and approaches to domestic violence in this multicultural society making the transition from communism were not only different but, in some ways, competed with each other. Successfully organizing a conference that brought representatives of these three groups together, Snajdr emphasized that, to reveal a more accurate picture of the occurrence of domestic violence and to more effectively address the problem, both the government and the Western-oriented nongovernmental organizations (NGOs) needed to heighten their awareness of Kazakhstan's cultural diversity and be more sensitive to local culturally based responses. As we see in the Bringing It Back Home feature, competing values in varying responses to domestic violence is the subject of debate both in the larger society and within the anthropological community.

▌▌MEDICAL ANTHROPOLOGY

Despite the many important advances in preventing disease and improving health care that have been made over the past several hundred years, the Western medical model has serious limitations in dealing with health issues in different cultures and among different ethnic, racial, and class populations in the United States (Helman 1998/1991). **Medical anthropology** draws upon social, cultural, biological, and linguistic anthropology to better understand those factors that influence health and well-being. It is concerned with the experience of disease, disability, and related concepts such as aging, as well as the distribution, prevention, and treatment of various health-related processes (Anthropology News 2009).

medical anthropology A subfield of anthropology that draws upon social, cultural, biological, and linguistic anthropology to better understand those factors that influence health and illness; concerned with the experience, distribution, prevention, and treatment of disease.

Medical anthropologists adapt the holistic and ethnographic approaches of anthropology to the study of health and disease in diverse societies. Although modern biomedicine tends to regard diseases as universal entities, regardless of their contexts, medical anthropologists have found that concepts of disease and medicine are best understood in their particular cultural and historical contexts.

Economics also plays a significant role in explaining comparative incidences of health and the treatment of illness. The degree to which people in different societies have access to basic resources such as food, water, sanitation, and medical care, which is based on economic resources, is a critical determinant of health (Baer, Singer, and Susser 1997). This focus on unequal access to basic life conditions and medical care has resulted in medical anthropology becoming more critical and engaged in advocacy.

Paul Farmer (2003), who is both an anthropologist and a medical doctor, is an active and widely known medical anthropologist (Kidder 2003; SANA 2003). He helped found Partners in Health (PIH), an international health and social justice organization that specializes in the medical treatment of people in some of the poorest communities in the world. PIH began in the Central Plateau of Haiti, where Farmer worked as a student. His Haitian hospital and clinic provide free treatment to people with infectious diseases such as HIV/AIDS and multidrug-resistant tuberculosis. PIH is now a worldwide organization that uses novel, community-based treatment strategies for infectious and curable diseases in places like Haiti, Peru, and Rwanda.

If Paul Farmer (2003) only treated patients in the poorest places on earth, he would still be a hero. In addition to implementing successful health care strategies for the poor, Farmer also writes widely for both the academic community and the public, expressing his view that the globally unequal distribution of suffering and illness, for example, the risks and treatment of infectious diseases, can be explained by the unequal distribution of power. The title of one of Farmer's most recent books, *Pathologies of Power: Health, Human Rights and the New War on the Poor*, clearly articulates Farmer's theory.

Early on in his career, Paul Farmer expressed his view that anthropology is less an academic discipline than a tool for intervention (Nesbett 2006). Now, Farmer writes, lectures, and raises funds to motivate governments to understand the relationship between power; ethnic, gender, and economic inequalities; violence against the poor; and effective medical care.

Like many engaged anthropologists, Farmer's ethnographic perspective locates potentially successful health strategies based on local cultures, but he also suggests how government bureaucracies and wealthy, powerful elites must do more to address the most basic human right: the right to survive (Democracy Now, 2008).

HIV/AIDS

An important aspect of medical anthropology relates to the spread and treatment of HIV/AIDS. Medical anthropologists call attention to the ecological, political, cultural, biological, and economic factors that contribute to its spread, particularly among disadvantaged populations (Feldman 2008; 2009; Himmelgreen and Romero-Daza 2008; Singer 2008). Studies of these factors can help government and nongovernmental agencies formulate more effective interventions.

The most significant forms of behavior implicated in the transmission of HIV/AIDS are heterosexual and same-sex sexual relations (see Feldman 2009). As a result, many preventive interventions target sexual relationships: incorporating abstinence, sexual fidelity, and condom use, alone or in combination. As anthropological research makes clear, however, these intimate relationships are shaped both by culture and by the political economy. For example, there is overwhelming evidence that condom use inhibits the

Medical anthropologist Douglas Feldman doing field research in Zambia. Feldman's project was aimed at HIV/AIDS prevention through a culturally sensitive educational approach aimed at changing normative behavior among Zambian adolescents.

spread of AIDS. But condom use is significantly shaped by cultural values and norms regarding intimate relationships. In the Philippines, for example, exotic dancers who exchange sex for money are willing to use condoms with one-time customers, but not for "regulars" with whom they hope to have long-term relationships (Ratliff 1999).

Gender inequality is another factor centrally implicated in the spread of AIDS. Where women are nearly powerless or economically dependent on men, they are less likely to insist on behavioral changes, such as marital fidelity or condom use, that inhibit the spread of AIDS. In southern Africa, for example, where AIDS infection rates are extremely high, 55 to 60 percent of AIDS victims are women. The Ju/'hoansi people of Namibia are an exception to this statistic. According to anthropologists Richard Lee and Ida Susser (2008), the significantly lower rate of AIDS among Ju/'hoansi women is due to their economic autonomy. Ju/'hoansi women assertively declared that they would have no hesitation in refusing to have sex with a man who would not wear a condom. Lee and Susser note, however, that as a changing economy introduces more outsiders into the formerly somewhat isolated Ju/'hoansi area, AIDS infection, though still low, has increased.

Anthropological ethnography and interventions have also occurred with regard to the use of illegal drugs, especially among intravenous drug users in the United States, among whom needle sharing for intravenous drug use is a significant cause of AIDS infection. Although anthropologists have demonstrated that needle sharing is an important cause of the spread of AIDS and have suggested effective programs of government distribution of clean needles, local political opposition has blocked such efforts (Singer, Irizarry, and Schensul 1991; Heimer et al. 1996). The failure of such reform has resulted in an increase in syringe sharing, a black market in syringes, and the increased spread of AIDS (Broadhead, Van Hulst, and Heckathorn 1999).

EXPLOITED CHILDREN

American and European movie audiences were shocked by the portrayal of childhood in Mumbai in the 2008 film *Slumdog Millionaire*, which seems the very opposite of what childhood should be. For the middle and upper classes in both wealthy and poor countries, childhood is constructed as a time of life distinct and separate from adulthood, in which children should be in school, not working, especially not in activities like manufacturing, begging, or sex work. A universalist conception of childhood is enshrined in the United Nations Convention on the Rights of the Child, which declares that children should "grow up in a family environment, in an atmosphere of happiness, love and understanding . . . protected from economic exploitation and from performing any work that is likely to be hazardous or to interfere with the child's education, or to be harmful to . . . [their] development." These cultural views are not universal, however, and perhaps as many as one billion children worldwide live in conditions similar to those portrayed in *Slumdog Millionaire*, and 100 million of these live on the streets.

Working Children in Brazil

Anthropologist Mary Kenny (2007) studied child workers in Olinda, a town of about 400,000 in northeastern Brazil, which is a tourist destination because of the preservation of some of its 17th-century Portuguese colonial heritage. It is also, however, deeply impoverished, with approximately 60 percent of its population living in *favelas* (shantytowns) or other poor neighborhoods, in two- and three-room homes made of brick, wood, paper, and tin, each housing an average of ten people. Throughout the favela, there are "open cement drains filled with a grey liquid with bubbles on top, emitting a wretched stench that never quits" (Kenny 2007:90).

Most of the work for adult residents of the favela is low paid and difficult to find. Some men are day laborers, while others wash cars or sell peanuts and ice pops; women sometimes work as laundresses, hairdressers, or seamstresses. None of these jobs earns enough money to support even a small family and thus the labor of even very young children becomes essential. Children under the age of 12 sell small items, guard cars, carry goods, wash dishes, beg, and pick up garbage. The conditions in these occupations jeopardize the health of both children and adults through exposure to a wide range of diseases, infections, parasites, and rodents. Horrors abound at the garbage dumps, for example; at least two human bodies are found there each week (Kenny 2007: 105). However, with the labor of children, a family of garbage pickers can earn enough to survive, and children and adults often find food that is still edible in the dumps.

Children under 12 can also make money as beggars. Dalva is a 12-year-old who organizes the four younger children in her family to beg from tourists in the old colonial district of town. Because Dalva's parents produce very little income, her family survives only because of her abilities to beg. She says: "If I don't work, my family will go hungry. . . . I can take it. It's my fate" (p. 108). Although Dalva gives her parents most of the money she and the younger children receive, she does retain some for herself to buy a variety of food and small items during her workday. Although Dalva lives with her mother and her sometimes-present father, Dalva's income-generating abilities effectively make her a household head. While working children do sometimes go to school, school is expensive, as even with free tuition, students require proper clothes and school supplies that most families cannot afford.

Sex Workers in New York

Although we may be more likely to associate the exploitation of children with other countries, child exploitation also exists in the United States. Applied anthropologist Richard Curtis et al. (2008) studies exploited youth in commercial sex markets in New York City. Curtis's research is aimed at providing city agencies with information on the attitudes, orientations, and behaviors of these youth, as well as demographic statistics, that will improve the effectiveness of various social service programs aimed at addressing the needs of these populations. Young sex workers, whose numbers may run into the millions nationwide, are mainly runaways and homeless youth, children who have been sexually or physically and emotionally abused, who have minimal education, who cannot find legitimate employment, and who are thus vulnerable to manipulation and control by profit-seeking adults, whether as customers or as pimps.

Vigorous law enforcement in New York has been successful in decreasing the street-level sex market, but the sex business has adapted by diversifying and expanding its use of cell phones and the Internet to conduct business. Curtis's team used surveys, in addition to traditional ethnography, to carry out their research, as the youth sex market is geographically dispersed throughout the city. The research team was given training in the cultures of several different neighborhoods in New York that had been established as youth sex markets by Curtis's previous in-depth ethnographic research. They also interviewed police and social service providers, and those in other city agencies that are involved in youth activities.

The study resulted in some important and unexpected findings. Young sex workers came from diverse ethnic backgrounds; black youth formed the largest single group, but there were also significant numbers of Hispanics, including Puerto Ricans and Dominicans, as well as almost one-quarter of the population who self-identified as "multiracial." There was also an unexpectedly high proportion of white male "traveler" youth, young men who engage in homosexual relations, move from city to city, who rely on each other for survival, and who have limited contact with sex workers from other ethnic groups. A surprising number of the exploited youth also identified as transgender; these youth also formed their own tightly knit social networks.

About one-third of the youth interviewed were homeless and living on the street, but this was less true for girls than boys, and least true of the transgender respondents. Many of the other youth still lived at home or with friends; again, this was truer of girls than boys. Boys, then, seemed much more solitary and disconnected from others, including family members, than girls. Given the designation of the study as one of exploited youth, an unexpected finding was that the introduction into the sex market was more often a friend or an acquaintance, rather than a stranger. This was especially true for transgendered youth. Most of the youth interviewed indicated that pimps played no role in their sex work; pimps played a more important role for girls entering the sex market than for boys. Although pimps were often violent, some girls commented on their necessity for both commercial advantage and protection. At least one-quarter of the youth entered the sex market by being unexpectedly propositioned on the street by a stranger.

Although economic desperation and the need to survive or economically help their families was an important context for many of these youth to enter the sex market, especially given their lack of education and opportunity for other work, the study also found that the glamorizing of "the life" in the media, such as MTV, was also a factor in attracting almost 10 percent of the study participants. Thus, for many of these youth, adult exploitation did not force them into the "game," but rather a fascination with and curiosity about a lifestyle. Further, although these youthful sex workers spent most of their money on essentials such as food, shelter, and drugs (including cigarettes), items such as upscale clothing, music, movies, and electronics also consumed a significant part of their income.

Most of the youth blamed themselves for their predicaments, but they also gave suggestions about the kind of help they could use in changing their lives. One of their main priorities was finding safe and stable long-term housing. The lack of a job was also frequently cited as an issue motivating youth to enter or stay in the sex market, even though their participation filled some of them with feelings of shame, stigma, degradation, and loneliness. Most of the youth expressed a wish to leave the "life," if given the opportunity, though some did not.

The conditions poor children in Olinda, Brazil, and commercial youth sex workers in New York experience are disturbing in many ways, not least because they challenge our contemporary notions of childhood. In places like Olinda, families can survive only because of the income-generating activities of their children, who in fact have higher earning abilities than adults. The role of youth sex workers in New York, although less essential to many of their families, nevertheless also is significantly related to poverty.

The studies of Olinda and New York raise some similar questions about the role of outside help for such youth. In Olinda's favelas, the efforts of well-intentioned reformers, which are based around middle-class norms, are often ineffective, or worse yet, work against the interests of the children. Reformers promote policies intended to keep families together, but the families of Olinda's poor are often brutally exploitative of children. Reformers promote education, but education is not only expensive, it reduces the time children can spend earning money and thus threatens their families' survival. Further, education is only economically valuable when it provides access to higher-paying jobs, which is not the case in the favelas.

The many failures of social services in New York to some degree echo those of Olinda; indeed, in one case, several youth sex workers noted that their temporary shelter was their entry into the commercial sex market. What Kenny's and Curtis's studies clearly demonstrate is that the exploitation of children and youth is a symptom of poverty. Kenny noted that although child advocates drawn from the middle and wealthy classes promote the elimination of child labor, child laborers themselves advocate for better wages and more secure jobs, demands also made by adults from the same areas "who work in conditions as damaging to health and as exploitative as those faced by their children" (Kenny 2007:216). The desire for secure jobs at decent wages is also central to providing a path out of the "life" for youthful New York City sex workers, though the so-called glamour of the life expressed by some of the New York City youth has no parallel in Olinda. Both studies show that although these young people live in terrible conditions and are exploited, they are also able to use their wits and the resources available to them to maintain their independence and a degree of control over their lives. In Olinda, New York City, and other cities around the world, anthropology makes a difference by describing the complex contexts of poverty, the ways in which they entrap children, and by exposing how well-meaning but often flawed constructions of the problem become obstacles to effective solutions.

ADVOCATING FOR WORKERS

An anthropology of work is today an important component of applied anthropology (see, for example, Chapter 5 of Stull and Broadway 2004). In some cases, such as that of Ann Dunham's work among women in Indonesia and Pakistan (2009; see also p. 198, Chapter 8), anthropologists go beyond ethnographic description and become advocates for the people they study.

Pun Ngai, a Hong Kong anthropologist, combines her ethnographic research with advocating for female factory workers in China. The expansion of global capitalism and the sweatshop working conditions in factories that produce goods for a global market particularly affect women. Pun Ngai spent six months tightening screws in computer hardware at an electronics factory in Shenzhen, People's Republic of China, as part of her ethnographic study of how dagongmei, or "working girls," are responding to the pressure of China's increasing participation in the global economy (Tsui 2000).

The factory directors hoped Dr. Pun's work would teach them what the workers want so they would know better how to deal with them. They expected Pun to work largely through perusing the company's documents on its operation and personnel. They were astounded when she announced that she would work on the line and live with the workers, using anthropological participant observation to understand the factory. Although initially suspicious of Pun, the dagongmei soon made her a confidante, sharing complaints about their work, hopes for the future, and desires for intimate personal relationships.

An important part of the multinational factory workforce, and particularly of the Asian economic "miracle," consists of young women workers. Anthropologists have played important roles in improving the conditions and economic potential of young women, as it has been demonstrated that a key factor in economic development is the education and treatment of women.

Pun soon experienced the actual factory work as a monotonous routine. The dagongmei spend 15 hours a day on the factory floor, sleep in dormitory-type accommodations called cage houses, and suffer many physical ailments from their work, such as menstrual pain and anemia. Those who weld microchips suffer eyesight problems, and those who wash plates with acids are constantly at risk of chemical poisoning. Accommodation and other expenses are deducted from their already low wages. They are also overcharged for medical and other services and consumer goods.

The dagongmei work and live under very strict rules: They have to wait their turn to go to the restroom, they are thoroughly searched before they are allowed to leave the factory premises, and security guards wielding electric batons guard their locked quarters at night. Urban factories recruit dagongmei as cheap labor but when unemployment increases, the first thing people want to do is send the dagongmei back to their rural villages. After years of urban living and participation in a consumer-oriented global lifestyle, dagongmei find it difficult to readapt to village life.

Dagongmei receive little sympathy in China, especially from men who say they are taking away their jobs. In fact, times are getting harder for dagongmei. With China's admission to the World Trade Organization and the opening up of its agricultural market, more people are rushing to the cities. Urban unemployment is high and getting higher, thousands of workers have been downsized as a result of the privatization of factories, and factories themselves are now closing by the thousands as part of the worldwide recession and the steep decline in the global demand for Chinese-made goods.

In spite of all these hardships, dagongmei see advantages in their factory work. It expands their world and permits some escape from the rigid patriarchal structure of the village. Dagongmei enjoy having boyfriends, keeping up with the latest fashions, and searching for the secrets of success, especially in the form of making money and maybe finding a husband (Chang 2008). Some dagongmei, by pooling their earnings, have managed to open small factories. Others have ambitions for a business career, or to improve their education. Urban migration offers the opportunity to take a computer class or learn some English, which can lead to switching jobs and earning more money. Indeed, it may be that dagongmei are at the cutting edge of a changing Chinese culture: moving from traditional commitments and filial loyalty to the cultural values of upward social mobility, individualism, and the pursuit of a more prosperous future. However, Pun cautions, out of 70 million dagongmei, few succeed.

Dr. Pun has followed up her field study with a continuing commitment to improving conditions for dagongmei in China. She represents the interests of dagongmei at labor conferences, fighting for their rights. Multinational corporations' desires for cheap labor will lead to more women working in the global factory. Anthropologists such as Pun Ngai are trying to make sure their rights are protected when they do.

BRINGING IT BACK HOME:
CULTURE, THE CULTURAL DEFENSE, AND DOMESTIC VIOLENCE

Edward Snadjr's ethnography of Kazakhstan calls attention to both the value and the problems of invoking culture as an explanation of domestic violence, an issue that is also becoming problematic in the United States. On the one hand, anthropologists have frequently been used as expert witnesses as part of a "**cultural defense**" of men from other cultures who are charged with domestic violence, in an attempt to avoid or mitigate punishment (Renteln 2004; Norgren and Nanda 2006). The cultural defense has mainly been used in court where defendants are members of subcultural, often immigrant groups in the United States, where patriarchal practices or the linking of honor and sexual purity are central to the culture. The cultural defense has mainly been used for defendants who have killed their

cultural defense A legal argument that attempts to mitigate conviction and sentencing in criminal cases by invoking the influence of culture on behavior; mainly used to defend men who assault women in cases of domestic violence.

wives, daughters, or other female relatives whom they claim have sullied their male "honor" or family's reputation through sexual transgressions. In many of these cases, perpetrators have successfully used the cultural defense to avoid or reduce punishment (Winkelman 1996).

As a result of the use of the cultural defense, many women's groups and legal scholars have protested that there should be only one standard of justice, which should not be affected by a defendant's cultural background. In this view, a court's decision to take culture into account in mitigating sentences for domestic violence sends out the dangerous message that immigrant women cannot be fully protected by American law.

In addition to raising ethical issues about anthropological participation, some anthropologists claim that, in accepting a cultural defense, lawyers, judges, and the media rely on an outdated concept of culture as static and as wholly determinative of individual behavior, in contrast to the more complex view generally held by contemporary anthropology (Demian 2008; also see Chapter 3).

Anthropology then, can make a difference, *not* by reinforcing the idea that "culture made me do it" is a valid excuse for domestic violence, but rather in raising awareness about the complexity of culture and by helping to implement culturally and linguistically sensitive responses to victims of domestic violence.

▨▨ YOU DECIDE

1. Given the dominant anthropological view that culture is diverse, dynamic, multifaceted, and shapes but does not determine behavior, should the cultural defense be permitted as a mitigating factor in criminal cases involving domestic violence? Why or why not?
2. What in your view would be the most effective local and/or national responses to domestic violence in the United States: social services, laws and law enforcement, counseling, mediation? What might be some unforeseen consequences of each of these responses?
3. What in your view might be the most effective way of using anthropological expertise to decrease the rate of domestic violence?

▨▨ CHAPTER SUMMARY

1. Ethnography, advocacy, and the comparative and holistic perspectives all work to give anthropology an important role in understanding contemporary issues and improving the lives of people throughout the world.

2. Anthropology, with its emphasis on understanding the relation between biology and culture, adds to our knowledge about race as a cultural construction.

3. The study of human remains by archaeologists and by forensic anthropologists adds to our understanding of history and culture and contributes to human rights issues by identifying victims of genocide or governmental violence.

4. Anthropology has been influential in reshaping museum exhibits of indigenous arts so that it more nearly reflects the role of that art in the lives of the people who produced it.

5. Anthropology educates people about racism, as in Melissa Checker's ethnography of pollution in Hyde Park, Georgia.

6. Ethnography enhances our understanding of the complicated ways in which culture intersects with domestic violence and helps craft more effective responses to its victims.

7. Medical anthropologists contribute a cultural perspective to understanding illness and health and advocate for those whose poverty prevents them from accessing the medical resources they need.

8. Studies of exploited children in Brazil and the United States indicate the importance of anthropology in exposing the complex nature of this social problem and creating effective solutions based on the reality of children's lives rather than universalistic, upper-middle-class cultural norms.

9. Participant observation of work situations and advocacy for workers is a growing anthropological contribution both in the United States and abroad.

▌▌▌ KEY TERMS

African Burial Ground National Monument
Cultural defense
Environmental justice

Forensic anthropology
Medical anthropology
Public anthropology
RACE Project

GLOSSARY

acephalous Lacking a government head or chief.

achieved status A social position that a person chooses or achieves on his or her own.

adaptation A change in the biological structure or lifeways of an individual or population by which it becomes better fitted to survive and reproduce in its environment.

affinal Relatives by marriage; in-laws.

age grades Specialized associations, based on age, that stratify a society by seniority.

age set A group of people of similar age and sex who move through some or all of life's stages together.

agglutinating language A language that allows a great number of morphemes per word and has highly regular rules for combining morphemes.

agriculture A form of food production in which fields are in permanent cultivation using plows, animals, and techniques of soil and water control.

allophone Two or more different phones that can be used to make the same phoneme in a specific language.

ambilineal descent A form of bilateral descent in which an individual may choose to affiliate with either the father's or mother's descent group.

animism The notion that all objects, living and nonliving, are imbued with spirits.

anthropological linguistics The study of language and its relation to culture.

anthropological theory A set of propositions about which aspects of culture are critical, how they should be studied, and what the goal of studying them should be.

anthropology The scientific and humanistic study of human beings.

antistructure The socially sanctioned use of behavior that radically violates social norms; frequently found in religious ritual.

apartheid The South African system of multiple exclusive racial groups—black, white, colored, and Asian—that were formally recognized, segregated, treated differently in law and life, and occupied different and almost exclusive statuses within the society.

applied anthropology The application of anthropology to the solution of human problems.

archaeology The subdiscipline of anthropology that focuses on the reconstruction of past cultures based on their material remains.

arranged marriage The process by which senior family members significantly control the choice of their children's spouses.

artifacts (in communications studies) Communication by clothing, jewelry, tattoos, piercings, and other visible body modifications.

ascribed status A social position into which a person is born.

assimilation The process by which immigrants abandon their cultural distinctiveness and become mainstream Americans.

assimilation model a model of U.S. ethnicity that holds that people should abandon their cultural traditions and become wholly absorbed in mainstream American culture.

authority The ability to cause others to act based on characteristics such as honor, status, knowledge, ability, respect, or the holding of formal public office.

avunculocal residence System under which a married couple lives with the husband's mother's brother.

balanced reciprocity The giving and receiving of goods of nearly equal value with a clear obligation of a return gift within a specified time limit.

band A small group of people related by blood or marriage, who live together and are loosely associated with a territory in which they forage.

bifurcation A principle of classifying kin under which different kinship terms are used for the mother's side of the family and the father's side of the family.

bigman A self-made leader who gains power through personal achievements rather than through political office.

bilateral descent System of descent under which individuals are equally affiliated with their mother's and their father's descent groups.

bilocal residence System under which a married couple has the choice of living with the husband's family or the wife's family.

biological (or physical) anthropology The subdiscipline of anthropology that studies people from a biological perspective, focusing primarily on aspects of humankind that are genetically inherited.

bound morpheme A unit of meaning that must be associated with another.

bride service The cultural rule that a man must work for his bride's family for a variable length of time either before or after the marriage.

bridewealth Goods presented by the groom's kin to the bride's kin to legitimize a marriage (formerly called "bride price").

bureaucracy Administrative hierarchy characterized by specialization of function and fixed rules.

call system The form of animal communication composed of a limited number of sounds that are tied to specific stimuli in the environment.

capital Productive resources that are used with the primary goal of increasing their owner's financial wealth.

capitalism An economic system in which people work for wages, land and capital goods are privately owned, and capital is invested for profit.

cargo system A ritual system common in Central and South America in which wealthy people are required to hold a series of costly ceremonial offices.

caste system A system of stratification based on birth or ascribed status in which social mobility between castes is not possible.

chiefdom A society with social ranking in which political integration is achieved through an office of centralized leadership called the chief.

chronemics The study of the different ways that cultures understand time and use it to communicate.

citizenship Those people invested by the state with rights and duties, based on criteria such as residence or other group affiliations.

clan A unilineal kinship group whose members believe themselves to be descended from a common ancestor but who cannot trace this link through known relatives.

class A category of people who all have about the same opportunity to obtain economic resources, power, or prestige and who are ranked relative to other categories.

class system A form of social stratification in which the different strata form a continuum and social mobility is possible.

closed system (social stratification) a stratification system based primarily on ascription.

code switching Moving seamlessly and appropriately between two different languages.

cognitive anthropology A theoretical position in anthropology that focuses on the relationship between the mind and society.

collaborative ethnography Ethnography that gives priority to cultural consultants on the topic, methodology, and written results of fieldwork.

collateral kin Kin descended from a common ancestor but not in a direct ascendant or descendant line, such as cousins or siblings.

colonialism The active possession of a foreign territory and the maintenance of political domination over that territory.

colony A territory under the immediate political control of a nation-state.

communitas A state of perceived solidarity, equality, and unity among people sharing a religious ritual, often characterized by intense emotion.

comparative linguistics The science of documenting the relationships between languages and grouping them into language families.

compensation A payment demanded by an aggrieved party to compensate for damage.

composite (compound) family An aggregate of nuclear families linked by a common spouse.

conflict theory A perspective on social stratification that focuses on inequality as a source of conflict and change.

conjugal tie The relationship between a husband and wife formed by marriage.

consanguineal Related by birth.

consultant A person from whom anthropologists gather data. Also known as an informant or sometimes an interlocutor.

contagious magic The belief that things once in contact with a person or object retain an invisible connection with that person or object.

conventionality The notion that, in human language, words are only arbitrarily or conventionally connected to the things for which they stand.

core vocabulary A list of 100 or 200 terms that designate things, actions, and activities likely to be named in all the world's languages.

corporate descent groups Permanent kinship groups that have an existence beyond the individuals who are members at any given time.

corvée labor Unpaid labor required by a governing authority.

cosmology A system of beliefs that deals with fundamental questions in the religious and social order.

cross-cousin marriage Marriage between an individual and the child of his or her mother's brother or father's sister.

cultural anthropology The study of human thought, behavior, and lifeways that are learned rather than genetically transmitted and that are typical of groups of people.

cultural construction of gender The idea that gender characteristics are the result of historical, economic, and political forces acting within each culture.

cultural defense A legal argument that attempts to mitigate conviction and sentencing in criminal cases by invoking the influence of culture on behavior; mainly used to defend men who assault women in cases of domestic violence.

cultural ecology A theoretical position in anthropology that focuses on the adaptive dimension of culture.

cultural relativism The notion that cultures should be analyzed with reference to their own histories and values rather than according to the values of another culture.

culture The learned behaviors and symbols that allow people to live in groups; the primary means by which humans adapt to their environment; the ways of life characteristic of a particular human society.

culture and personality A theoretical position in anthropology that held that cultures could best be understood by examining the patterns of child rearing and considering their effect on adult lives and social institutions.

culture shock Feelings of alienation and helplessness that result from rapid immersion in a new and different culture.

descent The culturally established affiliation between a child and one or both parents.

descent group A group of kin who are descendants of a common ancestor, extending beyond two generations.

deviants Those who transgress society's rules.

diffusion The spread of cultural elements from one culture to another.

displacement The capacity of all human languages to describe things not happening in the present.

divination A religious ritual performed to find hidden objects or information.

division of labor The pattern of apportioning different tasks to different members of a society.

dominant culture The culture with the greatest wealth and power in a society that consists of many subcultures.

double descent The tracing of descent through both matrilineal and patrilineal links, each of which is used for different purposes.

dowry Presentation of goods by the bride's kin to the family of the groom or to the couple.

Dutch East India Company A joint stock company chartered by the Dutch government to control all Dutch trade in the Indian and Pacific oceans. Also known by its Dutch initials VOC for Verenigde Ostendische Compagnie.

ecological functionalism A theoretical position in anthropology that focuses on the relationship between environment and society.

economic system The norms governing production, distribution, and consumption of goods and services within a society.

economics The study of the ways in which the choices people make combine to determine how their society uses its resources to produce and distribute goods and services.

efficiency (in food production) Yield per person per hour of labor invested.

egalitarian society A society in which no individual or group has more privileged access to resources, power, or prestige than any other.

ego (in kinship studies) The person from whose perspective a kinship chart is viewed.

elites The social strata that has differential access to all culturally valued resources, whether power, wealth, or prestige, and possessively protects its control over these resources.

emic (perspective) Examining societies using concepts, categories, and distinctions that are meaningful to members of that culture.

enculturation The process of learning to be a member of a particular cultural group.

endogamy A rule prescribing that a person must marry within a particular group.

environmental justice A movement to expose and address the problems of environmental pollution among poor, powerless, and minority communities.

essentialism a view of ethnicity that holds that ethnic groups are distinguished by essential, historically rooted, and emotionally experienced cultural differences.

ethnic boundaries The perceived cultural attributes by which ethnic groups distinguish themselves from others.

ethnic groups Categories of people who see themselves as sharing an ethnic identity that differentiates them from other groups or from the larger society as a whole.

ethnic identity The sense of self a person experiences as a member of an ethnic group.

ethnobotany A focus within anthropology that examines the relationship between humans and plants in different cultures.

ethnocentrism Judging other cultures from the perspective of one's own culture. The notion that one's own culture is more beautiful, rational, and nearer to perfection than any other.

ethnography The major research tool of cultural anthropology; includes both fieldwork among people in a society and the written results of such fieldwork.

ethnology The attempt to find general principles or laws that govern cultural phenomena.

ethnomedicine A focus within anthropology that examines the ways in which people in different cultures understand health and sicknesses as well as the ways they attempt to cure disease.

ethnoscape   Global distribution of people associated with each other by history, kinship, friendship, and webs of mutual understandings.

ethnoscience   A theoretical position in anthropology that focuses on recording and examining the ways in which members of a culture use language to classify and organize their cognitive world.

etic (perspective)   Examining societies using concepts, categories, and rules derived from science; an outsider's perspective.

exogamy   A rule specifying that a person must marry outside a particular group.

extended family   Family based on blood relations extending over three or more generations.

factions   Informal alliances within well-defined political units such as lineages, villages, or organizations.

firm   An institution composed of kin and/or nonkin that is organized primarily for financial gain.

foraging (hunting and gathering)   Fishing, hunting, and collecting vegetable food.

forensic anthropology   The application of biological anthropology to the identification of skeletalized or badly decomposed human remains.

functionalism (theoretical position in anthropology   The anthropological theory that specific cultural institutions function to support the structure of a society or serve the needs of its people.

functionalism (theory of inequality)   A theoretical position in anthropology, common in the first half of the 20th century, that focuses on finding general laws that identify different elements of society, show how they relate to each other, and demonstrate their role in maintaining social order.

fundamentalism   A proclamation of reclaimed authority over a sacred tradition that is to be reinstated as an antidote for a society that is believed to have strayed from its cultural moorings.

gender   A cultural construction that makes biological and physical differences into socially meaningful categories that seem reasonable and appropriate.

gender ideology   The totality of ideas about sex, gender, the natures of men and women, including their sexuality, and the relations between the genders.

gender role   The cultural expectations of men and women in a particular society, including the division of labor.

gender stratification   The ways in which gendered activities and attributes are differentially valued and related to the distribution of resources, prestige, and power in a society.

generalized reciprocity   Giving and receiving goods with no immediate or specific return expected.

globalization   The integration of resources, labor, and capital into a global network.

glottochronology   A statistical technique that linguists have developed to estimate the date of separation of related languages.

god (deity)   A named spirit who is believed to have created or to have control of some aspect of the world.

gossip   A generally negative and morally laden verbal exchange taking place in a private setting concerning the conduct of absent third parties.

government   An interrelated set of status roles that become separate from other aspects of social organization, such as kinship, in exercising control over a population.

great vowel shift   A change in the pronunciation of English language that took place between 1200 and 1600.

gross national income (GNI)   The total market value of all goods and services produced in a country.

haptics   The analysis and study of touch.

Heeren XVII   The Lords Seventeen, members of the board of directors of the Dutch East India Company.

hegemony   The (usually elite) construction of ideologies, beliefs, and values that attempt to justify the stratification system in a state society.

hijra   An alternative gender role in India conceptualized as neither man nor woman.

historical particularism   A theoretical position in anthropology associated with American anthropologists of the early 20th century that focuses on providing objective descriptions of cultures within their historical and environmental context.

holism   In anthropology, an approach that considers culture, history, language, and biology essential to a complete understanding of human society.

horticulture   Production of plants using a simple, nonmechanized technology and where the fertility of gardens and fields is maintained through long periods of fallow.

household   A group of people united by kinship or other links who share a residence and organize production, consumption, and distribution among themselves.

human paleontology   The focus within biological anthropology that traces human evolutionary history.

Human Relations Area Files   An ethnographic database that includes cultural descriptions of more than 300 cultures.

imitative magic   The belief that imitating an action in a religious ritual will cause the action to happen in the material world.

incest taboo   A prohibition on sexual relations between relatives.

indigenous peoples   Groups of people who have occupied a region for a long time but who have a minority position and usually little or no influence in the government of the nation-state that ultimately controls their land.

industrialism The process of the mechanization of production.

informant A person from whom anthropologists gather data. Also known as a consultant or sometimes an interlocutor.

inheritance The transfer of property between generations.

innovation An object or a way of thinking or behaving that is new because it is qualitatively different from existing forms.

interpretive anthropology A theoretical position in anthropology that focuses on using humanistic methods, such as those found in the analysis of literature, to analyze culture and discover the meaning of culture to its participants.

isolating language A language with relatively few morphemes per word and fairly simple rules for combining them.

joint stock company A firm that is managed by a centralized board of directors but is owned by shareholders.

kindred A unique kin network made up of all the people related to a specific individual in a bilateral kinship system.

kinesics The study of body position, movement, facial expressions, and gaze.

kinship A culturally defined relationship established on the basis of blood ties or through marriage.

kinship system The totality of kin relations, kin groups, and terms for classifying kin in a society.

kinship terminology The words used to identify different categories of kin in a particular culture.

kula ring A pattern of exchange among trading partners in a ring of islands off Papua New Guinea.

law A means of social control and dispute management through the systematic application of force by a politically constituted authority.

leadership The ability to direct an enterprise or action.

leveling mechanism A practice, value, or form of social organization that evens out wealth within a society.

levirate The custom whereby a man marries the widow of a deceased brother.

lexicon The total stock of words in a language.

life chances The opportunities that people have to fulfill their potential in society.

liminal The stage of a ritual, particularly a rite of passage, in which one has passed out of an old status but has not yet entered a new one.

lineage A group of kin whose members trace descent from a known common ancestor.

magic A religious ritual believed to produce a mechanical effect by supernatural means. When magic is done correctly, believers think it must have the desired effect.

mahu An alternative gender role in Tahiti.

mana Religious power or energy that is concentrated in individuals or objects.

manhood puzzle The question of why in almost all cultures masculinity is viewed not as a natural state but as a problematic status to be won through overcoming obstacles.

market exchange An economic system in which goods and services are bought and sold at a money price determined primarily by the forces of supply and demand.

marriage The customs, rules, and obligations that establish a special relationship between sexually cohabiting adults, between them and any children they take responsibility for, and between the kin of the married couple.

matriarchy A female-dominated society in which all important public and private power is held by women.

matrilineage A lineage formed by descent in the female line.

matrilineal descent A rule that affiliates a person to kin of both sexes related through females only.

matrilocal residence System under which a husband lives with his wife's family after marriage.

mediation A form of managing disputes that uses the offices of a third party to achieve voluntary agreement between disputing parties.

medical anthropology A subfield of anthropology that draws upon social, cultural, biological, and linguistic anthropology to better understand those factors that influence health and illness; concerned with the experience, distribution, prevention, and treatment of disease.

menarche A woman's first menstruation.

messianic Focusing on the coming of an individual who will usher in a utopian world.

millenarian Belief that a coming catastrophe will signal the beginning of a new age and the eventual establishment of paradise.

minimal pair Two words that differ in only one sound but have different meanings.

modernization theory A model of development holding that some nations are poor because their societies are traditional. Such nations should achieve wealth by attempting to repeat the historical experience of today's wealthy nations.

monoculture plantation An agricultural plantation specializing in the large-scale production of a single crop to be sold on the market.

monogamy A rule that permits a person to be married to only one spouse at a time.

monotheism Belief in a single god.

morpheme The smallest unit of language that has a meaning.

morphology A system for creating words from sounds.

multiculturalism The view that cultural diversity is a positive value that should be incorporated into national identity and public policy.

multinational corporation (MNC) A corporation that owns business enterprises in more than one nation, able to seek the most profitable venues to produce and market its goods and services regardless of national boundaries.

myths (sacred narratives) Stories of historical events, heroes, gods, spirits, and creation that members of a religious tradition hold to be holy and true.

nation-state A sovereign, geographically based state that identifies itself as having a distinctive national culture and historical experience.

negative reciprocity Exchange conducted for the purpose of material advantage and the desire to get something for nothing.

neoliberalism Political and economic policies promoting free trade, individual initiative, and minimal government regulation of the economy and opposing state control or subsidy to industries and all but minimal aid to impoverished individuals.

neolocal residence System under which a couple establishes an independent household after marriage.

nomadic pastoralism A form of pastoralism in which the whole social group (men, women, children) and their animals move in search of pasture.

nonunilineal (cognatic) descent A system of descent in which both the father's and the mother's lineages have equal claim to the individual.

norms Shared ideas about the way things ought to be done; rules of behavior that reflect and enforce culture.

nuclear family A family organized around the conjugal tie (the relationship between husband and wife) and consisting of a husband, a wife, and their children.

open stratification system one based primarily on achievement and where there is mobility between social strata.

organic analogy The comparison of societies to living organisms.

parallel-cousin marriage Marriage between the children of a parent's same-sex siblings (mother's sisters, father's brothers).

participant observation The fieldwork technique that involves gathering cultural data by observing people's behavior and participating in their lives.

pastoralism A food-getting strategy that depends on the care of domesticated herd animals.

patriarchy A male-dominated society in which all important public and private power is held by men.

patrilineage A lineage formed by descent in the male line.

patrilineal descent A rule that affiliates a person to kin of both sexes related through males only.

patrilocal residence System under which a bride lives with her husband's family after marriage.

peasants Rural cultivators who produce for the subsistence of their households but are also integrated into larger, complex state societies.

phone Smallest identifiable unit of sound made by humans and used in any language.

phoneme The smallest significant unit of sound in a language.

phonology The sound system of a language.

pillage To strip an area of money, goods, or raw materials through the threat or use of physical violence.

plasticity The ability of human individuals or cultural groups to change their behavior with relative ease.

political ideology The shared beliefs and values that legitimize the distribution and use of power in a particular society.

political organization The patterned ways in which power is legitimately used in a society to regulate behavior, maintain social order, make collective decisions, and deal with social disorder.

political process The ways in which individuals and groups use power to achieve public goals.

polyandry A rule permitting a woman to have more than one husband at a time.

polygamy A rule allowing more than one spouse.

polygyny A rule permitting a man to have more than one wife at a time.

polytheism Belief in many gods.

population density The number of people inhabiting a unit of land (usually given as people per square mile or kilometer).

postmodernism A theoretical position in anthropology that focuses on issues of power and voice. Postmodernists suggest that anthropological accounts are partial truths reflecting the backgrounds, training, and social positions of their authors.

potlatch A form of redistribution involving competitive feasting practiced among Northwest Coast Native Americans.

power The ability to impose one's will on others.

prayer Any conversation held with spirits and gods in which people petition, invoke, praise, give thanks, dedicate, supplicate, intercede, confess, repent, and bless.

prestige Social honor or respect.

priest One who is formally elected, appointed, or hired to a full-time religious office.

primatology The focus within biological anthropology that is concerned with the biology and behavior of nonhuman primates.

private/public dichotomy A gender system in which women's status is lowered by their almost exclusive cultural identification with the home and children, whereas men are identified with public, prestigious economic, and political roles.

productive resources Material goods, natural resources, or information used to create other goods or information.

productivity (food production) Yield per person per unit of land.

productivity (linguistics) The idea that humans can combine words and sounds into new, meaningful utterances they have never before heard.

prophets persons who create new religious ideas or call for a purification of existing religious practices.

proxemics The study of the cultural use of interpersonal space.

public anthropology Anthropology that aims to communicate with nonanthropological audiences and to have an impact on critical issues of wide social significance.

race A culturally constructed category based on *perceived* physical differences.

RACE Project A traveling museum exhibition and website emphasizing race as a cultural construction and the ways in which race is assigned meanings in American culture.

racism The belief that some human populations are superior to others because of inherited, genetically transmitted characteristics.

rank society A society characterized by institutionalized differences in prestige but no important restrictions on access to basic resources.

rebellion The attempt of a group within society to force a redistribution of resources and power.

reciprocity A mutual give-and-take among people of equal status.

redistribution Exchange in which goods are collected and then distributed to members of a group.

reincorporation the third phase of a rite of passage during which participants are returned to their community with a new status.

religion A social institution characterized by sacred stories, symbols, and symbolism; the proposed existence of immeasurable beings, powers, states, places, and qualities; rituals and means of addressing the supernatural; specific practitioners; and change.

respondent A person from whom anthropologists collect data. Also known as informant, consultant, or sometimes interlocutor.

revolution An attempt to overthrow the existing political structure and put another type of political structure in its place.

rite of intensification A ritual structured to reinforce the values and norms of a community and to strengthen group identity.

rite of passage A ritual that moves an individual from one social status to another.

ritual A ceremonial act or a repeated stylized gesture used for specific occasions involving the use of religious symbols.

sacrifice An offering made to increase the efficacy of a prayer or the religious purity of an individual.

Sapir-Whorf hypothesis The hypothesis that perceptions and understandings of time, space, and matter are conditioned by the structure of a language.

secret societies West African societies whose membership is secret or whose rituals are known only to society members. Their most significant function is the initiation of boys and girls into adulthood.

sedentary Settled, living in one place.

semantics The system of a language that relates words to meaning.

separation the first stage of a rite of passage in which individuals are removed from their community or status.

sex the biological differences between male and female.

shaman An individual socially recognized as being able to mediate between the world of humanity and the world of gods or spirits but who is not a recognized official of any religious organization.

social complexity The number of groups and their interrelationships in a society.

social constructionism a view of ethnicity that holds that ethnic groups emerge and change based on specific historical conditions.

social differentiation The relative access individuals and groups have to basic material resources, wealth, power, and prestige.

social mobility Movement from one social class to another.

social stratification A social hierarchy resulting from the relatively permanent unequal distribution of goods and services in a society.

society A group of people who depend on one another for survival or well-being as well as the relationships among such people, including their status and roles.

sociolinguistics The study of the relationship between language and culture and the ways language is used in varying social contexts.

sorcery The conscious and intentional use of magic.

sororate The custom whereby, when a man's wife dies, her sister is given to him as a wife.

state A hierarchical, centralized form of political organization in which a central government has a legal monopoly over the use of force.

stratified society A society characterized by formal, permanent social and economic inequality in which some people are denied access to basic resources.

structural adjustment A development policy promoted by Western nations, particularly the United States, that requires poor nations to pursue free market reforms in order to get new loans from the International Monetary Fund and the World Bank.

subculture A group within a society that shares norms and values significantly different from those of the dominant culture.

subsistence strategies The pattern of behavior used by a society to obtain food in a particular environment.

succession The transfer of office or social position between generations.

surrogate motherhood A variety of reproductive technologies in which a woman helps a couple to have a child by acting as a biological surrogate, carrying an embryo to term.

sweatshop Generally a pejorative term for a factory with working conditions that may include low wages, long hours, inadequate ventilation, and physical, mental, or sexual abuse of its workers.

swidden (slash-and-burn) cultivation A form of cultivation in which a field is cleared by felling the trees and burning the brush.

symbol Something that stands for something else. Central to language and culture.

symbolic anthropology A theoretical position in anthropology that focuses on understanding cultures by discovering and analyzing the symbols that are most important to their members.

syncretism The merging of elements of two or more religious traditions to produce a new religion.

syntax A system of rules for combining words into meaningful sentences.

Tirailleurs Senegalais Senegalese Riflemen. An army that existed from 1857 to 1960 composed largely of soldiers from French African colonies led by officers from metropolitan France.

totem An object, an animal species, or a feature of the natural world that is associated with a particular descent group.

totemism religious practices centered around animals, plants, or other aspects of the natural world held to be ancestral or to have other intimate relationships with members of a group.

transhumant pastoralism A form of pastoralism in which herd animals are moved regularly throughout the year to different areas as pasture becomes available.

tribe A culturally distinct population whose members consider themselves descended from the same ancestor.

two-spirit An alternative gender role in native North America (formerly called berdache).

unilineal descent A rule specifying that membership in a descent group is based on links through either the maternal line or the paternal line, but not both.

universal grammar A basic set of principles, conditions, and rules that form the foundation of all languages.

values Shared ideas about what is true, right, and beautiful.

VOC See Dutch East India Company.

warfare (war) A formally organized and culturally recognized pattern of collective violence directed toward other societies or between segments within a larger society.

wealth The accumulation of material resources or access to the means of producing these resources.

witchcraft The ability to harm others by harboring malevolent thoughts about them; the practice of sorcery.

xanith An alternative gender role in Oman on the Saudi Arabian peninsula.

REFERENCES

Abdo, Geneive. 2006. *Mecca and Main Street: Muslim Life in America after 9/11.* New York: Oxford University Press.

Aberle, David F., et al. 1963. "The Incest Taboo and Mating Patterns of Animals." *American Anthropologist* 65:253–265.

Adam, Nigel. 2007. "Lost Tribe Happy in Modern World." *Herald Sun,* February 3.

Adams, Kathleen M. 1990. "Cultural Commoditization in Tana Toraja, Indonesia." *Cultural Survival Quarterly* 40(1):31–34.

Adams, Kathleen M. 1993. "Theologians, Tourists and Thieves: The Torajan Effigy of the Dead in Modernizing Indonesia." *Kyoto Journal* 22:38–45.

Adams, Kathleen M. 1995. "Making-Up the Toraja? The Appropriation of Tourism, Anthropology, and Museums for Politics in Upland Sulawesi, Indonesia." *Ethnology* 34:143–152.

Adams, Kathleen M. 2006. *Art as Politics: Re-Crafting Identities, Tourism, and Power in Tana Toraja, Indonesia.* Honolulu: University of Hawai'i Press.

Adetunji, Jimoh I. 2006. "Nigeria: An End to Gas Flaring." *E Magazine: The Environmental Magazine* 17(4):38–39.

Akcam, Taner. 2006. *A Shameful Act: The Armenian Genocide and the Question of Turkish Responsibility,* trans. by Paul Bessemer. New York: Metropolitan Books/Henry Holt & Company.

Akom, A. A. 2008. "Toward an Eco-Pedagogy: Urban Youth Use Digital Media to Combat Environmental Racism." *Anthropology Newsletter,* November, p. 51.

Ali, Hirsi Ayaan. 2006. *The Caged Virgin: An Emancipation Proclamation for Women and Islam.* New York: Free Press.

Allen, Theodore W. 1997. *The Invention of the White Race* (Vols. 1 and 2). London: Verso.

Allitt, Patrick N. 2002. *Victorian Britain.* Chantilly, VA: Teaching Co.

Almond, Gabriel, Emmanuel Sivan, and R. Scott Appleby. 1995. "Fundamentalism: Genus and Species." In E. Marty and R. Scott Appleby (Eds.), *Fundamentalisms Comprehended* (pp. 399–424). Chicago: University of Chicago Press.

Alonso, Ana Maria. 1994. "The Politics of Space, Time and Substance: State Formation, Nationalism, and Ethnicity." In B. Siegel (Ed.), *Annual Review of Anthropology* (Vol. 23, pp. 379–405). Stanford, CA: Stanford University Press.

Amabile, T., et al. 2010. "Breakthrough Ideas for 2010." *Harvard Business Review* 88(1–2):41–57.

American Anthropological Association. 1998. *Code of Ethics of the American Anthropological Association.* Available at www.aaanet .org/committees/ethics/ ethcode.htm.

Ammon, Paul R., and Mary S. Ammon. 1971. "Effects of Training Black Preschool Children in Vocabulary Versus Sentence Construction." *Journal of Educational Psychology* 62(5):421–426.

Anagnost, Ana. 1989. "Transformations of Gender in Modern China." In S. Morgen (Ed.), *Gender in Anthropology: Critical Reviews for Research and Teaching* (pp. 313–342). Washington DC: American Anthropological Association.

Anderson, Benedict. 1991. *Imagined Communities: Reflections on the Origin and Spread of Nationalism.* New York: Verso.

Anderson, Elijah. 1999. *Code of the Streets.* New York: W.W. Norton.

Anthropology News. 2009. "Aging and the Life Course." *Anthropology News* 50(8).

Appadurai, Arjun. 1990. "Disjunction and Difference in the Global Cultural Economy." In Mike Featherstone (Ed.), *Global Culture: Nationalism, Globalization, and Modernity* (pp. 295–310). London: Sage.

Archibold, Randal C. 2006. "Border Fence Must Skirt Objections From Arizona Tribe." *New York Times,* September 20, p. A24.

Artz, G., P. Orazem, and D. Otto. "Measuring the Impact of Meat Packing and Processing Facilities in the Nonmetropolitan Midwest: A Difference-in-Differences Approach."

American Journal of Agricultural Economics 89(3):557–570.

Atran, Scott. 2003. "Genesis of Suicide Terrorism." *Science* 299(5612): 1534–1539.

Atran, Scott. 2007. "The Nature of Belief." *Science* 317(5837):456.

Baer, Hans A., Merrill Singer, and Ida Susser. 1997. *Medical Anthropology and the World System: A Critical Perspective.* Westport, CT: Bergin & Garvey.

Bagchi, Amiya Kumar. 2002. "The Other Side of Foreign Investment by Imperial Powers: Transfer of Surplus from Colonies." *Economic and Political Weekly* 37(23):2229–2238.

Bajaj, Vikas, and Ron Nixon. 2006. "Subprime Loans Going from Boon to Housing Bane." *New York Times,* December 6, p. C1.

Balikci, Asen. 1970. *The Netsilik Eskimo.* Prospect Heights, IL: Waveland.

Barber, Benjamin R. 2006. "The Uncertainty of Digital Politics: Democracy's Uneasy Relationship with Information Technology." In D. Stanley Eitzen and Maxine Baca Zinn (Eds.), *Globalization: The Transformation of Social Worlds* (pp. 61–68). Belmont, CA: Thomson/Wadsworth.

Barfield, Thomas J. 1993. *The Nomadic Alternative.* Englewood Cliffs, NJ: Prentice Hall.

Barker, Randolph, Robert W. Herdt, and Beth Rose. 1985. *The Rice Economy of Asia.* Washington DC: Resources for the Future.

Barnes, Virginia Lee, and Janice Boddy. 1995. *Aman: The Story of a Somali Girl.* New York: Vintage.

Barnes-Dean, Virginia Lee. 1989. "Clitoridectomy and Infibulation." *Cultural Survival Quarterly* 9(2):26–30.

Barnett, Homer. 1953. *Innovation: The Basis of Cultural Change.* New York: McGraw-Hill.

Barth, Fredrik. 1998/1969. *Ethnic Groups and Boundaries: The Social Organization of Culture Difference.* Prospect Heights, IL: Waveland.

Basso, Keith. 1979. *Portraits of "The Whitemen."* New York: Cambridge University Press.

Basson, Lauren L. 2008. *White Enough to be an American? Race Mixing, Indigenous People, and the Boundaries of State and Nation.* Chapel Hill: University of North Carolina Press.

Bawaya, Michael. 2010. "An Examination of Slavery." *American Archaeology,* Summer, pp. 12–18.

Behringer, Wolfgang. 2004. *Witches and Witch-Hunts: A Global History.* Cambridge, MA: Polity Press.

Benedict, Ruth. 1948. "Anthropology and the Humanities." *American Anthropologist* 50(4):585–593.

Benedict, Ruth. 1961/1934. *Patterns of Culture.* Boston: Houghton and Mifflin.

Berdan, Frances F. 1982. *The Aztecs of Central Mexico: An Imperial Society.* New York: Holt, Rinehart, and Winston.

Bereiter, Carl, and Siegfried Engelmann. 1966. *Teaching Disadvantaged Children in Preschool.* Englewood Cliffs: Prentice Hall.

Berreman, Gerald D. 1988. "Race, Caste, and Other Invidious Distinctions in Social Stratification." In J. Cole (Ed.), *Anthropology for the Nineties: Introductory Readings* (pp. 485–518). New York: Free Press.

Besnier, Niko. 1996. "Polynesian Gender Liminality Through Time and Space." In G. Herdt (Ed.), *Third Sex, Third Gender: Beyond Sexual Dimorphism in Culture and History* (pp. 285–328). New York: Zone.

Besnier, Niko. 2009. *Gossip and the Everyday Production of Politics.* Honolulu, HI: University of Hawai'i Press.

Beteille, Andre. 1998. *Society and Politics in India: Essays in a Comparative Perspective.* New Delhi: Oxford India.

Bhagwati, Jagdish. 1996. "The Demand to Reduce Domestic Diversity Among Trading Nations." In Jagdish Bhagwati and R. E. Hudec (Eds.), *Fair Trade and Harmonization.* Cambridge: MIT Press.

Bialostok, Steve. 2009. "Revisiting Class on Campus: Patching the Pipeline." *Anthropology News,* March, p. 43.

Bickerton, Derek. 1998. "Catastrophic Evolution: The Case for a Single Step from Protolanguage to Full Human Language." In James Hurford, M. Studdert-Kennedy, and C. Knight (Eds.), *The Evolutionary Emergence of Language: Social Function and the Origins of Linguistic Form* (pp. 341–358). Cambridge: Cambridge University Press.

Bittman, Mark. 2008. "The Meat of the Matter." *Dallas Morning News,* February 10.

Blackwood, Evelyn. 1998. *Female Desires: Same-Sex Relations and Transgender Practices across Cultures.* New York: Columbia University Press.

Blumenfield, Tami. 2004. "Walking Marriages." *Anthropology Newsletter* 45(5).

Boas, Franz. 1906. "Some Philological Aspects of Anthropological Research." *Science* 23:641–645.

Bodley, John H. 1999. *Victims of Progress* (4th ed.). Mountain View, CA: Mayfield.

Bodley, John H. 2000. *Cultural Anthropology: Tribes, States, and the Global System* (3rd ed.). Mountain View, CA: Mayfield.

Boellstorff, Tom. 2004. "Playing Back the Nation: *Waria,* Indonesian Transvestites." *Cultural Anthropology* 19:159–195.

Bonvillain, Nancy. 1997. *Language, Culture, and Communication* (2nd ed.). Englewood Cliffs, NJ: Prentice Hall.

Borgerhoff Mulder, Monique. 1995. "Bridewealth and Its Correlates: Quantifying Changes over Time." *Current Anthropology* 36:573–603.

Bornstein, Avram S. 2002. *Crossing the Green Line Between the West Bank and Israel.* Philadelphia: University of Pennsylvania Press.

Borofsky, Robert. 1994. "On the Knowledge and Knowing of Cultural Activities." In R. Borofsky (Ed.), *Assessing Cultural Anthropology* (pp. 331–347). New York: McGraw-Hill.

Borofsky, Robert. 2005. *Yanomami: The Fierce Controversy and What We Might Learn From It.* Berkeley, CA: University of California.

Bourgois, Philippe. 1996. "Confronting Anthropology, Education, and Inner-City Apartheid." *American Anthropologist* 98:249–265.

Bourgois, Philippe, and Jeff Schonberg. 2009. *Righteous Dopefiend.* Berkeley: University of California Press.

Bowen, John Richard. 2007. *Why the French Don't Like Headscarves: Islam, the State, and Public Space.* Princeton: Princeton University Press.

Bowerman, M. 1996. "Learning How to Structure Space for Language: A Cross-Linguistic Perspective." In P. Bloom, M. A. Peterson, L. Nadel, and M. F. Garrett (Eds.), *Language and Space* (pp. 385–436). Cambridge, MA: MIT Press.

Bowles, Samuel, Herbert Gintis, and Melissa Osborne Groves (Eds.). 2005. *Unequal Changes: Family Background and Economic Success.* Princeton: Princeton University Press.

Boxer, C. R. 1965. *The Dutch Seaborne Empire 1600–1800.* New York: Knopf.

Boyd-Bowman, Peter. 1975. "A Sample of Sixteenth Century 'Caribbean' Spanish Phonology." In William Milan, John Staczek, and Juan Zamora (Eds.), *1974 Colloquium on Spanish and Portuguese Linguistics* (pp. 1–11). Washington: Georgetown University Press.

Boynton, Robert S. 2006. "The Plot Against Equality" (book review of *The Trouble With Diversity: How We Learned to Love Identity and Ignore Inequality,* Walter Benn Michaels). *The Nation,* December 25, pp. 23 ff.

Bracken, Christopher. 1997. *The Potlatch Papers: A Colonial Case History.* Chicago: University of Chicago Press.

Brain, James L. 1989. "An Anthropological Perspective on the Witchcraze." In Jean R. Brink, A. P. Coudert, and M. C. Horowitz (Eds.), *The Politics of Gender in Early Modern Europe* (pp. 15–27). Kirksville, MO: Sixteenth Century Journal Publishers.

Brandes, Stanley. 1981. "Like Wounded Stags: Male Sexual Ideology in an Andalusian Town." In S. B. Ortner and H. Whitehead (Eds.), *Sexual Meanings: The Cultural Construction of Gender and Sexuality* (pp. 216–239). Cambridge: Cambridge University Press.

Brandt, Deborah. 2008. *Tangled Routes: Women, Work, and Globalization on the Tomato Trail* (2nd ed.). Lanham: Rowman.

Bremner, Brian. 2006. "What's It Going to Cost to Clean Up China?" *Business Week.* Available at www.businessweek.com/globalbiz/content/sep2006/gb20060927_774622.htm?chan5top1news_top1news1 index_global1business.

Brettell, Caroline B. 2003. *Anthropology and Migration: Essays on Transnationalism, Ethnicity, and Identity.* Walnut Creek, CA: Altamira.

Brettell, Caroline B. 2007. "Adjustment of Status, Remittances, and Return: Some Observations on 21st Century Migration Processes." *City and Society* 19(1):47–59.

Breusers, Mark. 1999. *On the Move: Mobility, Land Use and Livelihood Practices on the Central Plateau in Burkina Faso.* Münster, Hamburg and London: LIT Verlag.

Briggs, Jean L. 1991. "Expecting the Unexpected: Canadian Inuit Training for an Experimental Lifestyle." *Ethos* 19(3):259–287.

Briggs, Jean L. 1999. *Inuit Morality Play: The Emotional Education of a Three-Year-Old.* New Haven: Yale University Press.

Broadhead, Robert, Yael Van Hulst, and Douglas Heckathorn. 1999. "Termi-

nation of an Established Needle Exchange: A Study of Claims and Their Impact." *Social Problems* 46(1):48–56.

Brondo, Keri Vacanti. 2010. "Practicing Anthropology in a Time of Crisis: 2009 Year in Review." *American Anthropologist* 112(2)(June):208–218.

Brosius, Peter J. 1999. "Green Dots, Pink Hearts: Displacing Politics from the Malaysian Rain Forest." *American Anthropologist* 101:36–57.

Brown, Dorothy. 2009. "Two Americas, Two Tax Codes," *New York Times,* March 9, p. A23.

Brown, Drusilla, Alan Deardorff, and Robert Stern. 2003. "The Effects of Multinational Production on Wages and Working Conditions in Developing Countries." National Bureau of Economic Research, Working Paper 9669. Cambridge, MA: National Bureau of Economic Research. Available at http://www.nber.org/papers/w9669.

Brown, Judith. 1965. "A Cross Cultural Study of Female Initiation Rites." *American Anthropologist* 65:837–855.

Brown, Judith. 1975. "Iroquois Women: An Ethnohistoric Note." In R. R. Reiter (Ed.), *Toward an Anthropology of Women* (pp. 235–251). New York: Monthly Review Press.

Brown, Karen McCarthy. 1991. *Mama Lola: A Vodou Priestess in Brooklyn.* Berkeley, CA: University of California Press.

Brumfiel, Elizabeth. 1991. "Weaving and Cooking: Women's Production in Aztec Mexico." In J. M. Gero and M. W. Conkey (Eds.), *Engendering Archaeology: Women and Prehistory* (pp. 224–251). Cambridge, MA: Basil Blackwell.

Brumfiel, Elizabeth M. 2006. "Cloth, Gender, Continuity, and Change: Fabricating Unity in Anthropology." *American Anthropologist* 108(4): 862–877.

Bruun, Thilde Bech, Andreas de Neergaard, Deborah Lawrence, and Alan

D. Ziegler. 2009. "Environmental Consequences of the Demise in Swidden Cultivation in Southeast Asia: Carbon Storage and Soil Quality." *Human Ecology* 37(3):375–388.

Bryant, Vaughn M. 2003. "Árchaeology: Invisible Clues to New World Plant Domestication." *Science* 299(5609):1029–1030.

Burton, John W. 1992. "Representing Africa: Colonial Anthropology Revisited." *Journal of Asian and African Studies* 27:181–201.

Burton, Thomas G. 1993. *Serpent-Handling Believers*. Knoxville, TN: University of Tennessee Press.

Buruma, Ian. 2006. *Murder in Amsterdam: The Death of Theo van Gogh and the Limits of Tolerance*. New York: Penguin.

Cagan, Jonathan, and Craig M. Vogel. 2002. *Creating Breakthrough Products: Innovation from Product Planning to Program Approval*. Upper Saddle River: Prentice Hall.

Callaway, Ewen. 2010. "Neanderthal Genome Reveals Interbreeding with Humans." *New Scientist,* May 6.

Calman, Neil, Charmaine Ruddock, Maxine Golub, and Lan Le. 2005. *Separate and Unequal: Medical Apartheid in New York City*. New York: Institute for Urban Family Health.

Canadian Broadcasting Company. 1982. *Ear Pull Hoopla. Broadcast March 21, 1982*. Available at http://archives.radio-canada.ca/IDC-1-41-1194-6705/sports/arcticgames/clip4.

Cancian, Frank. 1989. "Economic Behavior in Peasant Communities." In Stuart Plattner (Ed.), *Economic Anthropology* (pp. 127–170). Stanford, CA: Stanford University Press.

Cannon, Walter B. 1942. "The 'Voodoo' Death." *American Anthropologist* 44:169–180.

Carneiro, Robert. 1970. "A Theory of the Origin of the State." *Science* 169:733–738.

Carneiro, Robert. 1981. "The Chiefdom: Precursor of the State." In Grant Jones and Robert Kautz (Eds.), *The Transition to Statehood in the New World* (pp. 37–79). Cambridge: Cambridge University Press.

Carr, Nicholas. 2010. *The Shallows: What the Internet Is Doing to Our Brains*. New York: WW. Norton & Co.

Carroll, Joseph. 2005. "Who Supports Marijuana Legalization?" *Gallup Poll Tuesday Briefing,* November 1.

Casasanto, Daniel. 2008. "Who's Afraid of the Big Bad Whorf? Cross-linguistic Differences in Temporal Language and Thought." *Language Learning* 58(Suppl. 1):63–79.

Cashdan, Elizabeth. 1989. "Hunters and Gatherers: Economic Behavior in Bands." In S. Plattner (Ed.), *Economic Anthropology* (pp. 21–48). Stanford, CA: Stanford University Press.

Center for Muslim-Jewish Engagement. 2007. III&E. Available at www.usc.edu/dept/MSA/human-relations/womeninislam/whatishijab.html (accessed September 16, 2007).

Cerroni-Long, E. L. 1993. "Teaching Ethnicity in the USA: An Anthropological Model." *Journal of Ethno-Development* 2(1):106–112.

Cerroni-Long, E. L. 1995. "Introduction." In E. L. Cerroni-Long (Ed.), *Insider Anthropology* (Napa Bulletin, Vol. 16). Washington, DC: American Anthropological Association.

Chagnon, Napoleon. 1997. *Yanomamo* (5th ed.). Fort Worth, TX: Harcourt Brace Jovanovich.

Chan, Dennis et al. 2009. "The Clinical Profile of Right Temporal Lobe Atrophy." *Brain.* 132:1287–1298.

Chance, John K., and William B. Taylor. 1985. "Cofradias and Cargos: An Historical Perspective on the Mesoamerican Civil-Religious Hierarchy." *American Ethnologist* 12(1):1–26.

Chance, Norman. 1990. *The Inupiat and Arctic Alaska: An Ethnography of Development*. Fort Worth, TX: Holt, Rinehart and Winston.

Chang, Leslie T. 2008. Factory Girls: From Village to City in a Changing China. New York: Spiegel & Grau.

Chapman, Mary M. 2008. "Black Workers in Auto Plants Losing Ground." *New York Times,* December 30, p. A1.

Chavez, Leo R. 1998. *Shadowed Lives: Undocumented Immigrants in American Society*. Belmont, CA: Wadsworth.

Checker, Melissa. 2005. *Polluted Promises: Environmental Racism and the Search for Justice in a Southern Town*. New York: New York University Press.

Checker, Melissa. 2009. "Anthropology in the Public Sphere: 2008: Emerging Trends and Significant Impacts." *American Anthropologist* 111(2): 162–169.

Chelala, Cesar. 2006. "Chronically Hungry Children of America." *Japan Times,* September 18.

Chelala, Cesar. 2009. "Turkey and Armenia: Beginning of a New Era?" *Common Ground News Service,* September 29.

Cherrington, Mark. 2008. "Indigenous Peoples Take Action Against Climate Change." *Anthropology News,* September, p. 31.

Chibnik, Michael. 2005. "Experimental Economics in Anthropology: A Critical Assessment." *American Ethnologist* 32(2):198–209.

Chomsky, Noam. 1965. *Syntactic Structures*. London: Mouton.

Chomsky, Noam. 1975. *The Logical Structure of Linguistic Theory*. New York: Plenum Press.

Cissé, Almahady. 2007. "Mali: Wood—The Gift That Can't Keep On Giving." *Inter Press Service (Johannesburg),* April 13. Available at ipsnews.net/news.asp?idnews=37339.

Clark, Lauren and Ann Kingsolver. n.d. "Briefing Paper on Informed Consent." *AAA Committee on Ethics.* Available at www.aaanet.org/committees/ethics/bp5.htm.

Clendinnen, Inga. 1991. *Aztecs: An Interpretation*. Cambridge: Cambridge University Press.

Cleaveland, A. A., J. Craven, and M. Dadfelser. 1979. *Universals of Culture*. New York: Global Perspectives in Education.

Cohen, Yehudi. 1971. *Man in Adaptation: The Institutional Framework*. Chicago: Aldine.

Cole, Alistair, and Gino Raymond. 2006. *Redefining the French Republic*. Manchester: Manchester University Press.

Coleman, Michael C. 1999. "The Responses of American Indian Children and Irish Children to the School, 1850s–1920s: A Comparative Study in Cross-Cultural Education." *American Indian Quarterly* 23(3/4):83–112.

Condon, Richard G., with Julia Ogina and the Holman Elders. 1996. *The Northern Copper Inuit: A History*. Toronto: University of Toronto Press.

Conklin, Beth A. 1995. "'Thus Are Our Bodies, Thus Was Our Custom': Mortuary Cannibalism in an Amazonian Society." *American Ethnologist* 22(1):75–101.

Connolly, Bob, and Robin Anderson. 1987. *First Contact: New Guinea's Highlanders Encounter the Outside World*. New York: Penguin.

Conway-Long, Don. 1994. "Ethnographies and Masculinities." In Harry Brod and Michael Kaufman (Eds.), *Theorizing Masculinities* (pp. 61–81). Thousand Oaks, CA: Sage.

Coquery-Vidrovitch, Catherine. 1988. *Africa: Endurance and Change South of the Sahara*. Berkeley, CA: University of California Press.

Corak, Miles. 2004. *Generational Income Mobility in North America and Europe*. Cambridge, UK: Cambridge University Press.

Corbett, Greville G. 2008. "Number of Genders." In Martin Haspelmath,

Matthew S. Dryer, David Gil, and Bernard Comrie (Eds.), *The World Atlas of Language Structures Online*. Munich: Max Planck Digital Library, Chapter 30. Available online at wals.info/feature/30 (accessed on August, 19, 2010).

Costa, LeeRay, and Andrew Matzner. 2007. *Male Bodies, Women's Souls: Personal Narratives of Thailand's Transgendered Youth*. Binghamton, NY: Haworth Press.

Cotter, Holland. 2009. "Putting 'Primitive' to Rest." *New York Times*, June 5, p. C1.

Covington, Dennis. 1995. *Salvation on Sand Mountain: Snake Handling and Redemption in Southern Appalachia*. Reading, MA: Addison-Wesley.

Crespin, Pamela. 2005. "The Global Transformation of Work." *Anthropology News* 46(3):20–21.

Cronk, Lee. 1999. *That Complex Whole: Culture and the Evolution of Human Behavior*. Boulder, CO: Westview Press.

Cronk, Lee, Drew Gerkey, and William Irons. 2009. "Interviews as Experiments: Using Audience Effects to Examine Social Relationships. *Field Methods* 21(4):331–346.

Cunningham, Lawrence S., John Kelsay, R. Maurice Barineau, and Heather Jo McVoy. 1995. *The Sacred Quest: An Invitation to the Study of Religion* (2nd ed.). Englewood Cliffs, NJ: Prentice Hall.

Curtis, Lewis P. 1968. *Anglo-Saxons and Celts: A Study of Anti-Irish Prejudice in Victorian England*. Bridgeport: University of Bridgeport.

Curtis, Richard, Karen Terry, Meredith Dank, Kirk Dombrowski, and Bilal Khan. 2008. "The Commercial Sexual Exploitation of Children in New York City. Vol. l: The CSEC Population in New York City: Size, Characteristics and Needs." Report submitted to the National Institute of Justice, United States Department of Justice.

Dalton, George. 1961. "Economic Theory and Primitive Society." *American Anthropologist* 63:1–25.

Danfulani, Umar Habila Dadem. 1999. "Exorcising Witchcraft: The Return of the Gods in New Religious Movements on the Jos Plateau and the Benue Regions of Nigeria." *African Affairs* 98(391):167–193.

Daniel, G. Reginald. 2006. *Race and Multiraciality in Brazil and the United States: Converging Paths?* University Park: Pennsylvania State University Press.

Darian-Smith, Eve. 2004. *New Capitalists: Law, Politics and Identity Surrounding Casino Gaming on Native American Land*. Belmont: Wadsworth.

Das, Raju. 1998. "The Green Revolution, Agrarian Productivity and Labor." *International Journal of Urban and Regional Research* 22(1):122–135.

Das, Subhamoy. 2009. "Hindus Protest Sony's Hanuman Game." *Subhamoy's Hinduism Blog. About.com: Hinduism*. Available at hinduism.about.com/b/2009/04/22/hindus-protest-sonys-hanuman-game.htm (accessed August 20, 2010).

Daugherty, Mary L. 1976. "Serpent-Handling as Sacrament." *Theology Today* 33:232–243.

Deák, Istvan. 2002. "The Crime of the Century," *New York Review of Books*, September 26, p. 48.

de Bellaigue, Christopher. 2007. "Turkey at the Turning Point?" *New York Review of Books*, October 25, p. 69.

Delcore, Henry D. 2007. "The Racial Distribution of Privilege in a Thai National Park." *Journal of Southeast Asian Studies* 38(1):83–105.

Demian, Melissa. 2008 "Fictions of Intention in the 'Cultural Defense'." *American Anthropologist* 110: 432–442.

Democracy Now. 2008, May 28. "Dr. Paul Farmer Challenges Profit-Driven Medical System While Bringing Healthcare to Poor Communities Worldwide." Radio interview.

De Vos, George, and Lola Romanucci-Ross. 1995. "Ethnic Identity: A Psychocultural Perspective." In Lola Romanucci-Ross and George A. De Vos (Eds.), *Ethnic Identity: Creation, Conflict, and Accommodation* (3rd ed., pp. 349–380). London: Sage.

De Waal, Alex. 2002. "Anthropology and the Aid Encounter." In Jeremy MacClancy (Ed.), *Exotic No More: Anthropology on the Front Lines* (251–269). Chicago: University of Chicago Press.

Dewey, Alice, and Geoffrey White. 2008. "Ann Dunham: A Personal Reflection." *Anthropology Newsletter*, November, p. 20.

Diamond, Jared. 1992. "The Arrow of Disease." *Discover* 13(10):64–73.

Diamond, Jared. 1998. *Guns, Germs, and Steel: The Fate of Human Societies*. New York: W.W. Norton.

di Leonardo, Micaela. 1984. *The Varieties of Ethnic Experience: Kinship, Class, and Gender among California Italian-Americans*. Ithaca, NY: Cornell University Press.

di Leonardo, Micaela. 1998. *Exotics at Home: Anthropologies, Others, American Modernity*. Chicago: University of Chicago Press.

di Leonardo, Micaela. 2003. "Margaret Mead and the Culture of Forgetting." *American Anthropologist* 105(3): 592–595.

Divale, William Tulio, and Marvin Harris. 1976. "Population, Warfare and the Male Supremacist Complex." *American Anthropologist* 78:521–538.

Dominguez, Martin, and Pasko Rakic. 2009. "Language Evolution: The Importance of Being Human." *Nature* 462:169–170.

Dove, Michael R. 2009. "Dreams from his Mother." *New York Times*, August 11, p. A1.

Dozon, Jean-Pierre. 1985. "Les Bété: une creation coloniale." In J. L. Amselle and E. M'bokolo (Eds.), *Au Coeur de l'ethnie* (pp. 49–85). Paris: Editions La Decouverte.

Duncan, David Ewing. 1995. *Hernando de Soto: A Savage Quest in the Americas*. New York: Crown.

Duncan, David James. 2000. "Salmon's Second Coming." *Sierra* March/April:30–41.

Dunham, S. Ann, Alice G. Dewey, Nancy I. Cooper, and Maya Soetoro-Ng. 2009. *Surviving Against the Odds: Village Industry in Indonesia*. Durham, NC: Duke University Press.

Durkheim, Émile. 1961/1915. *The Elementary Forms of the Religious Life*. New York: Collier.

Durning, Alan Thein. 1994. "The Conundrum of Consumption." In L. A. Mazur (Ed.), *Beyond the Numbers: A Reader on Population, Consumption, and the Environment* (pp. 40–47). Washington, DC: Island Press.

Durrenberger, E. Paul. 2001. "Explorations of Class and Consciousness in the U.S." *Journal of Anthropological Research* 57(1):41–60.

Durrenberger, E. Paul, and Dimitra Doukas. 2008. "Gospel of Wealth, Gospel of Work: Counterhegemony in the U.S. Working Class." *American Anthropologist*, 110(2): 214–224.

Earle, Timothy K. 1987. "Chiefdoms in Archaeological and Ethnological Perspective." *Annual Reviews in Anthropology* 16:279–308.

Early, John D., and Thomas N. Headland. 1998. *Population Dynamics of a Philippine Rain Forest People: The San Ildefonso Agta*. Gainesville, FL: University Press of Florida.

Eckert, Penelope. 1989. *Jocks and Burnouts: Social Categories and Identity in the High School*. New York: Teacher's College Press.

Eckert, Penelope. 2004. "Language and Gender in Adolescence." In Janet Holmes and Miriam Meyerhoff (Eds.), *The Handbook of Language and Gender. Blackwell Reference Online*. Accessed May 28, 2010.

Eckholm, Eric. 2007. "Boys Cast Out by Polygamists Find New Help." *New York Times*, September 9.

Economist, The. 2007. "The Good Consumer." *The Economist*, January 17.

Eggan, Fred. 1950. *The Social Organization of Western Pueblos*. Chicago: University of Chicago Press.

Elkin, A. P. 1967. "The Nature of Australian Totemism." In J. Middleton (Ed.), *Gods and Rituals* (pp. 159–176). Garden City, NY: Natural History Press.

Eller, Jack David. 2006. *Violence and Culture: A Cross-Cultural and Interdisciplinary Approach*. Belmont, CA: Wadsworth.

El Saadawi, Nawal. 1980. *The Hidden Face of Eve*. London: Zed Books.

Ember, Carol. 1983. "The Relative Decline in Women's Contribution to Agriculture with Intensification." *American Anthropologist* 85(2): 285–304.

Ember, Carol R., and Melvin Ember. 2005. "Explaining Corporal Punishment of Children: A Cross-Cultural Study." *American Anthropologist* 107(4):609–619.

Ember, Melvin, and Carol R. Ember. 1971. "The Conditions Favoring Matrilocal vs. Patrilocal Residence." *American Anthropologist* 73:571–594.

Engelmann, Siegfried, and Therese Engelmann. 1966. *Give Your Child a Superior Mind: A Program for the Preschool Child*. New York: Simon and Schuster.

Ensminger, Jean. 2002. "Experimental Economics: A Powerful New Method for Theory Testing in Anthropology." In Jean Ensminger (Ed.), *Theory in Economic Anthropology* (pp. 59–78). Walnut Creek: Altamira.

Erickson, Jon. 1995. *The Human Volcano: Population Growth as Geologic Force*. New York: Facts on File.

Estioko-Griffin, Agnes. 1986. "Daughters of the Forest." *Natural History* 5:37–42.

Evans, Peter. 2000. "Fighting Marginalization with Transnational Networks: Counter Hegemonic Globalization." *Contemporary Sociology* 29:230–241.

Evans-Pritchard, E. E. 1958/1937. *Witchcraft, Oracles, and Magic among the Azande.* Oxford: Clarendon Press.

Evans-Pritchard, E. E. 1968/1940. *The Nuer.* Oxford: Clarendon Press.

Ewing, Katherine Pratt, ed. 2008. *Being and Belonging: Muslims in the United States since 9/11.* New York: Russell Sage Foundation.

Fábrega, Horacio. 1997. *Evolution of Sickness and Healing.* Berkeley, CA: University of California Press.

Farmer, Paul. 2003. *Pathologies of Power: Health, Human Rights and the New War on the Poor.* Berkeley, CA: University of California Press.

Feinberg, Richard. 1986. "Market Economy and Changing Sex-Roles on a Polynesian Atoll." *Ethnology* 25:271–282.

Feinberg, Richard. 1994. "Contested Worlds: Politics of Culture and the Politics of Anthropology." *Anthropology and Humanism* 19:20–35.

Feldman, Douglas, ed. 2008. *AIDS, Culture and Africa.* Gainesville: University of Florida Press.

Feldman, Douglas A., ed. 2009. *AIDS, Culture, and Gay Men.* Gainesville, FL: University of Florida Press.

Ferguson, R. Brian. 1992. "A Savage Encounter: Western Contact and the Yanomamo War Complex." In R. B. Ferguson and N. L. Whitehead (Eds.), *War in the Tribal Zone: Expanding States and Indigenous Warfare* (pp. 199–227). Santa Fe, NM: School of American Research Press.

Ferraro, Gary P. 1994. *The Cultural Dimension of International Business* (2nd ed.). Englewood Cliffs, NJ: Prentice-Hall.

Fetto, John. 1999. "Six Billion Served." *American Demographics* June:14.

Fix, Michael, and Jeffrey Passel. 1994. *Immigration and Immigrants: Setting the Record Straight.* Washington, DC: Urban Institute.

Flamm, Bruce L. 2002. "Faith Healing by Prayer: Review of Cha, KY, Wirth, DP, Lobo, RA. Does Prayer Influence the Success of In Vitro Fertilization-Embryo Transfer?" *Scientific Review of Alternative Medicine* 6(1):47–50.

Fluehr-Lobban, Carolyn. 2005. "Cultural Relativism and Universal Rights in Islamic Law." *Anthropology News* 46(9):23.

Fondacaro, Steve, and Montgomery McFate. 2008. "In Memoriam—Michael Bhatia." Available at http://humanterrainsystem.army.mil/bhatia.html.

Forbes. 2009a. "NBA Team Valuations #1 Los Angeles Lakers." Available at www.forbes.com/lists/2009/32/basketball-values-09_Los-Angeles-Lakers_320250.html. Accessed August 20, 2010.

Forbes 2009b. "The 400 Richest Americans: #37 Philip Anschutz." Available at www.forbes.com/lists/2009/54/rich-list-09_Philip-Anschutz_DSAK.html. Accessed August 20, 2010.

Forbes. 2010. "SportsMoney: Kobe Bryant: King of the Court." Available at blogs.forbes.com/sportsmoney/2010/06/18/kobe-bryant-king-of-the-court. Accessed August 20, 2010.

Ford, James D, Barry Smit, and Johanna Wandel. 2006. "Vulnerability to Climate Change in the Arctic: A Case Study from Arctic Bay, Canada." *Global Environmental Change* 16:145–60.

Fordham, Signithia. 1999. "Dissin' 'the Standard': Ebonics and Guerrilla Warfare at Capital High." *Anthropology & Education Quarterly* 30(3):272–93.

Fortune. 2006. *Global 500.* Available at money.cnn.com/magazines/fortune/global500/2005/.

Foster, Robert J. 1991. "Making National Cultures in the Global Ecumene." *Annual Reviews of Anthropology* 20:235–260.

Frank, Robert, and Phillip J. Cook. 1996. *The Winner-Take-All Society: Why the Few at the Top Get So Much More Than the Rest of Us.* New York: Penguin.

Frankenberg, Ruth. 1993. *White Women, Race Matters: The Social Construction of Whiteness.* Minneapolis: University of Minnesota Press.

Fredrickson, George M. 2009. *Diverse Nations: Explorations in the History of Racial and Ethnic Pluralism.* New York: Paradigm.

Freed, Ruth S., and Stanley A. Freed. 1985. "The Psychomedical Case History of a Low-Caste Woman of North India." *Anthropological Papers of the American Museum of Natural History* 60(2):102–228.

Fried, Morton. 1967. *The Evolution of Political Society.* New York: Random House.

Friedl, Ernestine. 1975. *Women and Men: An Anthropologist's View.* New York: Holt, Rinehart and Winston.

Friedman, Ariella, and Judith Todd. 1994. "Kenyan Women Tell a Story: Interpersonal Power of Women in Three Subcultures in Kenya." *Sex Roles* 31:533–546.

Friedman, Jonathan. 1992. "The Past in the Future: History and the Politics of Identity." *American Anthropologist* 94:837–859.

Friedman, Jonathan, ed. 2003. *Globalization, the State, and Violence.* Walnut Creek, CA: AltaMira.

Fry, Douglas P., and Kaj Bjorkqvist (Eds.). 1997. *Cultural Variation and Conflict Resolution: Alternatives to Violence.* Mahwah, NJ: Erlbaum.

Geertz, Clifford. 1973a. "Deep Play: Notes on the Balinese Cockfight." In C. Geertz (Ed.), *The Interpretation of Cultures* (pp. 412–453). New York: Basic Books.

Geertz, Clifford, ed. 1973b. *The Interpretation of Cultures.* New York: Basic Books.

Geertz, Clifford. 2008/1973. "Deep Play: Notes on a Balinese Cock-fight." In R. Jon McGee and Richard L. Warms (Eds.), *Anthropological Theory: An Introductory History.* Boston: McGraw-Hill.

Geographical. 2005. "The Fertile Century." *Geographical* 77(3):50–51.

Ghosh, Anjan. 1991. "The Structure of Structure, or Appropriation of Anthropological Theory." *Review* 14(1):55–77.

Gibbs, James L., Jr. 1988. "The Kpelle Moot: A Therapeutic Model for the Informal Settlement of Disputes." In J. B. Cole (Ed.), *Anthropology of the Nineties* (pp. 347–359). New York: Free Press.

Gibbs, W. Wayt. 2002. "Saving Dying Languages." *Scientific American* 287:78–86.

Gibson, Margaret A. 1997. "Ethnicity and School Performance: Complicating the Immigrant/Involuntary Minority Typology." *Anthropology and Education Quarterly* 28(3):431–454.

Gibson, Margaret A., and John Ogbu. 1991. *Minority Status and Schooling: A Comparative Study of Immigrant and Involuntary Minorities.* New York: Garland.

Gilbert, Aubrey L., Terry Regier, Paul Kay, and Richard B. Ivry. 2006. "Whorf Hypothesis Is Supported in the Right Visual Field but Not the Left." *Proceedings of the National Academy of Sciences* 103(2):489–494.

Gilbert, Matthew. 2007. "Farewell, Sweet Ice." *The Nation,* May 7, pp. 26–27.

Gilmore, David D. 1990. *Manhood in the Making: Cultural Concepts of Masculinity.* New Haven, CT: Yale University Press.

Gilmore, David D. 1996. "Above and Below: Toward a Social Geometry of Gender." *American Anthropologist* 98:54–66.

Ginsburg, Faye. 1989. *Contested Lives: The Abortion Debate in an American Community.* Berkeley, CA: University of California Press.

Glazer, Nathan, and Daniel P. Moynihan. 1970. *Beyond the Melting Pot* (2nd ed.). Cambridge, MA: MIT.

Glick-Schiller, Nina, Linda Basch, and Christina Szanton-Blanc (Eds.). 1992. *Towards a Transnational Perspective on Migration: Race, Class, Ethnicity and Nationalism Reconsidered.* New York: New York Academy of Sciences.

Gmelch, George. 2000. "Baseball Magic." In James Spradley and David McCurdy (Eds.), *Conformity and Conflict* (pp. 322–331). Boston: Allyn and Bacon.

Godelier, Maurice. 1993. "L'Occident, miroir brisé: une evaluation partielle de l'anthropologie sociale assortie de quelques perspectives." *Annales* 48:1183–1207.

Goldschmidt, Walter R. 1986. *The Sebei: A Study in Adaptation.* New York: Holt, Reinhart and Winston.

Goldstein, Donna. 1999. "'Interracial' Sex and Racial Democracy in Brazil: Twin Concepts?" *American Anthropologist* 101:563–578.

Goodale, J. 1971. *Tiwi Wives.* Seattle, WA: University of Washington Press.

Goodstein, Laurie. 2009. "Poll Finds U.S. Muslims Thriving, but Not Content." *New York Times,* March 1, p. 11.

Goody, Jack. 1995. *The Expansive Moment: Anthropology in Britain and Africa 1918–1970.* Cambridge: Cambridge University Press.

Gordon, Peter. 2004. "Numerical Cognition Without Words: Evidence from Amazonia." *Science* 306(5695):496–499.

Gore, Al. 2006. *An Inconvenient Truth: The Planetary Emergency of Global Warming and What We Can Do About It.* New York: Melcher Media/Rodale. Also available on DVD. Hollywood, CA: Paramount.

Graham, Laura R. 2006. "Anthropologists Are Obligated to Promote Human Rights and Social Justice: Especially Among Vulnerable Communities." *Anthropology News* 47(7):4–5.

Graham, Laura, Alexandra Jaffe, Bonnie Urciuoli, and David Valentine. 2007. "Why Anthropologists Should Oppose English Only Legislation in the U.S." *Anthropology News* 48(1):32–33.

Gramsci, Antonio. 1971. *Selections from the Prison Notebook,* ed. and trans. by Quentin Hoare and Goffry Nowell-Smith. London: Lawrence and Wishart.

Gray, John. 2005. "The World Is Round." *New York Review of Books* 52(13).

Green, Richard E., et al. 2010. "A Draft Sequence of the Neandertal Genome." *Science* 328(5979):710–722.

Greenberg, James B. 1997. "A Political Ecology of Structural-Adjustment Policies: The Case of the Dominican Republic." *Culture & Agriculture* 19(3):85–93.

Greenhalgh, Susan. 2005. "Globalization and Population Governance in China." In Aihwa Ong and Stephen J. Collier (Eds.), *Global Assemblages: Technology, Politics, and Ethics as Anthropological Problems* (pp. 354–372). Malden, MA.

Greenhalgh, Susan. 2007a. "China's Future with Fewer Females." *China from the Inside.* Washington, DC: Public Broadcasting Service. Available at www.pbs.org/kqed/chinainside/women/population.html.

Greenhalgh, Susan. 2007b. *Just One Child: Science and Policy in Deng's China.* Berkeley: University of California Press.

Grosfoguel, Ramon. 2003. *Colonial Subjects: Puerto Ricans in a Global Perspective.* Berkeley: University of California Press.

Gruenbaum, Ellen. 2001. *The Female Circumcision Controversy: An Anthropological Perspective.* Philadelphia, PA: University of Pennsylvania Press.

Gu Baochang, Wang Feng, Guo Zhigang, Zhang Erli. 2007. "China's Local and National Fertility Policies at the End of the Twentieth Century." *Population and Development Review* 33(1):129–148.

Guillermoprieto, Alma. 2006. "A New Bolivia?" *New York Review of Books* 53(13):36.

Gutmann, Matthew C. 1996. *The Meanings of Macho: Being a Man in Mexico City.* Berkeley, CA: University of California Press.

Hackenberg, Robert. 2000. "Advancing Applied Anthropology: Joe Hill in Cyberspace: Steps Toward Creating 'One Big Union.'" *Human Organization* 59(3):365–369.

Hacker, Jacob. 2002a. *The Divided Welfare State: The Battle Over Public and Private Social Benefits in the United States.* New York: Cambridge.

Hadden, Jeffrey K., and Anson Shupe. 1989. "Is There Such a Thing as Global Fundamentalism?" In Jeffrey K. Hadden and Anson Shupe (Eds.), *Secularization and Fundamentalism Reconsidered* (pp. 109–122). New York: Paragon House.

Haines, David. 2007. "Labor, Migration, and Anthropology: Reflections From the Work of Philip L. Martin." *City and Society* 19(1):60–71.

Hale, Sondra. 1989. "The Politics of Gender in the Middle East." In S. Morgen (Ed.), *Gender and Anthropology: Critical Reviews for Research and Teaching* (pp. 246–267). Washington, DC: American Anthropological Association.

Hall, Edward T. 1959. *The Silent Language.* Greenwich, CT: Fawcett.

Hall, Edward T. 1966. *The Hidden Dimension.* New York: Doubleday.

Hall, Edward T. 1968. "Proxemics." *Current Anthropology* 9:83–109.

Hall, Edward T. 1983. *The Dance of Life: The Other Dimension of Time.* New York: Anchor/Doubleday.

Halperin, Rhoda H. 1990. *The Livelihood of Kin: Making Ends Meet "The Kentucky Way."* Austin, TX: University of Texas Press.

Handler, Richard. 1988. *Nationalism and the Politics of Culture in Quebec.* Madison, WI: University of Wisconsin Press.

Hansen, Edward C. 1995. "The Great Bambi War: Tocquevillians versus Keynesians in an Upstate New York County." In J. Schneider and R. Rapp (Eds.), *Articulating Hidden Histories: Exploring the Influence of Eric R. Wolf* (pp. 142–155). Berkeley, CA: University of California Press.

Harrell, Steven. 2001. "Review of *A Society without Fathers or Husbands: The Na of China.* By Cai Hua." *American Anthropologist.* 104(3):982–983.

Harries, Patrick. 1987. "The Roots of Ethnicity: Discourse and the Politics of Language Construction in South-East Africa." *African Affairs* 87:25–52.

Harris, Marvin. 1966. "The Cultural Ecology of India's Sacred Cattle." *Current Anthropology* 7:51–66.

Harris, Marvin. 1989. *Our Kind: Who We Are, Where We Came From, Where We Are Going.* New York: Harper Perennial.

Harrison, David, ed. 1992. *Tourism and the Less Developed Countries.* London/New York: Belhaven/Wiley & Sons.

Harrison, Faye V. 2009. "The Paradox of Democracy in the New Racial Domain." *Anthropology News,* January, p. 15.

Harrison, Paul, and Fred Pearce. 2000. *AAAS Atlas of Population and Environment.* Victoria Dompka Markham (Ed.). American Association for the Advancement of Science and the University of California Press. Available at atlas.aaas.org/.

Hart, C. W. M. 1967. "Contrasts between Pre-Pubertal and Post-Pubertal Education." In R. Endelman (Ed.), *Personality and Social Life* (pp. 275–290). New York: Random House.

Hart, C. W. M., and Arnold R. Pilling. 1960. *The Tiwi of North Australia.* New York: Holt, Rinehart and Winston.

Hartigan, John. 1997. "Establishing the Fact of Whiteness." *American Anthropologist* 99:495–505.

Haskins, Ron, Julie Isaacs, and Isabel Sawhill. 2008. "Getting Ahead or Losing Ground: Economic Mobility in America." Economic Mobility Project. The Pew Foundation. Available at http://www.brookings.edu/multimedia/video/2008/0220_mobility_sawhill.aspx.

Hefner, Robert. 2002. "Global Violence and Indonesian Muslim Politics." *American Anthropologist* 104(3):754–765.

Heimer, Robert, Ricky Bluthenthal, Merill Singer, and Kaveh Khoshnood. 1996. "Structural Impediments to Operational Syringe-Exchange Programs." *AIDS Public Policy Journal* 11:169–184.

Helft, Miguel, and Michael Wines. 2010. "Google Faces Fallout as China Reacts to Site Shift." *New York Times*, March 24, p. B1.

Helman, Cecil G. 1998/1991. "Medicine and Culture: Limits of Biomedical Explanation." In G. Ferraro (Ed.), *Applying Cultural Anthropology: Readings* (pp. 3–6). Belmont, CA: Wadsworth.

Henrich, Joseph, et al. 2004. *Foundations of Human Sociality: Economic Experiments and Ethnographic Evidence From 15 Small-Scale Societies.* Oxford: Oxford University Press.

Herdt, Gilbert H. 1981. *Guardians of the Flutes: Idioms of Masculinity.* New York: McGraw-Hill.

Herdt, Gilbert H. 1987. *The Sambia.* New York: Holt, Rinehart and Winston.

Herdt, Gilbert H., ed. 1996. *Third Sex, Third Gender: Beyond Sexual*

Dimorphism in Culture and History. New York: Zone.

Hester, Marianne. 1988. "Who Were the Witches?" *Studies in Sexual Politics* 26–27:1–22.

Hill, Jane H. 1998. "Language, Race, and White Public Space." *American Anthropologist* 100:680–689.

Himmelgreen, David A., and Nancy Romero-Daza. 2008. "Food Security and the Battle against HIV/AIDS." *Anthropology News,* October, p. 13.

Hobsbawm, Eric, and Terence Ranger (Eds.). 1983. *The Invention of Tradition.* Cambridge: Cambridge University Press.

Hochschild, Adam. 1998. *King Leopold's Ghost.* New York: Houghton Mifflin.

Hochschild, Adam. 2005. "In the Heart of Darkness." *New York Review of Books,* October 6, pp. 39–42.

Hoebel, E. Adamson. 1960. *The Cheyennes: Indians of the Great Plains.* New York: Holt.

Hoebel, E. Adamson. 1974. *The Law of Primitive Man.* New York: Henry Holt.

Holthouse, David. 2005. "Arizona Showdown." *Southern Poverty Law Center Intelligence Report,* Summer.

Horowitz, Irving L., ed. 1967. *The Rise and Fall of Project Camelot.* Cambridge, MA: MIT Press.

Horsley, Richard A. 1979. "Who Were the Witches? The Social Roles of the Accused in the European Witch Trials." *Journal of Interdisciplinary History* 9:689–715.

Horst, Heather A., and Daniel Miller. 2006. *The Cell Phone: An Anthropology of Communication.* New York: Berg.

Hua, Cai. 2001. *A Society without Fathers or Husbands: The Na of China.* Cambridge, MA: Zone Books.

Hughey, Matthew W. 2009. "Cinethetic Racism: White Redemption and Black Stereotypes in 'Magical Negro' Films." *Social Problems* 56(3):543–577.

Human Rights Watch. 2001. *Human Rights in Saudi Arabia: A Deafening Silence.* Available at hrw.org/backgrounder/mena/saudi/.

Human Rights Watch. 2004. "'Political Shari'a'? Human Rights and Islamic Law in Northern Nigeria." *Human Rights Watch* 16(9)A.

Igoe, Jim. 2004. *Conservation and Globalization: A Study of the National Parks and Indigenous Communities from East Africa to South Dakota.* Belmont, CA: Thomson/Wadsworth.

Intergovernmental Panel on Climate Change, 2007. "Summary for Policymakers." In Solomon, Sl, D. Qin, M. Maning, Z. Chen, M. Marquis, K.B. Averyt, M. Tignor, and H. L. Miller (Eds.) *Climate Change 2007: The Physical Science Basis. Contributions of Working Group I to the Fourth Assessment Report of the Intergovernmental Panel on Climate Change.* Cambridge: Cambridge University Press.

Investment Company Institute. 2005. *Equity Ownership in America.* Washington, DC: Investment Company Institute.

Ireland, Doug. 2005. "Why is France Burning?" *The Nation,* November 28.

Isaacman, Allen. 1996. *Cotton Is the Mother of Poverty: Peasants, Work, and Rural Struggle in Colonial Mozambique (1938–1961).* Portsmouth, NH: Heinemann.

Ishemo, Shubi L. 1995. "Cultural Response to Forced Labour and Commodity Production in Portugal's African Colonies." *Social Identities* 1(1):95–110.

Jenkins, Richard. 2002. "Imagined but Not Imaginary: Ethnicity and Nationalism in the Modern World." In Jeremy MacClancy (Ed.), *Exotic No More: Anthropology on the Front Lines* (pp. 114–128). Chicago: University of Chicago Press.

Johnstone, Brick, and Bret A. Glass. 2008. "Support for a Neuropsychological Model of Spirituality in

Persons with Traumatic Brain Injury. *Zygon* 43(4):861–74.

Jones, Delmos J. 1995. "Anthropology and the Oppressed: A Reflection on 'Native' Anthropology." In E. L. Cerroni-Long (Ed.), *Insider Anthropology* (Napa Bulletin, Vol. 16, pp. 58–70). Washington, DC: American Anthropological Association.

Judt, Tony. 2005. *Postwar: A History of Europe Since 1945.* New York: Penguin.

Kakutani, Michiko. 2010. "Texts without Context: The Internet Mashes Up Everything We Know About Culture." *New York Times,* March 21, p. AR1.

Kaplan, Flora E. S., ed. 1997. *Queens, Queen Mothers, Priestesses, and Power: Case Studies in African Gender.* New York: New York Academy of the Sciences.

Karlen, Arno. 1995. *Man and Microbes: Disease and Plagues in History and Modern Times.* New York: G. P. Putnam's Sons.

Kaufman, Stuart. 2001. *Modern Hatreds: The Symbolic Politics of Ethnic War.* New York: Cornell University Press.

Keen, Andrew. 2007. *The Cult of the Amateur: How Today's Internet is Killing Our Culture.* New York: Doubleday.

Kelly, Gail P. 1986. "Learning to Be Marginal: Schooling in Interwar French West Africa." *Journal of Asian and African Studies* 21:171–184.

Kenny, Mary. 2007. *Hidden Heads of Households: Child Labor in Northeast Brazil.* Peterborough, Ontario: Broadview Press.

Kepel, Gilles. 2005. *The Roots of Radical Islam.* London: Saqi.

Kidder, Tracy. 2003. *Mountains Beyond Mountains: The Quest of Dr. Paul Farmer, A Man Who Would Cure the World.* New York: Random House.

Kilbride, Philip L. 1994. *Plural Marriage for Our Times: A Reinvented Option?* Westport, CT: Bergin and Garvey.

Kilbride, Philip L. 2004. "Plural and Same Sex Marriage." *Anthropology News* 45(5):17.

Kilbride, Philip L. 2006. "African Polygyny: Family Values and Contemporary Changes." In Aaron Podolefsky and Peter J. Brown (Eds.), *Applying Cultural Anthropology: An Introductory Reader* (5th ed., pp. 201–208). Mountain View, CA: Mayfield.

Kim, Jim Yong, Joyce V. Millen, Alec Irwin, and John Gershman. 2000. *Dying for Growth: Global Inequality and the Health of the Poor.* Monroe, ME: Common Courage Press.

Kimmelman, Michael. 2010a. "D.I.Y. Culture." *New York Times,* April 18, p. A1.

Kimmelman, Michael. 2010b. "Pardon My French: The Globalization of a Language." *New York Times,* April 25, p. A1.

Klein, Laura F. 1976. "'She's One of Us, You Know': The Public Life of Tlingit Women: Traditional, Historical, and Contemporary Perspectives." *Western Canadian Journal of Anthropology* 6(3):164–183.

Klein, Laura F. 1995. "Mother as Clanswoman: Rank and Gender in Tlingit Society." In L. F. Klein and L. A. Ackerman (Eds.), *Women and Power in Native North America* (pp. 28–45). Norman, OK: University of Oklahoma Press.

Klein, Laura F., and Lillian A. Ackerman (Eds.). 1995. *Woman and Power in Native North America.* Norman, OK: University of Oklahoma Press.

Kluckhohn, Clyde. 1959. "The Philosophy of the Navaho Indians." In M. H. Fried (Ed.), *Readings in Anthropology* (Vol. 2). New York: Crowell.

Kofinas, Gary. 2007. *Subsistence Hunting in a Global Economy.* Retrieved June 12, 2007. Available at http://arcticcircle.uconn.edu/NatResources/subsistglobal.html.

Kohn, Hans. 1958. "Reflections on Colonialism." In R. Strausz-Hupe and H. W. Hazard (Eds.), *The Idea of Colonialism* (pp. 2–16). New York: Praeger.

Krakauer, Jon. 2003. *Under the Banner of Heaven: A Story of Violent Faith.* New York: Doubleday.

Krause, J. et al. 2007. "The Derived FOXP2 Variant of Modern Humans was Shared with Neandertals." *Current Biology* 17(21):1908–1912.

Krauss, Michael E. 1992. "The World's Languages in Crisis." *Language* 68(1): 6–10.

Kristoff, Nicholas, and Sheryl WuDunn. 2000. "The Cheers for Sweatshops." *New York Times,* September 24.

Kulick, Don. 1998. *Travesti: Sex, Gender, and Culture among Brazilian Transgendered Prostitutes.* Chicago: University of Chicago Press.

Labov, William. 1972. *Language in the Inner City.* Philadelphia: University of Pennsylvania Press.

Labov, William, Sharon Ash, and Charles Boburg. 2005. *Atlas of North American English: Phonetics, Phonology and Sound Change.* Berlin: Mouton de Gruyter.

LaFraniere, Sharon. 2009. "Chinese Bias for Baby Boys Creates a Gap of 32 Million." *New York Times,* April 10.

Lamphere, Louise, ed. 1992. *Structuring Diversity: Ethnographic Perspectives on the New Immigration.* Chicago: University of Chicago Press.

Lamphere, Louise. 2005. "The Domestic Sphere of Women and the Public World of Men: The Strength and Limitations of an Anthropological Dichotomy." In Caroline B. Brettell and Carolyn F. Sargent (Eds.), *Gender in Cross-Cultural Perspective* (4th ed., pp. 86–94). Upper Saddle River, NJ: Pearson/Prentice Hall.

Lapidus, Ira M. 1988. *A History of Islamic Societies.* Cambridge: Cambridge University Press.

Lareau, Annette. 2003. *Unequal Childhoods: Class, Race, and Family Life.* Berkeley, CA: University of California.

Lassiter, Luke Eric. 2004. "Collaborative Ethnography." *AnthroNotes* 25(1):1–9.

Leacock, Eleanor Burke. 1981. *Myths of Male Dominance.* New York: Monthly Review Press.

Leathers, Dale G. 1997. *Successful Nonverbal Communication* (3rd ed.). Boston: Allyn and Bacon.

LeDuff, Charlie. 2006. "Dreams in the Dark at the Drive-through Window." *New York Times,* November 27, p. A12.

Lee, Richard B. 1984. *The Dobe !Kung.* New York: Holt, Rinehart and Winston.

Lee, Richard B. 2000. "Indigenism and Its Discontents: Anthropology and the Small Peoples at the Millennium." Keynote address at the annual meeting of the American Ethnological Society, Tampa, Florida, March 2000.

Lee, Richard B. 2003. *The Dobe Ju/'hoansi* (3rd ed.). Belmont, CA: Wadsworth.

Lee, Richard B., and Ida Susser. 2008. "Confounding Conventional Wisdom: The Ju/'hoansi and HIV/AIDS." In Douglas A. Feldman (Ed.), *AIDS, Culture, and Africa.* Gainesville, FL: University of Florida Press.

Lefever, Harry G. 1996. "When the Saints Go Riding In: Santeria in Cuba and the United States." *Journal for the Scientific Study of Religion* 35:318–330.

Leighton, Ralph. 2000. *Tuva or Bust!: Richard Feynman's Last Journey.* New York: W. W. Norton and Company.

Lemert, Edwin M. 1997. *The Trouble with Evil: Social Control at the Edge of Morality.* Albany, NY: State University of New York Press.

Lepowsky, Maria. 1993. *Fruit of the Motherland: Gender in an Egalitarian Society.* New York: Columbia University Press.

Lesser, Alexander. 1933. *The Pawnee Ghost Dance Hand Game: Ghost Dance*

Revival and Ethnic Identity. Lincoln, NE: University of Nebraska.

Levine, Mark, and Penny Roberts (Eds.). 1999. *The Massacre in History.* New York: Berghahn.

Levine, Mary Ann, and Rita Wright. 1999. "COSWA Corner." *Society for American Archaeology Bulletin* 17(2).

Levinson, David. 1989. "Family Violence in Cross-Cultural Perspective." *Frontiers of Anthropology* (Vol. 1). Newbury Park, CA: Sage.

Levinson, David. 1996. *Religion: A Crosscultural Dictionary.* New York: Oxford University Press.

Lévi-Strauss, Claude. 1969/1949. *The Elementary Structures of Kinship.* Boston: Beacon Press.

Lewchuk, Wayne A. 1993. "Men and Monotony: Fraternalism as a Managerial Strategy at the Ford Motor Company." *Journal of Economic History* 53(4):824–856.

Lewis, Richard D. 1996. *When Cultures Collide: Managing Successfully Across Cultures.* London: Nicholas Brealey.

Lewis, Tom. 1991. *Empire of the Air: The Men Who Made Radio.* New York: Harper Perennial.

Lexington. 2005. "Minding About the Gap." *The Economist,* June 9.

Lichtenberg, Judith. 1994. "Population Policy and the Clash of Cultures." In L. A. Mazur (Ed.), *Beyond the Numbers: A Reader on Population, Consumption, and Environment* (pp. 273–280). Washington, DC: Island Press.

Lindquist, Danille Christensen. 2006. "'Locating' the Nation: Football Game Day and American Dreams in Central Ohio." *Journal of American Folklore* 119(4):444–488.

Lindstrom, Lamont. 1993. *Cargo Cult: Strange Stories of Desire from Melanesia and Beyond.* Honolulu, HI: University of Hawaii Press.

Lobao, Linda, and Katherine Meyer. 2001. "The Great Agricultural Transition: Crisis, Change, and Social Consequences of Twentieth Century U.S. Farming." *Annual Review of Sociology* 27:103–124.

Lockwood, Victoria. 2005. "The Impact of Development on Women: The Interplay of Material Conditions and Gender Ideology." In Caroline B. Brettell and Carolyn F. Sargent (Eds.), *Gender in Cross Cultural Perspective* (4th ed., pp. 500–514). Upper Saddle River, NJ: Prentice Hall.

London, Mark, and Brian Kelly. 2007. *The Last Forest: The Amazon in the Age of Globalization.* New York: Random House.

Lovejoy, Paul E. 1983. *Transformations in Slavery: A History of Slavery in Africa.* Cambridge: Cambridge University Press.

Luo, Michael. 2009. "Forced Down the Job Ladder, From Executive Pay to Hourly Wage." New York Times, March 1, p. A1.

Lutkehaus, Nancy C., and Paul B. Roscoe, eds. 1995. *Gender Rituals: Female Initiation in Melanesia.* New York: Routledge.

MacClancy, Jeremy. 2002. "Paradise Postponed: The Predicaments of Tourism." In Jeremy MacClancy (Ed.), *Exotic No More: Anthropology on the Front Lines* (pp. 418–429). Chicago: University of Chicago Press.

MacCormack, Carol P. Hoffer. 1974. "Madam Yoko: Ruler of the Kpa Mende Confederacy." In Michele Z. Rosaldo and Louise Lamphere (Eds.), *Woman, Culture and Society* (pp. 171–187). Stanford: Stanford University Press.

Malinowski, Bronislaw. 1929a. "Practical Anthropology." *Africa* 2:22–38.

Malinowski, Bronislaw. 1929b. *The Sexual Life of Savages.* New York: Harcourt, Brace and World.

Malinowski, Bronislaw. 1948. *Magic, Science, and Religion and other Essays.* New York: Free Press.

Malinowski, Bronislaw. 1984/1922. *Argonauts of the Western Pacific.* Prospect Heights, IL: Waveland.

Malinowski, Bronislaw. 1992/1954. *Magic, Science, and Religion.* Prospect Heights, IL: Waveland.

Mallaby, Sebastian. 2010. "The Politically Incorrect Guide to Ending Poverty." *The Atlantic,* July/August 2010.

Malveaux, Julianne. 2005. "Sweatshops Aren't History Just Yet." *USA Today,* March 18.

Manhein, Mary H. 1999. *The Bone Lady: Life as a Forensic Anthropologist.* Baton Rouge: LSU Press.

Manji, Irshad. 2003. *The Trouble with Islam: A Wakeup Call for Honesty and Change.* Toronto, Canada: Random House Canada.

Manjoo, Farhad. 2008. *True Enough: Learning to Live in a Post-Fact Society.* Hoboken, NJ: John Wiley & Sons.

Maples, William R., and Michael Browning. 1995. *Dead Men Do Tell Tales: The Strange and Fascinating Cases of a Forensic Anthropologist.* New York: Random House.

Marcus, George E., and Michael M. J. Fischer. 1986. *Anthropology as Culture Critique: An Experimental Moment in the Human Sciences.* Chicago: University of Chicago Press.

Marcus, George E., and Fred R. Myers, eds. 1995. *The Traffic in Culture: Refiguring Art and Anthropology.* Berkeley, CA: University of California Press.

Marlowe, Frank W. 2004. "Marital Residence Among Foragers." *Current Anthropology* 45(2):277–284.

Marshall, Donald. 1971. "Sexual Behavior on Mangaia." In D. S. Marshall and R. C. Suggs (Eds.), *Human Sexual Behavior: Variations in the Ethnographic Spectrum* (pp. 163–172). New York: Basic Books.

Marshall, Mac. 1979. *Weekend Warriors.* Palo Alto, CA: Mayfield.

Martin, Emily. 1987. *The Woman in the Body.* New York: Beacon Press.

Martin, M. K., and Barbara Voorhies. 1975. *Female of the Species.* New York: Columbia University Press.

Martin, Philip. 2007. "Managing Labor Migration in the 21st Century." *City and Society* 19(1):5–18.

Maskus, Keith. 1997. "Should Core Labor Standards be Imposed through International Trade Policy?" *World Bank Working Paper 1817.* Washington, DC: World Bank. Available at www.worldbank.org/research/trade/wp1817.html.

Mateu-Gelabert, Pedro, and Howard Lune. 2007. "Street Codes in High School: School as an Educational Deterrent." *City & Community* 6(3):173–191.

Matsumoto, David, and Tsutomu Kudoh. 1993. "American-Japanese Cultural Differences in Attributions of Personality Based on Smiles." *Journal of Nonverbal Communication* 17(4):231–243.

Matthews, Richard. 1997. "The Ebonic Plague Will Kill America Yet." *Atlanta Journal and Constitution,* January 23, p. A18.

Matthiessen, Peter. 2007. "Alaska: Big Oil and the Whales." *New York Review of Books,* November 22: 57–64.

Matzner, Andrew. 2001. *'O Au No Keia: Voices from Hawai'i's Mahu and Transgender Communities.* Philadelphia, PA: XLibris.

Mauss, Marcel. 1990/1924. *The Gift: Form and Reason of Exchange in Archaic Societies* (W. D. Halls, Trans.). New York: W.W. Norton.

Maybury-Lewis, David. 1997. *Indigenous Peoples, Ethnic Groups, and the State.* Boston: Allyn and Bacon.

McGee, R. Jon. 1990. *Life, Ritual, and Religion Among the Lacandon Maya.* Belmont, CA: Wadsworth.

McIntosh, Peggy. 1999. "White Privilege: Unpacking the Invisible Knapsack." In A. Podolefsky and P. J. Brown (Eds.), *Applying Cultural Anthropology: An Introductory Reader* (4th ed., pp. 134–137). Mountain View, CA: Mayfield.

Mead, Margaret. 1963/1935. *Sex and Temperament in Three Primitive Societies.* New York: Dell.

Mead, Margaret. 1971/1928. *Coming of Age in Samoa.* New York: Morrow. (Originally published 1928.)

Meier, Matt S., and Feliciano Ribera. 1993. *Mexican Americans/American Mexicans: From Conquistadors to Chicanos.* New York: Hill & Wang.

Melendez, Edwin. 1993. *Colonial Subjects: Critical Perspectives on Contemporary Puerto Ricans.* Boston: South End Press.

Merrick, Amy. 2004. "Gap Offers Unusual Look at Factory Conditions." *Wall Street Journal,* May 12.

Merry, Sally E. 1981. *Urban Danger: Life in a Neighborhood of Strangers.* Philadelphia: Temple University Press.

Messenger, John C. 1971. "Sex and Repression in an Irish Folk Community." In D. S. Marshall and R. C. Suggs (Eds.), *Human Sexual Behavior: Variations in the Ethnographic Spectrum* (pp. 3–37). New York: Basic Books.

Meyer, Stephen. 2004. "The Degradation of Work Revisited: Workers and Technology in the American Auto Industry, 1900–2000." *Automobile in American Life and Society.* Available at www.autolife.umd.umich .edu/Labor/L_Overview/L_Overview3.htm.

Mintz, Sidney W. 1985. *Sweetness and Power: The Place of Sugar in Modern History.* New York: Penguin.

Monaghan, Leila. 1997. "Ebonics Discussion Continues." *Anthropology Newsletter* 38(2):44–45.

Monger, Randall. 2010. "U.S. Legal Permanent Residents: 2009." *Annual Flow Report: Office of Immigration Statistics, United States Department of Homeland Security.* Washington, DC: Government Printing Office.

Montagu, Ashley. 1978. *Touching: The Human Significance of the Skin* (2nd ed.). New York: Harper and Row.

Mooney, James. 1973/1896. *The Ghost-Dance Religion and the Sioux Outbreak of 1890.* Glorieta, NM: Rio Grande Press.

Moore, Molly. 1998. "To Guatemalan Scientist, Dead Men Do Tell Tales." *Washington Post,* July 19, p. A22.

Moore, Sally Falk. 1978. *Law as Process: An Anthropological Approach.* London: Routledge and Kegan Paul.

Morgan, Marcyliena. 2004. "Speech Community." In Alassandro Duranti (Ed.), *A Companion to Linguistic Anthropology* (pp. 3–33). Malden, MA: Blackwell.

Moser, Caroline. 1993. *Gender Planning and Development: Theory, Practice, and Training.* New York: Routledge.

Muhammad, Dedrick. 2008. "Race and Extreme Inequality." *The Nation,* June 30, p. 26.

Mullin, Molly H. 1995. "The Patronage of Difference: Making Indian Art, Not Ethnology." In George E. Marcus and Fred R. Myers (Eds.), *The Traffic in Culture: Refiguring Art and Anthropology* (pp. 166–200). Berkeley, CA: University of California Press.

Munn, Nancy D. 1990. "Constructing Regional Worlds in Experience: Kula Exchange, Witchcraft and Gawan Local Events." *Man* 25: 1–17.

Murdock, George Peter. 1949. *Social Structure.* New York: Free Press.

Murphy, Joseph M. 1989. *Santeria: An African Religion in America.* Boston: Beacon Press.

Murphy, Robert. 1964. "Social Distance and the Veil." *American Anthropologist* 66:1257–1273.

Murphy, Yolanda, and Robert Murphy. 1974. *Women of the Forest.* New York: Columbia University Press.

Myerhoff, Barbara G. 1974. *Peyote Hunt: The Sacred Journey of the Huichol Indians.* Ithaca: Cornell University Press.

Myerhoff, Barbara. 1978. *Number Our Days.* New York: Simon and Schuster.

Myers, Fred. 1986. *Pintupi Country, Pintupi Self: Sentiment, Place, and Politics among Western Desert Aborigines.* Washington, DC: Smithsonian Institution Press.

Myers, Fred R. 2006. "The Unsettled Business of Tradition, Indigenous Being, and Acrylic Painting." In Eric Venbrux, Pamela Sheffield Rosi, and Robert L. Welsch (Eds.), *Exploring World Art* (pp. 177–200). Long Grove, IL: Waveland.

Myers, Steven Lee, Andrew C. Revkin, Simon Romero, and Clifford Krauss. 2005. "Old Ways of Life Are Fading as the Arctic Thaws." *New York Times,* October 20, p. A1.

Nader, Laura. 2006. "Human Rights and Moral Imperialism: A Double-Edged Story." *Anthropology News* 47(7):6.

Nagashima, Kenji, and James A. Schellenberg. 1997. "Situational Differences in Intentional Smiling: A Cross-Cultural Exploration." *Journal of Social Psychology* 137:297–301.

Nagengast, Carole. 1994. "Violence, Terror, and the Crisis of the State." In B. J. Siegel (Ed.), *Annual Review of Anthropology* (Vol. 23, pp. 109–136). Stanford, CA: Stanford University Press.

Naimark, Norman. 2001. *Fires of Hatred: Ethnic Cleansing in Twentieth-Century Europe.* Cambridge, MA: Harvard University Press.

Nanda, Serena. 1999. *Neither Man nor Woman: The Hijras of India* (2nd ed.). Belmont, CA: Wadsworth.

Nanda, Serena. 2000a. "Arranging a Marriage in India." In P. R. DeVita (Ed.), *Stumbling Towards Truth: Anthropologists at Work* (pp. 196–204). Prospect Heights, IL: Waveland.

Nanda, Serena. 2000b. *Gender Diversity: Crosscultural Variations.* Prospect Heights, IL: Waveland.

Nanda, Serena. 2004. "South African Museums and the Creation of a New National Identity." *American Anthropologist* 106(2):379–384.

Nanda, Serena, and Joan Young Gregg. 2009. *The Gift of a Bride: A Tale of Anthropology, Matrimony, and Murder.* Lanham (MD): Rowman Altamira.

Narasimhan, Sakuntala. 1990. *Sati: Widow Burning in India.* New York: Anchor/Doubleday.

Narayan, Kirin. 1993. "How Native Is a 'Native' Anthropologist?" *American Anthropologist* 95:671–686.

Nash, June. 1970. *In the Eyes of the Ancestors: Belief and Behavior in a Mayan Community.* New Haven: Yale University Press.

Nash, June. 1993. "Introduction: Traditional Arts and Changing Markets in Middle America." In June Nash and Helen Safa (Eds.), *Crafts in the World Market* (pp. 1–24). Albany: State University of New York Press.

Nash, June. 1994. "Global Integration and Subsistence Insecurity." *American Anthropologist* 96:7–30.

Nash, Manning. 1961. "The Social Context of Economic Choice in a Small Society." *Man* 219:186–191.

Nayar, Baldev Raj, and T. V. Paul. 2003. *India in the World Order: Searching for Major Power Status.* Cambridge: Cambridge University Press.

Neckerman, Kathryn M., ed. 2004. *Social Inequality.* New York: Russell Sage Foundation.

Nelson, Edward William. 1983. *The Eskimo About Bering Strait.* Washington: Smithsonian Institution Press.

Nesbett, Richard. 2006. "Violence and Global Health." *Anthropology News* 47(9):23.

Netting, Robert. 1977. *Cultural Ecology.* Menlo Park, CA: Cummings.

New York Times. 2005. *Class Matters.* New York: *New York Times.*

New York Times. 2009. "Remade in America: The Newest Immigrants and Their Impact." March 15, p. A20.

Newman, Katherine S. 1999. *Falling from Grace: Downward Mobility in an Age of Affluence* (2nd ed.). Berkeley: University of California.

Newman, Katherine, and Victor Chen. 2007. *The Missing Class: Portraits of the Near Poor in America.* Boston: Beacon.

Newman, Katherine S., and Victor Chen. 2007. *The Missing Class: Portraits of the Near Poor in America.* Boston, MA: Beacon.

Newman, Philip L. 1977. "When Technology Fails: Magic and Religion in New Guinea." In James P. Spradley and David W. McCurdy (Eds.), *Conformity and Conflict: Readings in Cultural Anthropology* (3rd ed.). Boston: Little Brown.

Newson, L. 1999. "Disease and Immunity in the Pre-Spanish Philippines." *Social Science and Medicine* 48: 1833–1850.

Nguyen, Tram. 2005. *We Are All Suspects Now: Untold Stories from Immigrant Communities after 9/11.* Boston: Beacon Press.

Nicolaisen, Ida. 2006. "Anthropology Should Actively Promote Human Rights." *Anthropology News* 47(7):6.

Nike. 2005. *Disclosure List.* Available at www.nike.com/nikebiz/gc/mp/pdf/disclosure_list_2005-06.pdf.

Nisbett, Richard E. 2007. "All Brains Are the Same Color." *New York Times,* December 9, Section 4 (Science), p. 11.

Nobles, Melissa. 2000. *Shades of Citizenship: Race and the Census in Modern Politics.* Palo Alto, CA: Stanford University Press.

Norbeck, Edward. 1974. *Religion in Human Life: Anthropological Views.* Prospect Heights, IL: Waveland.

Norgren, Jill. 1996. *The Cherokee Cases: The Confrontation of Law and Politics.* New York: McGraw-Hill.

Norgren, Jill, and Serena Nanda. 1996. *American Cultural Pluralism and Law* (2nd ed.). New York: Praeger.

Norgren, Jill, and Serena Nanda. 2006. *American Cultural Pluralism and Law* (3rd ed.). Westport, CT: Praeger.

Offiong, Daniel A. 1983. "Witchcraft among the Ibibio of Nigeria." *African Studies Review* 26:107–124.

Ogbu, John. 1978. "African Bride-wealth and Women's Status." *American Ethnologist* 5:241–260.

O'Kelly, Charlotte G., and Larry S. Carney. 1986. *Women and Men in Society: Cross-Cultural Perspectives on Gender Stratification.* Belmont: Wadsworth.

Oliver, Mary Beth. 2003. "Race and Crime in the Media: Research From a Media Effects Tradition." In A. Valdivia (Ed.), *A Companion to Media Studies* (pp. 421–436). London: Blackwell Publishing.

Ong, Aihwa. 1989. "Center, Periphery, and Hierarchy: Gender in Southeast Asia." In S. Morgen (Ed.), *Gender and Anthropology: Critical Reviews for Research and Teaching* (pp. 294–303). Washington, DC: American Anthropological Association.

Onishi, Norimitsu. 2010. "Internet Grows in Indonesia, as Does a Debate on Its Limits." *New York Times*, April 20, p. A6.

Oreskes, Naomi. 2004. "The Scientific Consensus on Climate Change." *Science* 306(5702):1686.

Organization for Economic Cooperation and Development. 2007. *United States Donor Information.* Available at www.oecd.org/dataoecd/25/16/43193218.pdf.

Oriard, Michael. 1993. *Reading Football: How the Popular Press Created an American Spectacle.* Chapel Hill: University of North Carolina Press.

Otterbein, Keith F. 2010. "Nobel Peace Prize—Passed Over Again." *General Anthropology: Bulletin of the General Anthropology Division*, Spring, p. 1.

Ottley, Bruce L., and Jean G. Zorn. 1983. "Criminal Law in Papua New Guinea: Code, Custom and the Courts in Conflict." *American Journal of Comparative Law* 31:251–300.

Overbey, Mary Margaret. 2007. "RACE Are We So Different? A New Public Education Program." *AnthroNotes* 28(1, Spring):15–17.

Page, Tim. 2007. "Parallel Play: A Life of Restless Isolation Explained." *New Yorker,* August 20.

Paiement, Jason J. 2007. "Anthropology and Development." *National Association for the Practice of Anthropology Bulletin* 27(1):196–223.

Palkovich, Anna M. 1994. "Historic Epidemics of the American Pueblos." In C. S. Larsen and G. R. Milner (Eds.), *In the Wake of Contact: Biological Responses to Conquest* (pp. 87–95). New York: Wiley.

Paredes, Anthony J., ed. 2006. Introduction to In Focus: The Impact of the Hurricanes of 2005 on New Orleans and the Gulf Coast of the United States. *American Anthropologist* 108(4):637–642.

Patterson, Orlando. 2006. "A Poverty of the Mind." *New York Times,* March 26.

Peacock, James, et al. 2007. "AAA Commission on the Engagement of Anthropology with the U.S. Security and Intelligence Communities Final Report November 4, 2007." Washington, DC: American Anthropological Association.

Peacock, Nadine R. 1991. "Rethinking the Sexual Division of Labor: Reproduction and Women's Work among the Efe." In M. di Leonardo (Ed.), *Gender and the Crossroads of Knowledge: Feminist Anthropology in the Postmodern Era* (pp. 339–360). Berkeley, CA: University of California Press.

Peoples, James G. 1990. "The Evolution of Complex Stratification in Eastern Micronesia." *Micronesia Suppl.* 2:291–302.

Peregrine, Peter N., Carol R. Ember, and Melvin Ember. 2004. "Universal Patterns in Cultural Evolution: An Empirical Analysis Using Guttman Scaling." *American Anthropologist* 106(1):145–149.

Perez, Agnes, and Susan Pollack. 2008. *Fruit and Tree Nuts Outlook.* Washington, DC: USDA Economic Research Service FTS-332. Available at www.ers.usda.gov/Publications/fts/2008/05MAY/FTS332.pdf.

Perlez, Jane, and Lowell Bergman. 2005. "Tangled Strands in Fight Over Peru Gold Mine." *New York Times*, October 25, p. A1.

Perlez, Jane, and Kirk Johnson. 2005. Behind Gold's Glitter: Torn Lands and Pointed Questions." *New York Times*, October 24, A1.

Petersen, Charles. 2010. "In the World of Facebook." *New York Review of Books*, Feb. 25, p. 8.

Pew Research Center. 2007. "Muslim Americans: Middle Class and Mostly Mainstream." Available at http://pewsocialtrends.org/2007/05/22/muslim-americans-middle-class-and-mostly-mainstream/. Accessed November 15, 2010.

Peyrefitte, Alain. 1992. *The Immobile Empire* (Jon Rothschild, Trans.). New York: Knopf.

Pilkington, Ed. 2010. "South Park Censored After Threat of Fatwa over Muhammad Episode." *Guardian. co.uk.* Available at www.guardian.co.uk/tv-and-radio/2010/apr/22/south-park-censored-fatwa-muhammad. Accessed August 20, 2010.

Pinker, Steven. 1994. *The Language Instinct.* New York: William Morrow.

Pitts, Leonard. 2007. "At Large, Replying to Those E-mails about Vick." *Miami Herald,* Sept. 12.

Plattner, Stuart. 1989. "Marxism." In S. Plattner (Ed.), *Economic Anthropology* (pp. 379–396). Stanford, CA: Stanford University Press.

Polyani, Karl. 1944. *The Great Transformation.* New York: Holt, Rinehart and Winston.

Popper, Karl R. 2002/1963. *Conjectures and Refutations: The Growth of Scientific Knowledge.* London: Routledge.

Population Reference Bureau. 2005. *2005 World Population Data Sheet.* Washington, DC: Population Reference Bureau. Available at www.prb.org/pdf05/05WorldDataSheet_Eng.pdf.

Potash, Betty. 1989. "Gender Relations in Sub-Saharan Africa." In S. Morgen (Ed.), *Gender and Anthropology: Critical Reviews for Research and Teaching* (pp. 189–227). Washington, DC: American Anthropological Association.

Prah, Kwesi K. 1990. "Anthropologists, Colonial Administrators, and the Lotuko of Eastern Equatoria, Sudan: 1952–1953." *African Journal of Sociology* 3(2):70–86.

Press, Eyal. 2007. "The Missing Class." *The Nation,* July 26.

Price, David. 2008. "Soft Power, Hard Power and the Anthropological 'Leveraging' of Cultural 'Assets': Distilling the Politics and Ethics of Anthropological Counterinsurgency." In John Kelly, Sean Mitchell, Bea Jauregui, and Jeremy Walton (Eds.), *Anthropology and Global Counterinsurgency.* Chicago: University of Chicago Press.

Price, David H. 2010. "Blogging Anthropology: Savage Minds, Zero Anthropology, and AAA Blogs." *American Anthropologist,* 112(1):140–141.

Price, Sally. 1989. *Primitive Art in Civilized Places.* Chicago: University of Chicago Press.

Price, Sally. 2007. *Paris Primitive: Jacques Chirac's Museum on the Quai Branly.* Chicago: University of Chicago Press.

Radcliffe-Brown, A. R. 1965/1952. *Structure and Function in Primitive Society.* New York: Free Press.

Ragoné, Helena. 1994. *Surrogate Motherhood: Conception in the Heart.* Boulder, CO: Westview.

Rasmussen, Susan. 2005. "Pastoral Nomadism and Gender: Status, Prestige, Economic Contribution, and Division of Labor among the Tuareg of Niger." In Caroline B. Brettell and Carolyn F. Sargent (Eds.), *Gender in Cross-Cultural Perspective* (4th ed., pp. 155–168). Upper Saddle River, NJ: Pearson/Prentice Hall.

Rasmussen Reports. 2010. "87% Say English Should be U.S. Official Language." *Rasmussen Reports,* May 11. www.rasmussenreports.com/public_content/politics/general_politics/may_2010/87_say_english_should_be_us_official_language. Accessed August 20, 2010.

Ratliff, Eric A. 1999. "Women as 'Sex-Workers,' Men as 'Boyfriends': Shifting Identities in Philippine Go-Go Bars and Their Significance in STD/AIDS Control." *Anthropology and Medicine* 6(1):79–101.

Reed, Jr., Adolph. 2006. "Undone by Neoliberalism." *The Nation,* September 18, p. 26.

Remnick, David. 2010. *The Bridge: The Life and Rise of Barack Obama.* New York: Knopf.

Renfrew, Colin, April McMahon, and Larry Trask (Eds.). 2000. *Time Depth in Historical Linguistics* (Vols. 1 and 2). Cambridge: McDonald Institute for Archaeological Research.

Renteln, Alison D. 2004. *The Cultural Defense.* New York: Oxford.

Republic of Indonesia. 1997. "Issues and Perspectives: A Solution to Java's Overcrowding." Embassy of the Republic of Indonesia in London—United Kingdom. Available at www.indonesianembassy.org.uk/transmigration-7.htm.

Rerkasem, Kanok, et al. 2009. *"Consequences of Swidden Transitions for Crop and Fallow Biodiversity in Southeast Asia."* *Human Ecology* 37:347–60.

Revolutionary Association of the Women of Afghanistan, http://www.rawa.org [8]

Ricklefs, Merle C. 1990. "Balance and Military Innovation in 17th Century Java." *History Today* 40(11):40–47.

Roberts, Alan H., D. G. Kewman, L. Mercier, and M. Hovell. 1993. "The Power of Nonspecific Effects in Healing: Implications for Psychosocial and Biological Treatments." *Clinical Psychology Review* 13:375–391.

Roberts, Sam. 2010. "Facing a Financial Pinch, and Moving Back Home." *New York Times,* March 22, p. A20.

Rohde, Douglas, Steve Olson, and Joseph T. Chang. 2004. "Modelling the recent common ancestry of all living humans." *Nature* 431:562–566.

Romer, Paul. 2009. "Paul Romer's Radical Idea: Charter Cities." *TED.* Available online at www.ted.com/talks/paul_romer.html. Accessed August 20, 2010.

Rosaldo, Michelle Z., and Louise Lamphere. 1974. "Introduction." In M. Z. Rosaldo and L. Lamphere (Eds.), *Women, Culture and Society* (pp. 1–16). Stanford, CA: Stanford University Press.

Roscoe, Paul. 2003. "Margaret Mead, Reo Fortune, and Mountain Arapesh Warfare." *American Anthropologist* 105(3):581–591.

Roscoe, Will. 1991. *The Zuni Man-Woman.* Albuquerque: University of New Mexico Press.

Roscoe, Will. 1995. "Strange Craft, Strange History, Strange Folks: Cultural Amnesia and the Case of Lesbian and Gay Studies." *American Anthropologist* 97:448–452.

Rosman, Abraham, and Paula G. Rubel. 1971. *Feasting with Mine Enemy: Rank and Exchange among Northwest Coast Societies.* Prospect Heights, IL: Waveland.

Rothenberg-Aalami, Jessica. 2004. "Coming Full Circle? Forging Missing Links along Nike's Integrated Production Networks." *Global Networks* 4(4):335–354.

Rothstein, Edward. 2010. "A Burial Ground and Its Dead Are Given Life." *New York Times,* Feb. 26, p. A1.

Roybal, Joe. 2007. "Big Beef Buyers." *Beef Magazine.* Available at http://beefmagazine.com/mag/beef_big_beef_buyers/index.html.

Sacks, Karen Brodkin. 1982. *Sisters and Wives.* Westport, CT: Greenwood.

Sacks, Oliver. 1995. *An Anthropologist on Mars: Seven Paradoxical Tales.* New York: Knopf.

Sage, George H. 1999. "Justice Do It! The Nike Transnational Advocacy Network: Organization, Collective Actions, and Outcomes." *Sociology of Sport Journal* 16:206–235.

Sahlins, Marshall. 1961. "The Segmentary Lineage: An Organization of Predatory Expansion." *American Anthropologist* 63:332–345.

Sahlins, Marshall. 1971. "Poor Man, Rich Man, Big Man, Chief." In J. P. Spradley and D. W. McCurdy (Eds.), *Conformity and Conflict* (pp. 362–376). Boston: Little, Brown.

Sahlins, Marshall. 1972. *Stone Age Economics.* Chicago: Aldine.

Salzman, Philip. 1999. *The Anthropology of Real Life: Events in Human Experience.* Prospect Heights, IL: Waveland.

Salzman, Philip C. 2000. *Black Tents of Baluchistan.* Washington, DC: Smithsonian.

Salzmann, Zdenek. 1993. *Language, Culture and Society.* Boulder, CO: Westview Press.

Sanchez, Rene. 1997. "Ebonics Debate Comes to Capitol Hill; 'Political Correctness Gone Out of Control,' Sen. Faircloth Says." *Washington Post,* January 24, p. A15.

Sanday, Peggy Reeves. 1981. *Female Power and Male Dominance.* New York: Cambridge University Press.

Sanday, Peggy Reeves. 1992. *Fraternity Gang Rape: Sex, Brotherhood, and Privilege on Campus.* New York: New York University Press.

Sanghavi, Prachi, Kavi Bhatta, and Veena Das. 2009. "Fire-Related Deaths in India in 2001: A Retrospective Analysis of Data." *The Lancet* (early online publication), 2 March: 1–2.

Sang-Hun, Choe. 2010. "North Koreans Use Cellphones to Bare Secrets." *New York Times,* March 29, p. 1A.

SAPRIN. 2004. *Structural Adjustment: The SAPRI Report.* London: Zed Books.

Scaglion, Richard. 1981. "Homicide Compensation in Papua New Guinea: Problems and Prospects." In Law Reform Commission of Papua New Guinea Monograph, 1. New Guinea: Office of Information.

Scammell, G. V. 1989. *The First Imperial Age.* London: HarperCollins Academic.

Schensul, Stephen L. 1997. "The Anthropologist in Medicine: Critical Perspectives on Cancer and Street Addicts." *Reviews in Anthropology* 26(1):57–69.

Schepartz, L. A. 1993. "Language and Modern Human Origins." *Yearbook of Physical Anthropology* 36:91–96.

Schlegel, Alice, and Herbert Barry III. 1991. *Adolescence: An Anthropological Inquiry.* New York: Free Press (Macmillan).

Schmidt-Vogt, Dietrich, et al. 2009. "An Assessment of Trends in the Extent of Swidden in Southeast Asia." *Human Ecology* 37:269–80.

Schneider, Harold K. 1973. "The Subsistence Role of Cattle among the Pokot in East Africa." In E. P. Skinner (Ed.), *Peoples and Cultures of Africa.* Garden City, NY: Natural History Press.

Schneider, Jane. 2002. "World Markets: Anthropological Perspectives." In Jeremy MacClancy (Ed.), *Exotic No More: Anthropology on the Front Lines.* Chicago: University of Chicago Press.

Scott, James. 1992. *Domination and the Arts of Resistance: Hidden Transcripts.* New Haven, CT: Yale University Press.

Scott, Janny. 2005. "Life at the Top in America Isn't Just Better, It's Longer." *New York Times,* May 16.

Seddon, Judith S. 1993. "Possible or Impossible?: A Tale of Two Worlds in One Country." *Yale Journal of Law and Feminism* 5(2):265–288.

Seitlyn, David. 1993. "Spiders In and Out of Court, or 'The Long Legs & the Law': Styles of Spider Divination in Their Sociological Contexts." *Africa* 63:219–240.

Service, Elman. 1962. *Primitive Social Organization.* New York: Random House.

Service, Elman. 1971. *Profiles in Ethnology.* New York: Harper and Row.

Shanklin, Eugenia. 1994. *Anthropology and Race.* Belmont, CA: Wadsworth.

Sheehan, John. 1982. *The Enchanted Ring: The Untold Story of Penicillin.* Cambridge, MA: MIT Press.

Sheriff, Robin E. 2001. *Dreaming Equality: Color, Race and Racism in Urban Brazil.* East Brunswick, NJ: Rutgers University Press. 2001.

Shih, Chuan-Kang. 2001. "Genesis of Marriage among the Moso and Empire-Building in Late Imperial China." *Journal of Asian Studies* 60(2):381–412.

Shostak, Marjorie. 1983. *Nisa: The Life and Words of a !Kung Woman.* New York: Random House.

Simeone, William E. 1995. *Rifles, Blankets, and Beads: Identity, History, and the Northern Athapaskan Potlatch.* Norman, OK: University of Oklahoma Press.

Singer, Merrill. 2008. "The Perfect Epidemiological Storm: Food Insecurity, HIV/AIDS and Poverty in Southern Africa." *Anthropology News,* October, p. 12.

Singer, Merrill, Ray Irizarry, and Jean J. Schensul. 1991. "Needle Access as an AIDS Prevention Strategy for IV Drug Users: A Research Perspective." *Human Organization* 50:142–153.

Slackman, Michael. 2007. "In Egypt, a New Battle Begins Over the Veil." *New York Times,* January 28.

Smedley, Audrey. 1998. "'Race' and the Construction of Human Identity." *American Anthropologist* 100:690–702.

Smith, Roberta. 2005. "From a Mushroom Cloud, a Burst of Art Reflecting Japan's Psyche." *New York Times,* April 8, p. E33.

Snajdr, Edward. 2005. "Gender, Power, and the Performance of Justice: Muslim Women's Responses to Domestic Violence in Kazakhstan." *American Ethnologist* 32(22):294–311.

Snajdr, Edward. 2007. "Ethnicizing the Subject: Domestic Violence and the Politics of Primordialism in Kazakhstan." *Journal of the Royal Anthropological Institute (N.S.)* 13:603–620.

Society for Anthropology of North America (SANA). 2003. Available at http://sananet.org/.

Sokoloff, Natalie, and Christina Pratt (Eds.). 2005. *Domestic Violence at the Margins: Readings on Race, Class, Gender, and Culture.* New Brunswick, NJ: Rutgers University Press.

Southern Baptist Convention. 2006. Resolution 5 of the SBC Meeting, 2006, June 13–14: "On Alcohol Use in America." Available at http://www.sbc.net/resolutions/ amResolution.asp?ID=1156.

Sponsel, Leslie E., ed. 1995. *Indigenous Peoples and the Future of Amazonia: An Ecological Anthropology of an Endangered World.* Tucson: University of Arizona Press.

Spradley, James. 1970. *You Owe Yourself a Drunk.* Boston: Little, Brown.

Squires, Susan, and Bryan Byrne. 2002. *Creating Breakthrough Ideas: The collaboration of anthropologists and designers in the product development industry.* Westport (CN): Bergin and Garvey.

Stannard, David E. 2005. *Honor Killing: Race, Rape, and Clarence Darrow's Spectacular Last Case.* New York: Penguin.

Stanyon, Roscoe, Marco Sazzini, and Donata Luiselli. 2009. "Timing the First Human Migration into Eastern Asia." *Journal of Biology* 8:18.

Stearns, M. L. 1975. "Life Cycle Rituals of the Modern Haida." In D. B. Carlisle (Ed.), *Contributions to Canadian Ethnology* (pp. 129–169). Ottawa: National Museum of Man.

Steiner, Christopher B. 1994. *African Art in Transit.* New York: Cambridge University Press.

Steiner, Christopher B. 1995. "The Art of the Trade: On the Creation of Value and Authenticity in the African Art Market." In G. E. Marcus and F. R. Myers (Eds.), *The Traffic in Culture: Refiguring Art and Anthropology* (pp. 151–165). Berkeley, CA: University of California Press.

Steiner, Christopher B. 2002. "Art/Anthropology/Museums: Revulsions and Revolutions. In Jeremy MacClancy (Ed.), *Exotic No More: Anthropology on the Front Lines* (pp. 400–417). Chicago: University of Chicago Press.

Stern, Pamela R. 1999. "Learning to Be Smart: An Exploration of the Culture of Intelligence in a Canadian Inuit Community." *American Anthropologist* 101:502–514.

Sternberg, Esther. 2002. "Walter B. Cannon and 'Voodoo' Death: A Perspective from 60 Years On." *American Journal of Public Health* 92: 1564–1566.

Stevens, Jr., Phillips. 2006. "Women's Aggressive Use of Genital Power in Africa." *Transcultural Psychiatry* 43(4):592–599.

Stolberg, Sheryl Gay. 1999. "Black Mother's Mortality Rate is Under Scrutiny." *New York Times,* August 8, p. A1.

Stolcke, Verena. 1995. "Talking Culture: New Boundaries, New Rhetorics of Exclusion in Europe." *Current Anthropology* 36:1–7.

Stone, Linda, and Caroline James. 2005. "Dowry, Bride-Burning, and Female Power in India." In C. B. Brettell and C. F. Sargent (Eds.), *Gender in Cross-Cultural Perspective* (4th ed., pp. 312–320). Upper Saddle River, NJ: Prentice Hall.

Stonich, Susan C., Douglas L. Murray, and Peter R. Rossart. 1994. "Enduring Crises: The Human and Environmental Consequences of Nontraditional Export Growth in Central America." *Research in Economic Anthropology* 15:239–274.

Strathern, Marilyn. 1995. *Women in Between: Female Roles in a Male World: Mount Hagen, New Guinea.* Latham, MD: Rowman and Littlefield.

Strum, Philippa, ed. 2005. *Muslims in the United States: Identity, Influence, Innovation.* Washington, DC: Woodrow Wilson International Center for Scholars.

Strum, Philippa, ed. 2006. *American Arabs and Political Participation.* Washington, DC: Woodrow Wilson International Center for Scholars.

Strum, Philippa. 2010. *Mendez v. Westminister: School Desegregation and Mexican-American Rights.* Lawrence, Kansas: University of Kansas Press.

Strum, Philippa, and Danielle Tarantolo (Eds.). 2003. *Muslims in the United States: Demography, Beliefs, Institutions.* Washington, DC: Woodrow Wilson International Center for Scholars.

Stull, Donald D., and Michael J. Broadway. 2004. *Slaughterhouse Blues: The Meat and Poultry Industry in North America.* Belmont, CA: Wadsworth.

Sunstein, Cass. 2006. *Infotopia: How Many Minds Produce Knowledge.* New York: Oxford University Press.

Tang, Tiffany. 2007. "The Major-Career Connection." *Business Today Online Journal,* Wednesday, February 28.

Tavernise, Sabrina. 2008. "Putting a Dent in a Law against Insulting Turkishness." *New York Times,* January 25, p. A4.

Temple University. 2009. "Earliest Evidence of Domesticated Maize Discovered: Dates Back 8,700 Years." *ScienceDaily* 25 (March):3.

Tessman, Irwin, and Jack Tessman. 2000. "Efficacy of Prayer: A Critical Examination of Claims." *Skeptical Inquirer* 24(2):31–33.

Thompson, A. C. 2009. "Katrina's Hidden Race War." *The Nation,* January 5, pp. 11–18.

Time. 2010. "The 2010 Time 100." *Time* 175(18).

Todaro, Michael, and Stephen C. Smith. 2003. *Economic Development* (8th ed.). Harlow, UK: Pearson Addison Wesley.

Trachtman, Michael G. 2009. *The Supremes' Greatest Hit, Revised and Updated Edition: The 37 Supreme Court Cases that Most Directly Affect Your Life.* New York: Sterling Publishing.

Tsui, Clarence. 2000. "A Hong Kong Anthropologist Spent Months at a Mainland Electronic Plant to Study Lives of Its Female Workers: Hardship, Hope and Dreams in a Factory." *South China Morning Post,* January 9, p. 1.

Turnbull, Colin. 1968. "The Importance of Flux in Two Hunting Societies." In R. B. Lee and I. DeVore (Eds.), *Man the Hunter* (pp. 132–137). Chicago: Aldine.

Turnbull, Colin. 1981. "East African Safari." *Natural History Magazine,* March, p. 26.

Turner, Victor. 1967. *The Forest of Symbols: Aspects of Ndembu Ritual.* Ithaca: Cornell University Press.

Turner, Victor. 1969. *The Ritual Process: Structure and Antistructure.* Chicago: Aldine.

Tyler, Stephen A. 1986. "Post-Modern Ethnography: From Document of the Occult to Occult Document." In James Clifford and George E. Marcus (Eds.), *Writing Culture: The Poetics and Politics of Ethnography* (pp. 122–140). Berkeley: University of California Press.

UNEP/GRID-Arendal. 2008. "Population Distribution in the Circumpolar Arctic, by Country (including Indigenous Population)," UNEP/GRID-Arendal Maps and Graphics Library. Available at http://maps.grida.no/go/graphic/population-distribution-in-the-circumpolar-arctic-by-country-including-indigenous-population1. Accessed November 1, 2010.

United Nations. 2003. *The 2003 Revision and World Urbanization Prospects.* Available at esa.un.org/unup.

United Nations Environmental Programme. 2004. *Childhood Pesticide Poisoning.* Châtelaine, Switzerland: UNEP Chemicals, International Environment House.

University of Virginia. 2006. *Choosing and Using Your Major.* Publication of University of Virginia, Office of Career Services. Available at http://www.career.virginia.edu/students/resources/handouts/choosing_a_major.pdf.

U.S. Bureau of Labor Statistics. 2010. "Education Pays." *Education Projections.* Available at www.bls.gov/emp/ep_chart_001.htm. Accessed August 20, 2010.

U.S. Census Bureau. 2008. *Statistical Abstract.* Available at www.census.gov/compendia/statab/.

U.S. Department of Labor. 2010. *A Profile of the Working Poor, 2008.* US Bureau of Labor Statistics, Report 1022.

Van Biema, David, and Jeff Chu. 2006. "Does God Want You To Be Rich?" *Time,* September 18.

van Donge, Jan Kees. 1992. "Agricultural Decline in Tanzania: The Case of the Uluguru Mountains." *African Affairs* 91:73–94.

van Gennep, Arnold. 1960/1909. *The Rites of Passage.* Chicago: University of Chicago Press.

Vayda, Andrew P. 1976. *War in Ecological Perspective.* New York: Plenum.

Venbrux, Eric, Pamela Sheffield Rosi, and Robert L. Welsch (Eds.). 2006. *Exploring World Art.* Long Grove, IL: Waveland.

Verdon, Michel, and Paul Jorion. 1981. "The Hordes of Discord: Australian Aboriginal Social Organization Reconsidered." *Man* 16(1):90–107.

Victor, David A. 1992. *International Business Communication.* New York: Harper Collins.

Vincent, Susan. 1998. "The Family in the Household: Women, Relationships, and Economic History in Peru." *Research in Economic Anthropology* 19:179–187.

Viswanathan, Gauri. 1988. "Currying Favor: The Politics of British Educational and Cultural Policy in India, 1813–1854." *Social Text* 19–20(Fall):85–104.

Volkman, Toby Alice. 1984. "Great Performances: Toraja Cultural Identity in the 1970s." *American Ethnologist* 11(1):152–168.

Wali, Alaka. 2010. "Ethnography for the Digital Age: http://www.YouTube/Digital Ethnography (Michael Wesch)." *American Anthropologist* 112(1):147–148.

Walker, Deward E. 1967. Nez Perce Sorcery." *Ethnology* 6(1):66–96.

Wall, Diana diZerega, and Anne-Marie Cantwell. 2004. *Touring Gotham's Archaeological Past: 8 Self-Guided Walking Tours through New York City.* New Haven, CN: Yale University Press.

Wallace, Anthony. 1970. *Death and Rebirth of the Seneca.* New York: Knopf.

Wallace, Anthony. 1999. *Jefferson and the Indians: The Tragic Fate of "The First Americans."* Cambridge, MA: Harvard University Press.

Wallerstein, Immanuel. 1995. *Historical Capitalism.* London: Verso.

Walley, Christine J. 1997. "Searching for 'Voices': Feminism, Anthropology, and the Global Debate over Female Genital Operations." *Cultural Anthropology* 12:405–438.

Walsh, Eileen Rose. 2004. "Desensationalizing the Mosou." *Anthropology Newsletter* 45(4).

Warner, Melinda. 2010. "My Tea-Stained Weekend: An Evangelical Conservative Turned Progressive Goes to the Tea Party Convention." *Huffington Post,* February 9. Available at http://www.huffingtonpost.com/melinda-warner/my-tea-stained-weekend-an_b_455810.html. Accessed August 20, 2010.

Warren, Kay B., and Susan C. Bourque. 1989. "Women, Technology, and Development Ideologies: Frameworks and Findings." In S. Morgen (Ed.),

Gender and Anthropology: Critical Reviews for Research and Teaching (pp. 382–410). Washington, DC: American Anthropological Association.

Weiner, Annette B. 1976. *Women of Value, Men of Renown: New Perspectives on Trobriand Exchange.* Austin: University of Texas Press.

Wenzel, George W. 2009. "Canadian Inuit Subsistence and Ecological Instability—If the Climate Changes, Must the Inuit?" *Polar Research* 28:89–99.

Wesch, Michael. 2007. "An In-Depth Look at the Cyber-Phenomenon of Our Time: Web 2.0 (Interview with Virginia Buege)." *Lawlor Review* 15(2):10–16.

White, Benjamin. 1980. "Rural Household Studies in Anthropological Perspective." In H. Binswanger, R. Evenson, C. Florencio, and B. White (Eds.), *Rural Household Studies in Asia* (pp. 3–25). Singapore: Singapore University Press.

White, Geoffrey M. 1997. "Introduction: Public History and National Narrative." *Museum Anthropology* 21(1):3–6.

White, Jenny B. 1994. *Money Makes Us Relatives.* Austin, TX: University of Texas Press.

Whitehead, Harriet. 1981. "The Bow and the Burden Strap: A New Look at Institutionalized Homosexuality in Native North America." In S. B. Ortner and H. Whitehead (Eds.), *Sexual Meanings: The Cultural Construction of Gender and Sexuality* (pp. 80–115). Cambridge: Cambridge University Press.

Whiting, John, Richard Kluckhohn, and Albert Anthony. 1967. "The Function of Male Initiation Ceremonies at Puberty." In R. Endelman (Ed.), *Personality and Social Life* (pp. 294–308). New York: Random House.

Whorf, Benjamin L. 1941. "The Relation of Habitual Thought and Behavior to Language." In Leslie Spier (Ed.), *Language, Culture and Personality* (pp. 75–93). Menasha, WI: Sapir Memorial Publication Fund.

Wikan, Unni. 1977. "Man Becomes Woman: Transsexualism in Oman as a Key to Gender Roles." *Man* (new series) 12:304–319.

Wilk, Richard, ed. 2006. *Fast Food/Slow Food: The Cultural Economy of the Global Food System.* Lanham, MD: Altamira Press.

Williams, Trevor. 1984. *Howard Florey: Penicillin and After.* Oxford: Oxford University Press.

Williams, Walter. 1986. *The Spirit and the Flesh* (2nd ed.). Boston: Beacon Press.

Williams, Walter. 1996. "Amazons of America: Female Gender Variance." In Caroline B. Brettell and Carolyn F. Sargent (Eds.), *Gender in Cross-Cultural Perspective* (2nd ed., pp. 202–213). Upper Saddle River, NJ: Prentice Hall.

Williams, Walter L. 2009. "Strategies for Challenging Homophobia in Islamic Malaysia and Secular China." *Nebula*, March, 6(1). Available at nobleworld.biz/nebulaarchive.html.

Winkelman, Michael. 1996. "Cultural Factors in Criminal Defense Proceedings." Human Organization 55:154.

Wolf, Eric R. 1982. *Europe and the People Without History.* Berkeley, CA: University of California Press.

Wong, Edward. 2008. "Factories Shut, China Workers Are Suffering." *New York Times,* November 14, p. A1.

Woodburn, James. 1968. "An Introduction to Hadza Ecology." In R. B. Lee and I. DeVore (Eds.), *Man the Hunter* (pp. 49–55). Chicago: Aldine.

Woodburn, James. 1998. "Sharing Is Not a Form of Exchange: An Analysis of Property-Sharing in Immediate Return Hunter-Gatherer Societies." In C. M. Hann (Ed.), *Property Relations: Renewing the Anthropological Tradition* (pp. 48–63). Cambridge: Cambridge University Press.

World Bank. 1992. *Development and the Environment: World Development Report 1992.* New York: Oxford University Press.

World Bank. 2006. *Global Economic Prospects. Economic Implications of Remittances and Migration.* Washington, DC: World Bank. Available at econ.worldbank.org/external/default/main?pagePK=64165259&theSitePK=469372&piPK=6416 5421&menuPK=64166322&entit yID=000112742_20051114174928.

World Bank. 2008. *World Development Indicators Database.* Washington, DC: World Bank. Available at http://siteresources.worldbank.org/DATA-STATISTICS/Resources/GNI.pdf.

World Bank Group Archives. 2003. *Robert Strange McNamara.* Washington, DC: World Bank. Available at http://go.worldbank.org/44V9497H50.

Worthman, Carol M. 1995. "Hormones, Sex, and Gender." In William Durham, E. Valentine Daniel, and Bambi Schieffelin (Eds.), *Annual Review of Anthropology* (Vol. 24, pp. 593–618). Stanford, CA: Stanford University Press.

Yardley, Jim. 2006. "China's Path to Modernity, Mirrored in a Troubled River." *New York Times*, November 19, p. A1.

Zaloom, Caitlin. 2006. *Out of the Pits: Trading and Technology from Chicago to London.* Chicago: University of Chicago Press.

Zeegers, Maurice, Frans van Poppel, Robert Vlietinck, Liesbeth Spruijt, and Harry Ostrer. 2004. "Founder Mutations Among the Dutch." *European Journal of Human Genetics* 12:591–600.

Ziegler, Alan D., et al. 2009. "Environmental Consequences of the Demise in Swidden Cultivation in Montane Mainland Southeast Asia: Hydrology and Geomorphology." *Human Ecology* 37:361–73.

Zoepf, Katherine. 2008. "In Booming Gulf, Some Arab Women Find Freedom in the Skies." *New York Times,* December 22, p. A1.

PHOTO CREDITS

INDEX